REAL WORLD

MICRO

EDITED BY ROB LARSON, ALEJANDRO REUSS, BRYAN SNYDER, CHRIS STURR,

AND THE *DOLLARS & SENSE* COLLECTIVE

REAL WORLD MICRO, TWENTY-THIRD EDITION

Published by:
Economic Affairs Bureau, Inc. d/b/a *Dollars & Sense*
89 South St., Suite LL02, Boston, MA 02111
617-447-2177; dollars@dollarsandsense.org.
For order information, contact Economic Affairs Bureau or visit: www.dollarsandsense.org.

Real World Micro is edited by the *Dollars & Sense* Collective, which also publishes *Dollars & Sense* magazine and the classroom books *Microeconomics: Individual Choice in Communities, Real World Macro, Current Economic Issues, The Economic Crisis Reader, Real World Globalization, America Beyond Capitalism, Labor and the Global Economy, Real World Latin America, Real World Labor, Real World Banking and Finance, The Wealth Inequality Reader, The Economics of the Environment, Introduction to Political Economy, Unlevel Playing Fields: Understanding Wage Inequality and Discrimination, Striking a Balance: Work, Family, Life,* and *Grassroots Journalism.*

The 2016 *Dollars & Sense* Collective:
Betsy Aron, Nancy Banks, Nina Eichacker, Peter Kolozi, John Miller, Jawied Nawabi, Kevin O'Connell, Alejandro Reuss, Dan Schneider, Zoe Sherman, Bryan Snyder, Chris Sturr, Jeanne Winner

Co-editors of this volume: Rob Larson, Alejandro Reuss, Bryan Snyder, and Chris Sturr
Design and layout: Chris Sturr; Cover design and layout: Alejandro Reuss

Printed in U.S.A

CONTENTS

CHAPTER 5 • MARKET FAILURE I: MARKET POWER

CHAPTER 6 • MARKET FAILURE II: EXTERNALITIES

CHAPTER 7 • LABOR MARKETS

CHAPTER 8 • THE DISTRIBUTION OF INCOME AND WEALTH

CHAPTER 9 • TAXATION

CHAPTER 10 • TRADE AND DEVELOPMENT

CHAPTER 11 • POLICY SPOTLIGHT: GENERATIONAL WAR?

INTRODUCTION

It sometimes seems that the United States has not one, but two economies. The first economy exists in economics textbooks and in the minds of many elected officials. It is a free-market economy, a system of promise and plenty, a cornucopia of consumer goods. In this economy, people are free and roughly equal, and each individual carefully looks after him- or herself, making uncoerced choices to advance his or her economic interests. Government is but an afterthought in this world, since almost everything that people need can be provided by the free market, itself guided by the reassuring "invisible hand."

The second economy is described in the writings of progressives, environmentalists, union supporters, and consumer advocates as well as honest business writers who recognize that real-world markets do not always conform to textbook models. This second economy features vast disparities of income, wealth, and power manifested in a system of class. It is an economy where employers have power over employees, where large firms have the power to shape markets, and where large corporate lobbies have the power to shape public policies. In this second economy, government sometimes adopts policies that ameliorate the abuses of capitalism and other times does just the opposite, but it is always an active and essential participant in economic life.

If you are reading this introduction, you are probably a student in an introductory college course in microeconomics. Your textbook will introduce you to the first economy, the harmonious world of free markets. *Real World Micro* will introduce you to the second.

Why "Real World" Micro?

A standard economics textbook is full of powerful concepts. It is also, by its nature, a limited window on the economy. What is taught in most introductory economics courses today is in fact just one strand of economic thought—neoclassical economics. Fifty years ago, many more strands were part of the introductory economics curriculum, and the contraction of the field has imposed limits on the study of economics that can confuse and frustrate students. This is particularly true in the study of microeconomics, which looks at markets for individual goods or services.

Real World Micro is designed as a supplement to a standard neoclassical textbook. Its articles provide vivid, real-world illustrations of economic concepts. But beyond that, our mission is to address two major sources of confusion in the study of economics at the introductory level.

The first source of confusion is the striking simplification of the world found in orthodox microeconomics. Standard textbooks describe stylized economic

1

interactions between idealized buyers and sellers that bear scant resemblance to the messy realities of the actual economic activity that we see around us. There is nothing wrong with simplifying. In fact, every social science must develop simplified models; precisely because reality is so complex, we must look at it a little bit at a time in order to understand it. Still, these simplifications mystify and misrepresent actual capitalist social relations and excise questions of race, gender, and class from the analysis.

Mainstream economic analysis calls to mind the story of the tipsy party-goer whose friend finds him on his hands and knees under a streetlight. "What are you doing?" asks the friend. "I dropped my car keys across the street, and I'm looking for them," the man replies. "But if you lost them across the street, how come you're looking over here?" "Well, the light's better here." In the interest of greater clarity, economics often imposes similar limits on its areas of inquiry.

As the title *Real World Micro* implies, one of our goals is to confront mainstream microeconomic theory with a more complex reality to direct attention to the areas not illuminated by the streetlight, and particularly to examine how inequality, power, and environmental imbalance change the picture. The idea is not to prove the standard theory "wrong," but to challenge you to think about where the theory is more and less useful, and why markets may not operate as expected.

This focus on real-world counterpoints to mainstream economic theory connects to the second issue we aim to clarify. Most economics texts uncritically present key assumptions and propositions that form the core of standard economic theory. They offer much less exploration of a set of related questions: What are alternative propositions about the economy? Under what circumstances will these alternatives more accurately describe the economy? What differences do such propositions make? Our approach is not to spell out an alternative theory in detail, but to raise questions and present real-life examples that bring these questions to life. For example, textbooks carefully lay out "consumer sovereignty," the notion that consumers' wishes ultimately determine what the economy will produce. But can we reconcile consumer sovereignty with an economy where one of the main products in industries such as soft drinks, cars, and music is consumer desire itself? We think it is valuable to see ideas like consumer sovereignty as debatable propositions and that requires hearing other views in the debate.

In short, our goal in this book is to use real-world examples from today's economy to raise questions, stimulate debate, and dare you to think critically about the models in your textbook.

What's in This Book

Real World Micro is organized to follow the outline of a standard economics text. Each chapter leads off with a brief introduction, including study questions for the entire chapter, and then provides several short articles from *Dollars & Sense* magazine and other sources that illustrate the chapter's key concepts.

Here is a quick overview:

Chapter 1, Perspectives on Microeconomic Theory, starts off the volume by taking a hard look at the strengths and weaknesses of actual markets, with special attention to weaknesses that standard textbooks tend to underemphasize.

Chapter 2, Supply and Demand, presents real-world examples of supply and demand in action. *Dollars & Sense* authors question the conventional wisdom on topics such as price volatility, affordability of essential goods like food (and issues of hunger), and price regulations like the minimum wage and rent control.

Chapter 3, Consumers, raises provocative questions about utility theory and individual consumer choice. What happens when marketers shape buyers' tastes? What happens when important information is hidden from consumers? How can consumer decisions include broader considerations like environmental sustainability or labor conditions? What roles should government play in consumer protection?

Chapter 4, Firms, Production, and Profit Maximization, illustrates how business strategies to maximize profits may come at the expense of the social good, and challenges students to think about different ways of organizing firms. The chapter considers issues like executive compensation, and the relation between the profit motive and essential goods like food and health care.

Chapter 5, Market Failure I: Market Power, explores market power and monopoly, just one example of the unequal power relationships that pervade our economic system. The chapter critiques market power in such industries as pharmaceuticals, banking, and agriculture, but also questions whether small business prevalence would be an improvement.

Chapter 6, Market Failure II: Externalities, addresses cases where processes of production, exchange, and consumption affect not only the parties to those transactions, but also third parties (especially negatively). It considers how public policy should address cases where such spillover effects create a divergence between private and social costs and benefits.

Chapter 7, Labor Markets, examines the ways in which labor-market outcomes can be affected by unionization, globalization, and a host of other factors largely left out of the standard supply-and-demand models. Among the issues discussed are the reasons for union decline, the causes of high unemployment today, the rise of "contingent" labor arrangements, and possible ways to improve labor conditions domestically and internationally.

Chapter 8, The Distribution of Income and Wealth, discusses the causes and consequences of inequality, countering the mainstream view that inequality is good for growth. The chapter examines the contours of inequality, with particular attention to race and gender. It questions conventional views attributing rising inequality to technological change and globalization, and considers the impact of a changing balance of power between workers and employers. And it dealw sith issues of wealth and poverty, both domestic and global.

Chapter 9, Taxation, explores issues of incomes, wealth, and taxation, including who actually pays taxes and at what rates. It also explores whether changes in taxes lead to changes in economic behavior and outcomes. This proposition is explored in the areas of taxes on high-income individuals and their effects on savings and investment, as well as taxes on financial transactions and effects on speculative activity. Finally, it discusses new controversies over growing inequality and the possibility of international taxation on accumulated wealth.

Chapter 10, Trade and Development, covers key issues in trade policy and the world economy. The chapter's articles question the value of free trade and foreign investment for development, consider the role of currency markets in global trade outcomes, address the impacts of globalization on workers (in both high-income and low-income countries), and discuss issues of development and environmental protection.

Chapter 11, Policy Spotlight: Generational War?, explores major policy and social issues related to "intergenerational equity"—the distribution of economic benefits and costs between generations, including the older versus the younger today and current generations versus those yet to be born. It considers issues including investments in education, pensions and Social Security, government debt, and climate change.

Chapter 1

PERPECTIVES ON MICROECONOMIC THEORY

INTRODUCTION

Economics is all about tradeoffs. The concept of "opportunity cost" reminds us that in order to make a purchase, or even to make use of a resource that you control (such as your time), you must give up other possible purchases or other possible uses. Markets broaden the range of possible tradeoffs by facilitating exchange between people who do not know each other, and in many cases never meet at all. Think of buying a pair of athletic shoes in Atlanta from a company based in Los Angeles that manufactures shoes in Malaysia and has stockholders all over the world. As the idea of gains from trade suggests, markets allow many exchanges that make both parties better off.

But markets have severe limitations as well. The economic crisis that began in 2008 has made those limitations all too clear. Even lifelong free-marketeers such as former Federal Reserve chair Alan Greenspan have been forced to question their belief in the "invisible hand."

In the chapter's first article, economist Marty Wolfson critiques a mainstream "free market" ideology that views markets as delivering to each person their just rewards, based on their talent or effort. In fact, he argues, markets are often structured in ways that stack the deck in favor of the wealthy and powerful (Article 1.1).

Markets and price determination, in neoclassical economics, have been idealized into an elegant, utility-maximizing perfection. Chris Tilly, in "Shaking the Invisible Hand" (Article 1.2), uncovers the curious assumptions necessary to allow for the market mechanism to be the most efficient allocator of scarce resources. He provides us with eight "Tilly Assumptions" underlying perfectly functioning markets. If any of these assumptions is violated, then there is a possibility of "market failure," or less-than-optimal market results.

In "Pursuing Profits—Or Power?" (Article 1.3), James K. Boyce questions the assumption that the firm seeks to maximize profits alone. In Boyce's view, a great deal of business behavior (especially political behavior) suggests that corporate decision-makers often put the pursuit of power above profits.

Alejandro Reuss provides us with a clear discussion of the idealized neoclassical view of exchange, with a particular focus on labor markets, in "Freedom, Equity, and Efficiency" (Article 1.4). Ideal neoclassical markets offer the promise of freedom of choice, equity (fairness), and efficiency, but often fail to deliver on all three counts. Reuss walks us through these neoclassical standards and contrasts them to the not-so-rosy reality of unrestrained labor-market competition.

In "Sharing the Wealth of the Commons" (Article 1.5), Peter Barnes focuses our attention on the oft-ignored forms of wealth that we do not own privately, but are held in various "commons." He challenges the way that conventional economists view the environment and other goods that are shared by many people.

An interview with economist Juliet Schor (Article 1.6) explores the causes behind U.S. consumerism. Schor looks beyond some of the "usual suspects"—like advertising—by linking the rise of consumerism to labor-market forces that have prevented the reduction of work time. She argues that future changes in U.S. consumption behavior, and therefore long-term environmental sustainability, depend on reducing hours of work.

Discussion Questions

1. (General) What things should not be for sale? Beyond everyday goods and services, think about human bodies, votes, small countries, and other things that might be bought and sold. How do you draw the line between what should be bought and sold and what should not?

2. (General) If not markets, then what? What are other ways to organize economic activity? Which ways are most likely to resolve the problems brought up in this chapter?

3. (Article 1.1) Wolfson argues that markets, far from being "free," are often rigged in favor of the wealthy and powerful. What are some examples?

4. (Article 1.2) Write out the eight "Tilly Assumptions" and corresponding realities using Tilly's exact terms for the assumptions. Are these assumptions reasonable?

5. (Article 1.2) For each of the eight "Tilly Assumptions," explain how the market mechanism would fail if the assumption were violated.

6. (Article 1.3) Boyce argues that firms frequently put power before profits. If greater power goes hand in hand with higher profits, how can we tell what aim firms are actually pursuing?

7. (Article 1.4) According to neoclassical theory, how do markets deliver "efficient" results if all "barriers" to exchange are removed? In what sense are these results "efficient"?

8. (Article 1.4) How is the word "freedom" defined by neoclassical economists? What freedoms do they argue workers lose under regulated labor markets? How does this compare to your view of what kinds of freedoms are valuable?

9. (Article 1.4) Does the unfettered operation of the market mechanism deliver "equity" to society? In your view, what would fair labor-market processes or outcomes look like?

10. (Article 1.5) Barnes says that we take for granted an enormous number of resources—including the natural environment, but also the laws and institutions that make economic activity possible. Is his point the same as saying that there are market failures, such as pollution externalities, that prevent markets from taking into account the full value of the environment?

11. (Article 1.6) Schor argues that, far from being the consequence of human beings' inherently insatiable wants, consumerism is the result of various social and institutional factors. What does she see as the key factors pushing people to consume more and more? What are the main reasons, in her view, that consumer behavior in the United States has differed from that in other countries?

Article 1.1

"FREE MARKET" OUTCOMES ARE NOT FAIR—AND NOT FREE

BY MARTY WOLFSON
November/December 2012

"Since 1980, the U.S. government has reduced its intervention in the U.S. economy, which has become much more of a free market. Conservatives applaud this development because they think that free-market outcomes reward talent and hard work; progressives object to the income inequality of free-market outcomes and want to use government tax and transfer policy to reduce inequality."

Most people, whether conservative or progressive, would probably agree with this statement. This framing of the issue, however, plays into a right-wing story in which conservatives are the defenders of (free) market outcomes, including the success of the rich who have made it "on their own"; meanwhile, the "dependent poor" look to the government for handouts. This has been a basic element of the right-wing playbook for a long time. Then-presidential candidate Mitt Romney was drawing on this narrative when he complained about the 47% of the U.S. population "who are dependent upon government ... who believe that government has a responsibility to care for them."

This view has two main themes: 1) Because the U.S. free-market economy rewards talent and hard work, the middle class should emulate the wealthy for their success, not vilify them; and 2) those who have been failures in the market want the government to take care of them by redistributing income from those who have been successful. We can see these themes play out on all sorts of political issues. They form, for example, the basis for the attacks on the Affordable Health Care Act (or "Obamacare"). Middle-class Americans, in the conservative view, are being taxed—forced to pay—to provide health insurance for those "unsuccessful" elements of the population who have not earned it themselves.

The conservative argument assumes that the outcomes we observe are the result of a free-market economy. However, the right-wing objective has not been to create a free market; it has been to rig government policy and the market so as to redistribute income towards large corporations and the wealthy.

For example, conservatives themselves want to use government policy to bring about a different distribution of income from what we have now—a distribution that is more favorable to corporations and the very rich. A central policy objective for conservatives, ever since the Reagan Administration, has been to cut taxes on the wealthy. And by cutting government revenue, they have been able to make the argument that government programs for the poor and the middle class need to be cut in order to balance the budget.

Also, conservatives have eliminated restrictions on corporations and protections for workers, consumers, and the environment. They have attacked barriers to international capital mobility, deregulated industries, and reduced government regulations aimed at ensuring a safe workplace and a healthy environment.

Because conservative policies have often taken the form of reducing government programs and regulations, the ideology of a free market has been useful in rationalizing them. Other conservative interventions, however, have been less able to fit into the free-market mold, and therefore are especially revealing of conservatives' genuine aims.

When the financial crisis of 2008 threatened the survival of the large banks, they were quick to ask for the government to intervene with a large bailout. The "right-to-work" law recently passed in Indiana, designed to deprive unions of financial resources, is an explicit rejection of a market outcome—the private agreement between management and union to require all workers to pay their "fair share" of the costs of union representation. "Free-trade" agreements, ostensibly designed to eliminate restrictions on the movement of goods and capital, have nonetheless continued to restrict the free movement of people. Even the repeal of financial regulations in the 1980s and 1990s, ostensibly a free-market endeavor, created the anti-competitive giant financial firms that demanded to be bailed out in 2008.

The realization that the economy is rigged to benefit the rich and large corporations takes away the force of the right-wing argument that progressives want to use government to "vilify" the "successful" and reward the "slothful and incompetent." When the game has been rigged, it is wrong to say that the market simply rewards talent and hard work, and the outcomes that result can hardly be called fair. When the market outcomes that we observe are unfair, we need to both change the rules for how the economy works and use the government to restore fairness. ❏

Sources: Dean Baker, *The End of Loser Liberalism: Making Markets Progressive* (2011); Transcript of Mitt Romney video, *Mother Jones*, September 17, 2012 (motherjones.com).

Article 1.2

SHAKING THE INVISIBLE HAND
The Uncertain Foundations of Free-Market Economics

BY CHRIS TILLY
November 1989; updated March 2011

> "It is not from the benevolence of the butcher, the brewer or the baker that we expect our dinner, but from their regard to their own interest... [No individual] intends to promote the public interest... [rather, he is] led by an invisible hand to promote an end which was no part of his intention."
>
> —*Adam Smith, The Wealth of Nations, 1776*

Seen the Invisible Hand lately? It's all around us these days, propping up conservative arguments in favor of free trade, deregulation, and tax-cutting.

Today's advocates for "free," competitive markets echo Adam Smith's claim that unfettered markets translate the selfish pursuit of individual gain into the greatest benefit for all. They trumpet the superiority of capitalist free enterprise over socialist efforts to supplant the market with a planned economy, and even decry liberal attempts to moderate the market. Anything short of competitive markets, they proclaim, yields economic inefficiency, making society worse off.

But the economic principle underlying this fanfare is shaky indeed. Since the late 19th century, mainstream economists have struggled to prove that Smith was right—that the chaos of free markets leads to a blissful economic order. In the 1950s, U.S. economists Kenneth Arrow and Gerard Debreu finally came up with a theoretical proof, which many orthodox economists view as the centerpiece of modern economic theory.

Although this proof is the product of the best minds of mainstream economics, it ends up saying surprisingly little in defense of free markets. The modern theory of the Invisible Hand shows that given certain assumptions, free markets reduce the wasteful use of economic resources—but perpetuate unequal income distribution.

To prove free markets cut waste, economists must make a number of far-fetched assumptions: there are no concentrations of economic power; buyers and sellers know every detail about the present and future economy; and all costs of production are borne by producers while all benefits from consumption are paid for by consumers (see box for a complete list). Take away any one of these assumptions and markets can lead to stagnation, recession, and other forms of waste—as in fact they do.

In short, the economic theory invoked by conservatives to justify free markets instead starkly reveals their limitations.

The Fruits of Free Markets

The basic idea behind the Invisible Hand can be illustrated with a story. Suppose that I grow apples and you grow oranges. We both grow tired of eating the same fruit all the time and decide to trade. Perhaps we start by trading one apple for one orange. This exchange satisfies both of us, because in fact I would gladly give up more than one apple to get an orange, and you would readily pay more than one orange for an apple. And as long as swapping one more apple for one more orange makes us both better off, we will continue to trade.

Eventually, the trading will come to a stop. I begin to notice that the novelty of oranges wears old as I accumulate a larger pile of them and the apples I once had a surplus of become more precious to me as they grow scarcer. At some point, I draw the line: in order to obtain one more apple from me, you must give me more than one orange. But your remaining oranges have also become more valuable to you. Up to now, each successive trade has made both of us better off. Now there is no further exchange that benefits us both, so we agree to stop trading until the next crop comes in.

Note several features of this parable. Both you and I end up happier by trading freely. If the government stepped in and limited fruit trading, neither of us would be as well off. In fact, the government cannot do anything in the apple/orange market that will make both of us better off than does the free market.

Adding more economic actors, products, money, and costly production processes complicates the picture, but we reach the same conclusions. Most of us sell our labor time in the market rather than fruit; we sell it for money that we then use to buy apples, oranges, and whatever else we need. The theory of the Invisible Hand tells us a trip to the fruit stand improves the lot of both consumer and seller; likewise, the sale of labor time benefits both employer and employee. What's more, according to the theory, competition between apple farmers insures that consumers will get apples produced at the lowest possible cost. Government intervention still can only make things worse.

This fable provides a ready-made policy guide. Substitute "Japanese autos" and "U.S. agricultural products" for apples and oranges, and the fable tells you that import quotas or tariffs only make the people of both countries worse off. Change the industries to airlines or telephone services, and the fable calls for deregulation. Or re-tell the tale in the labor market: minimum wages and unions (which prevent workers from individually bargaining over their wages) hurt employers and workers.

Fruit Salad

Unfortunately for free-market boosters, two major short-comings make a fruit salad out of this story. First, even if free markets perform as advertised, they deliver only one benefit—the prevention of certain economically wasteful practices—while preserving inequality. According to the theory, competitive markets wipe out two kinds of waste: unrealized trades and inefficient production. Given the right assumptions, markets ensure that when two parties both stand to gain from a trade, they make that trade, as in the apples-and-oranges story. Competition compels producers to search for the most efficient, lowest-cost production methods—again, given the right preconditions.

Though eliminating waste is a worthy goal, it leaves economic inequality untouched. Returning once more to the orchard, if I start out with all of the apples and oranges and you start out with none, that situation is free of waste: no swap can make us both better off since you have nothing to trade! Orthodox economists acknowledge that even in the ideal competitive market, those who start out rich stay rich, while the poor remain poor. Many of them argue that attempts at redistributing income will most certainly create economic inefficiencies, justifying the preservation of current inequities.

But in real-life economics, competition does lead to waste. Companies wastefully duplicate each other's research and build excess productive capacity. Cost-cutting often leads to shoddy products, worker speedup, and unsafe working conditions. People and factories stand idle while houses go unbuilt and people go unfed. That's because of the second major problem: real economies don't match the assumptions of the Invisible Hand theory.

Of course, all economic theories build their arguments on a set of simplifying assumptions about the world. These assumptions often sacrifice some less important aspects of reality in order to focus on the economic mechanisms of interest.

Assumptions and Reality

The claim that free markets lead to efficiency and reduced waste rests on eight main assumptions. However, these assumptions differ sharply from economic reality. (Assumptions 1, 3, 4, and 5 are discussed in more detail in the article.)

ASSUMPTION ONE: *No market power.* No individual buyer or seller, nor any group of buyers or sellers, has the power to affect the market-wide level of prices, wages, or profits.
REALITY ONE: Our economy is dotted with centers of market power, from large corporations to unions. Furthermore, employers have an edge in bargaining with workers because of the threat of unemployment.

ASSUMPTION TWO: *No economies of scale.* Small plants can produce as cheaply as large ones.
REALITY TWO: In fields such as mass-production industry, transportation, communications, and agriculture, large producers enjoy a cost advantage, limiting competition.

ASSUMPTION THREE: *Perfect information about the present.* Buyers and sellers know everything there is to know about the goods being exchanged. Also, each is aware of the wishes of every other potential buyer and seller in the market.
REALITY THREE: The world is full of lemons—goods about which the buyer is inadequately informed. Also, people are not mind-readers, so sellers get stuck with surpluses and willing buyers are unable to find the products they want.

ASSUMPTION FOUR: *Perfect information about the future.* Contracts between buyers and sellers cover every possible future eventuality.
REALITY FOUR: Uncertainty clouds the future of any economy. Futures markets are limited.

But in the case of the Invisible Hand, the theoretical preconditions contradict several central features of the economy.

For one thing, markets are only guaranteed to prevent waste if the economy runs on "perfect competition": individual sellers compete by cutting prices, individual buyers compete by raising price offers, and nobody holds concentrated economic power. But today's giant corporations hardly match this description. Coke and Pepsi compete with advertising rather than price cuts. The oil companies keep prices high enough to register massive profits every year. Employers coordinate the pay and benefits they offer to avoid bidding up compensation. Workers, in turn, marshal their own forces via unionization—another departure from perfect competition.

Indeed, the jargon of "perfect competition" overlooks the fact that property ownership itself confers disproportionate economic power. "In the competitive model," orthodox economist Paul Samuelson commented, "it makes no difference whether capital hires labor or the other way around." He argued that given perfect

---

ASSUMPTION FIVE: *You only get what you pay for.* Nobody can impose a cost on somebody else, nor obtain a benefit from them, without paying.
REALITY FIVE: Externalities, both positive and negative, are pervasive. In a free market, polluters can impose costs on the rest of us without paying. And when a public good like a park is built or roads are maintained, everyone benefits whether or not they helped to pay for it.

ASSUMPTION SIX: *Price is a proxy for pleasure.* The price of a given commodity will represent the quality and desirability and or utility derived from the consumption of the commodity.
REALITY SIX: "Conspicuous Consumption" (Veblen) and or "snob effects" will often distort prices from underlying utility and marketers will try to position commodities accordingly.

ASSUMPTION SEVEN: Self-interest only. In economic matters, each person cares only about his or her own level of well-being.
REALITY SEVEN: Solidarity, jealousy, and even love for one's family violate this assumption.

ASSUMPTION EIGHT: No joint production. Each production process has only one product.
REALITY EIGHT: Even in an age of specialization, there are plenty of exceptions to this rule. For example, large service firms such as hospitals or universities produce a variety of different services using the same resources.

—*Chris Tilly and Bryan Snyder*

competition among workers and among capitalists, wages and profits would remain the same regardless of who does the hiring. But unemployment—a persistent feature of market-driven economies—makes job loss very costly to workers. The sting my boss feels when I "fire" him by quitting my job hardly equals the setback I experience when he fires me.

Perfect Information?

In addition, the grip of the Invisible Hand is only sure if all buyers and sellers have "perfect information" about the present and future state of markets. In the present, this implies consumers know exactly what they are buying—an assumption hard to swallow in these days of leaky breast implants and chicken à la Salmonella. Employers must know exactly what skills workers have and how hard they will work—suppositions any real-life manager would laugh at.

Perfect information also means sellers can always sniff out unsatisfied demands, and buyers can detect any excess supplies of goods. Orthodox economists rely on the metaphor of an omnipresent "auctioneer" who is always calling out prices so all buyers and sellers can find mutually agreeable prices and consummate every possible sale. But in the actual economy, the auctioneer is nowhere to be found, and markets are plagued by surpluses and shortages.

Perfect information about the future is even harder to come by. For example, a company decides whether or not to build a new plant based on whether it expects sales to rise. But predicting future demand is a tricky matter. One reason is that people may save money today in order to buy (demand) goods and services in the future. The problem comes in predicting when. As economist John Maynard Keynes observed in 1934, "An act of individual saving means—so to speak—a decision not to have dinner today. But it does not necessitate a decision to have dinner or to buy a pair of boots a week hence...or to consume any specified thing at any specified date. Thus it depresses the business of preparing today's dinner without stimulating the business of making ready for some future act of consumption." Keynes concluded that far from curtailing waste, free markets gave rise to the colossal waste of human and economic resources that was the Great Depression—in part because of this type of uncertainty about the future.

Free Lunch

The dexterity of the Invisible Hand also depends on the principle that "You only get what you pay for." This "no free lunch" principle seems at first glance a reasonable description of the economy. But major exceptions arise. One is what economists call "externalities"—economic transactions that take place outside the market. Consider a hospital that dumps syringes at sea. In effect, the hospital gets a free lunch by passing the costs of waste disposal on to the rest of us. Because no market exists where the right to dump is bought and sold, free markets do nothing to compel the hospital to bear the costs of dumping—which is why the government must step in.

Public goods such as sewer systems also violate the "no free lunch" rule. Once the sewer system is in place, everyone shares in the benefits of the waste disposal, regardless of whether or not they helped pay for it. Suppose sewer systems were sold in a free market, in which each person had the opportunity to buy an individual share. Then any sensible, self-interested consumer would hold back from buying his or her fair share—and wait for others to provide the service. This irrational situation would persist unless consumers could somehow collectively agree on how extensive a sewer system to produce—once more bringing government into the picture.

Most orthodox economists claim that the list of externalities and public goods in the economy is short and easily addressed. Liberals and radicals, on the other hand, offer a long list: for example, public goods include education, health care, and decent public transportation—all in short supply in our society.

Because real markets deviate from the ideal markets envisioned in the theory of the Invisible Hand, they give us both inequality and waste. But if the theory is so far off the mark, why do mainstream economists and policymakers place so much stock in it? They fundamentally believe the profit motive is the best guide for the economy. If you believe that "What's good for General Motors is good for the country," the Invisible Hand theory can seem quite reasonable. Business interests, government, and the media constantly reinforce this belief, and reward those who can dress it up in theoretical terms. As long as capital remains the dominant force in society, the Invisible Hand will maintain its grip on the hearts and minds of us all. ❑

Article 1.3

PURSUING PROFITS—OR POWER?

BY JAMES K. BOYCE
July/August 2013

Do corporations seek to maximize profits? Or do they seek to maximize power? The two may be complementary—wealth begets power, power begets wealth—but they're not the same. One important difference is that profits can come from an expanding economic "pie," whereas the size of the power pie is fixed. Power is a zero-sum game: more for me means less for you. And for corporations, the pursuit of power sometimes trumps the pursuit of profits.

Take public education, for example. Greater investment in education from pre-school through college could increase the overall pie of well-being. But it would narrow the educational advantage of the corporate oligarchs and their privately schooled children—and diminish the power that comes with it. Although corporations could benefit from the bigger pie produced by a better-educated labor force, there's a tension between what's good for business and what's good for the business elite.

Similarly, the business elite today supports economic austerity instead of full-employment policies that would increase growth and profits. This may have something to do with the fact that austerity widens inequality, while full employment would narrow it (by empowering workers). If we peel away the layers of the onion, at the core again we find that those at the top of the corporate pyramid put power before profits.

As one more example, consider the politics of government regulation. Corporations routinely pass along to consumers whatever costs they incur as a result of regulation. In the auto industry, for instance, the regulations that mandated seat belts, catalytic converters, and better fuel efficiency added a few hundred dollars to car prices. They didn't cut automaker profit margins. If the costs of regulation are ultimately borne by the consumer, why do they face such stiff resistance from the corporations? The answer may have less to do with profits than with power. Corporate chieftains are touchy about their "management prerogatives." They simply don't like other folks telling them what to do.

In a famous 1971 memorandum to the U.S. Chamber of Commerce, future Supreme Court Justice Lewis Powell wrote, "The day is long past when the chief executive office of a major corporation discharges his responsibility by maintaining a satisfactory growth of profits." To counter what he described as an attack on the American free-enterprise system by labor unions, students, and consumer advocates, Powell urged CEOs to act on "the lesson that political power is necessary; that power must be assiduously cultivated; and that when necessary, it must be used aggressively and with determination." He was preaching to a receptive choir.

The idea that firms single-mindedly maximize profits is an axiom of faith of neoclassical Econ 101, but alternative theories have a long history in the broader profession. Thorstein Veblen, John Maynard Keynes, and Fred Hirsch all saw an individual's position relative to others as a key motivation in economic behavior.

Today a sound-bite version of this idea is encountered on bumper stickers: "He Who Dies with the Most Toys Wins."

In his 1972 presidential address to the American Economics Association, titled "Power and the Useful Economist," John Kenneth Galbraith juxtaposed the role of power in the real-world economy to its neglect in orthodox economics: "In eliding power—in making economics a nonpolitical subject—neoclassical theory ... destroys its relation with the real world."

On the free-marketeer side of the ideological spectrum, the pursuit of power is depicted as a pathology distinctive to the State. "Chicago school" economist William Niskanen theorized that public-sector bureaucrats seek to maximize the size of their budgets, taking this as a proxy for "salary, perquisites of the office, public reputation, power, patronage, ease of managing the bureau, and ease of making changes." He called this "the peculiar economics of bureaucracy."

But the pursuit of power isn't unique to government bureaucracies. It's commonplace in corporate bureaucracies, too. In his presidential address, Galbraith made the connection: "Between public and private bureaucracies—between GM and the Department of Transportation, between General Dynamics and the Pentagon—there is a deeply symbiotic relationship."

Recognizing the real-world pursuit of power not only helps us understand behavior that otherwise may seem peculiar. It also redirects our attention from the dichotomy between the market and the state toward a more fundamental one: the divide between oligarchy and democracy. ❏

Sources: Sarah O'Connor, "OECD warns of rising inequality as austerity intensifies," *Financial Times*, May 15, 2013 (ft.com); Lewis F. Powell, Jr., "Confidential Memorandum: Attack on American Free Enterprise System," Aug. 23, 1971 (law.wlu.edu); John Kenneth Galbraith, "Power and the Useful Economist," *American Economic Review*, March 1973; William A. Niskanen, "The Peculiar Economics of Bureaucracy," *American Economic Review*, May 1968.

Article 1.4

FREEDOM, EQUITY, AND EFFICIENCY
Contrasting Views of Labor Market Competition

BY ALEJANDRO REUSS
April 2012

The basic world-view of neoclassical economists is that, in markets, people engage voluntarily in exchanges with each other, and that this means market exchanges leave both parties better off. If someone cannot be forced to make a trade, they will only do so if it leaves them at least a little better off than they would have been otherwise. Left to their own devices, people will find and exhaust all the possibilities for trades that boost the overall social well-being. Policies that interfere with people's ability to make voluntary trades, then, can only subtract from the well-being of society as a whole.

The neoclassical narrative depends on many (often unspoken) *assumptions*. Individuals must be rational and self-interested. The assumption of "rationality" means they must act in ways that further their objectives, whatever these objectives may be. The assumption of "self-interest" means that, in making decisions, they must only take into account benefits and costs to themselves. They must have perfect information about all factors (past, present, and future) that could affect their decisions. Their actions must not affect any "third parties" (anyone other than those directly involved in the exchange and agreeing to its terms). There must be many buyers and sellers, so that no single buyer or seller (and no group of buyers or sellers colluding together) can impose the prices they want. Several other assumptions may also be important.

The Neoclassical View

Implicitly, the neoclassical story appeals to ideas about freedom, equity (fairness), and efficiency. Very few people would say they are against any of these virtues, but different people embrace different definitions. Different people, for example, have different ideas about what people should have the freedom to do, and what "freedoms" would impinge on the freedoms, rights, or well-being of others. So really the issue is, when neoclassical economists say that unregulated market competition is desirable, for example, as a matter, of "freedom," what view of freedom are they basing this on?

Freedom

By "freedom," neoclassical economists mean freedom from force or threat of force. They would recognize that someone making an exchange when threatened with violence—when confronted with "an offer they can't refuse," in the *Godfather* sense of that phrase—is not really engaging in a voluntary transaction. That person could very well make an exchange leaving them worse off than they would have been otherwise (except that they may have saved their own neck). On the other hand, suppose a person is faced only with very undesirable alternatives to engaging in a trade. Suppose they have "no choice" but to accept a job, because the alternative is to starve. Neoclassical economists would point out that these circumstances are not of the potential employer's making. It is quite unlike, in their view, conditions that are directly imposed by the other party (like having a gun held to one's head). If the impoverished worker accepts a job offer, even at a very low wage or under very bad working conditions, the neoclassical economist would argue that this is evidence that he or she really is made better off by the exchange. Restricting his or her freedom to engage in this exchange, in the neoclassical view, only makes him or her worse off.

Equity

Neoclassical economists argue that restrictions on market competition can unfairly benefit some market participants (buyers or sellers) or potential market participants at the expense of others. This kind of equity concern enters into neoclassical theory in several ways:

First, restrictions on competition may affect the ability of different people (or firms) to participate in a market—to offer what they have for sale or to bid on what others offer for sale. Suppose that the government issues special licenses to some people or firms that permit them to engage in a certain trade, like driving a taxi, while denying such licenses to others. (Such policies create "barriers to entry," in the language of neoclassical economics.) Such restrictions are, in the neoclassical view, unfair to the unlucky (or less-influential) individuals or firms who do not receive licenses and so are locked out of the market.

Second, restrictions may affect the ability of different people to use whatever advantage they may have, to compete in a market. A price floor, for example, prevents lower-cost sellers from using their cost advantage (their willingness to accept a lower price) to compete in the market. In the neoclassical view, this favors higher-cost sellers at the expense of their lower-cost competitors.

Third, restrictions may affect the ability of sellers to fetch the highest price they can, constrained only by competition from other sellers, and of buyers to pay the lowest price they can, constrained only by bidding from other buyers. A price floor, by restricting producers from competing on price (preventing any from offering prices below the floor), may favor producers in general at the expense of consumers. By the same token, a price ceiling (a maximum legal price) may favor consumers at the expense of producers.

Efficiency

In the neoclassical view, a resource is used "efficiently" as long as the benefit from using that resource is greater than the cost. Let's think about a company—say, an auto company—that has to decide how many machines to rent or how many workers to hire for its operations. It will consider how many extra cars it can produce if it rents one additional machine, or hires one additional worker. The company will figure out how much income it will get from the sale of those additional cars. That is, it will multiply the number of additional cars by the price it will get per car. Ultimately, it will compare this extra income against the rental cost paid for the machine, or the wage paid to the worker. The company will rent a machine, or hire a worker, as long as the extra income it gets is more than the additional cost it has to pay.

In the neoclassical view, this is "efficient" not only from the standpoint of the company, but from the standpoint of society as a whole. If the cost of using an extra machine or hiring an extra worker is less than value of the extra cars produced, the use of the machine or worker is also "efficient" from the standpoint of society as a whole.

There's just one more problem. In the neoclassical view, for private actors to make decisions that are also "efficient" form the standpoint of society as a whole, the prices they base their decisions on have to be the *right* prices. That is, each price has to reflect the true cost of a good to society as a whole. So how do we know, in this view, what is the "right price"?

The "Right" Wage

Let's look at an example using, in the language of neoclassical economics, the "price of labor" (or wage). Suppose that the going wage in a certain place is $20 per hour. According to neoclassical economists, a company will hire a worker as long as the extra benefit it gets from each extra hour of labor (the extra units produced times the price the company gets per unit) is at least as much as the additional cost it pays for that extra hour of labor ($20). Suppose, however, that the wage was only this high because there were barriers to competition in the labor market. If the wage without barriers would have only been, say, $10, then a company would hire an extra worker as long as the extra benefit it got from each extra hour of labor was at least $10 per hour.

How do we know whether the "right" wage is $20 or $10? In the view of neoclassical economists, the right wage—like any other right price—reflects the true cost to society of the good involved (here, an hour of labor). The cost of labor is whatever pains the worker endures as a result of that hour of work. This includes having to show up for work, when one might prefer to be someone else, having to follow the employer's orders, when one would rather be "doing one's own thing," putting up with the conditions at work, which could be dangerous, unhealthy, or unpleasant, and so on. It is competition in the labor market that makes workers reveal what they really require to compensate them for the burdens of labor.

If the price of labor, due to barriers to labor-market competition, is "too high," then employers will use "too little" labor. If the wage is $20, due to barriers, then employers will not hire an extra hour of labor unless it results in the production of at least $20 of additional goods. As a result of the inflated price of labor, society will have turned its back on who-knows-how-many opportunities to get between $10 and $20 of goods at a true cost of $10 worth of labor. In other words, wages that are inflated by barriers to competition result in an "inefficient" use of resources.

Critiques of the Neoclassical View

Economists associated with different schools of thought may use normative concepts like "freedom," "equity," or "efficiency," but mean something very different by these ideas than what neoclassical economists mean. (Some may choose not to use these terms, and instead invoke other normative concepts, like "justice," "equality," "the good life," and so on.) Here, however, we will focus on contrasts with the neoclassical views of freedom, equity, and efficiency described above.

Freedom

Neoclassical economists emphasize workers' freedom of choice to accept low wages, long hours, bad working conditions, and so on. Workers would not accept those conditions, they argue, unless doing so would leave them better off than they would be otherwise. In this view, institutions like unions or policies like minimum-wage laws interfere with workers' freedom to make a deal that would leave them better off.

Many liberal and almost all radical economists, on the other hand, emphasize how the conditions that an individual will "freely" accept depend on the alternatives available to them. If the only alternative is to starve in the street, most people would work even very long hours, under very bad conditions, for very low pay. Instead of seeing these workers as having "freely" accepted such agreements, however, one could view them as lacking any real freedom to *refuse* these conditions.

Union contracts, minimum-wage laws, and other restraints on competition between workers do, indeed, restrict each individual worker's "freedom" to accept lower wages, worse conditions, and so on, just as neoclassical economists argue. However, this view ignores the benefit to each worker—that these institutions also *protect* each worker from other workers undercutting him or her. Instead of seeing restraints on labor competition as robbing workers of the freedom to accept lower wages or worse conditions, one can instead see them as giving workers the freedom to demand higher wages or better conditions.

Equity

Barriers to labor-market competition, neoclassical economists argue, favor some workers at the expense of others and workers at the expense of consumers. An alternative view is that restraints on labor-market competition allow workers to get a better deal (higher pay, better conditions, etc.) from employers. The absence of these restraints, on the other hand, may result in higher profits for employers while relegating workers to lower pay and worse conditions. Which outcome one prefers depends on how one values benefits to one group of people (workers) compared to benefits to another (employers).

There are several reasons that someone might favor the interests of workers over those of employers, and therefore approve of changes that benefit workers even if these benefits come at the expense of employers:

1. **Ideas of "fairness" based on social "custom" or "convention."** In most societies where people work for wages, there are evolving ideas about what is a "fair" wage or "decent" living. Partly, such ideas may be based on what people have become accustomed to in the past. Partly, they may reflect expectations that conditions of life will improve over time, and especially from one generation to the next.

2. **Commitment to greater economic and social equality.** People who get most of their income from property (ownership of businesses, land or buildings, or financial wealth) are likely to be at the top of the income ladder. Most of the people at the bottom or in the middle, on the other hand, get most of their income from work. Therefore, changes that benefit workers as a group (at the expense of employers) tend to bring about a more equal distribution of income in society.

3. **Ideas about who creates and deserves to keep society's wealth.** Some "radical" economists argue that labor is the source of all new wealth produced in society. Owners of property take a piece of this wealth by controlling things (like farms, mines, factories, etc.) that everyone else needs in order to work and live. In this view, there is no such thing as a "fair" distribution of income between workers and employers, since the employing class exists only by virtue of taking part of what workers produce.

Much of the history of labor movements around the world centers on attempts to *restrain* competition between workers, to keep workers from undercutting each other on the wages or conditions they will accept, and therefore to benefit workers as a group. Unions, for example, are compacts by which each member agrees *not* to accept a lower wage or worse conditions than the other members. Unions also set conditions on hours, benefits, and conditions of work. No individual can bargain a lower wage or worse conditions, in order to get a job, and thereby force other workers to do the same. Labor legislation like the minimum-wage laws, maximum hours (or overtime) laws, and laws regulating labor conditions, likewise, all restrain competition between workers.

Efficiency

We have already described one concept of efficiency used by neoclassical economists: The key idea is that resources are used if (and only if) the benefit to society is greater than the cost. Neoclassical economists also use another concept of efficiency: An efficient condition is one in which nobody can be made better off without making someone worse off. This definition, pioneered by the Italian neoclassical economist Vilfredo Pareto, is known as "Pareto efficiency." The two definitions are connected: If resources were being wasted (used inefficiently), they could be used to make someone better off without making anyone worse off.

Neoclassical economists call a *change* that makes some people better off without making anyone worse off a "Pareto improvement." There are very few changes in public policies, however, that make some people better off while literally making nobody worse off. Most policy changes, potentially affecting millions of people, make some people better off and others worse off. In these cases, neoclassical economists apply what they call the "compensation test." They compare the benefits to the "winners" from some change in public policy to the losses to the "losers." If the total gains are greater than the total losses, neoclassical economists argue, the winners could compensate the losers—and leave everyone at least a little better off.

In most cases where there are both winners and losers due to a change in public policy, however, the winners do not actually compensate the losers. These are not, then, actual efficiency improvements in the sense that some people are made better off while nobody is made worse off. Restraints on labor-market competition, for example, may benefit workers at the expense of their employers. (Eliminating such policies, meanwhile, may have the opposite effect.)

Judging whether these changes are for the better, then, involves weighing the benefits to some people against the losses to others. How one resolves such an issue depends on one's normative ideas, or values, about whose interests should take precedence. In other words—which side are you on? ❑

Article 1.5

SHARING THE WEALTH OF THE COMMONS

BY PETER BARNES
November/December 2004

We're all familiar with private wealth, even if we don't have much. Economists and the media celebrate it every day. But there's another trove of wealth we barely notice: our common wealth.

Each of us is the beneficiary of a vast inheritance. This common wealth includes our air and water, habitats and ecosystems, languages and cultures, science and technologies, political and monetary systems, and quite a bit more. To say we share this inheritance doesn't mean we can call a broker and sell our shares tomorrow. It does mean we're responsible for the commons and entitled to any income it generates. Both the responsibility and the entitlement are ours by birth. They're part of the obligation each generation owes to the next, and each living human owes to other beings.

At present, however, our economic system scarcely recognizes the commons. This omission causes two major tragedies: ceaseless destruction of nature and widening inequality among humans. Nature gets destroyed because no one's unequivocally responsible for protecting it. Inequality widens because private wealth concentrates while common wealth shrinks.

The great challenges for the 21st century are, first of all, to make the commons visible; second, to give it proper reverence; and third, to translate that reverence into property rights and legal institutions that are on a par with those supporting private property. If we do this, we can avert the twin tragedies currently built into our market-driven system.

Defining the Commons

What exactly is the commons? Here is a workable definition: The commons includes all the assets we inherit together and are morally obligated to pass on, undiminished, to future generations.

This definition is a practical one. It designates a set of assets that have three specific characteristics: they're (1) inherited, (2) shared, and (3) worthy of long-term preservation. Usually it's obvious whether an asset has these characteristics or not.

At the same time, the definition is broad. It encompasses assets that are natural as well as social, intangible as well as tangible, small as well as large. It also introduces a moral factor that is absent from other economic definitions: it requires us to consider whether an asset is worthy of long-term preservation. At present, capitalism has no interest in this question. If an asset is likely to yield a competitive return to capital, it's kept alive; if not, it's destroyed or allowed to run down. Assets in the commons, by contrast, are meant to be preserved regardless of their return.

This definition sorts all economic assets into two baskets, the market and the commons. In the market basket are those assets we want to own privately and manage for profit. In the commons basket are the assets we want to hold in common and manage for long-term preservation. These baskets then are, or ought to be, the yin and yang of economic activity; each should enhance and contain the other. The role of the state should be to maintain a healthy balance between them.

The Value of the Commons

For most of human existence, the commons supplied everyone's food, water, fuel, and medicines. People hunted, fished, gathered fruits and herbs, collected firewood and building materials, and grazed their animals in common lands and waters. In other words, the commons was the source of basic sustenance. This is still true today in many parts of the world, and even in San Francisco, where I live, cash-poor people fish in the bay not for sport, but for food.

Though sustenance in the industrialized world now flows mostly through markets, the commons remains hugely valuable. It's the source of all natural resources and nature's many replenishing services. Water, air, DNA, seeds, topsoil, minerals, the protective ozone layer, the atmosphere's climate regulation, and much more, are gifts of nature to us all.

Just as crucially, the commons is our ultimate waste sink. It recycles water, oxygen, carbon, and everything else we excrete, exhale, or throw away. It's the place we store, or try to store, the residues of our industrial system.

The commons also holds humanity's vast accumulation of knowledge, art, and thought. As Isaac Newton said, "If I have seen further it is by standing on the shoulders of giants." So, too, the legal, political, and economic institutions we inherit—even the market itself—were built by the efforts of millions. Without these gifts we'd be hugely poorer than we are today.

To be sure, thinking of these natural and social inheritances primarily as economic assets is a limited way of viewing them. I deeply believe they are much more than that. But if treating portions of the commons as economic assets can help us conserve them, it's surely worth doing so.

How much might the commons be worth in monetary terms? It's relatively easy to put a dollar value on private assets. Accountants and appraisers do it every day, aided by the fact that private assets are regularly traded for money.

This isn't the case with most shared assets. How much is clean air, an intact wetlands, or Darwin's

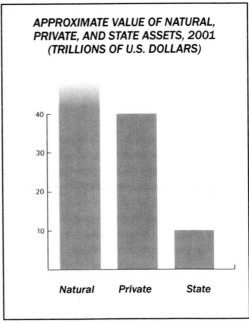

APPROXIMATE VALUE OF NATURAL, PRIVATE, AND STATE ASSETS, 2001 (TRILLIONS OF U.S. DOLLARS)

theory of evolution worth in dollar terms? Clearly, many shared inheritances are simply priceless. Others are potentially quantifiable, but there's no current market for them. Fortunately, economists have developed methods to quantify the value of things that aren't traded, so it's possible to estimate the value of the "priceable" part of the commons within an order of magnitude. The surprising conclusion that emerges from numerous studies is that the wealth we share is worth more than the wealth we own privately.

This fact bears repeating. Even though much of the commons can't be valued in monetary terms, the parts that can be valued are worth more than all private assets combined.

It's worth noting that these estimates understate the gap between common and private assets because a significant portion of the value attributed to private wealth is in fact an appropriation of common wealth. If this mislabeled portion was subtracted from private wealth and added to common wealth, the gap between the two would widen further.

Two examples will make this point clear. Suppose you buy a house for $200,000 and, without improving it, sell it a few years later for $300,000. You pay off the mortgage and walk away with a pile of cash. But what caused the house to rise in value? It wasn't anything you did. Rather, it was the fact that your neighborhood became more popular, likely a result of the efforts of community members, improvements in public services, and similar factors.

Or consider another fount of private wealth, the social invention and public expansion of the stock market. Suppose you start a business that goes "public" through an offering of stock. Within a few years, you're able to sell your stock for a spectacular capital gain.

Much of this gain is a social creation, the result of centuries of monetary-system evolution, laws and regulations, and whole industries devoted to accounting, sharing information, and trading stocks. What's more, there's a direct correlation between the scale and quality of the stock market as an institution and the size of the private gain. You'll fetch a higher price if you sell into a market of millions than into a market of two. Similarly, you'll gain more if transaction costs are low and trust in public information is high. Thus, stock that's traded on a regulated exchange sells for a higher multiple of earnings than unlisted stock. This socially created premium can account for 30% of the stock's value. If you're the lucky seller, you'll reap that extra cash—in no way thanks to anything you did as an individual.

Real estate gains and the stock market's social premium are just two instances of common assets contributing to private gain. Still, most rich people would like us to think it's their extraordinary talent, hard work, and risk-taking that create their well-deserved wealth. That's like saying a flower's beauty is due solely to its own efforts, owing nothing to nutrients in the soil, energy from the sun, water from the aquifer, or the activity of bees.

The Great Commons Giveaway

That we inherit a trove of common wealth is the good news. The bad news, alas, is that our inheritance is being grossly mismanaged. As a recent report by the advocacy group Friends of the Commons concludes, "Maintenance of the commons is terrible, theft is rampant, and rents often aren't collected. To put it bluntly, our common wealth—and our children's—is being squandered. We are all poorer as a result."

Examples of commons mismanagement include the handout of broadcast spectrum to media conglomerates, the giveaway of pollution rights to polluters, the extension of copyrights to entertainment companies, the patenting of seeds and genes, the privatization of water, and the relentless destruction of habitat, wildlife, and ecosystems.

This mismanagement, though currently extreme, is not new. For over 200 years, the market has been devouring the commons in two ways. With one hand, the market takes valuable stuff from the commons and privatizes it. This is called "enclosure." With the other hand, the market dumps bad stuff into the commons and says, "It's your problem." This is called "externalizing." Much that is called economic growth today is actually a form of cannibalization in which the market diminishes the commons that ultimately sustains it.

Enclosure—the taking of good stuff from the commons—at first meant privatization of land by the gentry. Today it means privatization of many common assets by corporations. Either way, it means that what once belonged to everyone now belongs to a few.

Enclosure is usually justified in the name of efficiency. And sometimes, though not always, it does result in efficiency gains. But what also results from enclosure is the impoverishment of those who lose access to the commons, and the enrichment of those who take title to it. In other words, enclosure widens the gap between those with income-producing property and those without.

Externalizing—the dumping of bad stuff into the commons—is an automatic behavior pattern of profit-maximizing corporations: if they can avoid any out-of-pocket costs, they will. If workers, taxpayers, anyone downwind, future generations, or nature have to absorb added costs, so be it.

For decades, economists have agreed we'd be better served if businesses "internalized" their externalities—that is, paid in real time the costs they now shift to the commons. The reason this doesn't happen is that there's no one to set prices and collect them. Unlike private wealth, the commons lacks property rights and institutions to represent it in the marketplace.

The seeds of such institutions, however, are starting to emerge. Consider one of the environmental protection tools the United States currently uses, pollution trading. So-called cap-and-trade programs put a cap on total pollution, then grant portions of the total, via permits, to each polluting firm. Companies may buy other firms' permits if they want to pollute more than their allotment allows, or sell unused permits if they manage to pollute less. Such programs are generally supported by business because they allow polluters to find the cheapest ways to reduce pollution.

Public discussion of cap-and-trade programs has focused exclusively on their trading features. What's been overlooked is how they give away common wealth to polluters.

To date, all cap-and-trade programs have begun by giving pollution rights to existing polluters for free. This treats polluters as if they own our sky and rivers. It means that future polluters will have to pay old polluters for the scarce—hence valuable—right to dump wastes into nature. Imagine that: because a corporation polluted in the past, it gets free income forever! And, because ultimately we'll all pay for limited pollution via higher prices, this amounts to an enormous transfer of wealth—trillions of dollars—to shareholders of historically polluting corporations.

In theory, though, there is no reason that the initial pollution rights should not reside with the public. Clean air and the atmosphere's capacity to absorb pollutants are "wealth" that belongs to everyone. Hence, when polluters use up these parts of the commons, they should pay the public—not the other way around.

Taking the Commons Back

How can we correct the system omission that permits, and indeed promotes, destruction of nature and ever-widening inequality among humans? The answer lies in building a new sector of the economy whose clear legal mission is to preserve shared inheritances for everyone. Just as the market is populated by profit-maximizing corporations, so this new sector would be populated by asset-preserving trusts.

Here a brief description of trusts may be helpful. The trust is a private institution that's even older than the corporation. The essence of a trust is a fiduciary relationship. A trust holds and manages property for another person or for many other people. A simple example is a trust set up by a grandparent to pay for a grandchild's education. Other trusts include pension funds, charitable foundations, and university endowments. There are also hundreds of trusts in America, like the Nature Conservancy and the Trust for Public Land, that own land or conservation easements in perpetuity.

If we were to design an institution to protect pieces of the commons, we couldn't do much better than a trust. The goal of commons management, after all, is to preserve assets and deliver benefits to broad classes of beneficiaries. That's what trusts do, and it's not rocket science.

Over centuries, several principles of trust management have evolved.

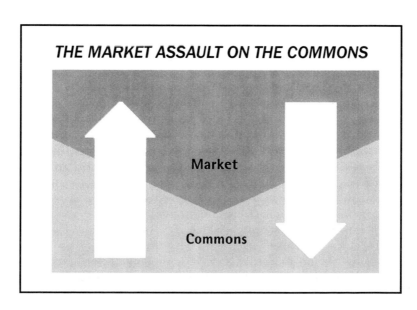

THE MARKET ASSAULT ON THE COMMONS

Market

Commons

These include:

- Trustees have a fiduciary responsibility to beneficiaries. If a trustee fails in this obligation, he or she can be removed and penalized.
- Trustees must preserve the original asset. It's okay to spend income, but don't invade the principal.
- Trustees must assure transparency. Information about money flows should be readily available to beneficiaries.

Trusts in the new commons sector would be endowed with rights comparable to those of corporations. Their trustees would take binding oaths of office and, like judges, serve long terms. Though protecting common assets would be their primary job, they would also distribute income from those assets to beneficiaries. These beneficiaries would include all citizens within a jurisdiction, large classes of citizens (children, the elderly), and/or agencies serving common purposes such as public transit or ecological restoration. When distributing income to individuals, the allocation formula would be one person, one share. The right to receive commons income would be a nontransferable birthright, not a property right that could be traded.

Fortuitously, a working model of such a trust already exists: the Alaska Permanent Fund. When oil drilling on the North Slope began in the 1970s, Gov. Jay Hammond, a Republican, proposed that 25% of the state's royalties be placed in a mutual fund to be invested on behalf of Alaska's citizens. Voters approved in a referendum. Since then, the Alaska Permanent Fund has grown to over $28 billion, and Alaskans have received roughly $22,000 apiece in dividends. In 2003 the per capita dividend was $1,107; a family of four received $4,428.

What Alaska did with its oil can be replicated for other gifts of nature. For example, we could create a nationwide Sky Trust to stabilize the climate for future generations. The trust would restrict emissions of heat-trapping gases and sell a declining number of emission permits to polluters. The income would be returned to U.S. residents in equal yearly dividends, thus reversing the wealth transfer built into current cap-and-trade programs. Instead of everyone paying historic polluters, polluters would pay all of us.

Just as a Sky Trust could represent our equity in the natural commons, a Public Stock Trust could embody our equity in the social commons. Such a trust would capture some of the socially created stock-market premium that currently flows only to shareholders and their investment bankers. As noted earlier, this premium is sizeable—roughly 30% of the value of publicly traded stock. A simple way to share it would be to create a giant mutual fund—call it the American Permanent Fund—that would hold, say, 10% of the shares of publicly traded companies. This mutual fund, in turn, would be owned by all Americans on a one share per person basis (perhaps linked to their Social Security accounts).

To build up the fund without precipitating a fall in share prices, companies would contribute shares at the rate of, say, 1% per year. The contributions would be the price companies pay for the benefits they derive from a commons asset, the large, trusted market for stock—a small price, indeed, for the hefty benefits. Over time, the mutual fund would assure that when the economy grows, everyone benefits. The top 5% would still own more than the bottom 90%, but at least every American would have some property income, and a slightly larger slice of our economic pie.

Sharing the Wealth

The perpetuation of inequality is built into the current design of capitalism. Because of the skewed distribution of private wealth, a small self-perpetuating minority receives a disproportionate share of America's nonlabor income.

Tom Paine had something to say about this. In his essay "Agrarian Justice," written in 1790, he argued that, because enclosure of the commons had separated so many people from their primary source of sustenance, it was necessary to create a functional equivalent of the commons in the form of a National Fund. Here is how he put it:

> There are two kinds of property. Firstly, natural property, or that which comes to us from the Creator of the universe—such as the earth, air, water. Secondly, artificial or acquired property—the invention of men. In the latter, equality is impossible; for to distribute it equally, it would be necessary that all should have contributed in the same proportion, which can never be the case …. Equality of natural property is different. Every individual in the world is born with legitimate claims on this property, or its equivalent.

Enclosure of the commons, he went on, was necessary to improve the efficiency of cultivation. But:

> The landed monopoly that began with [enclosure] has produced the greatest evil. It has dispossessed more than half the inhabitants of every nation of their natural inheritance, without providing for them, as ought to have been done, an indemnification for that loss, and has thereby created a species of poverty and wretchedness that did not exist before.

The appropriate compensation for loss of the commons, Paine said, was a national fund financed by rents paid by land owners. Out of this fund, every person reaching age 21 would get 15 pounds a year, and every person over 50 would receive an additional 10 pounds. (Think of Social Security, financed by commons rents instead of payroll taxes.)

A Progressive Offensive

Paine's vision, allowing for inflation and new forms of enclosure, could not be more timely today. Surely from our vast common inheritance—not just the land, but the atmosphere, the broadcast spectrum, our mineral resources, our threatened habitats and water supplies—enough rent can be collected to pay every American over age 21 a modest annual dividend, and every person reaching 21 a small start-up inheritance.

Such a proposal may seem utopian. In today's political climate, perhaps it is. But consider this. About 20 years ago, right-wing think tanks laid out a bold agenda.

They called for lowering taxes on private wealth, privatizing much of government, and deregulating industry. Amazingly, this radical agenda has largely been achieved.

It's time for progressives to mount an equally bold offensive. The old shibboleths—let's gin up the economy, create jobs, and expand government programs—no longer excite. We need to talk about fixing the economy, not just growing it; about income for everyone, not just jobs; about nurturing ecosystems, cultures, and communities, not just our individual selves. More broadly, we need to celebrate the commons as an essential counterpoise to the market.

Unfortunately, many progressives have viewed the state as the only possible counterpoise to the market. The trouble is, the state has been captured by corporations. This capture isn't accidental or temporary; it's structural and long-term.

This doesn't mean progressives can't occasionally recapture the state. We've done so before and will do so again. It does mean that progressive control of the state is the exception, not the norm; in due course, corporate capture will resume. It follows that if we want lasting fixes to capitalism's tragic flaws, we must use our brief moments of political ascendancy to build institutions that endure.

Programs that rely on taxes, appropriations, or regulations are inherently transitory; they get weakened or repealed when political power shifts. By contrast, institutions that are self-perpetuating and have broad constituencies are likely to last. (It also helps if they mail out checks periodically.) This was the genius of Social Security, which has survived—indeed grown—through numerous Republican administrations.

If progressives are smart, we'll use our next New Deal to create common property trusts that include all Americans as beneficiaries. These trusts will then be to the 21st century what social insurance was to the 20th: sturdy pillars of shared responsibility and entitlement. Through them, the commons will be a source of sustenance for all, as it was before enclosure. Life-long income will be linked to generations-long ecological health. Isn't that a future most Americans would welcome? ❑

Article 1.6

THE FUTURE OF WORK, LEISURE, AND CONSUMPTION

AN INTERVIEW WITH JULIET SCHOR
May/June 2014

Economist Juliet Schor is known worldwide for her research on the interrelated issues of work, leisure, and consumption. Her books on these themes include The Overworked American: The Unexpected Decline of Leisure, The Overspent American: Upscaling, Downshifting, and the New Consumer, *and* Plenitude: The New Economics of True Wealth *(retitled* True Wealth *for its paperback edition). She is also a professor of sociology at Boston College.* —Eds.

DOLLARS & SENSE: We wouldn't expect patterns of work, leisure, and consumption to change overnight, but we're now more than half a decade into a profound crisis. Obviously it's had a big impact on employment, incomes, and so forth, but do you see any lasting changes emerging?

JULIET SCHOR: Some of the trends that were pretty significant before the crash have abated. I'm thinking most particularly about what I've called the "fast fashion model" of consumption—cheap imports of manufactured goods that people were acquiring at accelerating rates, the acceleration of the fashion cycle, and the cycle of acquisition and discard. The trend was people buying things, holding them for shorter and shorter periods of time and then discarding them either into some kind of household storage, into a waste stream, or into secondary markets. You had an amazing period of acquisition of consumer goods. I first started looking at this in the realm of apparel, but it was also in consumer electronics, ordinary household appliances, and pretty much across the board in consumer goods.

Of course, a lot of it was financed by debt or longer working hours, but manufactured goods just became so cheap. The idea that you could buy a DVD player for $19—and yes, people were trampling each other in the stores on Black Friday to get them—but that's just an extraordinary period. So that has changed, because the economics of that have changed. Going forward, I don't think we're going to see that level of availability of cheap goods that we saw before. So I think that cycle has slowed down.

The other big thing has been the bifurcation of the consumer market. That's something that's been going on for a long time—the falling out of the middle as a result of the decline of the middle class, the growth of a really low-end in the consumer market with dollar stores and a retail sector where even Walmart is considered expensive. The other side was the expansion of the hyper-luxury market.

Trends in income and wealth are reflected in the consumer sphere. There's more reluctance to take on debt, so debt-fueled consumer buying is lessened. There's also less availability of consumer credit for households now. The other big thing that I've been looking at is the rise of "alternative cultures" of consumption; that is, people moving out of the branded, advertised goods and the mass-produced lifestyles that dominated in the last couple of decades into more ecologically aware lifestyles with more artisanal and self-production.

D&S: Stepping back and looking more broadly at the emergence of this mass consumer culture in the United States after the Second World War, what do you see that are the key factors that are at the root of consumer capitalism in the United States? It seems a little facile to focus too narrowly on just advertising. Some scholars point to mass media images and what kinds of lifestyles people aspire to. Galbraith pointed more generally to the relentless stream of new products fueling new desires—the so-called "dependence effect." How do you see those influences, as well as others, sorting out?

JS: I don't want to completely dismiss factors like the old monopoly capital idea or the advertising and marketing story, which is that shortfalls of demand led to a big effort to get people to buy things, but I don't buy that story, for the most part. If you think about the postwar period, you had a labor market in which firms were unwilling to use productivity growth to reduce hours of work, and I wrote a book about that, *The Overworked American*. Part of that was about firms and why they don't want to do that. So in the post-war period, you have, from the labor market side, a situation where all productivity growth is getting channeled into income— into expansion of output—so it goes to wages and profits.

Now, of course, workers aren't getting the benefits of productivity growth, but in the post-war era, they did. There were contracts that were explicitly tied—3% productivity, 3% real wage growth. So that creates consumer demand, because that income is getting into people's pockets. Now you can ask the question: Why don't they save it? I don't think it's advertising, primarily, that determines why people didn't save more. There, I think, you have to look at social competition, and the fact that you have an unequal society in which how you live, what you buy, and what you have are important determinants of social position. Rising income gives you a constantly rising norm, and people consume to keep up with that norm. I think it would have played out more or less similarly if there weren't any advertising. The products might have been different but this sort of "consumer escalator," the fact that you have growing levels of consumption, is really coming much more from the production side. So in that way, I'm much more Marxian than Keynesian, I would say.

D&S: Turning to the contrast between the United States and other high-income capitalist countries, especially in terms of the shape of the labor movement and the role of the state: How did working hours get reduced in other countries? In France or Germany, for example, the average employed person works about 300 hours less per year than in the United States. So that strikes me as quite central, in your analysis, in terms of understanding consumption patterns in different countries.

JS: In the United States in the post-war period, the state devoted a lot of energy to the promotion of consumption, whether it was the highway system or suburbanization. That was in part out of a fear of the "Keynesian problem" of inadequate demand after the Second World War. In Europe, I guess I would point to two things. First, after the war, they had a supply-side problem, which was that they had to rebuild productive capacity rather than what we had, which was the demand-side problem. So our state was much more oriented to promoting consumption than European states, which were more oriented towards rebuilding their societies. In Europe, working hours continued to fall and they didn't in the United States.

That's the way you need to think about it—everybody was on a common trajectory of work-hours decline from about 1870. Of course, the United States was the leader in all of that. We had the shortest working hours and we were the first ones to put in reforms of working hours: The United States was the leader on no Sunday work, no Saturday work, etc. I think the factors are the role of trade unions—both that trade unions were much stronger in Europe and also that in the United States, trade unions turned against the reduction of working hours after the Second World War. That has to do mostly with the Cold War, and with the conservative nature of U.S. trade unions. So in the 1950s, the AFL-CIO became—"hostile" may be too strong a word—became extremely disinterested in the idea of shorter hours of work. That's something that did not happen in Europe.

The other thing is that the incentives facing firms in the United States were really different, in terms of U.S. employers having much higher per worker fixed costs, because of health insurance. There are some European countries where health insurance is provided at the firm level, but mostly not. In the United States that turns out to be a powerful disincentive to reduce working hours, and it becomes a powerful incentive for raising working hours. The growth in inequality, which is more pronounced in the United States, also raised working hours. I think those are the key factors which lead the United States and Europe to diverge quite rapidly on the issue of work time. That divergence turns out to have all sorts of very important consequences.

One of the things you have seen in the patterns of leisure time activities in the United States is you've got time-stressed households doing really money-intensive things like going to the Caribbean for three days, or spending a lot of money to "de-stress," or spending money to reward themselves for working so hard. So we definitely have quite a bit of that in the United States because work is so demanding and stressful and that shapes the leisure patterns. You get what economists call goods- or income-intensive leisure.

D&S: If we think of consumption behavior as social—as aiming to enhance a person's social status—can we think of any important social constraints on the amounts or patterns of consumption? If many people disapprove of polluting or wasteful forms of consumption, like the Hummer, can we observe a social constraint on that? Or, in what are very difficult economic times for a lot of people, is there any effect on people reining in unseemly levels of luxury consumption?

JS: Well, I'll start with the latter. I was reading about and experiencing people's reluctance to engage in ostentatious displays at the time of the crash, and in its early aftermath. I think, by now, that didn't last very long. One of the things about the most ostentatious stuff is that we're increasingly a gated society, so the wealthy are consuming lavishly outside of the view of the ordinary and the poor. There is certainly less celebration of it, and you see it less in the culture now than before the crash, for sure. The Hummers are a very interesting case. I have a friend who did research on the war between Hummer drivers and the Prius drivers, the Prius drivers being referred to as "pious" drivers by the Hummer folks. Now the Hummer vehicle has collapsed as a consumer product. Hummer drivers were subjected to a lot of social disapproval. It also became economically less-desirable when the price of gas went up.

There is definitely a rising ecological consciousness that is attempting to moralize consumption in ways that yield social approval or disapproval of low-carbon versus high-carbon lifestyles. It isn't mainstream yet. It's much more prevalent in highly educated groups, it tends to be more bicoastal, it's a kind of "forward trend" in the consumer culture. You do see more and more, as you move into the mainstream, people attempting to do more ecologically. I think there's widespread sentiment about that. Then, of course, you also have so many people who are just trying to make ends meet that they feel it is not possible for them to think about ecological impact. Of course, the irony is that the people who are just trying to make ends meet are the ones with the low carbon footprints, but the discourse of environmental impact is permeating through consumer culture.

D&S: Going back to something about advertising: It seems to have become more pervasive, both in terms of physical spaces that are filled with advertising and products advertised to users. In the last couple of decades, we've seen the advent of direct marketing of prescription pharmaceuticals, for example, directly to the people who will end up using them. There's a pushback, such as criticism of advertising to children, but it seems largely that there's widespread tolerance of this pervasiveness of advertising in daily life.

JS: This is a little counterintuitive, but part of why advertising has become so pervasive is that the core of advertising, which is television spots, have become so unimportant. People don't have to watch them anymore, and that's huge for advertisers. I think the 30- or 60-second TV spots are much more powerful than the kinds of things that advertisers have moved towards in terms of the spatial expansion of advertising. I think that advertising on the web is much less powerful. So, that's one of the paradoxes of advertising in the contemporary moment: the moment when advertising is much more pervasive in terms of space and place, is a moment when it's much less powerful. Advertisers have been able to move in a few directions that have been productive for them, like word of mouth advertising, and so forth, but those forms are also being delegitimized. People know the person sitting next to them in a bar telling them to drink this vodka might be paid by the company.

Prescription drugs are a big exception, because that came about as a regulatory change. Drug companies weren't allowed to advertise directly to consumers before. If it weren't for pharmaceuticals and ads directed at kids, the advertising industry would be in big trouble. Now the kid story is, I think, a little bit different than the adult story, in the sense that you have a much more powerful approach to children now than you did in the past. The approach to children, I think, is a lot more effective than the approach to adults, which I think is declining in effectiveness. So, you can see a theme in what I'm saying about advertising. Today, I would say I feel less worried about advertising than I did before I started studying it. I think people tune it out. I don't want to go too far on this, but to me it's not where the main action is in terms of what's driving consumer patterns.

D&S: We see some examples of people, in their purchasing decisions, transcending a kind of narrow consumer mentality: They're thinking about environmental impacts, say, in buying a hybrid or electric car. In terms of other products they may be thinking about labor conditions, such as buying fair trade goods or no sweatshop apparel or footwear. On the other hand, one might look at this as reinforcing a core aspect of consumerist capitalism: That whatever it is that you may want, it's for sale and you can buy it.

JS: There's a debate in sociology and the social sciences more generally—because there are other disciplines that have weighed in on this question—about the critique of ethical consumption, political consumption, green consumption. Some argue that it's actually detrimental because it leads people to think that this purchasing behavior can solve problems, and it leads them to be less likely to join in collective solutions to environmental problems, labor problems, poverty, and development in the global South.

I did a study of that, and I used two different data sets: One was a random sample survey of all Americans. The other was an intentional survey of people who are political or ethical consumers, or what we called "conscious consumers," with about 2,000 participants. What we found is that there are actually very high levels of correlation between people engaging in this kind of purchasing and being socially and politically involved in trying to solve these problems in collective ways. And we also looked at the time sequencing and found a group of people who are politically involved already and then you add on this "walk the talk" aspect—if you're going to be fighting sweatshops, then don't buy sweatshop clothing, and if you're concerned about environmental impacts then you don't want to be buying things that are at odds with your values.

So you have people who were political first, then extended to their purchasing behavior, and you have people who got into both at around the same time, and you have people who moved in the other direction—who first did the conscious consuming and then became politically active. Certainly the idea that becoming a "green consumer" undermines your likelihood of engaging in collective action around this is not at all supported by the data in the United States, and there have also been some studies in Europe that show the same thing.

I think the fact of the matter is that changing marketplace behavior in the kind of society we have today is an important component in a broad-based campaign, whether it's on the environment or labor conditions or whatever. We see a lot of the NGOs involved in campaigns that have a market-based dimension—and those have been some of the most successful campaigns in recent years—because it's so hard to get the state to act to do these things, because it is captured by business. People have turned to the market in part because it's an arena where it looks like you can have some results, at least in the short term.

Ultimately, can you stop climate change through consumer behavior and through just market behavior? Definitely not. Can you ensure good working conditions merely by market-oriented activity? Definitely not. To think that it's sufficient is the real mistake, but I don't think that most people who work in this field, who try to work on transforming consumer behavior, have such a naïve view.

D&S: We've already talked about ways in which consumption is connected to people's lives at work, and the availability of leisure time, as well as some changes in patterns of consumption related to broader social objectives. What kinds of changes in consumption—and in the forces shaping consumption—do you envision?

JS: Well, I have a hard time thinking about the future without orienting all of my thinking about climate, because I just don't see much of a positive future unless we can address climate change very significantly. And that means, for wealthy countries, pretty radical emissions cuts in a pretty short period of time. It actually means that for most countries. So, as I think about the future, I think about what we could do both to address climate change through radical emissions reductions and also increase social justice, reduce inequality, and start solving the enormous problems that we have in this country. My most recent book, *True Wealth*, is about how to do that. Obviously, we need to get onto a renewable energy system, there's no question about that. We need a carbon tax or carbon regulation, and that's stuff that is very well known. What is not understood, I don't think, is that we can't successfully address climate change with a model in which we continue to try to expand the size of the economy.

We're going to have to deal with working hours, because that's the only way to stop expanding the size of the economy in any sensible way. So the core of what we need to do is to get back on the trajectory of using productivity growth to reduce hours of work. And that then opens up incredible possibilities in terms of rebalancing the labor market, integrating the unemployed, and having a fairer distribution of hours. We're talking about the distribution of income, but not about the distribution of hours, which is one of the things that drives the distribution of income. So, fair access to the work that exists, giving people more time off from work, and doing much more as a society—and probably a lot on the local and community level—to ensure basic needs for people.

With declining work hours, people's incomes are pretty much stabilized, so you need to bring the incomes of the bottom up, and you need to bring the incomes of the top down. Part of that has to be a redistribution of work opportunity and creating community provisioning of basic needs, like publicly owned utilities which provide power and heat for people at reasonable prices, enhanced public transportation, more public provisioning of food. There are really interesting things going on in global-South countries bringing farmers and consumers together in local food economies that are not just about high-priced organic food, which is what we have here, but low-priced food that ensures food security for people. So, shorter hours, basic needs being met—including housing, education, healthcare—that's the direction I would like to see us go, and I think that really it all flows out from a kind of commitment to climate protection. It could all flow out from a commitment to basic needs, too. They really integrate.

Time use is central, and I think you get a totally different culture of consumption if people's incomes are on a basically stabilized trajectory and what they're getting is more and more free time. So, you have a new culture of consumption that is not about the acquisition of the new, it's not the "work and spend" pattern as I've called it, it's not "throw away" or media driven, it's more "true materialist," where you really pay attention to the things you have, and it's a kind of earthier consumption. ❏

Chapter 2

SUPPLY AND DEMAND

INTRODUCTION

Textbooks tell us that supply and demand work like a well-oiled machine. The Law of Supply tells us that as the price of an item goes up, businesses will supply more of that good or service. The Law of Demand adds that as the price rises, consumers will choose to buy less of the item. Only one equilibrium price can bring businesses' and consumers' intentions into balance. Away from this equilibrium point, surpluses or shortages tend to drive the price back toward the equilibrium. Of course, government actions such as taxation or setting a price ceiling or floor can move the economy away from its market equilibrium, and create what economists call a "deadweight loss."

Marc Breslow argues that supply and demand do not always produce the best outcomes for society. He notes that the "price gouging" that we suffer during shortages or feared shortages—especially for hard-to-substitute goods like gasoline—is simply supply and demand at work (Article 2.1).

Timothy A. Wise and Marie Brill's "Fiddling in Rome While Our Food Burns" (Article 2.2) argues that the current demand for biofuels has significant negative unintended consequences—diverting agricultural resources away from food production and driving up food prices. It reminds readers the way that seemingly distinct markets are linked, and how factors that impact one market or industry can reverberate onto others.

The next two articles take on the mainstream textbook criticisms of price ceilings and price floors. Economist Ellen Frank questions the textbook models' conclusion that rent controls (and other price ceilings) lead to permanent shortages. She maintains that rent control helps to equalize power between landlords and tenants, and also to assure a supply of affordable housing (Article 2.3).

Does raising the minimum wage cause layoffs, as mainstream models imply? Economist Jeannette Wicks-Lim says no, arguing that the minimum wage could go to $15 without causing substantial job loss (Article 2.4). Looking at the fast-food industry, she reasons that the proposed minimum wage increase would cause modest price increases (which would cushion the impact of the wage-cost rise on employers), a modest decline in growth in the quantities of fast food demanded (due to the price rise), and an increase in hourly pay for fast-food workers more than off-setting a mild decline in hours worked.

Next, Dean Baker takes a look at the other end of the pay scale—the factors behind skyrocketing executive compensation at large corporations. Mainstream texts tell us to look at prices and incomes as the outcomes of supply and demand. Highly valued commodities (like highly productive labor) commands a higher price, due to these market forces. Is that the reason for high executive pay at U.S. corporations? No, says Baker. In "Corporate Cronyism: The Secret to Overpaid CEOs" (Article 2.5), he argues that it is not CEOs' individual productivity, but rather their relationship to other corporate directors, that explains the executive-pay mystery.

John Miller looks at another labor issue—the impact of immigration on wages—in his "Walled Off from Reality" (Article 2.6). Current economic research offers precious little evidence to support the common claim the immigration drives down wages. Miller explains, offering two other arguments about supply and demand. First, immigration means not only a greater supply of labor, but also more demand for goods and, in turn, for labor. Second, immigrants do not simply substitute for (and compete with) native-born workers, but often bring different and complementary skills.

Finally, in "The Airfare Mystery" (Article 2.5), Arthur MacEwan argues that "supply and demand" is just a starting point for understanding what causes variation in air fares. We need to delve deeper, according to MacEwan, into issues of market power (does a particular airline monopolize a particular route?), price discrimination (are some buyers, like business travelers, charged more than others?), and government intervention (what roles do taxes and subsidies play?).

Taken together, these articles call into question the claims that markets always operate efficiently and lead to the best social allocation of resources. The articles also imply a constructive role for the "visible hand" of government.

Discussion Questions

1. (General) Several of these articles call for a larger government role in regulating supply and demand. What are some possible results of expanded government involvement, positive and negative? On balance, do you agree that government should play a larger role?

2. (Article 2.1) Breslow says that shortages have different effects on prices in the short run and the long run. Explain the difference. How is this difference related to the concepts of elasticity of demand and elasticity of supply?

3. (Article 2.2) Wise and Brill argues that policies promoting biofuels production have significant impacts on food prices. Why is this this the case?

4. (Article 2.3) Frank states that because modern rent-control laws are "soft," they do not lead to housing shortages. Explain. Do you agree with her reasoning?

5. (Article 2.4) If the minimum wage is set above the market-clearing wage, according to textbook models, the quantity of labor supplied will be greater than the quantity demanded. That is, the result will be unemployment. What is Wicks-Lim's argument against the claim that minimum-wage laws create unemployment? If she is right, what is wrong with the textbook models?

6. (Article 2.5) Mainstream neoclassical theory explains prices and incomes as outcomes of market forces—supply and demand. What other forces, according to Baker, explain high CEO compensation?

7. (Article 2.6) Miller argues that immigration does not, in fact, drive down wages. How is this possible, if immigration means additional labor supply, and more supply of something (all other things being equal) drives down its price?

8. (Article 2.7) MacEwan sees "supply and demand" as a shorthand for the various kinds of forces operating in real-world markets. What kinds of influences does he describe that may affect air fares? Which have an impact mainly on the supply side? Which on the demand side?

Article 2.1

PRICE GOUGING: IT'S JUST SUPPLY AND DEMAND

BY MARC BRESLOW

October 2000, updated May 2015

Critics of the oil industry charge that the companies conspire to raise prices during shortages, ripping off consumers and gaining huge profits through illegal behavior. The industries respond that there is no conspiracy, prices rise due to the simple functioning of supply and demand in the market. The media debate the question: can evidence be found of a conspiracy? Or are rising prices simply due to increased costs as supplies are short? Politicians ask whether companies are guilty of illegal activity, and demand that investigations be opened.

What's going on? In reality, critics of the industries are missing the point of how a capitalist "free market" operates during times of shortages. The industry spokespersons are more on target in their explanations—but that doesn't mean what the companies are doing is okay. In fact, they *are* profiting at the expense of everyone who is forced to pay outrageous prices.

Both the media and public officials want to know whether rising costs of operation are causing the high prices, and therefore the companies are justified. Why? Because simple textbook economics says that in a competitive market we should get charged according to costs, with companies only making a "normal" profit. But a careful reading of the texts shows that this is only in the "long run" when new supplies can come into the market. In the short run, when a shortage develops, "supply and demand" can force prices up to unbelievable levels, especially for any product or service that is really a necessity. It doesn't have any relationship to the cost of supplying the item, nor does it take a conspiracy. The industry spokespeople are right that market pressures are the cause.

What confuses consumers is why a relatively small shortage can cause such a huge price jump, as it did for gasoline and electricity. Why, if OPEC reduces world oil supplies by only 1% or 2%, can the price of gasoline rise by perhaps 50%? Why shouldn't prices rise by the 1% or 2%? The answer lies in a common-sense understanding of what happens during a shortage. Everyone who owns a car, and still needs to get to work, drop the kids off at child care, and buy groceries, still needs to drive. In the short run, you can't sell your car for a more energy-efficient one, nor move someplace where public transit is more available, nor find a new day care center closer to home. Even if there are subways or buses available where you live, tight work and family time schedules probably make it difficult for you to leave the car at home.

So, as prices rise, everyone continues trying to buy as much gasoline as they did before (in technical terms, the "short-run price elasticity of demand" is very low). But there is 2% less gas available, so not everyone can get as much as they want. Prices will continue rising until some people drop out of the market, cutting back on their purchases because they simply can't afford to pay the higher prices. For something as essential to modern life as gasoline, this can take quite a price jump. If the price goes from $3.00 to $3.50 will you buy less? How about $4.00? Or $4.50? You can see the problem. Prices can easily rise by 50% before demand falls by the 2% needed for supply and demand to equalize.

Note that this situation has nothing to do with the costs of supplying gasoline, nor do oil companies in the United States have to conspire together to raise prices. All they have to do is let consumers bid for the available gasoline. Nothing illegal has taken place—OPEC is acting as a cartel, "conspiring," but the United States has no legal power over other countries. Profits can go up enormously, and they may be shared between OPEC, oil companies such as Exxon/Mobil and Royal Dutch Shell, and firms lower on the supply chain such as wholesalers and retail gas stations.

Housing is perhaps the worst of these situations, as no one should be forced to leave their home. But the "invisible hand" of the market will raise prices, and allocate housing, according to who has the greatest purchasing power, not who needs the housing. A highly-skilled computer programmer, moving into San Francisco from elsewhere, will get an apartment that some lesser-paid worker, maybe a public school teacher or a bus driver, has been living in, perhaps for many years.

In all these cases, the market has done what it does well—allocate sales to those who can afford to buy, without regard to need; and allocate profits to those who have a product in short supply, without regard to costs of production. The human costs to people of moderate- and low-incomes, who are priced out of the market, can be severe. But they can be prevented—by price controls that prevent price-gouging due to shortages. Such controls have been used many times in the United States—for rent in high-demand cities, for oil and gas during the "crises" of the 1970's, and for most products during World War II. Maybe it's time we made them a staple of sensible economic policy. ❑

Resources: "In Gas Prices, Misery and Mystery," Pam Belluck, *New York Times*, 6/14/2000; "Federal action sought to cut power prices from May," Peter J. Howe, *Boston Globe*, Aug. 24, 2000; "Industry Blames Chemical Additives for High Gas Prices," Matthew L. Wald, *New York Times*, June 26, 2000.

Article 2.2

FIDDLING IN ROME WHILE OUR FOOD BURNS

BY MARIE BRILL AND TIMOTHY A. WISE
October 2013; Al Jazeera

*This article first appeared on the Al Jazeera website, www.aljazeera.com.
Reprinted by permission.*

Rumor has it that the Roman emperor Nero played a fiddle and sang while Rome burned for five days in the Great Fire of 64 A.D. Nearly 2000 years later, at the very site where this devastating fire started so long ago, history is repeating itself, only the leaders doing the fiddling are delegates to the 40th meeting of the UN Committee on World Food Security (CFS). And what's burning is the world's food, in the engines of our cars.

Unfortunately this time, the fire didn't end in five days. Food-based biofuels have been burning for over a decade, the fires are growing in scale and intensity, and there is no end in sight.

It's not as if we haven't seen the warning signs. There have been three food price spikes in the last six years, with a wide range of studies implicating biofuels as a key driver of price volatility. How could it be otherwise? In the United States, 40% of our corn—fully 15% of the global corn supply—is now diverted to make ethanol, up from just 5% in 2000.

The food security impacts are multiple and severe. Because ethanol competes for corn with food and animal feed, it has a direct impact on the cost of food. Indeed, in 2008 global food prices doubled. This hurts poor consumers. Biofuels—from corn, sugar, soybeans, and other feedstocks—compete for land and water, putting added stress on scarce resources.

Most dramatically, biofuels producers have been key drivers of large-scale land acquisitions in African and other developing countries.

This is why the CFS put the issue of biofuels and food security on this year's agenda and commissioned an expert report to inform the decision. Indeed, the report confirmed the negative impacts of biofuels to date and recommended decisive action.

Our own report confirms that one of the main threats to our ability to feed the world in the future is the continued expansion of first generation biofuels.

No matter. At the CFS the fiddling began. Despite urgent statements from the floor about the negative impacts of biofuels on food security, the small group tasked to negotiate a set of principles and actions came up with weak principles and complete inaction. There was no acknowledgement of the negative impacts of biofuel policies and mandates in the United States and European Union, which have been instrumental in artificially stimulating and sustaining the bio-fuel industry.

Why the fiddling? Simple: the most powerful countries at the negotiating table were the same ones benefiting from the burning of food in our cars. Canada and the United States played the loudest, with the European Union, Brazil, and Argentina playing much the same tune. Only South Africa, a lonely voice, joined with civil society to speak for the victims of these policies.

Of course, the ones choosing the tune were powerful industry interests, from the biofuels companies themselves as well as the agribusiness firms capturing the benefits of high prices and subsidized demand for their products.

The CFS is supposed to be the principal international agency coordinating global responses to the food price crisis and dealing with the new realities of the rising and worrisome integration of food markets with fuel and financial markets. It has that clear mandate.

But instead of leading, the CFS decided to do nothing. The straightforward proposal that biofuels policies that harm food security should be reformed was categorically rejected. So too was any mention of the land and water impacts of runaway biofuels expansion.

The world is not waiting for the CFS to lead. Policy-makers around the world are beginning to contend with food-fuel competition. The U.S. Congress is under pressure to reform, or even repeal, its biofuels mandate. The European Union recently cut its own mandate in half, explicitly recognizing the negative impacts of food-based fuels.

Meanwhile, the fiddling continues, and the biofuels burn on.

More than 80 organizations from around the world signed an open letter urging the CFS to take action. Members of civil society formally involved in the CFS negotiations refused to endorse the resolution. "Small scale food producers have spoken powerfully here about the reality they are confronted with every day: that biofuels crops compete with their food production, for the land they till and for the water that sustains them," they stated in a press release. "[These] recommendations overwhelmingly defend the interests of the biofuels industry and legitimize violations of the right to food."

This no time for the CFS to fiddle in Rome. Our food is burning. In our cars. And hundreds of millions of people are going hungry. ❏

Sources: Food and Agriculture Organization of the United Nations, Committee on World Food Security – 40 Session, Oct. 7-11, 2013 (fao.org); Committee on World Food Security, "Biofuels and Food Security," 2013 (fao.org); Actionaid, "Rising to the Challenge: Changing Course to Feed the World in 2050" (actionaidusa.org).

Article 2.3

DOES RENT CONTROL HURT TENANTS?

BY ELLEN FRANK
March/April 2003

> Dear Dr. Dollar:
> *What are the merits of the argument that rent control hurts tenants by limiting the incentives to create and maintain rental housing?*
> —Sarah Marxer, San Francisco, Calif.

The standard story of rent control, laid out in dozens of introductory economics textbooks, goes like this. In the housing market, landlords are willing to supply more rental units when prices are high, and tenants are willing to rent more units when prices are low. In an unregulated market, competition should result in a market-clearing price at which the number of apartments landlords are willing and able to provide just equals the number tenants are willing and able to rent. Thus, when prices are allowed to rise to their correct level, shortages disappear. Rent controls, in this story, disrupt the market mechanism by capping rents at too low a level. Artificially low rents discourage construction and maintenance, resulting in fewer available apartments than would exist without the controls. At the same time, low rents keep tenants in the area, searching for apartments that don't exist. The result: permanent housing shortages in rent-controlled markets.

What's wrong with this story? Just about everything.

First, the story ignores the unequal power that landlords and tenants exercise in an unregulated market. Boston College professor Richard Arnott notes that tenants are, for a number of reasons, averse to moving. This gives landlords inordinate pricing power even in a market where housing is not in short supply—and in areas where vacancy rates are low, land is scarce, and "snob zoning" commonplace, landlords can charge truly exorbitant prices. In Boston, rent controls were eliminated in 1997, and average apartment rents have since climbed nearly 100%. The city's spiraling rents show that without controls, landlords can—and do—gouge tenants.

Second, rent control opponents misrepresent the structure of controls. As practiced in the real world, rent control does not place fixed caps on rent. New York City enacted an actual rent freeze after World War II, and a small number of apartments still fall under this "old-law" rent control. But most rent-controlled apartments in New York and all controlled apartments in other U.S. cities fall under what Arnott calls "second generation" or "soft" controls, which simply restrict annual rent increases. Soft rent controls guarantee landlords a "fair return" on their properties and require that owners maintain their buildings. They allow landlords to pass along maintenance costs, and many allow improvement costs to be recouped on an accelerated schedule, making building upkeep quite lucrative.

Consequently, controlled apartments are not unprofitable. And as Occidental College professor and housing specialist Peter Dreier points out, landlords won't walk away as long as they are making a decent return. Residential landlords are not very mobile: they have a long-term interest in their properties, and only abandon them when *market* rents fall below even controlled levels as a result of poverty, crime, or economic depression. Rent controls themselves do not foster abandonment or poor maintenance.

Third, all second-generation rent control laws—enacted chiefly in the 1970s—exempted newly constructed buildings from controls. Thus, the argument that controls discourage new construction simply makes no sense. As for the oft-heard complaint that developers fear that rent controls, once enacted, will be extended to new buildings, the 1980s and 1990s construction booms in New York, Boston, San Francisco, and Los Angeles—all cities with controls—indicate that developers aren't all that worried. There is plenty of housing and construction in cities with and without rent controls.

Nevertheless, even in many cities with rent controls, there is a shortage of *affordable* apartments. Market housing costs have been rising faster than wages for at least two decades. That some apartments in New York and San Francisco are still affordable to low- and middle-income families is due primarily to rent control.

Indeed, limited as they might be, rent controls deliver real benefits. They prevent price-gouging and ration scarce apartments to existing tenants. The money tenants save in rent can be spent in the neighborhood economy, benefiting local businesses. Meanwhile, more secure tenants create neighborhoods that are stable, safe, and economically diverse. And rent controls are essential if tenants are to have credible legal protection against slumlords: the legal right to complain about lack of heat or faulty plumbing is meaningless if landlords can retaliate by raising rents.

There are many problems with the U.S. housing market. High prices, low incomes, and lack of public housing or subsidies for affordable housing all contribute to homelessness and housing insecurity in major American cities. Rent control is not the cause of these problems, nor is it the whole solution. But along with higher wages and expanded public housing, it is part of the solution. As Dreier puts it, "Until the federal government renews its responsibility to help poor and working-class people fill the gap between what they can afford and what housing costs to build and operate, rent control can at least help to keep a roof over their heads." ❑

Resources: Richard Arnott, "Time for Revisionism on Rent Control?" *Journal of Economic Perspectives*, Winter 1995. Dreier and Pitcoff, "I'm a Tenant and I Vote," *Shelterforce*, July/August 1997 (nhi.org).

Article 2.4

IS A $15 MINIMUM WAGE ECONOMICALLY FEASIBLE?

BY JEANNETTE WICKS-LIM

July/August 2012

Campaigns like 15Now and Fight for $15 are bucking convention and demanding minimum-wage hikes far larger than what has been past practice. Take, for example, the Fair Minimum Wage Act of 2007—one of the larger sets of increases in the federal minimum. This Act raised the federal wage floor by 40% in three steps: from $5.15 to $5.85 in 2007, $5.85 to $6.55 in 2008, and $6.55 to today's minimum of $7.25 in 2009. A $15 minimum wage, on the other hand, represents a more-than-100% increase in the federal minimum. The result? The fight for $15 has decisively changed the terms of today's minimum-wage debate.

The ball got rolling in 2013 with the breakthrough $15 minimum ordinance in SeaTac, a suburb of Seattle, Wash. Since then, some of the country's largest cities, including Los Angeles, San Francisco, and Seattle, have followed suit, passing their own citywide $15 minimums. In June 2015, Massachusetts passed a statewide measure covering Medicaid-funded homecare aides. Later in the fall, New York State passed a $15 minimum wage law for fast-food workers. This sea change seems to have occurred over just the past couple of years, dramatically pivoting away from President Obama's soft pitches to raise the federal minimum to $9.00 in 2013 and, more recently, to $10.10 in 2015.

These developments are certainly a remarkable political turnaround, but are these wage hikes economically feasible?

The immediate pushback against these campaigns has questioned whether it's feasible to expect businesses to adjust to a minimum-wage hike of this size without generating major negative unintended consequences. This opposition to a $15 minimum comes not only from expected corners—e.g., self-interested restaurant-industry lobbyists from the National Restaurant Association—but also from many economists. The most widely discussed of the possible unintended consequence is the large-scale loss of jobs. Such an outcome would counteract the primary intended consequence of a $15 minimum wage—to improve the living standards of low-wage workers and their families. The rationale is that, if you raise the price of anything, the quantity demanded of that thing will fall. This is how people usually interpret the basic economic principle known as the "law of demand." That raises a serious concern that raising the wages of low-wage workers will cause their employers to cut back on staff, leaving the workers worse off—either unemployed or working fewer shifts.

The current state of research on this employment question, however, finds that minimum-wage increases do not produce significant job losses. This then raises an important policy question: Why haven't there been significant job losses when minimum wages have increased?

First, the basic law of demand actually says something quite different and more specific than just "if the price of something goes up, the quantity demanded of that thing goes down." It actually says that if the price of something goes up—and nothing else changes—the quantity demanded of that something goes down. In the real world, however, other things are changing all the time. Moreover, raising the minimum wage itself causes businesses to change how they operate (more on this below). As a result, the minimum wage's actual impact on jobs depends on what other factors are changing at the same time.

Here's a specific, relevant example: Seattle's 2013 ordinance calls for a series of progressive increases in its minimum wage, up to $15 by 2021 for most businesses. At the same time that the city adopted this new policy, the local economy had been growing (and continues to grow) at a healthy clip. This helps explain why, according to the *Puget Sound Business Journal*, "six months after the first wage increase to $11 per hour took effect, the fear of soaring payrolls shows no signs of killing the appetite of ... the Seattle restaurant world—for rapid expansion." The title of the article sums it up: "Apocalypse Not: $15 and the Cuts that Never Came." Employment growth in Seattle's restaurant industry has not slowed.

The main point is that if no significant job losses result from minimum wages, then it must be the case that employers find other ways to adjust to their higher labor costs. And, in fact, past research has found that businesses often cover the costs of these higher wages by raising prices, re-directing some of their normal revenue growth into raises for their lowest paid workers, and finding savings from lower worker turnover, as higher wages strengthen workers' commitment to their jobs. A minimum-wage hike, in other words, causes both employers and workers to act differently from how they would act in the absence of a minimum wage hike. Employers adopt new strategies to increase revenue to support higher wages, and the stronger loyalty of better-paid employees frees up revenue that would have been spent on recruiting, hiring, and training new workers. Put another way, the "all else equal" clause simply does not hold in the real world. It's important to note, too, that there are disadvantages for employers if they cut their workforce—a smaller staff can make it hard for a business to maintain or improve its existing level of operation and also to retain or expand its customer base.

Even though past minimum-wage hikes have been more modest than the $15 minimum of today's political campaigns, we can use the existing body of research to develop a well-informed view of whether it's feasible for businesses to adjust to a $15 minimum wage without shedding jobs. This is exactly what my colleague Robert Pollin and I explored in our research earlier this year—we examined the question of whether the national economy could adjust to $15 minimum wage while avoiding any major negative unintended consequences.

Our analysis focuses specifically on the situation of the fast-food industry—the industry expected to require the largest adjustments. According to the U.S. Department of Labor, the two occupations that make up more than 62% of the jobs in the fast-food industry—fast-food cooks and combined food prep and serving workers—are the lowest paid occupations. Half of cooks earned less than $8.87 and half of combined food-prep and serving workers earned less than $8.85 in 2014. If fast-food firms can adjust to a $15 minimum without any major negative unintended consequences, other less-affected industries should be able to adopt a $15 minimum more easily.

In our study, we provide a detailed analysis of the labor-cost increase the fast-food industry would face as a result of a $15 minimum wage, taking as our starting point the situation as of 2013. We then use existing empirical research to make reasonable assumptions about the variety of ways firms could absorb these cost increases without shedding jobs.

We estimate that a $15 minimum, phased in over four years, would raise the overall business costs of the average fast-food restaurant by about 3.4% per year. About half of this cost increase could be covered through raising prices by 3% per year and assuming that quantity demanded will fall by about 1.5% due to the higher prices. This would mean, for example, that the average McDonald's outlet could cover about half of its total cost increase by raising the price of a Big Mac by $0.15 per year for four years—for example, from $4.80 to an eventual $5.40.

The fall in demand due to these price increases, however, is small enough that it can be more than offset by the rise in demand for fast food furnished by a healthy, expanding economy. Consumers tend to consume more fast food as their income grows. Over the past 15 years, industry sales have been growing at a slightly faster pace than the overall economy, or about 2.5% per year. As a result, even with the price increases, the fast-food industry should grow and add jobs, just at a somewhat slower pace. But note: this slower job growth is less concerning than one initially may think. Workers' gains in earnings per hour as a result of a $15 minimum wage—averaging 60% across the fast-food workforce—far outstrip the loss in earnings due to 1.5% fewer fast-food work hours added to the economy.

The remaining half of the cost increase could then be covered through cost savings due to lower turnover and by channeling more of the fast-food revenue growth generated by the growing U.S. economy toward payroll. We also found that, after these adjustments are made—increased prices, reduced worker turnover, and a more equitable distribution of the gains from growth—businesses will not have to cut into their profit rate at all. In other words, fast-food restaurants could adjust to a $15 minimum wage without laying off workers and without shrinking the industry's profit margin—the least desirable option from the perspective of employers.

There is one other possible outcome to consider: Will employers try to avoid higher labor costs, over the longer term, by replacing some workers with machines? So far, the empirical evidence of such capital-labor substitution suggests no. Preliminary research by Chicago Federal Reserve economist Daniel Aaronson and his colleague Brian Phelan indicates that jobs with a high level of routine manual work—the lion's share of low-wage positions in the fast-food industry—are unlikely to be replaced by technology in response to minimum wage hikes. This indicates that fast-food employers will tend to look first to other ways to adjust to a $15 minimum wage, before replacing their workers with robots. Since there are other ways for fast-food firms to adjust to a $15 minimum wage—as described above—it seems unlikely that employers would seek technological substitutes for their workers.

Businesses should, in other words, be able to adjust to a $15 minimum wage without having to shed jobs, as long as it is implemented at a reasonable pace. Such a policy, should provide major benefits for the lowest-paid workers in the United States. ❑

Sources: Robert Pollin and Jeannette Wicks-Lim, "A $15 U.S. Minimum Wage: How the Fast Food Industry Could Adjust Without Shedding Jobs," Political Economy Research Institute, Working Paper #373 (2015).

Article 2.5

CORPORATE CRONYISM: THE SECRET TO OVERPAID CEOs

BY DEAN BAKER
February 2014; Truthout

It's hardly a secret that the heads of major corporations in the United States get mind-bending paychecks. While high pay may be understandable when a top executive turns around a failing company or vastly expands a company's revenue and profit, CEOs can get paychecks in the tens or hundreds of millions even when they did nothing especially notable.

For example, Lee Raymond retired from Exxon-Mobil in 2005 with $321 million. (That's 22,140 minimum wage work years.) His main accomplishment for the company was sitting at its head at a time when a quadrupling of oil prices sent profits soaring. Hank McKinnel walked away from Pfizer in 2006 with $166 million. It would be hard to identify his outstanding accomplishments.

But you don't have to be mediocre to get a big paycheck as a CEO. Bob Nardelli pocketed $240 million when he left Home Depot after six years. The company's stock price had fallen by 40% in his tenure, while the stock its competitor Lowe's had nearly doubled. And then we have the CEOs in the financial industry, heads of huge banks like Lehman's, Bear Stearns, and Merrill Lynch, or the insurer AIG. These CEOs took their companies to the edge of bankruptcy or beyond and still walked away with hundreds of millions of dollars in their pockets.

It's not hard to write contracts that would ensure that CEO pay bear a closer relationship to the company's performance. For example, if the value of Raymond's stock incentives at Exxon were tied to the performance of the stock of other oil companies (this can be done) then his going away package probably would not have been one-tenth as large. Also, there can be longer assessment periods so that it's not possible to get rich by bankrupting a company.

If anyone were putting a check on CEO pay, these sorts of practices would be standard, but they aren't for a simple reason. The corporate directors who are supposed to be holding down CEO pay for the benefit of the shareholders are generally buddies of the CEOs.

Corporate CEOs often have considerable input into who sits on their boards. (Some CEOs sit on the boards themselves.) They pick people who will be agreeable and not ask tough questions.

For example, corporate boards probably don't often ask whether they could get a comparably skilled CEO for lower pay, even though top executives of major companies in Europe, Japan, and South Korea earn around one-tenth as much as CEOs in the United States. Of course this is the directors' job. They are supposed to be trying to minimize what the company pays their top executives in the same way that companies try to cut costs by outsourcing production to Mexico, China, and elsewhere.

But friends don't try to save money by cutting their friends' pay. And when the directors themselves are pocketing hundreds of thousands of dollars a year for attending four to ten meetings, there is little incentive to take their jobs seriously.

Instead we see accomplished people from politics, academia, and other sectors collecting their pay and looking the other way. For example, we have people like Erskine Bowles who had the distinction of sitting on the boards of both Morgan Stanley and General Motors in the years they were bailed out by the government. And we have Martin Feldstein, the country's most prominent conservative economist, who sat on the board of insurance giant AIG when it nearly tanked the world's financial system. Both Bowles and Feldstein were well-compensated for their "work."

Excessive CEO pay matters not only because it takes away money that rightfully belongs to shareholders, which include pension funds and individuals with 401(k) retirement accounts. Excessive CEO pay is important because it sets a pattern for pay packages throughout the economy. When mediocre CEOs of mid-size companies can earn millions or tens of millions a year, it puts upward pressure on the pay of top executives in other sectors.

It is common for top executives of universities and private charities to earn salaries in the millions of dollars because they can point to executives of comparably sized companies who earn several times as much. Those close in line to the boss also can expect comparably bloated salaries. In other words, this is an important part of the story of inequality in the economy.

To try to impose the checks that don't currently exist, the Center for Economic and Policy Research (CEPR) has created Director Watch. This site will highlight directors like Erskine Bowles and Martin Feldstein who stuff their pockets while not performing their jobs.

CEPR also worked with Huffington Post to compile a data set that lists the directors for the Fortune 100 companies, along with their compensation, the CEOs' compensation, and the companies' stock performance. This data set is now available at the Huffington Post as "Pay Pals."

Perhaps a little public attention will get these directors to actually work for their hefty paychecks. The end result could be to bring a lot of paychecks for those at the top back down to earth. ❑

Sources: Director Watch, Center for Economic and Policy Research (cepr.net/blogs/director-watch); Pay Pals, Huffington Post (data.huffingtonpost.com/paypals).

Article 2.6

WALLED OFF FROM REALITY

Trump's claims about immigration economics are without merit.

BY JOHN MILLER
November/December 2015

> Mexico's leaders have been taking advantage of the United States by using illegal immigration to export the crime and poverty in their own country. The costs for the United States have been extraordinary: U.S. taxpayers have been asked to pick up hundreds of billions in healthcare costs, housing costs, education costs, welfare costs, etc. ... The influx of foreign workers holds down salaries, keeps unemployment high, and makes it difficult for poor and working class Americans—including immigrants themselves and their children—to earn a middle class wage.
> —"Immigration Reform That Will Make America Great Again," Donald Trump campaign website

Donald Trump's immigration plan has accomplished something many thought was impossible. He has gotten mainstream and progressive economists to agree about something: his claims about the economics of immigration have "no basis in social science research," as economist Benjamin Powell of Texas Tech's Free Market Institute put it. That describes most every economic claim Trump's website makes about immigration: that it has destroyed the middle class, held down wages, and drained hundreds of billions from government coffers. Such claims are hardly unique to Trump, among presidential candidates. Even Bernie Sanders has said that immigration drives down wages (though he does not support repressive nativist policies like those proposed by Trump and other GOP candidates).

Beyond that, even attempting to implement Trump's nativist proposals, from building a permanent border wall to the mass deportation of undocumented immigrants, would cost hundreds of billions of dollars directly, and forfeit the possibility of adding trillions of dollars to the U.S. and global economies by liberalizing current immigration policies. That's not counting the human suffering that Trump's proposals would inflict.

No Drag on the Economy

Even the most prominent economist among immigration critics, Harvard's George Borjas, recognizes that immigration has had a large positive effect on the U.S. economy. By his calculations, immigrant workers (documented and undocumented) add $1.6 trillion to the U.S. economy each year, or 11% of Gross Domestic Product (GDP). The great bulk that additional income (97.8% according to Borjas) goes to immigrant workers. But that still leaves what he calls an "immigrant surplus" of $35 billion a year, which goes to non-immigrants, including workers, employers, and other users of services provided by immigrants.

Others have emphasized the disproportionate impact that immigrants have had on innovation in the U.S. economy. A study for the Kauffman Foundation found that, in 2006, foreign nationals residing in the United States were named as inventors or co-inventors in over 25% of all U.S. patent applications. Around the same time, another study found that immigrants were the founders of over half of all Silicon Valley startups and almost one-third of Boston startups.

Immigrants Didn't Do It

U.S. workers have undoubtedly fallen on hard times. The reasons are manifold: slow economic growth; pro-rich, anti-worker, anti-poor policies; the decline of unions; "free-trade" globalization; and so on. But immigration isn't one of those reasons, especially when it comes to "the middle class." Not only has immigration benefitted the U.S. economy, but economists find no evidence that immigration causes a widespread decrease in the wages of U.S.-born workers.

Estimates vary, but the best economic studies point to the same conclusion: over the long run, immigration has not caused the wages of the average U.S.-born worker to fall. Immigration critic Borjas calculated that, from 1990 to 2010, immigrant labor pushed down the wages of (pre-existing) U.S. workers by 3.2% in the short run. But even he conceded that over the long run, wages of native-born and earlier immigrant workers recovered to their previous level. Other economists find immigration to have a positive long-run effect on wages. Gianmarco Ottaviano and Giovanni Peri found that, from 1990 to 2006, immigration reduced wages of native-born workers in the short run (one to two years) by 0.7%, while over the long run (ten years) immigration into the United States boosted wages 0.6%.

Neither Ottaviano and Peri's nor even Borjas's estimates of the wage effects of immigration are consistent with Trump's claim that immigration is destroying the middle class. But what happens when we look at the wages of native-born workers by level of education? The Ottaviano-Peri study shows, in the long run, immigration is associated with an increase in wages across all education levels. Borjas's study reports that immigration has negative effects on the wages of native-born college graduates and especially on workers with less than a high-school education (those at the "bottom" of the labor market, mostly in low-wage jobs), even in the long run. But again concedes a positive effect for the 60% of U.S. workers with either a high school degree or some college (but no degree).

These results are probably a headscratcher for anyone who has taken introductory economics. After all doesn't increasing the supply of labor, through immigration, drive down its price (the going wage)? Well, no.

Immigrant workers do add to the supply of labor. But the economic effects of immigration do not stop there. Immigrants largely spend their wages within the U.S. economy. Businesses produce more—and hire more workers—to meet the increased demand. The cost savings from hiring cheaper immigrant labor also frees up businesses to expand production and hire more workers overall. Both those effects increase the demand for labor, offsetting the effects of added labor supply.

Economist David Card concludes that, taking into account these demand-side effects, "the overall impacts on native wages are small—far smaller than the effects of other factors like new technology, institutional changes, and recessionary macro conditions that have cumulatively led to several decades of slow wage growth for most U.S. workers."

Complements or Substitutes?

The effect of immigration on native-born workers with less than a high-school education remains a matter of dispute. Borjas insists that the costs of immigration are visited disproportionately upon those with the least education (and, to a lesser extent, those with the most education). He estimates, in a couple of different studies, that over the long run the wages of native-born high school dropouts fell 3-5% due to immigration.

But these estimates rely on the assumption that immigrant and native-born workers are substitutes for each other, and therefore compete for the same jobs. But, in fact, their skills differ in important ways. The first is their command of English. The Immigrant Policy Institute found that approximately one-half of the 41 million immigrants ages five and older speak English less than "very well." In addition, immigrant workers often have culture-specific skills—from cooking to opera singing to soccer playing, to cite examples given by Ottaviano and Peri—that differ from those of native-born workers.

When Ottaviano and Peri accounted for the imperfect substitutability between immigrants and natives, the negative of effect of immigration on native high school dropouts disappeared, and their wages were shown to rise by 0.3% over the long run.

Giving More Than They Get

Nor is there a credible case that undocumented immigrants are draining the public coffers by consuming more public services than they pay for. Immigrants migrate to jobs, not to welfare, and are disproportionately of working age. They are not major beneficiaries of the most generous U.S. welfare-state programs—Social Security and Medicare, which serve the elderly, not the young or the poor. And undocumented immigrants are already ineligible for most government benefits. (Even documented immigrants are ineligible for many federal programs, at least for some years after their arrival.)

On top of that, immigrants, both documented and undocumented, do pay taxes. They pay sales taxes, payroll taxes, and often income taxes. And they pay far more in taxes than they receive in benefits. That puts Trump's outrage over $4.2 billion in "free tax credits … paid to illegal immigrants" in a different light. In 2009, the federal government did in fact pay $4.2 billion in child tax credits to low-income tax filers using an Individual Taxpayer Identification Number (ITIN), the vast majority of them undocumented immigrants. But that same year, those ITIN filers paid an estimated $12 billion into a Social Security system from which they are not eligible to collect any benefits.

Trillions Left on the Sidewalk

Before the 1882 Chinese Exclusion Act, the United States allowed completely free immigration into our country. Immigration from elsewhere remained unrestricted until the eve of World War I. And immigrants flooded into the country and contributed mightily to its economic development.

Liberalizing immigration policies, unlike Trump's proposed border wall or mass deportations, could once again benefit the U.S. economy. Economists Angel Aguiar and Terrie Walmsley found that deporting all undocumented Mexican immigrants from the United States would reduce U.S. GDP by about $150 billion, while granting legal status to unskilled, undocumented Mexican workers (without additional effective border enforcement) would raise it by nearly that amount. And the potential gain for the global economy from liberalizing immigration policies is far greater. In fact so large that economist Michael Clemens likens liberalizing immigration to picking up "trillion-dollar bills on the sidewalk."

Such policies would also specifically improve conditions for workers, immigrant and native, in the United States. Immigrant workers, especially the estimated eleven million undocumented immigrants, tend to have less bargaining power than native-born workers. A policy granting undocumented immigrants legal status would make it easier for them to insist on their rights at work, and to organize and form unions. That's why the AFL-CIO and unions like UNITE HERE and SEIU now favor it.

For those who remain concerned about the effects of immigration on U.S.-born low-wage workers, there are obvious policies that would improve the lot of all low-wage workers: Boosting the minimum wage, making it easier for workers to organize unions, and making the welfare state more generous and inclusive, so people don't have to accept whatever lousy job they can find. These are the policies that are called for, not keeping immigrants out. ❑

Sources: George Borjas, "Immigration and the American Worker: A Review of the Academic Literature," Center for Immigration Studies, April 2013; Vivek Wadhwa, Foreign-Born Entrepreneurs: An Underestimated American Resource," Kauffman Foundation, Nov. 24, 2008; Michael A. Clemens, "Economics and Emigration: Trillion-Dollars Bills on the Sidewalk?" *Journal of Economic Perspectives*, Summer 2011; Gianmarco Ottaviano and Giovanni Peri, "Rethinking the Effects of Immigration on Wages," National Bureau of Economic Research, August 2006; Gianmarco Ottaviano and Giovanni Peri, "Immigration and National Wages: Clarifying the Theory and Empirics," National Bureau of Economic Research, August 2008; Gianmarco Ottaviano and Giovanni Peri, "Rethinking the Effect of Immigration on Wages," *Journal of the European Economic Association*, February 2012; George Borjas and Lawrence Katz, "The Evolution of the Mexican-Born Workforce n the United States," in George Borjas, ed., *Mexican Immigration to the United States*, 2007; Benjamin Powell, "Why Trump's Wrong on Immigration," Independent Institute, Sept. 15, 2015; Angel Aguiar and Terrie Walmsley, "The Importance of Timing in the U.S. Response to Illegal Immigrants: A Recursive Dynamic Approach," Global Trade Analysis Project, Working Paper No. 75, 2013; David Card, "Comment: The Elusive Search For Negative Wage Impacts of Immigration," *Journal of the European and Economic Association*, February 2012; Glenn Kessler, "Trump's Immigration plan include many claims that lack context," *Washington Post*, Aug. 20, 2015; Linda Qiu, "Trump's says illegal immigrants get $4.2B in tax credits but doesn't count their taxes paid," PolitiFact, Aug. 18, 2015; Michael Greenstone and Adam Looney, "What Immigration Means for U.S. Employment and Wages," Brookings on Job Numbers, May 4, 2012; Jie Zong and Jeanne Batalova, "Frequently Requested Statistics on Immigrants and Immigration in the United States," Migration Policy Institute, Feb. 26, 2015.

Article 2.7

THE AIRFARE MYSTERY

BY ARTHUR MacEWAN
January/February 2014

> Dear Dr. Dollar:
> *Boston is 3,280 air miles from London, only 27% further than the 2,580 air miles from Boston to San Diego. So why does a flight from Boston to London cost more than twice as much as a flight from Boston to San Diego, 100% more, for the same dates? Is it just supply and demand?* —Kathleen M. Gillespie, Lexington, Mass.

Airfares do seem to pose a mystery. Supply and demand may help explain things, but these are really little more than categories into which explanations can be placed. If someone says that the flights to London are so expensive because supply is limited relative to demand, we have no real explanation until we explain why supply is limited.

On the surface, the high price of flights on the Boston-London route suggests that this is a very profitable route. So why don't more airlines fly this route more often, expanding supply, to get a share of the profits?

Beneath the surface (on travel web sites), it turns out that a large part of the price difference between these two routes is not the actual payment to the airline, but taxes and fees. I found one Boston-London-Boston trip for $1,082, where taxes and fees accounted for $656 of that total. On the Boston-San Diego-Boston flight, however, taxes and fees accounted for only $33 out of the $436 cost.

In general, European governments charge much higher taxes and fees than is the case in the United States. From an environmental perspective, the Europeans are probably on the right track, as air travel is an especially polluting (greenhouse gas-creating) form of travel. The European governments, however, may simply be motivated by the opportunity to capture revenue.

There are seemingly strange airline fare differences within the United States that are not explained by tax and fee differences. For example, a non-stop round-trip Boston-Detroit flight (630 miles each way) costs about twice as much as a non-stop Boston-Chicago flight (860 miles each way)—$458 compared to $230 for the same times and dates.

This difference is explained by the fact that Delta has a lock on the Boston-Detroit route, while United, American, US Airways, and Jet Blue all fly the Boston-Chicago route. That is, Delta is a monopoly on the Boston-Detroit route and can charge high fares without facing competition. (Northwest used to control this route until it merged with Delta a couple of years ago.)

Why have no other airlines entered this apparently lucrative Boston-Detroit route? That's not clear. Perhaps Delta has long-term leases on Detroit airport gates. Or perhaps other airlines, recognizing the economic and population decline of Detroit, believe this market has limited potential. Whatever the reason, it is clear that monopoly control of this route is the issue.

Also, the Boston-Detroit fare portends an ominous future as airline mergers reduce competition further. Following the Delta-Northwest merger, Continental and United came together. American Airlines and US Airways have also been moving toward a merger. In August, however, the federal government acted to block the move. "According to the Justice Department," reported the *New York Times*, the proposed merger "would substantially reduce competition in over 1,000 city pairs served by the two airlines."

While monopolistic situations and taxes and fees explain some of the "mystery" of airline fares, there is more. Flights and times that are heavily used by business travelers tend to have high fares because business travelers are less concerned about the price. This is partly because they often have limited flexibility, but also because airfares are deductible as a cost of business—i.e., the taxpayers pick up part of the tab.

Also, on a flight with the same airline, prices can change dramatically within a day or even within hours. Trying to book a flight one evening, the cheapest ticket I could find was about $600, but by the next morning I got the ticket for about $300. I suspect that in this case the airline (using computer-based forecasting) recognized that the flight was not filling up and therefore reduced the price to attract more customers.

And things can work in the other direction. Making a reservation at the last minute, the potential passenger is often faced with a very high fare because the airline views the traveler as having little flexibility. For example, if I make a reservation to fly Boston-Chicago-Boston, leaving tomorrow and returning two days later, the fare would be over $900, as compared to the $230 I would pay if I made the reservation a few weeks in advance.

So, yes, supply and demand can help explain the variation in airfares. But to really understand what is going on we need to know a good deal more. ❏

Sources: "Airline Merger Mania," *New York Times*, June 22, 2013; James B. Stewart, "For Airlines, It May Be One Merger Too Many," *New York Times*, Aug. 16, 2013.

Chapter 3

CONSUMERS

INTRODUCTION

The "two economies" described in the introduction to this book—the textbook economy and the economy portrayed by critics of the status quo—come into sharp contrast when we consider the theory of consumer choice. In the textbook model of consumer choice, rational individuals seek to maximize their well-being by choosing the right mix of goods to consume and allocating their "scarce" resources accordingly. They decide for themselves how much they would enjoy various things, and make their choices based on full information about their options. More of any good is always better, but diminishing marginal utility says that each additional unit of a good consumed brings less additional enjoyment than the one before. The theory attempts to assess the utility of each individual uniquely. Yet, we soon discover that it is difficult if not impossible to "measure pleasure" for a single individual and impossible to compare utility between individuals.

The first article in this chapter contends that the idea of consumer sovereignty—that consumer wishes determine what gets produced—does not fit the facts. Helen Scharber notes, in "The 800-Pound Ronald McDonald in the Room" (Article 3.1), how the advertising that saturates our daily lives constantly creates new wants. In recent years, advertisers have been increasingly targeting children in order to convince them to nag their parents into buying products they suddenly "need."

Deborah M. Figart's "Underbanked and Overcharged" (Article 3.2) argues that low-income communities are ill-served by both conventional banks and "alternative financial service providers" (AFSPs), such as check-cashing outlets. Low-income areas may lack convenient nearby outlets for conducting financial transactions, and community members typically face high fees and interest rates from both banks and AFSPs. Figart points to a possible solution: recent proposals for the revival of "postal banks" operated by the U.S. Postal Service.

The next article, "The Economics of Net Neutrality," turns to a service that most students consume daily—internet communications (Article 3.3). Rob Larson observes the growing controversies over net neutrality—whether internet service providers (ISPs) will have to treat all packets of information equally—and how a departure from this principle would allow ISPs to charge content providers and consumers more for the delivery of their information. While some have seen the net neutrality issue as a battle between giant corporations—the ISPs and the content providers (like Netflix, Google, and Facebook)—Larson argues that this understates the importance of grassroots movements defending net neutrality.

The next two articles focus on ways that consumers may go beyond narrow self-interested behavior—the direct benefits they get from goods and services, weighed against the price of acquiring them—and include things like labor conditions and environmental impacts in their decisions

First, economists Anita Dancs and Helen Scharber take a look at the criticisms of the "local food" movement coming from mainstream economists, who argue that a "10,000 mile diet" yields cheaper food at a lower environmental impact (Article 3.4). While Dancs and Scharber don't think that "locavores" have got it quite right, they argue that the unfettered markets championed by the mainstream economists would not lead to socially efficient or equitable food production or distribution. Their critique of pure market forces, though, extends to the belief that consumers "voting with their dollars" will be enough to create a desirable food system.

Next, in "Campus Struggles Against Sweatshops Continue" (Article 3.5), Sarah Blaskey and Phil Gasper turn our attention to activism around global labor conditions. They show how people on the consumption side, in this case students and faculty at U.S. colleges and universities, have banded together with workers on the other side of the world to fight "sweatshop" conditions in apparel production.

In the chapter's final article, "How to Take on the Card Sharks—and Win!" (Article 3.6), Jim Campen describes a rare case of successful consumer-protection regulation in recent U.S. history. Credit card regulation has reined in what were widely seen as deceptive and abusive practices, designed to extract as much money in fees and fines as possible from unsuspecting card holders.

Discussion Questions

1. (Article 3.1) Standard consumer theory still applies if advertising is simply a way to inform consumers. But critics suggest that advertising shapes our tastes and desires. Think of some of your recent purchases. For which purchases was advertising primarily a source of information, and for which was it more of a taste-shaper?

2. (Article 3.1) According to Scharber, what are the negative impacts of advertising directed at children? Would you support a law banning advertising to young children? Why or why not?

3. (Article 3.2) Why might private for-profit enterprises not supply desired services at affordable prices, as in the case of financial services in low-income communities? Is the establishment of public service providers a good solution?

4. (Article 3.3) Mainstream microeconomic theory includes the concept of "market

power," meaning that a particular buyer or seller is able to influence market prices (contrary to the first "Tilly assumption," Article 1.2). How does Larson's analysis take into account the existence of market power? Does it take into account other forms of power as well?

5. (Articles 3.4 and 3.5) How can consumers overcome the problem of "asymmetric information" in making purchases? Consider cases when consumers are interested in something (like environmental impact or labor conditions) that they cannot directly observe from the product itself.

6. (Articles 3.4 and 3.5) Why might people on the consumption side of a market (like apparel buyers) consider factors other than product price and quality in their purchasing decisions? Do you think changes in consumer purchasing behavior are enough to bring about social change, in terms of things like labor conditions and environmental impacts of production methods?

7. (Articles 3.6) Why does Campen think that government regulation was called for in the case of credit cards? Do you agree?

Article 3.1

THE 800-POUND RONALD McDONALD IN THE ROOM

BY HELEN SCHARBER
January 2007

When your child's doctor gives you advice, you're probably inclined to take it. And if 60,000 doctors gave you advice, ignoring it would be even more difficult to justify. Last month, the American Academy of Pediatrics (AAP) issued a policy statement advising us to limit advertising to children, citing its adverse effects on health. Yes, banning toy commercials might result in fewer headaches for parents ("Please, please, pleeeeeeease, can I have this new video game I just saw 10 commercials for????"), but the AAP is more concerned with other health issues, such as childhood obesity. Advertising in general—and to children specifically—has reached astonishingly high levels, and as a country, we'd be wise to take the doctors' orders.

Advertising to kids is not a new phenomenon, but the intensity of it is. According to Juliet Schor, author of *Born to Buy*, companies spent around $100 million in 1983 on television advertising to kids. A little more than 20 years later, the amount earmarked for child-targeted ads in a variety of media has jumped to at least $12 billion annually. That's over $150 per boy and girl in the United States. And it's not as though kids only see ads for action figures and sugary cereal; the other $240 billion spent on advertising each year ensures that they see ads for all kinds of products, everywhere they go. According to the AAP report, "the average young person views more than 3,000 ads per day on television, on the Internet, on billboards, and in magazines." Ads are also creeping into schools, where marketers have cleverly placed them in "educational" posters, textbook covers, bathroom stalls, scoreboards, daily news programs, and bus radio programming.

If advertising to children is becoming increasingly ubiquitous, it's probably because it's becoming increasingly profitable. Once upon a time, kids didn't have as much market power as they do today. The AAP report estimates that kids under 12 now spend $25 billion of their own money annually, teenagers spend another $155 billion, and both groups probably influence around $200 billion in parental spending. Not too surprising, considering that 62 percent of parents say their children "actively participate" in car-buying decisions, according to a study by J.D. Power & Associates. Marketers are also becoming more aware of the long-term potential of advertising to children. While they may not be the primary market now, they will be someday. And since researchers have found that kids as young as two can express preferences for specific brands, it's practically never too early to begin instilling brand loyalty.

But while small children have an incredible memory for commercial messages, they may not have developed the cognitive skills necessary to be critical of them. In 2004, the American Psychological Association (APA) also called for setting limits on advertising to kids, citing research that "children under the age of eight are unable to critically comprehend televised advertising messages and are prone to accept advertiser messages as truthful, accurate and unbiased." Many people take offense at the idea that we might be manipulated by marketing. Aren't we, after all, intelligent enough to make up our own minds about what to buy? The research cited by the APA, however, shows that children are uniquely vulnerable to manipulation by advertising. Marketers therefore should not be allowed to prey on them in the name of free speech.

Such invasive advertising to children is not only an ethical problem. The American Academy of Pediatrics cited advertising's effects on health through the promotion of unhealthy eating, drinking and smoking as the main motivation for setting limits. Children's health issues certainly merit attention. The Center for Disease Control, for example, has found that the prevalence of overweight children (ages 6 to 11) increased from 7 percent in 1980 to about 19 percent in 2004, while the rate among adolescents (ages 12 to 19) jumped from 5 percent to 17 percent. In addition to physical health problems, Schor argues that extensive marketing has negative effects on children's emotional well being. In her research for Born to Buy, Schor found links between immersion in consumer culture and depression, anxiety, low self esteem and conflicts with parents. The big push to consume can also lead to financial health problems, as many Americans know all too well, with credit card debt among 18 to 24-year-olds doubling over the past decade.

Not even the staunchest critics of marketing to children would argue that advertisements are completely at fault for these trends. Yet, the commercialization of nearly everything is negatively affecting children's well being in rather profound ways. Why, then, is hardly anyone paying attention to the 800-pound Ronald McDonald in the room? Perhaps it's because advertising appears to be a necessary evil or a fair tradeoff—maybe little Emma's school couldn't afford a soccer team without Coke on the scoreboard, for example. Or perhaps some would argue that parents who don't approve of the commercial culture should limit their kids' exposure to it. Increasingly invasive marketing techniques make it practically impossible to simply opt out of commercial culture, though. Thus, decisions to limit marketing to children must be made by the country as a whole. Sweden, Norway, Greece, Denmark, and Belgium have already passed laws curbing kid-targeted advertising, and according to 60,000 pediatricians, if we care about the health of our kids, we should too. ❑

Sources: American Association of Pediatrics, Policy Statement on Children, Adolescents, and Advertising, December 2006 (pediatrics.aappublications.org/cgi/content/full/118/6/2563); American Psychological Association, "Television Advertising Leads to Unhealthy Habits in Childen" February 2004 (releasees/childrenads.html); Jennifer Saranow, "Car makers direct more ads at kids," *Wall Street Journal*, November 9th, 2006 (www.commercialexploitation.org/news/carmakers.html); David Burke, "Two-year olds branded by TV advertising" (www.whitedot.org/issue/isssory.aps?slug=Valkenburg); Center for a New American Dream, *Kids and Commercialism* (www.newdream.org/kids/);; Juliet Schor, Born to Buy: The Commercialized Child and the New Consumer Culture (New York: Scribner, 2004); "Facts about Childhood Overweight," Center for Disease Control (www.cdc.gov/Healthy Youth/overweight/index.html).

Article 3.2

UNDERBANKED AND OVERCHARGED
Creating Alternatives to the "Alternative Financial Service Providers"

BY DEBORAH M. FIGART
July/August 2014

D riving down Atlantic Avenue, the main commercial thoroughfare in Atlantic City, N.J., one can easily count at least three times as many check-cashing outlets as banks. At these stores, you can cash your paycheck or government check (for a fee), send a wire transfer to a relative or friend overseas, or pay some bills.

Many traditionally African-American neighborhoods and poor census tracts, like this one, do not have a single bank nearby. The U.S. banking system is working for well-heeled customers. It isn't working for poor people.

Over 30 million households—more than one in four–are unbanked or underbanked. That means they have no access to traditional banking services or that they have a bank account but also rely on Alternative Financial Service Providers (AFSPs). According to the Federal Deposit Insurance Corporation's 2011 FDIC National Survey of Unbanked and Underbanked Households, the number of financially excluded households has increased since the publication of its first survey in 2009, with the number of unbanked alone increasing by over 800,000. The incidence of financial exclusion is highest among households that are African-American, Hispanic, lower-income, younger, or less-educated (see Figure 1).

The FDIC asked people why they had never had a bank account or why they had closed any prior account. Some reasons are listed in Figure 2. (Respondents were able to select more than one option.) Since the exact language of the FDIC's survey choices changed between 2009 and 2011, four reasons from the 2009 survey are included for further information.

FIGURE 1: PERCENTAGES OF HOUSEHOLDS, BY CHARACTERISTIC OF HOUSEHOLDER, UNBANKED OR UNDERBANKED, 2011

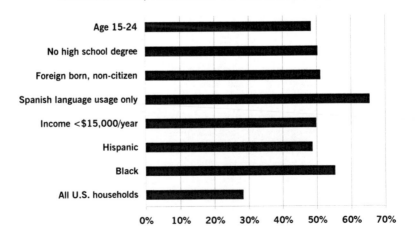

The responses suggest how difficult it is to survive at the lower end of the income distribution. Living paycheck to paycheck, the unbanked feel they do not have enough money to open and maintain a bank account, especially if there is a minimum balance requirement or the bank charges low-balance fees. The survey also reveals social barriers to being a bank customer. If your primary language is not spoken at the bank, for example, then you may feel banks are unwelcoming. This is one reason that over half of immigrant/non-citizen households, and that nearly two-thirds of households where only Spanish is spoken, are unbanked or underbanked

Logistical problems can be a major barrier. "Do I have the proper documents to open an account?" "Is there a bank near me that is convenient?" Banks and savings-and-loans ("thrifts") are under-represented in minority and low-income areas, and AFSPs cluster in those communities. (Scholars who study the issue call this the "spatial void hypothesis.") These spatial voids have only intensified since the 2008 financial crisis, as mainstream banks have ostensibly become more risk-averse—at least regarding low- and moderate-income households and communities.

Alternative financial services are big business in the United States, with an FDIC estimate of $320 billion in annual revenues. The sheer number of check-cashing outlets, payday lenders, auto-title lenders, and issuers of loans on anticipated tax refunds—over 13,000 according to the trade association Financial Service Centers of America—places them nearly on par numerically with banks and credit unions. (Combined, banks and credit unions number almost 15,000, according to the FDIC and National Credit Union Association.) AFSPs are not a "fringe" phenomenon in another sense—many are owned by large mainstream banks that have sought to profit in the market niches left unexploited by regular banking.

In states where check-cashing stores are regulated, fees are clearly posted in business locations, so it is fairly easy to determine the costs to customers. For example, cashing a

FIGURE 2: SOME REASONS HOUSEHOLDS DO NOT HAVE AN ACCOUNT OR CLOSED THEIR ACCOUNT, 2011 AND 2009

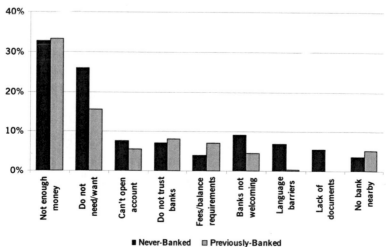

■ Never-Banked ▢ Previously-Banked

Note: The last four categories appeared only in the 2009 survey.

government check (or direct deposit services for these checks) costs 1-3% of the face value of the check. Paychecks from businesses typically carry a 1-5% fee. Determining the typical fees for transaction services in mainstream banks is more difficult because of complicated fee structures that are dependent upon minimum balances. For people with limited needs for transaction services, and who would risk low balance penalties if they used a mainstream bank, AFSPs may in fact be a reasonable alternative.

Fees for transaction services, however, pale in comparison to the cost of credit. To make ends meet, 12 million Americans rely on short-term payday loans each year, at interest rates of about 300-750% (annual percentage rate, or APR). (Thirty-five states allow payday lending.) For the average borrower, a two-week payday loan stretches into five months of debt, with total interest payments greater than the amount of the loan. Wanting in on the action, big banks have issued payday loans to their own customers.—terming them "deposit-advance loans," presumbaly to make them sound more legitimate.

With increased pressure from the new Consumer Financial Protection Bureau (CFPB) and the FDIC, the greedy practices of payday lenders, especially those operating on the internet, are gradually being investigated and curtailed. Now, banks are pulling back from deposit-advance loans. They are also beginning to cut off accounts for payday lenders and are allowing bank customers to halt automatic withdrawals to payday lending companies. What a difference the Dodd-Frank financial-regulation law and the CFPB are beginning to make.

U.S. Senator Elizabeth Warren (D-MA) wants to take the solutions to financial exclusion one step further, beyond regulatory protections against harmful lending and transaction practices. In a recent Huffington Post opinion piece, she urges a serious consideration of postal banks, backing a new report from the U.S. Postal Service (USPS) Office of the Inspector General. The Postal Service, she argues, could partner with banks to offer basic services, including bill paying, check cashing, and small loans.

The idea has precedents. The United States had a postal savings system for accepting and insuring small deposits from 1911 to 1967. The government was thought to be a safe place to stash savings. Savers were paid interest on money that the postal service accepted and redeposited in local banks. After World War II, banks offered higher interest rates to compete for deposits and postal deposits fell. The convenience of the local post office faded in importance as Americans increasingly enjoyed access to cars.

But the idea of postal banks is once again garnering widespread support (44% in favor vs. 37% opposed in a recent YouGov/Huffington Post poll). For millions of Americans, the local post office is one of the geographically closest retail outlets. Unlike private financial-service providers subject to patchy state-by-state regulations, federal postal banks would be regulated in all U.S. states. They would help ease the spatial void in poorer communities and guard against exploitative practices by unregulated banking "alternatives." ❏

Sources: 2011 FDIC National Survey of Unbanked and Underbanked Households, September 2012; FDIC National Survey of Unbanked and Underbanked Households, December 2009; Sen. Elizabeth Warren, "Coming to a Post Office Near You: Loans You Can Trust?" Huffington Post Blog, Feb. 1, 2014 (huffingtonpost.com); Office of the Inspector General, U.S. Postal Service, "Providing Non-Bank Financial Services for the Underserved," Report Number RARC-WP-14-2007, Jan. 27, 2014; Pew Charitable Trusts reports on Payday Lending in America (pewstates.org).

Article 3.3

THE ECONOMICS OF NET NEUTRALITY

BY ROB LARSON
July/August 2015

O n February 26, 2015, the Federal Communications Commission (FCC) made a headline-dominating decision to regulate Internet providers through "net neutrality" principles, in a milestone for freedom of information and for popular activism. The *Wall Street Journal* reported that the decision was the outcome of opposing forces, both representing a "backlash." The conservative paper had previously observed that if the agency moved forward with this regulatory stance, it would face a "Telecom Backlash" from Verizon, Comcast, AT&T, or their trade association, which had won court cases against the FCC's earlier efforts to impose some net neutrality rules.

But the smashing victory was driven by another force that the *Journal* elsewhere called a "Public Backlash"—engaged people and activist groups who were often themselves unsatisfied by the FCC's earlier positions. The FCC was swamped by the staggering volume of public comments filed—four million, with the press reporting that the "overwhelming majority of the comments supported common-carrier style rules," the central requirement of net neutrality. The activist success in this backlash-off was importantly aided by the telecom industry's own conflicting interests in the complex and rapidly evolving information marketplace, which created important opportunities for perceptive activists to exploit.

Not Neutering Net Neutrality

Net neutrality is the principle that data should be treated equally by network operators like Internet service providers (ISPs), the companies that transmit your online information packets through their cable or wireless services. This equality would rule out practices like an ISP blocking access to a website run by a competitor, or discrimination in service, where companies that can afford it get access to "fast lanes" that deliver their data more efficiently, while smaller sites that can't cough up the money get relegated to the slow lanes.

A lack of net neutrality standards would have two broad consequences. One has to do with the prices paid for Internet access at reasonable speeds. The concern is that ISPs would create an "artificial scarcity" (see glossary sidebar) in information markets, allowing them to charge significant amounts to firms that can pay. Artificial scarcity describes to markets where production technology allows for an abundant supply, plenty to satisfy the consumption requirements for the whole market, but in which suppliers are able to restrict the amount produced. This often applies to markets characterized by intellectual property laws, like copyrights or patents, which limit lawful production to companies holding these licenses and thus possessing a monopoly. Profits are elevated with higher prices, but this cuts off some part of the market from consumption, making the product or service "artificially" scarce. For example, without net neutrality an ISP might charge streaming movie firms for faster service, leading those firms to raise their prices to a level that some consumers can't afford.

The second point has less to do with relative prices and more to do with power. Having a degree of control over the flow of information through any medium, from phone service to TV to Internet access, grants a significant position of market power. The issue isn't as abstract as it sounds. In 2014, without any regulation to prevent it, Comcast and other broadband providers deliberately "throttled"—restricted— the data transmission for the popular video-streaming service Netflix, frustrating thousands of subscribers waiting for their programs to load. To end the blockade, Netflix agreed to pay the broadband providers tens of millions of dollars a year. This was a significant trigger for elevated public awareness of neutrality principles, as the cable firms had gone too far—they had gotten between America and its TV shows.

A Net Neutrality Glossary

Artificial scarcity: Most goods and services are necessarily "scarce," meaning that the labor and resources required to make them are limited in supply relative to demand. Others could be abundant, meaning there could be enough to meet demand, but producers limit supply, making them "artificially scarce." Many artificially scarce goods or services have negligible costs of production after development, for example drugs or software, but may be limited deliberately by an entity with market power, like the holder of a patent right.

Broadband: High-speed Internet access, via wired cable or fiber connection, a cell phone tower network, satellite service, or a local wireless hotspot.

Captured regulator: A government body created to regulate certain market practices in an industry, but which has become largely taken over by the industry itself, through lobbying or political action.

Common carrier: A provider of network services that obeys net neutrality rules, like the phone system under Title II classification.

Interconnection: The connections between networks, like those operated by ISPs and those operated by large content-providing firms, such as streaming video companies.

ISP: Internet service provider. Usually a private company (although a few embattled municipal networks exist) that runs a broadband network to consumers' computers and phones, transmitting data from content providers like websites.

Market power: The ability of a market actor (or combination of them) to influence prices or market conditions.

Net neutrality: The principle that all data traveling through information networks to consumers should be treated equally. Practices that violate the principle include throttling of data to collect payment, discrimination among users or types of data, or paid promotion to ensure faster delivery.

Network effect: A service used in a network gains value as more users join. (If everyone you need to contact regularly has a telephone, telephone service is worth more to you than if they did not.) This feature tends to create market concentration and monopoly.

Likewise, Comcast was found to be blocking use of BitTorrent, including downloads of public domain content like the King James Bible.

These relatively innocuous cases show the powerful potential of a for-profit network. Broadband firms and ISPs could force content producers to contribute a major new revenue stream, while those unable to pay could be neglected or, indeed, actively throttled. The cable and wireless firms would thus have major leverage over the flow of information through society. The business media saw that these stories, plus the industry's earlier court victories, "made clear that broadband access providers face few limitations on terms they can seek in negotiations with content companies." Timothy Berners-Lee, considered to be the inventor of the World Wide Web, called this market development "a fundamental shift in power in the Internet economy," driven by the growth of residential ISPs like Verizon and their buying up of other "backbone" network provider firms that used to deliver content. Crucially, this market concentration has made the ISPs into gatekeepers, a strong position since content lacks "any practical way to route around Verizon," for example. So rather than the net-neutral view—all data coming through the pipe should be treated equally—the possibility arises that "in a world where Netflix and Yahoo connect directly to residential ISPs, every Internet company will have its own separate pipe." Which would also make regulation far harder, all due to what Berners-Lee calls the "growing power of the residential broadband providers."

Net neutrality activists argue that this potential power-mongering mess can be resolved through the FCC reclassifying the broadband providers under Title II of the Telecommunications Act of 1934. This is the regulation historically applied to "common carriers" relied on by the broader society, like the phone lines (see sidebar). It was an important triumph when the FCC voted along party lines to reclassify Internet service (and the activist tactics that led to this victory will be reviewed shortly). The FCC's new rules conspicuously "forbear" to use the full regulatory apparatus of Title II, like price limits, keeping to a "light-touch" approach that leaves more freedom to the industry. But the main net neutrality provisions were confirmed, and the FCC in its rules frequently draws attention to the tsunami of public comments in justifying its decision: "Because the record overwhelmingly supports adopting rules and demonstrates that three specific practices invariably harm the open Internet—blocking, throttling, and paid prioritization—this order bans each of them, applying the same rules to both fixed and mobile broadband Internet access service."

Title II

Title II of the 1934 Communications Act requires network-operating companies to treat communications equally and not discriminate among users or with respect to content. The classic example is telephone service, where Title II requires that if you call your doctor, for example, your call can't be routed instead to another practice that paid the network operator. This means phone service is a "common carrier" of information, and the FCC's reclassification of the ISPs as common carriers means net neutrality principles will be instated for cable and wireless broadband markets.

Part of the FCC's calculation was the long- running trend in network-based industries to consolidate and create monopolies and oligopolies, one of the negative forms of what economists call "network effects." This creates uniquely compelling incentives to grow and absorb competitors, leaving many U.S. households with access to only one or two Internet providers. Communication scholar Tim Wu, coiner of the term "net neutrality," observed in his excellent history *The Master Switch* that "over the long haul, competition in the information industries has been the exception, monopoly the rule."

However, a good deal of uncertainty remains, including in significant areas like "interconnection," the connections between different networks and content firms in the "guts" of the Internet. The FCC rules allow paid agreements for interconnection between the networks and content firms for faster, high-capacity connections, which had once been arranged on a bartered, two-way basis. These "premium" arrangements are allowed, but now may be individually challenged by firms case by case, with the FCC ruling on their legality on a so-far unspecified basis. The Commission has held that such agreements must be "fair and reasonable," but has admitted that what will be allowed is unclear. However, even the ability to individually challenge this practice is relevant to net neutrality's core principle of non-discrimination in the treatment of data. As Netflix spokespeople have commented "Had such a process existed when we were battling with the ISPs last year, we definitely would have used it."

Bit Tyrants

The lineup of corporate forces on either side of the issue has attracted a good deal of attention. But with the information industry's fast evolution, the lines have shifted quickly and need to be carefully analyzed. The most common picture puts the cable and wireless ISPs, primarily Comcast, Verizon, TimeWarner Cable and AT&T on one side—eager to charge for fast-lane access to their networks—with content firms like Google, Facebook and Yahoo on the other—hoping to go on expanding their businesses without new tolls for net access.

This basic antagonism has indeed applied for some time, including in the FCC's previous attempts at net neutrality rules in 2010 (described below). It was reinforced by a 2014 open letter to the FCC—signed by dozens of tech firms, including titans like Google, Facebook, Amazon, Yahoo and Twitter—opposing Wheeler's "paid prioritization" scheme, and arguing against allowing "individualized bargaining and discrimination." The letter called the proposal "a grave threat to the Internet." This stance was enormously significant as it put major corporate weight on opposing sides, a more common market development than is widely understood, affecting areas from health care to climate change.

However, the market and technologies have swiftly evolved, and when President Obama made his November 2014 video statement supporting Title II reclassification, the business press observed that the online giants left the response to the lower-profile Internet Association, their trade group. The *National Journal*'s interpretation was that "Aside from the letter, the big Web companies like Facebook and Google mostly stayed on the sidelines of the debate." This "muted response" reflects the maturing of online markets and the growing market power of its largest firms.

Facebook, for example, is in a unique position to drive its millions of members to political action, but prefers to quietly position itself as an increasingly separate alternative to the Web. The eminent Tim Wu observes, "Many forms of content that once stood independent on the Web—personal pages, fan pages, e-vites, and so on—are now created instead on Facebook ... [U]nlike Web pages, Facebook pages are Facebook's property, and are deliberately not linked to the rest of the Web." To the alarm of neutrality supporters, this growing closed-off domain presumably encourages the company not to push too hard for the free and universal flow of information and Web traffic.

And Google itself is of unique importance due to its near-monopoly on search, a pivotal position that led Wu to call it the "Master Switch" of the whole Web, routing an enormous portion of internet traffic. Despite the company's reliance on an open system for users to search, the firm has followed the universal incentive to exploit its network monopoly, increasingly steering users to Google-owned services, prohibiting websites that use its search results from using others' (like Bing's), and making it more expensive for advertisers to also run ads on other search engines.

For these reasons, the Federal Trade Commission (FTC) staff wanted to bring antitrust action against the firm, but in an unusual move the Commission disregarded its staff's recommendations. In fact, the FTC concerns were only revealed when the information was accidentally released in the course of a Freedom of Information Act request. Unsurprisingly, Google had a "flurry" of meetings with administration figures as the FTC finished its investigation, and indeed now spends more on Washington lobbying than any other corporation, except Comcast.

Notably, Google is also moving toward becoming an ISP itself, with both its Google Fiber pilot projects in austin, Tex. and the Kansas City metro area, and its new phone service Google Fi. These developments mean the company is beginning to operate in both web traffic and web access, giving it conflicting allegiances in the debate. Indeed, after the Obama White House announced its support for common carrier rules, Google founder Eric Schmidt told an administration official that the position was a mistake. Even worse, in the proposed 2010 rule written by industry, Google agreed with Verizon that neutrality rules weren't necessary on wireless systems! As a *Wall Street Journal* headline put it, "Google and Net Neutrality: It's Complicated."

Among the several neoliberal objections to the common carrier designation are the Republican FCC Commissioner Ajit Pai's claim that the agency's reclassification was unnecessary since "The Internet is not broken." Those waiting impatiently in 2014 for Netflix to load when Comcast and other cable firms were throttling its data capacity might disagree. For their part, the cable and cellular ISPs claim that the threat of FCC interference will limit their infrastructure investments—meaning the networks will decrease their laying of cable and upgrading of network processes. But this claim is somewhat implausible in view of the staggering fact that the network giants make an absurd 97% profit margin on their bandwidth service, as *MIT Technology Review* reports. This cartoonish profit rate means that any mild regulatory burden is unlikely to overcome the enormous incentive to expand the business and swim in profit. Experience with net neutrality in Europe and elsewhere has borne this out.

Even the expected litigation against the FCC shows the industry's disunity. The major trade associations, the United States Telecom Association and the National Cable & Telecommunications Association, filed their lawsuits immediately after the decision. But Comcast surprised observers by saying it will not itself sue to block the action (although this was before its gigantic merger with Time Warner Cable was rejected by the Federal Trade Commission). The situation remains in flux, but industry conditions may be somewhat suited for reconciliation with the new agency rule, as the industry is expected to continue its ongoing consolidation despite the Comcast-TWC setback. The numerous mergers pending government approval may promote accommodation.

Bet the Net

Since the role of nominally open-network corporations like Google turns out to be somewhat over-hyped, the changed position of the White House and thus the FCC must be credited to another factor, and it's not too difficult to identify. The Commission received over four million comments on its proposed regulatory stance allowing "commercially reasonable" fast-lane treatment, with over 99% supporting strong net neutrality rules. The enormous volume of public comments repeatedly broke the FCC's comment facility, but was only the most dramatic component of the overall activism strategy that resulted in the victory at the FCC. Having brought about a rare triumph against corporate power-mongering, these tactics are worth some attention.

One crucial dimension of organizing around the issue was the effective combination of online and offline organizing, especially relevant to an issue like this that directly impacts the web environment. So while activists in groups like Free Press and the Electronic Frontier Foundation publicized the issue and steered alarmed Web users toward the FCC comment system, others made plans to increase the heat on public officials through "real-life" actions. Most dramatically, activists camped out in front of the FCC building in Washington D.C., an "occupy" tactic that ballooned from a pair of activists in sleeping bags to a tent city of dozens of people. This move was important, especially since the direct action was prepared for with extensive education and awareness-raising. The valuable Waging Nonviolence activist website quotes Malkia Cyrial with the Center for Media Justice: "All along we've been doing a lot of education and advocacy, but at this point we're ready to take direct action against these companies and target members of Congress." Likewise Kevin Zeese, an activist with Popular Resistance, said, "We don't like to occupy ... It's a tactic that we use very sparingly."

But the occupation—especially alarming to the FCC which is accustomed to bureaucratic invisibility—played a critical role, since reclassification of ISPs as Title II common carriers had previously been dismissed as "politically impossible." As Zeese puts it, "But when they say it's politically impossible, our job as activists is to make it politically doable." Demonstrations spread to regional FCC offices and the corporate headquarters of Comcast and Verizon.

The Open Internet Order

In 2010, AT&T, Verizon, Google, and their lobbyist attorneys wrote a bill for the FCC, banning the net neutrality violations of blocking and discrimination among data transmission. But a gigantic omission pointed toward the reason for the phone corporations' participation: The rule applied only to the "wired" Internet, meaning that part where service comes through a fiber or DSL line, not via a wireless signal. Wireless was and is the growth center of the industry, so this exemption meant AT&T and Verizon would be free to block, discriminate, and prioritize to their sleazy deal-making hearts' content. Ultimately, this half-neutered set of FCC rules was struck down in court in 2014, setting the stage for Wheeler's proposal for "commercially reasonable" prioritization, and the following deluge of public comments demanding neutrality.

The success of these activist tactics is especially impressive considering the FCC's long-standing reputation as a "captured" regulator. The FCC's chairman Tom Wheeler is himself a former cable industry lobbyist, and in 2010, the FCC's first attempt at a neutrality policy was literally written by the industry, as has become the standard in many industries. This "Open Internet Order" totally exempted the wireless net and was struck down after a Verizon suit in 2014 (see sidebar).

Of course, the main venue for organizing actions remained online, fitting for the subject and also reflecting the shift of civic engagement to Web venues, for better or worse. In September 2014, many prominent Web companies staged an "Internet Slowdown," replacing their normal home pages with a graphic of the ubiquitous spinning "loading" wheel, dramatizing the risks posed by fast- and slow-lanes to the flow of information. Participating firms included Web mid-weights like Mozilla, Kickstarter, WordPress, and of course Netflix. Notably absent were the heavyweights like Google, Facebook, or Apple, in line with their conflicting loyalties to the open net, outlined above.

Several of these tactics echo those used against previous attempts to restrain the open Web, like the copyright-mongering Stop Online Piracy Act in 2012, and the cable industry's attempts to persuade Congress to strip the FCC of its authority to stop paid prioritization in 2006. In the latter case, one of the most impressive episodes of online social action, activists assembled an alliance of left-wing, right-wing, and overtly apolitical groups to oppose the measures, including the online majors, consumer groups, MoveOn.org, Free Press, SEIU, the Christian Coalition of America, Gun Owners of America, the AARP, the American Library Association, and National Religious Broadcasters. This hugely broad coalition opposed the attempt by the cable and phone corporations to put up toll gates to reach their enormous networks. This activism was effective enough to kill the bills in Congress, foreshadowing what may be required to keep Congress from overriding the FCC order in the future.

In the end, the huge battle for net neutrality, and the major victory of getting the FCC to grudgingly support it despite major industry resistance, is a surprisingly happy chapter in a long story. The triumph at the FCC will require future activism, from the creative activists who got us this far, to defend it in Congress and future administrations, as well as in court. The left doesn't have a lot of triumphs to celebrate these days, so don't let this one go by.

Four million commenters can't be wrong! ❏

Sources: Ryan Knutson and Thomas Gryta, "FCC Likely To Catch Telecom Backlash," *Wall Street Journal*, Jan. 8 2015; Gautham Nagesh, "Net-Neutrality Proposal Faces Public Backlash," *Wall Street Journal*, July 14, 2014; Rebecca Ruiz and Steve Lohr, "F.C.C. Approves Net Neutrality Rules, Classifying Broadband Internet Service as a Utility," *New York Times*, Feb. 26 2015; Shalini Ramachandran, "Netflix to Pay Comcast for Smoother Streaming," *Wall Street Journal*, Feb. 23, 2014; Timothy B. Lee, "Comcast's deal with Netflix makes network neutrality obsolete," Washington Post, Feb. 23, 2014; Candace Clementa and Matt Wood, "Why Title II Reclassification for Net Neutrality Is the Biggest Deal Ever," Free Press, Feb. 4, 2015; Tim Wu, *The Master Switch* (Vintage, 2011); Drew Fitzgerald, "New Net Neutrality Rules Still Leave Some Questions Unanswered," *Wall Street Journal*, Feb. 25, 2015; Drew Fitzgerald, "For Netflix, One Net Neutrality Issue Remains Unclear," *Wall Street Journal*, Feb. 25, 2015; "Google, Facebook and Amazon write to FCC demanding true net neutrality," *The Guardian*, May 7, 2014; Gautham Nagesh, "Amazon, Google, Facebook and Others Disagree With FCC Rules on Net Neutrality," *Wall Street Journal*, May 7, 2014; Farhad Manjoo, "In Net Neutrality Push, Internet Giants on the Sidelines," *New York Times*, Nov. 11, 2014; Brendan Sasso, "Despite fierce opposition from the major Internet providers, the FCC is poised to seize expansive new regulatory powers," *National Journal*, Feb. 5, 2015; Rebecca Ruiz and Steve Lohr, "F.C.C. Approves Net Neutrality Rules, Classifying Broadband Internet Service as a Utility," *New York Times*, Feb. 26, 2015; David Talbot, "When Will the Rest of Us Get Google Fiber?" *MIT Technology Review*, Feb. 4, 2013; Mark Scott, "Dutch Offer Preview of Net Neutrality," *New York Times*, Feb. 26, 2015; Ryan Knutson and Thomas Gryta, "Telecom Industry Sues to Overturn Net Neutrality," *Wall Street Journal*, April 13, 2015; Ben Collins, "Comcast Now Says It Will Not Sue FCC," The Daily Beast, Feb. 26, 2015; Jay Cassano, "How activism won real net neutrality," *Waging Nonviolence*, Feb. 26, 2015; Lawrence Lessig and Robert McChesney, "No Tolls on the Internet," *Washington Post*, June 8, 2006; Jonathan Salant and Molly Peterson, "AT&T, Comcast Rout Google in 'Net Neutrality' Battle," Bloomberg News, July 20, 2006.

Article 3.4

DO LOCAVORES HAVE A DILEMMA?
Economists debate the local food movement.

BY ANITA DANCS AND HELEN SCHARBER
July/August 2015

Food produced on small farms close to where it is consumed—or "local food" for short—accounts for only about 2% of all the food produced in the United States today, but demand for it is growing rapidly. According to the U.S. Department of Agriculture, sales of food going directly from farmers' fields to consumers' kitchens have more than tripled in the past twenty years. During the same period, the number of farmers' markets in the United States has quintupled, and it's increasingly easy to talk about "CSAs"—community-supported agriculture operations where consumers pay up front for a share in the season's output—without explaining the acronym. The National Restaurant Association's "What's Hot" Chef Survey found that locally sourced meats and locally grown produce were the top two trends reported by chefs in 2014, followed by environmental sustainability.

But as local food has grown, so have the number of critics who claim that locavores have a dilemma. The dilemma, prominently argued by Pierre Desrochers and Hiroko Shimizu in their 2012 book *The Locavore's Dilemma: In Praise of the 10,000-mile Diet*, is that local food conflicts with the goal of feeding more people better food in an ecologically sustainable way. In other words, well-meaning locavores are inadvertently promoting a future characterized by less food security and greater environmental destruction. The critics are typically academics, and while not all of them are economists, they rely on economic arguments to support their claims that the globalized food chain has improved our lives.

Why are critics pessimistic about the trend toward local food? Their arguments hinge on what we call the CASTE paradigm—the idea that Comparative Advantage and economies of Scale justify global Trade and lead to greater Efficiency (see box).

Does Local Spinach Create Jobs?

Advocates of local food provide a host of reasons for its superiority, including its economic benefits. The mechanism for creating these benefits is what economists call the "multiplier effect": A dollar spent on local food results in a local farmer spending part of that dollar on other goods and services in the local economy, creating a virtuous circle of wealth and jobs. Despite clear evidence of the multiplier effect, critics argue that more wealth could be created overall through specialization and trade, because food can be grown with fewer resources, which frees up resources for creating wealth elsewhere.

In his 2008 article "Should We Buy Only Locally Grown Produce?" for the Ludwig von Mises Institute, economist Art Carden tries to illustrate the potential consequences of producing spinach locally in an area lacking comparative advantage in spinach production: "[T]he cultivation of spinach in Memphis will require more fertilizer, more rakes, more tillers, and more hoes than the cultivation of spinach in

---

The CASTE Paradigm

Efficiency, or maximizing benefits relative to costs, is the guiding principle in most economic analysis. For the critics, local food simply cannot be efficient because it does not take advantage of what we are calling "CASTE"—the idea that Comparative Advantage and economies of Scale justify global Trade and lead to greater Efficiency.

The theory of **comparative advantage**, developed by economist David Ricardo in the 19th century, says that because regions have different relative advantages in production, they should produce the goods and services that can be produced at the lowest opportunity cost. Even the best use of a resource—land, capital, time, labor—has an opportunity cost, which is the benefit that would have been gained from the next best use. Land devoted to growing food, for example, has a lower opportunity cost in Iowa than in New York City, since land in New York City is highly valued for office space or housing. So Iowa grows corn, this line of argument goes, because the alternatives are simply not as profitable to the owners of the land. As a rule, CASTE critics assert that food should be grown where it has the lowest opportunity cost, in places that tend *not* to be close to most potential consumers.

The concept of **economies of scale** suggests that larger farms can make more efficient use of modern-day farming methods than smaller ones. Someone cultivating an acre or two of rooftop garden in New York City, for example, cannot take advantage of the large tractors, harvesters and irrigation systems that can quickly plow, sow, fertilize and harvest a thousand acres of crops. Economies of scale help explain why the price of a bushel of corn is currently around $4, a price that might not be achievable by small farms producing diversified crops.

Taken together, the assumptions of comparative advantage and economies of scale lead to the conclusion that regions should specialize and **trade**. If Iowa's comparative advantage in corn production along with economies of scale in farm size allow it to produce corn more cheaply than other regions, economists say, it should specialize in corn and trade for other goods and services. New York City residents benefit from the inexpensively produced corn, and resources are freed up to use their land, labor, and capital to produce other goods. The idea that comparative advantage, economies of scale, and trade leads to the greatest **efficiency**—which we call the "CASTE" paradigm—is the foundation upon which modern economic thought has been built, and the critique of local food is just one recent example of how it has been applied.

California." Failing to exploit comparative advantage in food production, he concludes, "is, at its logical limit, a prescription for poverty and starvation."

In a 2010 blog post cheekily titled "Loco-vores," economist Steve Landsberg asks, "How can we possibly gather enough information to … reach a conclusion about which tomato imposes the fewest costs on our neighbors?" His response to the question is simple: the price. For Landsberg and other critics, the higher-priced local tomato signals higher opportunity costs from not exploiting regional advantages in land, labor, and other resources and not taking advantage of economies of scale offered by large global farms. In effect, goes the argument, we are all poorer by paying the higher prices of local spinach and tomatoes, since those higher prices eat into our ability to buy other goods and services.

Are Local Tomatoes Environmentally Destructive?

Local food does not only undermine economic efficiency, according to critics. The same CASTE concepts (see box) are used to argue against its supposed benefits in terms of environmental protection. Locavores have argued that transporting food long distances is bad environmental behavior and that reducing "food miles" is an important reason for buying local food. Critics point out that since food transport accounts for less than 5% of the carbon emissions embodied in food in the United States, it is better to exploit comparative advantage in growing conditions—reducing the use of land, water, chemicals, and energy—and engage in long-distance trade. For example, growing tomatoes in the UK reportedly produces three times the greenhouse gas emissions associated with importing them from Spain, since the extra energy and fertilizer required for greenhouse-grown tomatoes overwhelms the emissions savings from reduced transport. Further, individual car trips to farmers markets may cause more pollution than shipping large quantities of food via trucks or ships, which take advantage of economies of scale in transport.

The critics' environmental arguments go beyond debates over the importance of food miles. Economist Edward Glaeser, in a critique of the trend toward urban farming, estimates that urban population densities would need to be cut in half if just 7% of existing agricultural land were relocated to metro areas. Since lower population densities would lead to longer commutes, he argues that urban farming will increase rather than cut carbon emissions. In his book *Just Food*, agricultural historian James E. McWilliams argues that local food systems in water-scarce cities like Las Vegas and Santa Fe could only be created "through costly and environmentally damaging irrigation projects." Tyler Cowen, author of *An Economist Gets Lunch*, points to the failed Saudi wheat growing experiment in the 1980s that wasted hundreds of billions of cubic meters of water. According to Cowen, the international price of wheat at the time was $120 per ton while Saudi wheat, reflecting these high resource requirements, cost $500 per ton to produce. In sum, food grown in accordance with the principles of comparative advantage and economies of scale should save resources and reduce carbon emissions, all with the added upside of lower consumer prices.

Does That Local Squash Taste Better?

Surely, though, the critics would have a hard time using the CASTE paradigm to argue that global food tastes better than fresh, local food, right? Indeed, journalist Stephen Budiansky, whose main argument in his *New York Times* editorial "Math Lessons for Locavores" is that local food is inefficient, concedes the "pleasures and advantages to the palate and the spirit of eating what's local, fresh and in season." Yet, he notes, shorter food-supply chains do not deliver fresh fruits and vegetables in the middle of winter to most people. According to agricultural economist Jaysen Lusk in his 2013 book *The Food Police*, if the choice is fresh peaches from afar or nothing but squash all winter, his preference is clear: it's peaches. Other critics believe it is clear that relying more heavily on local food would lead to a less nutritious diet. Steven Sexton, an agricultural economist and author of several articles critiquing local food, argues that because there is a correlation between income, on one hand, and the consumption of fresh fruits and vegetables, on the other, the higher prices of local food would make consumers poorer and more reliant on unhealthy food.

In the view of locavores, shorter food supply chains and agricultural diversification also promise increased food security in the face of environmental change, political instability, and speculation in global markets. Not surprisingly, critics question these propositions as well. Economists suggest that exploiting a region's comparative advantage in food production through specialization, and taking advantage of economies of scale, is the only way to efficiently feed the nine to ten billion people we can expect to inhabit the planet by 2050. In addition, specialization and trade is billed as a way to reduce geographic-specific risks, in the face of environmental and political change. Desrochers and Shimizu remind us that "subsistence farmers periodically starve" and when "they escape famine, it is typically because relief efforts were able to deliver the products of large-scale monocultures grown in distant lands."

Do We Need More CASTE?

While critics argue that a sustainable and food-secure future requires a more thorough application of the CASTE paradigm, actual evidence that a sustainable food system requires increasing reliance on comparative advantage and economies of scale seems to be lacking. Economies of scale undeniably exist with respect to various inputs to agricultural production, but the concept is not synonymous with "bigger is better." A 2013 U.S. Department of Agriculture report praising the trend toward industrial farming and long-distance trade nonetheless noted that "most economists are skeptical that scale economies usefully explain increased farm sizes" partly because "crop production still covers a wide range of viable farm sizes."

Comparative advantage based on climatic and soil conditions also exists, but the anti-locavore literature presents little evidence that cost reductions are mainly brought about through natural sources of comparative advantage. Carden's claim that spinach is better grown in California than in Memphis should come with a footnote, since California's supposed comparative advantage in spinach production is made possible by federally subsidized, imported irrigation water. As we witness the unfolding drought crisis in California, it is hard to maintain that society benefits from growing so much spinach (or other water-intensive crops, like almonds) in the state.

Other important reasons for lower costs of food production may appear to be the result of comparative advantage, but instead highlight inequities in the food system. Florida's access to low-wage tomato pickers, for example, results in lower prices at American supermarkets—but these sources of comparative advantage are conspicuously absent from the critics' examples.

Locavores may also fault the CASTE paradigm for excessive "tradeoff thinking," which assumes any cost can be offset by any benefit. The assumption that all benefits (food, good soil, happiness) and all costs (inputs, pollution, psychological distress) might be measured and weighed against one another to make efficient decisions betrays the utilitarian philosophical basis of economics. It may seem like a reasonable way to make many decisions, but it is only one approach to making value

The Marginal Benefit of Marginal Thinking

The extent of problems in the food system would certainly seem to require a big shift, but economic analysis tends to focus on "marginal" changes—small, incremental changes at the margins, like whether or not to cultivate one more acre of land, or whether or not to employ one more worker—to the exclusion of more systemic ones. This tendency is rooted in the desire of 19th-century economists to mathematically formalize economics principles. It may seem logical for a farmer to only decide to farm an acre of marginal land if the additional revenue gained is greater than the additional costs. But this logic has had substantive effects on the questions economists ask, the problems they identify, and the solutions they propose.

To show how "marginal thinking" affects the local food debate, we can point to a study by agricultural economist Steven Sexton. He constructs what might be a useful low-tech study to estimate the land and inputs needed to grow more food locally, but he underpins his research with "marginalist" assumptions. Specifically, he calculates the resources that would be needed to produce corn, soy, and dairy in the *same* amounts and using the *same* methods that the United States currently does, with only a shift toward more local production. He finds that the shift would require more land and other resources. This hypothetical example assumes that the only change is where production happens and does not alter any other component of either the production methods or the products which are grown.

Most advocates for agricultural alternatives, however, are not seeking to reproduce the existing food system, just closer to where they live; they believe systemic changes are needed. Yet, the dominance of marginal thinking among economists prevents them from even considering systemic changes.

judgments. Many ecological economists, for example, believe that ecosystem limits cannot be ignored and are not simply costs that can be traded off against monetary benefits. For instance, we may decide that four degrees of warming would lead to an unacceptable amount of climate disruption, whether or not economists believed that the benefits of the associated fossil fuel use outweigh its costs.

Even for those who agree that weighing benefits against costs is a reasonable way to make decisions, in practice, and in the local food critiques in particular, benefits and costs that do not have market values are often ignored. In particular, the critics fail to take many external costs—those that producers and consumers impose on third parties, and are therefore not reflected in market prices—into account. These authors observe that the bulk of the environmental impacts from agriculture come from the production phase but only use this observation in discussing the merits of comparative advantage. They do not critically examine production practices that routinely poison farmworkers, deplete soil nutrients, destroy rural communities, breed herbicide-resistant weeds, impoverish farmers, and contaminate waterways destroying marine life and biodiversity.

Finally, the role of power in the food system is conspicuously absent from the CASTE analysis. Its absence is not surprising; power is a concept that does not fit easily into a framework focusing on the freedom of autonomous and equal individuals to make utility-maximizing decisions. In that framework, the market is simply an institution that coordinates production and distribution decisions through its near-magical capacity to gather information about consumers' preferences and producers' costs. Yet, looking through the conceptual lens of power relations—between agribusiness and contract farmers, farm owners and farmworkers, food corporations and low-income consumers, the government and immigrant workers—gives us a clearer picture of who determines what costs and benefits are created in the food system and how these costs and benefits are distributed. Paying attention to power allows for the possibility that the falling food prices attributed to comparative advantage and economies of scale may be related, instead, to the ability of the powerful to offload social and environmental costs onto the relatively powerless.

Buy Local? Why Local?

As the near absence of power in the CASTE analysis indicates, much of the disagreement between local food supporters and these critics can be chalked up to differences in the values underlying them. Most economists value efficiency above all else and believe that uncertain social and environmental costs can be traded off against other benefits. Meanwhile, locavores have different end goals—providing enough food for all and creating more resilient local economies while staying within ecological limits. So these groups, of course, tend to talk past each other. Yet both the CASTE analysis and its shortcomings suggest some items for a locavore's "to do" list, including acknowledging the real benefits the existing food system provides, understanding how power affects who receives these benefits, and realizing the political changes needed to make sure the food system benefits everyone.

Overlooking pressing social justice and ecological problems in the food system when making efficiency judgments, as economists have done, is not a balanced approach. The argument that local food activists have downplayed the benefits of the existing food system, however, is worth addressing. Many people do enjoy the diversity of foods that are now available year-round. Consumers in the northern United States are reluctant to give up citrus fruits and juices produced in the south, and many consumers desire fresh over preserved foods. Nutrition and lifespans have improved, thanks in part to increased food access. Likewise, because of inequalities—perpetuated, to be sure, by the system that allows agribusiness giants to profit year after year—higher-priced food would make food even more inaccessible to the nearly one in six Americans that is already food insecure.

It's possible to acknowledge the benefits of the existing industrialized food system without concluding, as the authors we have reviewed often do, that this is the best we can hope for. It's also possible to acknowledge these benefits while understanding that, in many cases, they are possible only because of costs imposed on already vulnerable groups of people. Only by having a clear view of who wins and who loses can we make informed, collective decisions that do not alienate or ignore important segments of the community.

These decisions to improve our food system will not likely come about purely through the market. Ironically, many locavores voice their preferences for a fair

Local Food or a Just and Sustainable Food System?

For most locavores, the impulse to "buy local" is rooted in the desire to reject the ailing industrial food system and to feel a greater connection to how food is grown. With its emphasis on location and scale, however, the locavore movement can unintentionally confuse its means—local and small-scale—with the end goal of building a better food system. But what would a better food system look like? Though different communities will have different priorities, some goals common to local food movement might include:

- Healthy people: The food system should provide safe, healthy food that nurtures people's bodies and minds.
- Accessibility: A wide variety of healthy food must be available to rich and poor alike.
- Decent work: The food system should ensure safe jobs and living wages for everyone working in it, including people working on farms, in food processing plants, and in stores and restaurants.
- Healthy ecosystems: Food should be grown and processed using less fossil fuel and fewer petrochemical fertilizers and pesticides, to prevent excess air and water pollution. A regenerative food system can help improve the quality of soil, water, and air.

Importantly, each of these goals must be placed ahead of profits. Keeping in mind such values and goals, which are at the root of "buy local" campaigns, is important both so that we can monitor progress toward them and remain open-minded about how to achieve them.

and sustainable food system mainly by exercising the consumer sovereignty that mainstream economists claim is the most important benefit of markets. Yet, simply "voting with our dollars" will not be enough to transform the current food system into a sustainable one. Even if the next twenty years brings another tripling of direct farm-to-consumer sales, local food will still be a sapling in the forest of big food. Knowing the farmers that grow your food may be worthwhile, but it's not enough.

Some changes that might not seem to have much to do with food at all can, in fact, contribute to building a just and sustainable food system. Environmental policies such as carbon and pollution taxes can help the prices of products come closer to reflecting their true social costs and provide incentives for more sustainable practices. Meanwhile, subsidies for renewable energy can help reduce the carbon footprint of food production and distribution. Such policies must be paired with others that address inequality, so that no one is forced to decide between buying healthy food and paying other bills. Expanding the SNAP program (formerly known as food stamps), raising the minimum wage, and increasing the earned income tax credit can all help increase food access, as can loftier goals like increasing top tax rates, guaranteeing jobs for all, and providing basic income guarantees. Shorter workweeks paired with good wages and benefits can also help move us toward a healthier food system, since many people simply do not have time to engage in food preparation or even learn what is in their food. These goals may not be easy to achieve, but because they can help improve the lives of so many people, they have the power to unite locavores with other social movements. By moving beyond the notion of shopping our way to a better world and embracing the wider set of changes necessary to increase social justice, locavores can help resolve dilemmas in the food system and beyond. ❏

Sources: Stephan Budiansky, "Math lessons for locavores," *New York Times*, Aug. 19, 2010 (nytimes.com); Art Carden, "Should we buy only locally grown produce?", Ludwig von Mises Institute, July 15, 2008 (mises.org); Tyler Cowen, *An Economist Gets Lunch: New Rules for Everyday Foodies* (Dutton Adult, 2012); Pierre Desrochers and Hiroko Shimizu, *The Locavore's Dilemma: In Praise of the 10,000-Mile Diet* (Public Affairs, 2012); Edward Glaeser, "The Locavore's Dilemma: Urban Farms Do More Harm Than Good to the Environment," *Boston Globe*, June 16, 2011 (boston.com); Steve Landsburg, "Loco-vores," The Big Questions, August 23, 2010 (thebigquestions.com); Jaysen Lusk, *The Food Police: A Well-Fed Manifesto About the Politics of Your Plate* (Crown Publishing Group, 2013); James MacDonald, Penni Korb, and Robert Hoppe, "Farm Size and the Organization of U.S. Crop Farming," Economic Research Report No. 152, USDA Economic Research Service, 2013; James E. McWilliams, *Just Food: Where Locavores Get It Wrong and How We Can Truly Eat Responsibly* (Little, Brown and Company, 2009); National Restaurant Association, "What's Hot: 2015 Culinary Forecast, Dec. 3, 2014 (restaurant.org); David Ricardo, *The Principles of Political Economy and Taxation* (J. M. Dent & Sons, Ltd., 1973 [1817]); Steven Sexton, "Does local production improve environment and health outcomes?", ARE Updates 13: 5–8, 2009;Paul Watkiss, et al., *The Validity of Food Miles as an Indicator of Sustainable Development*, REPORT ED50254. London, UK: Department of Environment, Food and Rural Affairs, 2005.

Article 3.5

CAMPUS STRUGGLES AGAINST SWEATSHOPS CONTINUE

Indonesian workers and U.S. students fight back against Adidas.

BY SARAH BLASKEY AND PHIL GASPER
September/October 2012

Abandoning his financially ailing factory in the Tangerang region of Indonesia, owner Jin Woo Kim fled the country for his home, South Korea, in January 2011 without leaving money to pay his workers. The factory, PT Kizone, stayed open for several months and then closed in financial ruin in April, leaving 2,700 workers with no jobs and owed $3.4 million of legally mandated severance pay.

In countries like Indonesia, with no unemployment insurance, severance pay is what keeps workers and their families from literal starvation. "The important thing is to be able to have rice. Maybe we add some chili pepper, some salt, if we can," explained an ex-Kizone worker, Marlina, in a report released by the Worker Rights Consortium (WRC), a U.S.-based labor-rights monitoring group, in May 2012.

Marlina, widowed mother of two, worked at PT Kizone for eleven years before the factory closed. She needs the severance payment in order to pay her son's high school registration fee and monthly tuition, and to make important repairs to her house.

When the owner fled, the responsibility for severance payments to PT Kizone workers fell on the companies that sourced from the factory—Adidas, Nike, and the Dallas Cowboys. Within a year, both Nike and the Dallas Cowboys made severance payments that they claim are proportional to the size of their orders from the factory, around $1.5 million total. But Adidas has refused to pay any of the $1.8 million still owed to workers.

Workers in PT Kizone factory mainly produced athletic clothing sold to hundreds of universities throughout the United States. All collegiate licensees like Adidas and Nike sign contracts with the universities that buy their apparel. At least 180 universities around the nation are affiliated with the WRC and have licensing contracts mandating that brands pay "all applicable back wages found due to workers who manufactured the licensed articles." If wages or severance pay are not paid to workers that produce university goods, then the school has the right to terminate the contract.

Using the language in these contracts, activists on these campuses coordinate nationwide divestment campaigns to pressure brands like Adidas to uphold previously unenforceable labor codes of conduct.

Unpaid back wages and benefits are a major problem in the garment industry. Apparel brands rarely own factories. Rather, they contract with independent manufacturers all over the world to produce their wares. When a factory closes for any reason, a brand can simply take its business somewhere else and wash its hands of any responsibilities to the fired workers.

Brands like Nike and Russell have lost millions of dollars when, pressed by United Students Against Sweatshops (USAS), universities haver terminated their contracts. According to the USAS website, campus activism has forced Nike to pay severance and Russell to rehire over 1,000 workers it had laid off, in order to avoid losing more collegiate contracts. Now many college activists have their sights set on Adidas.

At the University of Wisconsin (UW) in Madison, the USAS-affiliated Student Labor Action Coalition (SLAC) and sympathetic faculty are in the middle of a more than year-long campaign to pressure the school to terminate its contract with Adidas in solidarity with the PT Kizone workers.

The chair of UW's Labor Licensing Policy Committee (LLPC) says that Adidas is in violation of the code of conduct for the school's licensees. Even the university's senior counsel, Brian Vaughn, stated publicly at a June LLPC meeting that Adidas is "in breach of the contract based on its failure to adhere to the standards of the labor code." But despite the fact that Vaughn claimed at the time that the University's "two overriding goals are to get money back in the hands of the workers and to maintain the integrity of the labor code," the administration has dragged its feet in responding to Adidas.

Instead of putting the company on notice for potential contract termination and giving it a deadline to meet its obligations as recommended by the LLPC, UW entered into months of fruitless negotiations with Adidas in spring of 2012. In July, when these negotiations had led nowhere, UW's interim chancellor David Ward asked a state court to decide whether or not Adidas had violated the contract (despite the senior counsel's earlier public admission that it had). This process will delay a decision for many more months--perhaps years if there are appeals.

Since the Adidas campaign's inception in the fall of 2011, SLAC members have actively opposed the school's cautious approach, calling both the mediation process and the current court action a "stalling tactic" by the UW administration and Adidas to avoid responsibility to the PT Kizone workers. In response, student organizers planned everything from frequent letter deliveries to campus administrators, to petition drives, teach-ins, and even a banner drop from the administration building that over 300 people attended, all in hopes of pressuring the chancellor (who ultimately has the final say in the matter) to cut the contract with Adidas.

While the administration claims that it is moving slowly to avoid being sued by Adidas, it is also getting considerable pressure from its powerful athletics director, Barry Alvarez, to continue its contract with Adidas. As part of the deal, UW's sports programs receive royalties and sports gear worth about $2.5 million every year.

"Just look at the money—what we lose and what it would cost us," Alvarez told the *Wisconsin State Journal*, even though other major brands would certainly jump at the opportunity to replace Adidas. "We have four building projects going on. It could hurt recruiting. There's a trickle-down effect that would be devastating to our whole athletic program."

But Tina Treviño-Murphy, a student activist with SLAC, rejects this logic. "A strong athletics department shouldn't have to be built on a foundation of stolen labor," she told *Dollars & Sense*. "Our department and our students deserve better."

Adidas is now facing pressure from both campus activists in the United States and the workers in Indonesia--including sit-ins by the latter at the German and British embassies in Jakarta. (Adidas' world headquarters are in Germany, and the company sponsored the recent London Olympics.) This led to a meeting between their union and an Adidas representative, who refused to admit responsibility but instead offered food vouchers to some of the workers. The offer amounted to a tiny fraction of the owed severance and was rejected as insulting by former Kizone workers.

In the face of intransigence from university administrations and multinational companies prepared to shift production quickly from one location to another to stay one step ahead of labor-rights monitors, campus activism to fight sweatshops can seem like a labor of Sisyphus. After more than a decade of organizing, a recent fundraising appeal from USAS noted that "today sweatshop conditions are worse than ever."

Brands threaten to pull out of particular factories if labor costs rise, encouraging a work environment characterized by "forced overtime, physical and sexual harassment, and extreme anti-union intimidation, even death threats," says Natalie Yoon, a USAS member who recently participated in a delegation to factories in Honduras and El Salvador.

According to Snehal Shingavi, a professor at the University of Texas, Austin who was a USAS activist at Berkeley for many years, finding ways to build links with the struggles of the affected workers is key. "What I think would help the campaign the most is if there were actually more sustained and engaged connections between students here and workers who are in factories who are facing these conditions," Shingavi told *Dollars & Sense*. Ultimately, he said, only workers' self-activity can "make the kind of changes that I think we all want, which is an end to exploitative working conditions."

But in the meantime, even small victories are important. Anti-sweatshop activists around the country received a boost in September, when Cornell University President David Skorton announced that his school was ending its licensing contract with Adidas effective October 1, because of the company's failure to pay severance to PT Kizone workers. The announcement followed a sustained campaign by the Sweatfree Cornell Coalition, leading up to a "study in" at the president's office. While the contract itself was small, USAS described the decision as the "first domino," which may lead other campuses to follow suit. Shortly afterwards, Oberlin College in Ohio told Adidas that it would not renew its current four-year contract with the company if the workers in Indonesia are not paid severance.

Perhaps just as significant are the lessons that some activists are drawing from these campaigns. "The people who have a lot of power are going to want to keep that power and the only way to make people give some of that up is if we make them," Treviño-Murphy said. "So it's really pressure from below, grassroots organizing, that makes the difference. We see that every day in SLAC and I think it teaches us to be not just better students but better citizens who will stand up to fight injustice every time." ❏

Sources: Worker Rights Consortium, "Status Update Re: PT Kizone (Indonesia)," May 15, 2012 (workersrights.org); Andy Baggot, "Alvarez Anxiously Awaits Adidas Decision," *Wisconsin State Journal*, July 13, 2012 (host.madison.com); United Students Against Sweatshops (usas.org), PT Kizone update, June 15, 2012 (cleanclothes.org/urgent-actions/kizoneupdate).

Article 3.6

HOW TO TAKE ON THE CARD SHARKS—AND WIN!

New consumer-protection legislation has reined in predatory credit card lending.

BY JIM CAMPEN
November/December 2013

In the early 2000s, credit card companies, like other lenders, decided that there was lots of money to be made by exploiting vulnerable consumers. Up to that point, the credit card industry was a somewhat boring business that made its money by charging high—but not exorbitant—interest rates to borrowers who it judged likely to be able to make their monthly payments on time. Then, however, the giant banks that provide the bulk of the nation's credit cards switched to a business model based on what Elizabeth Warren, then a professor at Harvard Law School, memorably termed "tricks and traps." These were spelled out in the almost impossible-to-understand small print of the multi-page "agreements" that the banks provided to their customers. Anyone who did manage to read to the end found that the "agreement" allowed the credit card company to change any of its terms "at any time, for any reason."

The unfair and exploitative practices of the credit card companies, affecting millions of households, soon became widely known. Five years ago, it was almost impossible to avoid the avalanche of news articles, radio and TV reports, and Internet postings about them. Today, such stories are few and far between. This isn't because the media became bored with the story. It's because a powerful consumer movement publicized the abuses, built a strong campaign, and won two important legislative victories.

Tricks and Traps

Millions of consumers were enticed with offers of cards with "promotional" interest rates as low as 0% for the first few months and regular interest rates of between 12% and 14% after that, but ended up paying far more. They were slapped with late fees averaging over $33 each time their monthly payment arrived even one day late, even if the due date fell on a Sunday and their payment arrived on Monday. They faced stiff over-limit fees—sometimes multiple charges for a number of small purchases on the same day—if their charges exceeded their credit limit by even a single dollar, even though borrowers were generally not aware that they had exceeded their limit or that the credit card companies would authorize over-limit charges.

Most devastatingly, both of these minor mistakes were among those that could result in their interest rate being switched to a much higher "penalty rate." Some card companies adopted the policy of "universal default" whereby even a problem on an unrelated account (for example, being late on an electric bill) could result in a cardholder being subject to the penalty rate. By 2007, the average penalty rate was 16.9 percentage points higher than the regular interest rate, meaning that a 13% rate would jump to 29.9%.

Worst of all, the penalty rate applied not only to future purchases, but also to money already borrowed. For a household with the average 2008 credit card balance, about $10,700, this would result in additional interest charges of more than $1,800 per year. Once a household fell into this trap, it was almost impossible to get out—which is just the way the banks liked it.

Many of those trapped were low- and middle-income families who used their credit cards to pay for basic living expenses and unexpected medical bills. One recent survey, by the liberal policy organization Dēmos, found that two-fifths of such lower-income families used their credit cards in this way. Many other victims were college students, on their own for the first time, who fell prey to aggressive marketing on college campuses and ended up with debt that they couldn't repay as well as a damaged credit rating.

A Consumer Victory: The Credit CARD Act of 2009

As the credit card industry's abuses grew and spread, millions of outraged consumers demanded change. Led by a coalition of national consumer advocacy groups —including the Center for Responsible Lending, the Consumer Federation of America, Consumers Union, the National Consumer Law Center, and U.S. PIRG —a powerful grassroots movement pushed Congress to take action. The industry argued that the proposed legislation that eventually became the Credit Card Accountability, Responsibility, and Disclosure Act (known as the CARD Act) would end up hurting consumers by raising the cost and reducing the availability of credit card borrowing.

But credit card abuses were so widespread and so offensive that politicians were unwilling to defend them in the light of day. Although many Republicans worked behind the scenes to derail or weaken the bill, when the CARD Act came up for its final votes in May 2009, it passed overwhelmingly in both the Senate (90-5) and the House of Representatives (361-54).

The CARD Act effectively outlaws the worst of the credit card industry's tricks and traps. Most importantly, it prohibits retroactive interest rate increases on existing balances unless a borrower has missed two consecutive monthly payments on the account. And not only that: when a borrower is hit with a penalty rate, the company is required to restore the original interest rate if and when the borrower succeeds in making six consecutive on-time payments.

Late fees have been reduced by requiring that consumers have at least 21 days to make their payments, that payments due on a Sunday or holiday be regarded as on time if they arrive the next business day, that payments be due the same date each month, and that the fees be "reasonable and proportional." Over-limit fees are banned unless a cardholder opts-in to allow approval of charges over their credit limit, and are limited to one fee per month. The initial rate offered on a new account cannot be raised during the first year, and after that the borrower must be provided with 45-day advance notice and given the opportunity to cancel the card and pay off the existing balance over five years.

Credit card companies are prohibited from opening a new account or increasing a borrower's credit limit without assessing the consumer's ability to make timely loan payments. Those under 21 are given special protection from predatory credit card lenders by a prohibition on sending pre-approved offers of credit without advance permission, a ban on marketing on college campuses, and a new rule that no one under 21 years of age can get a card without either proving an independent ability to make the required monthly payments or obtaining a co-signer over 21.

Consumers Win Again: The CFPB

The enactment of the CARD Act was a major accomplishment. But simply passing laws doesn't make a difference unless those laws are enforced. And prohibiting existing abusive practices can't protect consumers against the credit card companies' endless ability to come up with imaginative new abuses that get around the law. The title of a December 2009 report from the Center for Responsible Lending spelled out the problem: "Dodging Reform: As Some Credit Card Abuses are Outlawed, New Ones Proliferate."

That's why a second consumer legislative victory—ensuring that the financial reform law passed in July 2010 (the Dodd-Frank Act) mandated the establishment of a Consumer Financial Protection Bureau (CFPB)—was perhaps even more important than the CARD Act itself.

The CFPB, which came into existence in July 2011, is charged not only with writing and enforcing the regulations that implement the CARD Act and other consumer-protection laws, but also with monitoring the operation of consumer-credit markets and taking action against unfair, deceptive, or abusive acts and practices. It seeks to improve consumers' ability to understand prices and risks upfront when shopping for credit, and to offer them a one-stop location for submitting complaints and seeking remedies for problems with credit card providers.

The Fruits of These Victories

That the CARD Act has produced major benefits for consumers, with none of the dire consequences predicted by the industry, has been documented in numerous reports and studies. For example, the group Consumer Action noted that while complaints about credit cards were regularly the number one reason for calls to its consumer hotline before 2009, they are no longer even among the top ten.

The most comprehensive assessment to date of the Act's impact on consumers and on the industry is provided by a major report released by the CFPB in October 2013. This report found that the average late fee had gone down from $33 to $27 and that over-limit fees had essentially disappeared. Together, these two changes were saving consumers an estimated $4 billion per year.

The CFPB also found that, while credit remains readily available to those with the ability to repay, the number of 18- to 20-year-olds with at least one credit card had fallen by half. (Meanwhile, of course, student loans have soared. These loans have their own problems, but at least their interest rates are much lower than those on credit cards and no repayment is required while students remain in school.)

The CFPB's publicly available consumer complaint database recorded over 36,000 complaints about credit cards in its first two years of operation, resulting in monetary payments to about 6,500 consumers, and increased public scrutiny of card-company performance. J. D. Power's 2013 *Credit Card Satisfaction Study* showed that customer satisfaction had risen every year since 2010, to the highest level since the study began in 2007.

The CFPB's report also highlighted areas where consumers continue to suffer from abusive practices of the credit card industry and promised to address these issues in a timely manner. In one of these areas—the selling of "add-on" products that purport to offer debt protection and identity protection—the CFPB has already required three big lenders (Chase, Capital One, and Discover) to refund over $700 million to consumers and to pay over $100 million in fines for deceptive marketing and charging for services that were never actually provided.

Crying Wolf

Data on what's happened during the three and one-half years since passage of the CARD Act demonstrate beyond any doubt what consumer advocates said at the time: that banks were "crying wolf," rather than warning of real dangers, when they predicted that the pending legislation would cause the cost of credit card borrowing to soar and their own profitability to plummet.

It is theoretically possible that all of the CARD Act's consumer benefits from the lower fees and rates noted earlier could have been offset by increases in other charges. This is what Jamie Dimon, CEO of JPMorgan Chase, was predicting when he said that "If you're a restaurant and you can't charge for the soda, you're going to charge more for the burger." But the CFPB investigated this possibility by measuring what it calls the "total cost of credit"—that is, it added up all fees and interest charges paid by credit card borrowers and calculated what percentage this represented of the total amount of credit card debt outstanding. The CFPB found that the total cost of credit declined from 16.4% in the last quarter of 2008 to 14.4% in the last quarter of 2012. It is impossible to know how much of this reduction is a result of the CARD Act, but it is crystal clear that predictions of an increase in borrowing costs were wrong.

Another October 2013 study on the impact of the CARD Act, this one by four academic economists, concluded that the resulting fee reductions have saved consumers $21 billion per year "with no evidence of an offsetting increase in interest charges or a reduction in access to credit." The savings were particularly great for the riskiest borrowers. While the fee reductions amounted to 2.8% of total credit card balances annually, they came to over ten percent of their credit card balances for the 17% of borrowers who were in the highest risk category as measured by their credit scores at the time they opened their accounts.

Did the consumer benefits from the CARD Act come at the expense of lender profitability? It's possible to get a remarkably clear answer to this question because the FDIC reports quarterly on the performance of different kinds of banks, categorized by specialization or size, and one of its categories consists of "credit card lenders." It turns out that all but one of the six largest credit card lenders (who together account for over two-thirds of total credit card balances) do their lending though separate banks that specialize in credit cards. This is true for Bank of

America, Chase, Capital One, Discover, and American Express; the only exception is Citibank.

Since 2010, "credit card banks" has been the most profitable single category, using the two measures of profitability reported by the FDIC—return on assets (ROA) and return on equity (ROE). In 2012, ROA was 3.14% for credit card banks, more than triple the 1.00% for all banks; ROE was 20.97% for credit card banks, more than double the 8.92% for all banks. The results for 2012 are very similar to those for 2011 and for the first half of 2013, and also to those for 2007, before the onset of the financial crisis and economic downturn.

Perhaps the credit card companies had been outsmarting themselves. A business model based on "tricks and traps" that aggressively pushed money into the hands of borrowers who lacked the ability to repay their debts may have worked in the short run, but ultimately was disastrous to the lenders themselves. Lending money only to those with the ability to repay it would seem like simple common sense. It's too bad that financial hardship for millions of borrowers, an act of Congress, and a new federal agency was necessary to make these lenders behave sensibly. ❏

Sources: The CARD ACT Report, October 1, 2013 (consumerfinance.gov); Sumit Agarwal, et al., "Regulating Consumer Financial Products: Evidence from Credit Cards"; Center for Responsible Lending (responsiblelending.org); Federal Deposit Insurance Corporation (FDIC), *Quarterly Banking Profile* (fdic.gov); Peter Dreier and Donald Cohen, "Credit Sharks Crying Wolf," The Cry Wolf Project, May 2009 (crywolfproject.org).

Chapter 4

FIRMS, PRODUCTION, AND PROFIT MAXIMIZATION

INTRODUCTION

How do producers make decisions? Textbooks describe a process that is rational, benign, and downright sensible. There is one best—least costly and most profitable—way to produce any given amount of goods or services. Given a particular scale of operations, there is one most profitable amount to produce. Businesses adjust their total output and the mix of inputs at the margin until they achieve these most profitable outcomes. They pay the going wage for labor, just as they pay the going price for any input. And when businesses have achieved the lowest possible costs, market competition ensures that they pass on savings to consumers.

This chapter describes a reality that is a bit more complicated, and in some ways uglier, than the textbook model. Very large companies are not the passive price-takers of neoclassical lore but do in fact affect the market-wide level of prices, profits, and wages, and manufacture their own demand. Thus, large corporations are the very embodiment of market power (violating Tilly Assumption #1, Article 1.2).

Alejandro Reuss starts things off with a primer on corporations (Article 4.1). He describes the ways that corporations are "special"—that is, different from other capitalist enterprises—and why they have become the dominant form of business organization in many countries. He concludes by discussing how corporations' economic power—their control over investment and employment—can translate into political power.

John Miller argues that the Trans-Pacific Partnership (TPP), a proposed "trade agreement" encompassing a dozen countries around the Pacific Rim, including the United States, is not really about trade at all (Article 4.2). Rather, like other so-called trade agreements, it is really about tilting the playing field of the global economy against workers and the broad public interest and in favor of big corporations.

In Article 4.3, "What's Good for Wal-Mart ...," John Miller provides a salient example of firms' market power. He suggests that there may not be just "one best way" for retail businesses, but rather two: a "high road" based on high levels of service, skilled, decently paid employees, and higher prices, as exemplified by the business model at Costco; and a "low road" that offers low prices, no frills, and a low-paid, high-turnover workforce, which is Walmart's business model. Despite

Walmart's growth and its position as the world's largest retailer, the author questions whether the business model has in fact proven beneficial for the U.S. economy as a whole.

Today's private equity firms engage in what used to be called "leveraged buyouts." Economists Eileen Appelbaum and Rosemary Batt offer a forceful critique, describing how private equity firms buy out target companies with borrowed money, load them up with debt, strip them of valuable assets, and pay themselves extraordinary dividends and fees. Meanwhile, they raise important questions about the boundaries of the firm. Private equity firms, Batt and Appelbaum note, "act as managers and employers of the companies they take over, even though the law treats them as passive investors in the companies they own." (Article 4.4)

The final two articles of the chapter consider two different forms of organization. Arthur MacEwan makes "A Case for Public Ownership" (Article 4.5). While textbook accounts of the firm focus almost exclusively on privately owned companies, public ownership of enterprises is widespread in capitalist economies. MacEwan describes the rationale for public ownership in sectors where market failures make private ownership undesirable, like utilities ("natural monopoly"), finance ("negative externalities"), and services such as firefighting and traffic control ("public goods").

Finally, economist Nancy Folbre looks at "Co-op Economics" (Article 4.6). Folbre considers not only the strengths of workers' cooperatives, in which the workers are also the owners of the firm, but also the problems that they face in growing and becoming more widespread.

Discussion Questions

1. (General) The authors of the articles in this chapter present various firm strategies as a choice, rather than an imperative. How does this compare with the standard microeconomic analysis of business decision-making?

2. (General) Miller suggests that we should change the rules of the competitive game to steer businesses toward better treatment of workers. Present-day capitalism already has some such rules (such as those forbidding slavery). What rule changes do articles in this chapter propose? What do you think of these proposals?

3. (Article 4.1) How do corporations differ from other capitalist firms? How should the fact that corporations are chartered by the government, and shareholders given special protections by law (such as limited liability), affect our attitudes about government regulation of corporate operations?

4. (Article 4.2) Most textbooks' accounts of firm profit-maximization focus on their decisions about how much output to produce and what factors of production to produce it. What does Miller's article suggest about other ways that firms may, in the real world, go about increasing their profits?

5. (Article 4.3) John Miller implies that there is more than one "best" way to organize production. Do you agree? If other ways of organizing production are equally good, why are certain ways dominant, at least in particular industries?

6. (Article 4.3) According to Cervantes (sidebar), how does Costco keep prices low while following very different labor practices?

7. (Article 4.4) Mainstream textbooks suggest that firms profit by offering something of positive value to the rest of society (like goods that consumers want). If private equity firms act in a way that is generally harmful, how do they profit?

8. (Article 4.5) MacEwan offers several arguments, rooted in the correction of market failures, for public ownership. Can you think of other ways that market failures might justify public ownership? Can you think of reasons not based in market failures?

9. (Article 4.6) Folbre proposes a dramatically different power structure at the level of the individual firm, with workers democratically controlling the enterprises where they work. Why does she think that this alternative structure could be desirable for workers and for society? If it is so desirable, why is it not more common?

Article 4.1

WHAT ARE CORPORATIONS?

BY ALEJANDRO REUSS
April 2012

When people use the word "corporation," they are usually referring to certain private, for-profit businesses, especially the largest businesses in the United States or other capitalist economies. When we think of corporations, we usually think of "big business." Besides size, people often picture other features of corporations when they hear the word. A corporation can have many shareholders—all part-owners of the company—instead of being owned by a single owner or a couple of partners. A corporation has a board of directors, elected by some or all of the shareholders, which may direct the overall way the corporation is managed. The board usually hires a few top executives, who then make decisions about how the corporation in managed on a day-to-day basis.

Corporations do not have to be large. There are corporations of all different sizes. Even a small company with a few employees could be a corporation. There are some large companies that are not corporations, but the very largest companies, which may have hundreds of thousands of employees and may sell billions of dollars of goods each year, are almost always corporations. Various different kinds of businesses can be corporations, including manufacturing companies (such as General Motors), retail companies (like Wal-Mart), or financial companies (like Bank of America or Liberty Mutual).

Even though some not for-profit entities are also—legally speaking—corporations, people usually use the word "corporation" as shorthand for for-profit companies like General Motors or Wal-Mart. A corporation, in this sense, is a particular type of capitalist enterprise—a "capitalist corporation."

What Is a Capitalist Enterprise?

By "capitalist enterprise," we just mean a private, for-profit business whose owners employ other people in exchange for wages. By this definition, a private business where a "self-employed" owner works, but which does not hire other people for wages, is not a capitalist enterprise.

In the United States and other similar economies, relatively few people are business owners. Farm workers do not usually own the farms where the work. Miners do not usually own the mines. Factory workers usually do not own the factories. People who work in shops or offices usually do not own those businesses. Most workers do not own the buildings where they go to work, the materials or tools they use, or the products they produce. Instead, they work for pay at capitalist enterprises that are owned by others.

Workers get paid a wage or salary by the owner of the business, who in turn owns whatever the worker produces using the materials and tools provided. The owners of a business, of course, do not usually want the goods that employees produce, but want to sell these goods. If a capitalist enterprise cannot sell these goods for more than what it cost to produce them, it cannot make a profit.

Even a business that makes a profit may not stay in business for very long if the profit is less than "normal" (whatever that may be). The owners may decide that it is not worth investing in that business, if it is possible for them to make a larger profit in another business. In addition, businesses that make higher profits can reinvest these profits to expand and modernize, and may put the less profitable business at a competitive disadvantage in the future. Therefore, owners of capitalist enterprises are under competitive pressure to make the most profit they can.

How Are Corporations Special?

In many ways, capitalist corporations are like other capitalist enterprises. However, corporations are also defined by their special legal status, which makes them different from other capitalist enterprises. Corporations are granted a "charter" by the government, which means that the corporation exists as a legal entity. (In the United States, state governments grant corporate charters.)

All the things that make corporations different from other capitalist enterprises are determined by government policy. Corporate law creates certain special privileges for corporations that other businesses do not have. It also imposes special obligations on corporations (especially those whose shares are bought and sold on the stock market). The most important of these special characteristics are "limited liability," the "fiduciary responsibility" of management to the corporation's shareholders, "public disclosure" requirements, and the corporate "governance" structure.

Limited Liability

If a corporation cannot pay its debts, it can declare bankruptcy, and the people it owes can get paid off from the sale of its assets, like the buildings or machinery it owns. If the proceeds are not enough to pay off all the debts, however, the shareholders are not responsible (not "liable") to pay the rest. This is what we mean by the term "limited liability." Someone who buys stock in a corporation is risking whatever they paid for the stock, but cannot lose more than this amount. If the corporation goes bankrupt, the shareholders' stock becomes worthless, but the shareholders cannot be forced, legally, to pay whatever debts the corporation has left unpaid.

The justification usually given for the legal principle of limited liability is that it promotes economic growth and development. The idea is that, if companies were limited to what an individual or family, or perhaps a couple of partners, could scrape together to start a business, they would not be able to operate at the scale that modern corporations do. They would not have enough money to buy expensive machinery, let alone buy large factories or put together huge assembly lines.

Even if the reason given for limited liability is to fuel economic growth, however, we should remember that this is also a big favor from the government for the people who own shares in corporations. First, limited liability means that the government gives the shareholders of a corporation a certain kind a protection from other people's claims against it. Second, it means that corporations may take bigger risks in hopes of bigger profits, since the shareholders are not on the hook for all the corporation's liabilities if these risks do not pay off.

Fiduciary Responsibility

A single person who fully owns an entire company (known as a "privately held" company) can use the company's funds for whatever he or she likes, whether that is expanding the company's operations or buying luxury cars. In contrast, corporate executives receive a salary and other compensation (often lavish, in the case of large companies) decided by the board of directors or a committee of the board. They are legally free to spend this income as they wish.

Corporate executives also control how company funds are spent, but are not free to treat corporate funds as their own. This means that the chief executive of a company is not legally entitled to use company funds to remodel his or her house, buy fancy cars, take expensive vacations, and so on. Of course, executives still fly on private jets, take "business trips" to exotic locales, enjoy fancy "business dinners," and so on, but they have to justify these as necessary costs of doing business. If shareholders think that executives have failed in their fiduciary responsibility, they can actually sue the company.

Some legal scholars and economists have extended this idea to the logical extreme that corporate managers are legally obligated to the shareholders and only the shareholders. In this view, management decisions must be guided by the sole objective of enhancing "shareholder value" (in effect, the profitability of the corporation, and therefore the value of an ownership stake in it). This means that they cannot put other people's interests ahead of those of the shareholders. According to the "shareholder value" doctrine, if managers decide to pay workers more than they really have to, they are giving away the company's (that is, the shareholders') money. Likewise, they have no legal duty to the broader community, beyond abiding by the law. They do not have to "give back," say, by funding schools, libraries, or parks in the communities where they operate.

The shareholder value doctrine is not new, and it is not just something that pro-business comentators have made up. The doctrine was clearly articulated no later than 1919, in a Supreme Court opinion (*Dodge v. Ford Motor Company*) no less. However, in practice, the courts have been reluctant to intervene in disputes between shareholders and management (in effect, declining to open up the can of worms of deciding what the right business decisions would be).

Public Disclosure

Corporations that sell shares of stock on the stock market are called "publicly traded corporations." Each time a corporation sells a share of its stock to an individual or another company, it raises some money. This is one way the company can finance its operations. In actual fact, most stock sales do not involve a corporation selling stock to a member of the public, but one member of the public selling shares to another (that is, resale of shares that a corporation had previously issued). Therefore, most stock sales do not result in any money going to the corporation that originally issued it.

By law, publicly traded companies have to disclose certain business information. They have to file forms with the government listing their officers (board members and top executives), the officers' compensation (salaries and other benefits), the company's profits or losses, and other information. The idea behind disclosure requirements is to protect shareholders or people who might consider purchasing shares in a company, often referred to as the "investing public."

In practice, corporate "insiders" (board members, top executives, etc.) have much more information about the financial condition of a corporation than members of the public. This has led to well-publicized scandals in recent years, such as the Enron case. Corporate executives sold the stock they owned when the price was high, knowing that in reality the company was not as profitable as the public thought, and that the stock price would soon plummet.

Corporate Governance

When an individual buys a share (or many shares) of a corporation, he or she gets certain property rights. Shareholders are not legally entitled to receive a share of the company's profits each year. The company management decides how much of this money to pay out to shareholders (as "dividends") and how much to keep. A corporation might keep cash reserves, use profits to buy existing businesses, use them to expand its existing operations (for example, by buying or renting additional factory or office buildings, buying new machinery, hiring additional workers, etc.). It is not necessarily preferable for shareholders to receive all or most of the company's profit for a year in the form of dividends. By using "retained earnings" to expand, a corporation may increase in overall value. This increases the value of an ownership share in the company (the value of the stock that shareholders own).

Shareholders have the right to sell their shares if and when they wish. This gives them a stake in the profitability of the corporation, since the price of a share (on the stock exchange) is likely to go higher the more profitable the company is. A shareholder who does not want to be a part owner of the company anymore is not entitled to sell back the shares to the company, nor to take "their" piece of the company with them. The corporation is not required to give the shareholder any tangible asset—the shareholder cannot claim any particular thing owned by the corporation—nor is the corporation forced to sell off tangible assets in order to pay a shareholder who does not want his or her shares anymore. This way, shareholders come and go, but the corporation itself stays intact.

Shareholders also have a say in the governance structure of the corporation. You can think of a corporation as a political entity, like a small (or, in some cases, not so small) country. Shareholders are like the citizens. They are entitled to attend annual shareholder meetings, where they can address questions or comments to the corporation's directors (board members) and executives. Shareholders are entitled to vote in elections to the board of directors (except for those holding certain classes of "nonvoting" or "preferred" stock). They can even run for election to the board of directors, if they so wish.

Corporate elections are different from government elections. First, in corporate elections, only shareholders are allowed to vote. The decisions made by a corporation's management may affect many other people—workers, people in communities where the corporation has operations, etc.. However, if they are not shareholders in the corporation, they are not entitled to vote. In addition, in corporate elections, different shareholders do not get the same number of votes. Rather, each shareholder gets a number of votes equal to the number of shares he or she owns (excluding nonvoting stock). Someone who owns one share gets one vote; 10 shares, 10 votes; 100 shares, 100 votes.

In practice, a large shareholder does not need to own anywhere near a majority of the shares to effectively control a company. People who own very few shares in a company, if disgruntled with the management, are more likely to just sell their shares than to devote a lot of time and energy to getting the management replaced. Relatively small shareholders, in fact, usually just sign away their voting rights to other, larger shareholders. This way, a very wealthy individual may have effective control of a company even though he or she "only" owns, say, 5% of the total shares. Keep in mind that 5% of the stock in the largest corporate giants could be worth billions of dollars.

Corporations, Economic Power, and Political Power

Large corporations are certainly among the most powerful entities in the U.S. economy and politics. We can start by classifying the power of large corporations into economic power, on the one hand, and political power, on the other. Economic power has to do with the ability of large corporations to dictate to others (other businesses, workers, etc.) the conditions under which they will do business. Political power has to do with their ability to get what they want from the government, including both favors they can get from the government and influence over the overall direction of government policy.

Mainstream or "neoclassical" economists do not talk about economic power very much. Mostly, they talk about "market" economies as if nobody exercised any power over anyone else—buyers and sellers engaging in voluntary exchanges, each free from any kind of coercion from other buyers or sellers. The main form of economic power neoclassical economists do talk about is "market power"—basically, the ability of a seller (or buyer) to dictate higher (or lower) prices to others, because of a lack of competition.

In the view of radical political economists, employers as a group have economic power in a different sense. Most of the economic activity in capitalist economies depends on the economic decisions made by capitalist enterprises, such as how much output to produce, how many people to hire, whether to buy new machines or new buildings (this is what economists mean by "investment"), and so on. If capitalist employers decide not to hire people to produce goods and services, many people will be unemployed. Tax collections will be low, and governments are likely to experience budget deficits, unless they dramatically cut spending. Moreover, if capitalist enterprises are not hiring, unemployment is high, and many people are afraid of losing their jobs, the party in power probably will not survive the next election.

If the owners and managers of capitalist enterprises do not like the kinds of economic policies the government is putting in place, they may decide not to hire or invest. In some cases, where capitalists feel very threatened by government policies, they may actually do this with the conscious political aim of bringing down the government. More often, a decline in employment and investment can arise from a simple decline in "business confidence." The owners and managers of capitalist enterprises become pessimistic about being able to sell their goods at a profit, and make a business decision to cut back on production, employment, and investment. The effect, however, can still be to force the government to bend over backwards to maintain profitable conditions for business, in order to avoid an economic downturn. This way, the economic power of capitalist enterprises over the whole economy can result in their getting the kinds of government policies that favor them. ❏

Article 4.2

TRANS-PACIFIC PARTNERSHIP: CORPORATE POWER UNBOUND

BY JOHN MILLER
July/August 2015

> The case [for opposing the Trans-Pacific Partnership] put forth by a showboating Sen. Elizabeth Warren is almost worse than wrong. It is irrelevant.
> Less than 10 percent of the AFL-CIO's membership is now in manufacturing. It's undeniable that American manufacturing workers have suffered terrible job losses. We could never compete with pennies-an-hour wages. Those low-skilled jobs are not coming back.
> Some liberals oddly complain that American efforts to strengthen intellectual property laws in trade deals protect the profits of U.S. entertainment and tech companies. What's wrong with that?
> Then we have Warren stating with a straight face that handing negotiating authority to Obama would "give Republicans the very tool they need to dismantle Dodd-Frank."
> —Froma Harrop, "The Left Is Wrong on Fast-Track Trade Issue," *Spokesman Review*, May 16, 2015.

The Trans-Pacific Partnership (TPP) sounds more like an international consortium of corporate law firms than a trade deal. That's for good reason. TPP is less about trade than about corporate-dominated globalization.

But that's all a mystery to Froma Harrop, liberal columnist, business writer, and robotic Obama supporter. (Obama has pushed hard for the TPP.) Why should the AFL-CIO, with so few members in manufacturing, oppose this trade deal, Harrop asks? And what so wrong with protecting corporate profits by enforcing intellectual property rights, as the TPP would?

The answer is: plenty. And that's especially true now that the Obama administration and both Republicans and corporate Democrats in Congress have engineered the passage of the "fast-track authority," guaranteeing an up or down vote for the TPP.

The TPP Is Not About Trade

The TPP is surely marketed as a trade deal. And economist after economist supporting TPP has touted it as a giant step toward free trade that will bestow benefits on all nations in just the way every student learns it will in introductory economics.

But what economists have to say about the virtues of free trade, as flawed as that may be, has little to do with the TPP. The TPP is not about free trade or even principally about the gains from trade.

The TPP would be the largest regional "trade" agreement ever. It involves twelve countries: the United States, Australia, Brunei, Canada, Chile, Japan, Malaysia, Mexico, New Zealand, Peru, Singapore, and Vietnam. Those dozen countries collectively produce 40% of global output (GDP).

But if trade is the hype, it is not the substance of the deal. To begin with, the TPP would do little to reduce barriers to trade in these countries, which are already quite low. The average tariff level in each of the twelve countries is lower than the world average (6.8% in 2012) and far lower than global tariff rates two decades ago. In addition, Australia, Canada, Chile, Mexico, Peru, and Singapore are already members of other free trade agreements with the United States. In 2014, nearly three-quarters (74%) of U.S. goods traded with the TPP group was with those six nations. As tariff levels have dropped, so have potential gains from further lowering tariffs, as envisioned by those who have drunk the free trade Kool-Aid served up by economists.

For instance, the Peterson Institute for International Economics, a Washington-based pro-free trade thinktank, estimates that the TPP would add $77.5 billion of income to the U.S. economy by 2025, a figure the Obama administration uses to make the case for the TPP. That number might sound impressive, but those gains would add just 0.38% to U.S. GDP over the next ten years. And it is undoubtedly an overestimate, for it relies on the assumption that the U.S. economy and the economies of its trading partners will be at full employment during those years.

The Obama Administration claims that the TPP would create 650,000 new jobs in the next decade. They get that number by dividing the $77.5 billion income gain from the TPP in the Peterson report by the average cost to a company when it hires an additional worker. But nowhere in its report does the Peterson Institute project that the TTP would create jobs. Rather, the position of the Peterson Institute, according to Fred Bergsten, its founder, is that "a trade agreement does not on balance, create, or destroy jobs, it alters the composition of the workforce."

Nor would the meager income gains produced by the TPP be widely shared. In a Center for Economic and Policy Research (CEPR) report, economist David Rosnick estimates that just the top 10% of U.S. workers would see real wage gains, if the Trans-Pacific Partnership were enacted. Worse yet, the real wages of a broad swath of middle-income U.S. workers (from the 35th percentile to the 80th percentile) would fall, even under Rosnick's most conservative assumptions about the likely effect of the TPP on inequality.

Losses from trade agreements have been visited upon the same groups, especially manufacturing workers, time and time again. For instance, labor economists Avraham Ebenstein, Ann Harrison, Margot McMillan, and Shannon Phillips have found that, between 1983 and 2002, globalization forced U.S. workers out of manufacturing into lower-paying jobs, reducing their real wage by 12% to 17%.

TPP is About Corporate Power

Why would the labor movement go all out to defeat the TPP with so few of its members in manufacturing, and with lost manufacturing jobs unlikely to return to the United States?

Economic journalist Robert Kuttner gave perhaps the best answer: "The labor movement is not motivated just by the loss of factory jobs but by the entire ideological assault on the security of ordinary wage earners and consumers." That's also what lies behind the complaints about how the TPP would protect corporate profits in what Nobel Prize winning economist Joseph Stiglitz calls a "secret corporate takeover."

At the heart of the TPP is an Investor-State Dispute Settlement (ISDS) process that would give corporations yet more power to make the economic rules that govern our lives. The settlement process would allow investors who think that a country's laws have reduced their profits to take their case before a "tribunal" of three private attorneys; that is, to sidestep the country's own legal system. Unlike national courts, which can order corporations to be compensated for losses of actual assets, ISDS tribunals would be empowered to order taxpayers to compensate corporation for losses of expected profits—even those projected decades into the future.

These are not just hypothetical concerns. In other free trade agreements, the ISDS process has enabled:

- Phillip Morris to sue Australia and Uruguay, arguing that warnings required on cigarette packages are cutting their profits.
- Nuclear power operator Vattenfall to sue Germany for $3.7 billion in lost future profits over the German government's decision to phase out nuclear power after the Fukushima nuclear disaster.
- The oil and gas company Lone Pine Resources Inc. to sue the Province of Quebec for $250 million (in Canadian dollars) after Quebec imposed a fracking moratorium.
- Veolia, French waste management company, to sue Egypt because the country raised the minimum wage, increasing Veolia's costs.
- A Dutch subsidiary of a Japanese bank to sue the Czech Republic, arguing that the country had violated its rights by extending its bailout program only to "too big to fail" banks.

Defenders of the ISDS process maintain that it will have little effect in the United States with its corporate friendly legal system that they call the "good rule of law." The U.S. government, they hasten to point out, has not lost an ISDS case. And President Obama, as Harrop emphasizes, has vehemently denied that he would ever sign an agreement that would threaten the Dodd-Frank financial reforms. But Obama's assurances are nearly meaningless. While he would have control over appointments to the ISDS tribunals, he would not be able to control what decisions his appointees reach, or who the Presidents who follows him appoint to the tribunals. And the "good rule of law" has not prevented Canada from having to pay out six ISDS claims brought by corporations. But whatever the ramifications for the United States, ISDS provisions shrink the "policy space" for other countries less inclined to have their governments constrained by what would pass muster with an ISDS tribunal.

Other TPP provisions would actually limit trade, not prompt it. Its provisions to enforce "intellectual property rights," which Harrop praises, would strengthen patents restricting the availability of prescription drugs. While a boon to big phrama, those provisions would drive up the cost of already expensive drugs to fight cancer and other diseases. Public health researchers Hazel Moir, Brigitte Tenni, Deborah Gleeson, and Ruth Lopert estimate that it would cut in half the share of Vietnam's AIDS patients who have access to life-saving antiretroviral drugs.

Not For Industry Alone

Just before the passage of fast track in June, Senator Elizabeth Warren (D-Mass.)—who led the fight against TPP in the Senate—warned against enacting more "trade agreements that offer gold-plated enforcement for giant corporations and meaningless promises for everyone else."

But TPP surely would do just that. Worse yet, it would exacerbate inequality and compromise democracy, as it exempts corporations from environmental and labor standards, or whatever laws interfere with their accumulation of profits.

Now that's not about the "good rule of law." It's about corporations using their power to evade the rule of law. ❏

Sources: Elizabeth Warren, "Trade agreements should not benefit industry only," *Boston Globe*, June 23, 2015; Robert Kuttner, "The Real Meaning of Obama's Trade Deal," *Huffington Post*, June 16, 2015; Joseph Stiglitz, "The Secret Corporate Takeover," Project Syndicate, May 13, 2015; Kevin Gallagher, "Saving Obama from a Bad Trade Deal," *The American Prospect*, March 4, 2015; Peter Petri and Michael Plummer, "The Trans-Pacifc Parternship and Asia-Pacific Integration," Peterson Institute for International Economics, June 2012; David Rosnick, "Gains from Trade?" Center for Economic and Policy Research, September 2013; Glen Kessler, "The Obama administration's illusionary job gains from the Trans-Pacific Partnership," *Washington Post*, Jan. 30, 2015; Peter Evans, "Our Delegation Stood Up to Bad Trade Deal," *Santa Fe New Mexican*, June 26, 2015; Avraham Ebenstein, Ann Harrison, Margaret McMillan, and Shannon Phillips, "Estimating the Impact of Trade and Offshoring on American Workers using the Current Population Surveys," *The Review of Economics and Statistics*, October 2014; Hazel Moir, Brigitte Tenni, Deborah Gleeson, and Ruth Lopert, "Assessing the impact of alternative patent systems on the cost of health care: the TPPA and HIV treatment in Vietnam," Asia-Pacific Innovation Conference, University of Technology Sydney, 27-29 November 2014.

Article 4.3

WHAT'S GOOD FOR WAL-MART . . .

BY JOHN MILLER
January/February 2006

"IS WAL-MART GOOD FOR AMERICA?"

It is a testament to the public relations of the anti-Wal-Mart campaign that the question above is even being asked.

By any normal measure, Wal-Mart's business ought to be noncontroversial. It sells at low costs, albeit in mind-boggling quantities. ...

The company's success and size ... do not rest on monopoly profits or price-gouging behavior. It simply sells things people will buy at small markups and, as in the old saw, makes it up on volume. ... You may believe, as do service-workers unions and a clutch of coastal elites—many of whom, we'd wager, have never set foot in Wal-Mart—that Wal-Mart "exploits" workers who can't say no to low wages and poor benefits. You might accept the canard that it drives good local businesses into the ground, although both of these allegations are more myth than reality.

But even if you buy into the myths, there's no getting around the fact that somewhere out there, millions of people are spending billions of dollars on what Wal-Mart puts on its shelves. No one is making them do it. ... Wal-Mart can't make mom and pop shut down the shop anymore than it can make customers walk through the doors or pull out their wallets.

What about the workers? ... Wal-Mart's average starting wage is already nearly double the national minimum of $5.15 an hour. The company has also recently increased its health-care for employees on the bottom rungs of the corporate ladder.

—*Wall Street Journal* editorial, December 3, 2005

"Who's Number One? The Customer! Always!" The last line of Wal-Mart's company cheer just about sums up the *Wall Street Journal* editors' benign view of the behemoth corporation. But a more honest answer would be Wal-Mart itself: not the customer, and surely not the worker.

The first retail corporation to top the Fortune 500, Wal-Mart trailed only Exxon-Mobil in total revenues last year. With 1.6 million workers, 1.3 million in the United States and 300,000 offshore, Wal-Mart is the largest private employer in the nation and the world's largest retailer.

Being number one has paid off handsomely for the family of Wal-Mart founder Sam Walton. The family's combined fortune is now an estimated $90 billion, equal to the net worth of Bill Gates and Warren Buffett combined.

But is what's good for the Walton family good for America? Should we believe the editors that Wal-Mart's unprecedented size and market power have redounded not only to the Walton family's benefit but to ours as well?

Low Wages and Meager Benefits

Working for the world's largest employer sure hasn't paid off for Wal-Mart's employees. True, they have a job, and others without jobs line up to apply for theirs. But that says more about the sad state of today's labor market than the quality of Wal-Mart jobs. After all, less than half of Wal-Mart workers last a year, and turnover at the company is twice that at comparable retailers.

Why? Wal-Mart's oppressive working conditions surely have something to do with it. Wal-Mart has admitted to using minors to operate hazardous machinery, has been sued in six states for forcing employees to work off the books (i.e., unpaid) and without breaks, and is currently facing a suit brought by 1.6 million current and former female employees accusing Wal-Mart of gender discrimination. At the same time, Wal-Mart workers are paid less and receive fewer benefits than other retail workers.

Wal-Mart, according to its own reports, pays an average of $9.68 an hour. That is 12.4% below the average wage for retail workers even after adjusting for geography, according to a recent study by Arindrajit Dube and Steve Wertheim, economists at the University of California's Institute of Industrial Relations and long-time Wal-Mart researchers. Wal-Mart's wages are nearly 15% below the average wage of workers at large retailers and about 30% below the average wage of unionized grocery workers. The average U.S. wage is $17.80 an hour; Costco, a direct competitor of Wal-Mart's Sam's Club warehouse stores, pays an average wage of $16 an hour.

Wal-Mart may be improving its benefits, as the *Journal*'s editors report, but it needs to. Other retailers provide health care coverage to over 53% of their workers, while Wal-Mart covers just 48% of its workers. Costco, once again, does far better, covering 82% of its employees. Moreover, Wal-Mart's coverage is far less comprehensive than the plans offered by other large retailers. Dube reports that according to 2003 IRS data, Wal-Mart paid 59% of the health care costs of its workers and dependents, compared to the 77% of health care costs for individuals and 68% for families the average retailer picks up.

A recent internal Wal-Mart memo leaked to the *New York Times* confirmed the large gaps in Wal-Mart's health care coverage and exposed the high costs those gaps impose on government programs. According to the memo, "Five percent of our Associates are on Medicaid compared to an average for national employees of 4 percent. Twenty-seven percent of Associates' children are on such programs, compared to a national average of 22 percent. In total, 46 percent of Associates' children are either on Medicaid or are uninsured."

A considerably lower 29% of children of all large-retail workers are on Medicaid or are uninsured. Some 7% of the children of employees of large retailers go uninsured, compared to the 19% reported by Wal-Mart.

Wal-Mart's low wages drag down the wages of other retail workers and shutter downtown retail businesses. A 2005 study by David Neumark, Junfu Zhang, and Stephen Ciccarella, economists at the University of California at Irvine, found that Wal-Mart adversely affects employment and wages. Retail workers in a community with a Wal-Mart earned 3.5% less because Wal-Mart's low prices force other businesses to lower prices, and hence their wages, according to the Neumark study. The same study also found that Wal-Mart's presence reduces retail employment by 2% to 4%. While other studies have not found this negative employment effect, Dube's research also reports fewer retail jobs and lower wages for retail workers in metropolitan counties with a Wal-Mart. (Fully 85% of Wal-Mart stores are in metropolitan counties.) Dube figures that Wal-Mart's presence costs retail workers, at Wal-Mart and elsewhere, $4.7 billion a year in lost earnings.

In short, Wal-Mart's "everyday low prices" come at the expense of the compensation of Wal-Mart's own employees and lower wages and fewer jobs for retail workers in the surrounding area. That much remains true no matter what weight we assign to each of the measures that Wal-Mart uses to keep its costs down: a just-in-time inventory strategy, its ability to use its size to pressure suppliers for large discounts, a routinized work environment that requires minimal training, and meager wages and benefits.

How Low are Wal-Mart's Everyday Low Prices?

Even if one doesn't subscribe to the editors' position that it is consumers, not Wal-Mart, who cause job losses at downtown retailers, it is possible to argue that the benefit of Wal-Mart's low prices to consumers, especially low-income consumers, outweighs the cost endured by workers at Wal-Mart and other retailers. Jason Furman, New York University economist and director of economic policy for the 2004 Kerry-Edwards campaign, makes just such an argument. Wal-Mart's "staggering" low prices are 8% to 40% lower than people would pay elsewhere, according to Furman. He calculates that those low prices on average boost low-income families' buying power by 3% and more than offset the loss of earnings to retail workers. For Furman, that makes Wal-Mart "a progressive success story."

But exactly how much savings Wal-Mart affords consumers is far from clear. Estimates vary widely. At one extreme is a study Wal-Mart itself commissioned by Global Insight, an economic forecasting firm. Global Insight estimates Wal-Mart created a stunning savings of $263 billion, or $2,329 per household, in 2004 alone.

At the other extreme, statisticians at the U.S. Bureau of Labor Statistics found no price savings at Wal-Mart. Relying on Consumer Price Index data, the BLS found that Wal-Mart's prices largely matched those of its rivals, and that instances of lower prices at Wal-Mart could be attributed to lower quality products.

Both studies, which rely on the Consumer Price Index and aggregate data, have their critics. Furman himself allows that the Global Insight study is "overly simplistic" and says he "doesn't place as much weight on that one." Jerry Hausman, the M.I.T. economist who has looked closely at Wal-Mart's grocery stores, maintains that the CPI data that the Bureau of Labor Statistics relies on systematically miss the savings offered by "supercenters" such as Wal-Mart. To show the difference between prices at Wal-Mart and at other grocers, Hausman, along with Ephraim Leibtag, USDA Economic Research Service economist, used supermarket scanner data to examine the purchasing patterns of a national sample of 61,500 consumers from 1988 to 2001. Hausman and Leibtag found that Wal-Mart offers many identical food items at an average price about 15%-25% lower than traditional supermarkets.

While Hausman and Leibtag report substantial savings from shopping at Wal-Mart, they fall far short of the savings alleged in the Global Insight study. The Hausman and Leibtag study suggests a savings of around $550 per household per year, or about $56 billion in 2004, not $263 billion. Still, that is considerably more than the $4.7 billion a year in lost earnings to retail workers that Dube attributes to Wal-Mart.

But if "Wal-Mart hurts wages, not so much in retail, but across the whole country," as economist Neumark told *BusinessWeek*, then the savings to consumers from Wal-Mart's everyday low prices might not outweigh the lost wages to all workers. (Retail workers make up just 11.6% of U.S. employment.)

Nor do these findings say anything about the sweatshop conditions and wages in Wal-Mart's overseas subcontractors. One example: A recent Canadian Broadcasting Corporation investigative report found that workers in Bangladesh were being paid less than $50 a month (below even the United Nation's $2 a day measure of poverty) to make clothes for the Wal-Mart private label, Simply Basic. Those workers included ten- to thirteen-year-old children forced to work long hours in dimly lit and dirty conditions sewing "I Love My Wal-Mart" t-shirts.

Making Wal-Mart Do Better

Nonetheless, as Arindrajit Dube points out, the relevant question is not whether Wal-Mart creates more savings for consumers than losses for workers, but whether the corporation can afford to pay better wages and benefits.

Dube reasons that if the true price gap between Wal-Mart and its retail competitors is small, then Wal-Mart might not be in a position to do better—to make

---

The Costco Alternative? Wall Street Prefers Wal-Mart

In an April 2004 online commentary, *BusinessWeek* praised Costco's business model but pointed out that Costco's wages cause Wall Street to worry that the company's "operating expenses could get out of hand." How does Costco compare to low-wage Wal-Mart on overhead expenses? At Costco, overhead is 9.8% of revenue; at Wal-Mart, it is 17%. Part of Costco's secret is that its better paid workers are also more efficient: Costco's operating profit per hourly employee is $13,647; each Wal-Mart employee only nets the company $11,039. Wal-Mart also spends more than Costco on hiring and training new employees: each one, according to Rutgers economist Eileen Appelbaum, costs the company $2,500 to $3,500. Appelbaum estimates that Wal-Mart's relatively high turnover costs the company $1.5 to $2 million per year.

Despite Costco's higher efficiency, Wall Street analysts like Deutsche Bank's Bill Dreher complain that "Costco's corporate philosophy is to put its customers first, then its employees, then its vendors, and finally its shareholders. Shareholders get the short end of the stick." Wall Street prefers Wal-Mart's philosopy: executives first, then shareholders, then customers, then vendors, and finally employees.

In 2004, Wal-Mart paid CEO Lee Scott $5.3 million, while a full-time employee making the average wage would have received $20,134. Costco's CEO Jim Senegal received $350,000, while a full-time average employee got $33,280. And *BusinessWeek* intimates that the top job at Costco may be tougher than at Wal-Mart. "Management has to hustle to make the high-wage strategy work. It's constantly looking for ways to repackage goods

up its wage and benefit gap and still maintain its price advantage. But if Wal-Mart offers consumers only minor price savings, then its lower wages and benefits hardly constitute a progressive success story that's good for the nation.

If Wal-Mart's true price gap is large (say, the 25% price advantage estimated by Hausman), then Wal-Mart surely is in a position to do better. For instance, Dube calculates that closing Wal-Mart's 16% overall compensation gap with other large retailers would cost the company less than 2% of sales. Raising prices by two cents on the dollar to cover those increased compensation costs would be "eminently absorbable," according to Dube, without eating away much of the company's mind-boggling $10 billion profit (2004).

Measures that set standards to force Wal-Mart and all big-box retailers to pay decent wages and provide benefits are beginning to catch on. Chicago, New York City, and the state of Maryland have considered or passed laws that would require big-box retailers to pay a "living wage" or to spend a minimum amount per worker-hour for health benefits. The Republican board of Nassau County on Long Island passed an ordinance requiring that all big-box retailers pay $3 per hour toward health care. Wal-Mart's stake in making sure that such proposals don't become law or spread nationwide goes a long way toward explaining why 80% of Wal-Mart's $2 million in political contributions in 2004 went to Republicans.

Henry Ford sought to pay his workers enough so they could buy the cars they produced. Sam Walton sought to pay his workers so little that they could afford to shop nowhere else. And while what was good for the big automakers was probably never good for the nation, what is good for Wal-Mart, today's largest employer, is undoubtedly bad for economic justice. ❏

---

into bulk items, which reduces labor, speeds up Costco's just-in-time inventory, and boosts sales per square foot. Costco is also savvier ... about catering to small shop owners and more affluent customers, who are more likely to buy in bulk and purchase higher-margin goods."

Costco's allegedly more affluent clientele may be another reason that its profit per employee is higher than Wal-Mart's and its overhead costs a lower percentage of revenue. However, Costco pays its employees enough that they could afford to shop there. As the BusinessWeek commentary noted, "the low-wage approach cuts into consumer spending and, potentially, economic growth."

—Esther Cervantes

Average Hourly Wage		Percentage of U.S. Workforce in Unions		Employees Covered by Company Health Insurance		Employees Who Leave After One Year	
Wal-Mart	Costco	Wal-Mart	Costco	Wal-Mart	Costco	Sam's Club*	Costco
$9.68	$16.00	0.0%	17.9%	48%	82%	21%	6%
* Sam's Club is the Wal-Mart unit that competes directly with Costco.							

Sources: "Is Wal-Mart Good for America?" *Wall Street Journal*, 12/3/05; "Gauging the Wal-Mart Effect," *WSJ*, 12/03/05; Arindrajit Dube & Steve Wertheim, "Wal-Mart and Job Quality—What Do We Know, and Should We Care?" 10/05; Jason Furman, "Wal-Mart: A Progressive Success Story," 10/05; Leo Hindery Jr., "Wal-Mart's Giant Sucking Sound," 10/05; A. Bernstein, "Some Uncomfortable Findings for Wal-Mart," *BusinessWeek* online, 10/26/05, and "Wal-Mart: A Case for the Defense, Sort of," *BusinessWeek* online, 11/7/05; Dube, Jacobs, and Wertheim, "The Impact of Wal-Mart Growth on Earnings Throughout the Retail Sector in Urban and Rural Counties," *Institute of Industrial Relations Working Paper*, UC Berkeley, 10/05; Dube, Jacobs, and Wertheim, "Internal Wal-Mart Memo Validates Findings of UC Berkeley Study," 11/26/05; Jerry Hausman and Ephraim Leibtag, "Consumer Benefits from Increased Competition in Shopping Outlets: Measuring the Effect of Wal-Mart," 10/05; Hausman and Leibtag, "CPI Bias from Supercenters: Does the BLS Know that Wal-Mart Exists?" *NBER Working Paper No. 10712*, 8/04; David Neumark, Junfu Zhang, and Stephen Ciccarella, "The Effects of Wal-Mart on Local Labor Markets," *NBER Working Paper No. 11782*, 11/05; Erin Johansson, "Wal-Mart: Rolling Back Workers' Wages, Rights, and the American Dream," American Rights at Work, 11/05; Wal-Mart Watch, "Spin Cycle"; CBC News, "Wal-Mart to cut ties with Bangladesh factories using child labour," 11/30/05; National Labor Committee, "10 to 13-year-olds Sewing 'I Love My Wal-Mart' Shirts," 12/05; Global Insight, "The Economic Impact of Wal-Mart," 2005.

Article 4.4

HOW PRIVATE EQUITY WORKS—AND WHY IT MATTERS

BY ROSEMARY BATT AND EILEEN APPLEBAUM
November/December 2015

Private equity (PE) firms are financial actors that raise billions of dollars in investment funds each year. They use these funds to buy out well-performing companies using high amounts of debt, take them private, and promise their investors outsized returns in the process. They advertise that they improve the operations of companies they buy. Sometimes they do. But more often PE firms engage in financial engineering techniques that extract wealth from companies and leave them more financially at risk than before—and sometimes bankrupt. While discredited as "leveraged buyouts" in the 1980s, these tactics have returned with a vengeance in the last fifteen years. And they are perfectly legal.

PE firms typically charge pension funds and other investors an annual management fee of 2% of capital committed to the private equity fund. Not satisfied with these payments for managing their private equity funds, PE firms also charge investors in their funds numerous other fees and expenses. This part isn't always legal: In May 2014, the Securities and Exchange Commission (SEC) revealed that its examinations of PE funds had uncovered numerous examples, some bordering on outright fraud, where PE firms had inappropriately charged fees and expenses to pension funds and other investors. In 2015, Fenway Partners, Blackstone, and KKR were the first PE firms to pay fines to the SEC to settle charges—a meager $80 million among the three.

Management fees are specified in contracts between private equity funds and the investors in these funds. But these are not the only fees that PE firms charge. They typically claim 20% of any profit the PE fund realizes on its investments as a bonus or performance fee. This performance fee—so-called "carried interest" taxed at half the rate of ordinary income—is generally not reported to investors. Private equity funds simply report returns net of these performance fees. But these fees cut deeply into the returns earned by pension funds and other private equity investors—and workers, retirees, and taxpayers have a right to know how large these payments are.

Private Equity: The Impact

Between 2000 and 2014, U.S. private equity firms invested $5.2 trillion in 32,200 leveraged buyouts that affected some 11.3 million workers in U.S. companies—considerably more than the number of workers who are currently union members. Over that period, the number of active PE firms globally grew from under 1,500 to over 3,500—a 143% rise. And, while PE investments fell sharply during the Great Recession, they have since largely recovered their pre-crisis levels. Currently, there are 3,883 U.S. private equity firms and 12,992 PE-owned companies headquartered in the United States.

In our book, *Private Equity at Work: How Wall Street Manages Main Street*, we explain how private equity firms have become such an important force in the economy and why regulators need to rein in their activities. That is because they are investors that actively manage the companies they buy, but are treated as passive investors and not held accountable for their actions. Before a company is ever purchased, the general partners of the PE fund (who make all decisions for the fund) develop a plan for how much debt can be leveraged on the company, how the company's cash flow will be used to service the debt, and how the PE firm will exit the company at a profit within a five-year window. They oversee company operations; make decisions that affect workers jobs, pay, and pensions—and then walk away. While law treats PE funds as investors, they behave as managers and employers in the companies they own.

Sometimes private equity does perform as advertised—providing access to management expertise and financial resources that help small companies grow and improve their competitiveness. Small companies have relatively few assets that can be mortgaged, but many opportunities for operational improvements in information technology, accounting, management, and distribution systems. Most PE investments, however, are in larger companies that already have modern management systems in place and also have substantial assets that can be mortgaged. Here, private equity firms use debt and financial engineering strategies to extract wealth from healthy companies, and workers, managers, and suppliers often pay the price. Job destruction outweighs job creation.

Private equity affects the lives of Americans in many ways —as workers, retirees, consumers, renters, and community members. Despite the fact that private equity ownership often leads to job and wage loss for workers, pension funds ("workers' capital") account for fully 35% of all investments in PE funds. Most workers do not know that their retirement savings are invested in these funds and may be putting other companies and their workers at risk. And despite the hype, these investments often don't yield the high returns for retirement funds that private equity firms promise. Moreover, since the Great Recession, private equity and hedge funds have bought up more than 100,000 troubled mortgages and are renting them back to people who lost their homes. In October 2015 alone, Blackstone

---

Case Study: Michael's Stores

Private Equity firms Bain and Blackstone used most of the tactics described here when they bought arts-and-crafts supplies retailer Michael's Stores in 2006 and took it private.

At the time, the company had 1,108 stores employing about 43,100 workers and $3.9 billion in sales. Its high sales revenue, healthy profits, and low debt made it an attractive takeover target. But the leveraged buyout saddled the chain with a $4 billion dollar debt. Bain and Blackstone also had Michael's sign a management services agreement through 2016 for an annual fee of $12 million—including a stipulation that if the company went public or was sold, the PE sponsors would continue to collect the fees for the remaining years of the contract even though the services would never be provided. In 2013, the PE funds did a dividend recapitalization, which yielded them $714 million, or about 70% of what the PE funds had invested. When Michael's went public in June 2014, it still carried long-term debt of $3.7 billion, and it had to pay the PE firms $30 million to cover the years remaining on the management services contract.

bought up 1000 rental units in New York City as well as the City's iconic rent-controlled Stuyvesant Town-Peter Cooper Village—making the PE firm one of the city's largest landlords.

How Do Private Equity Firms Make Money?

Debt, or "leverage," is at the core of the private equity business model. (Hence the term "leveraged buyout.") Debt multiplies returns on investment and the interest on the debt can be deducted from taxes owed by the acquired (or "portfolio") company. Private equity partners typically finance the buyout of a Main Street company with 30% equity coming from the PE fund and 70% debt borrowed from creditors—the opposite of the 30% debt and 70% equity typical of publicly traded companies. Private equity funds use the assets of the portfolio company as collateral, and put the burden of repaying the debt on the company itself.

The private equity firm also has very little of its own money at risk. The general partners of a PE fund typically put up $1 to $2 for every $100 that pension funds and other investors contribute. PE partners invest less than 1% of the purchase price of acquired companies (2% of the 30% equity is 0.02 x 0.30 = .006, or 0.6%). Yet they claim 20% of any gains from the subsequent sale of these companies.

In other words, PE firms play with other people's money—money contributed by pension funds and other investors in its funds and borrowed from creditors. Leverage magnifies investment returns in good times—and the general partners of the PE fund collect a disproportionate share of these gains. But if the debt cannot be repaid, the company, its workers, and its creditors bear the costs. The private equity business model is a low-risk, high-reward strategy for the PE firms and their partners.

Post buyout, PE firms often engage in financial engineering that further compromises their portfolio companies.

- They may have portfolio companies take out loans at "junk bond" rates and use the proceeds to pay themselves and their investors a dividend—a so-called "dividend recapitalization."

- They may sell company assets and claim the proceeds for themselves. They may split an asset-rich company into an operating company (OpCo) and a property company (PropCo) and sell off the real estate. Proceeds of the sale are used to repay the investors, while the operating company must lease back the property, often at inflated rates. Companies in cyclical industries are especially at risk of failure as owning their property provides a buffer against market downturns. For example, the Darden Restaurants sold its struggling Red Lobster restaurant chain to the PE firm Golden Gate, which immediately sold off most of Red Lobster's property and used the proceeds to repay most of the equity investment of the PE firm and its investors. The restaurants, however, now have to pay rent, and their annual earnings are cut substantially.

- They may "waive" the management fees they charge their limited partners in exchange for a higher share in the profits, which are then taxed at the

---

CalPERS (Finally) Releases Data on Performance Fees Paid to Private Equity

On November 24, 2015, CalPERS, the large California public employee pension fund, re-leased long-awaited figures on the amounts it has paid private equity firms in performance fees—so-called "carried interest" that is taxed at the lower capital gains rate rather than as ordinary income. For years, the pension fund failed to ask the PE firms for this informa-tion or to report on these fees. Recently this changed under pressure from unions, media, and the tax-paying public. As widely anticipated, the number is ginormous. Over the 25 years since 1990, CalPERS acknowledges it has paid $3.4 billion in performance fees—a number it admits understates the full amount paid.

Private equity has persuaded public pension funds that its high management and performance fees are warranted by exceptionally high returns on private equity invest-ments, but the evidence is weak. Moreover, because private equity investments are risky and require a 10-year commitment by pension fund investors, returns need to be high enough to be worth the risk and long-term investment—about three percentage points higher than stock market returns according to CalPERS benchmark. Unfortunately, half of the PE funds launched after 2005 have failed to beat this benchmark, and this is true of the PE funds in which CalPERS is invested. CalPERS's PE investments failed to beat its own benchmark in three-year, five-year and ten-year time frames.

More recently, having failed to meet their strategic objective to "maximize risk-adjusted rates of return," CalPERS staff proposed removing the requirement from the pension fund's PE policy. However, we and others concerned about the fund's risky invest-ments urged CalPERS board members to vote it down, which they did at their December 14 meeting.

---

much lower capital gains tax rate, rather than as ordinary income. The IRS recently released guidance making it crystal clear that this violates tax law.

- They may require portfolio companies to pay monitoring or "consulting" fees to the PE firm for unspecified services. Payment of the fees reduces the companies' cash cushion and puts them at risk in an economic downturn. The Securities and Exchange Commission (SEC) has found that many PE firms fail to share this fee income with their investors, as legally required. Moreover, in some cases where the monitoring fee contract fails to spec-ify the services to be provided, these payments may actually be dividends (which are not tax deductible) disguised as monitoring fees (which are)— and this tactic allows the portfolio company to reduce its tax liabilities.

- Monitoring-fee contracts typically have a term of ten years, even though the PE firms expect to re-sell portfolio companies in three to five years. As a result, at the time of the re-sale, the remaining years in the contract must be paid off, even though the PE firm will never provide any services once the company is sold.

What Happens to Companies and Workers?

The results of financial engineering are predictable. The high debt levels of highly leveraged companies make them much more likely to default on their loans or declare bankruptcy. And in cyclical industries, companies that have to pay rent rather than own their own property are more likely to go under in a recession. As we report in our book, a 2008 study by the World Economic Forum found that for the period 1980-2005, PE-owned companies were twice as likely to go bankrupt as comparable publicly owned companies. Another study of more than 2,000 highly leveraged companies found that, during the last recession (from 2007 to the first quarter of 2010), roughly a quarter of them defaulted on their debts. The financial crisis officially ended in 2009, but bankruptcies among private equity owned companies continued through 2015. Energy Future Holdings (EFH), for example, was acquired in 2007 by a PE consortium led by KKR and TPG and defaulted in 2014 with the largest debt for any leveraged buyout on record—$35.8 billion. By mid-2014, nine other private-equity owned companies defaulted on $6.5 billion in bonds and institutional loans. By 2014, defaults on the high-yield and leveraged loans that financed the 2004-2007 boom in leveraged buyouts affected a total of $120 billion (out of nearly $500 billion) in bonds and institutional loans.

In 2015, Harrah's (now known as Caesar's Entertainment) also declared bankruptcy. The company, with 30,440 unionized employees, was acquired in 2006 by Apollo Global Management and Texas Pacific Group (TPG Capital). By June of 2007, the casino chain's long-term debt had more than doubled. The gambling industry slumped in the recession and Harrah's struggled under its debt burden. The company cut staff, reduced hours, outsourced jobs, and scaled back operations, but in the end was not able to meet its debt obligations.

These examples of job loss following private equity takeovers are backed by rigorous economy-wide statistical studies by economists at Chicago, Harvard, and Maryland universities. One study, covering the period 1980-2005, found that post-buyout, private-equity-owned establishments and companies had significantly lower levels of employment and wages than their publicly traded counterparts. In the year of the PE buyouts, the target companies had higher levels of wages and employment growth than comparable public companies. Post-buyout, however, both wages and employment levels were lower in the PE-owned companies. Depending on the data and estimation techniques, PE-owned establishments registered employment levels that were, in the first two years after the buyout, 3.0 to 6.7% lower than similar establishments; after five years, 6% lower.

Bankruptcies of PE-owned companies threaten not only workers' jobs, but also their defined-benefit pensions. In typical bankruptcy proceedings, the pension plan can make its case for better treatment of workers under a court-approved Plan of Reorganization. If the bankrupt company is unable to fulfill its pension obligations, then an insurance program run by the Pension Benefit Guarantee Corporation (PBGC) provides employees with basic benefits, although not at the level they would have received had the pension remained solvent. In light of the higher rates of bankruptcy in PE-owned companies, the PGBC has disproportionately absorbed the pension liabilities of these companies.

Private equity firms have figured out a number of ways to take advantage of the bankruptcy code and more easily shift pension liabilities to the PBGC. One strategy is to use a special provision in the code—Section 363—that allows for the streamlined sale of company assets, including auctioning off the entire assets of a company

---

Dumping Pension Plans

A Sun Capital private equity fund bought Friendly's Ice Cream Restaurant chain in a leveraged buyout in 2007. Sun Capital immediately sold much of the company's real estate and leased the property back to Friendly's outlets. After a series of cutbacks and layoffs, it filed for bankruptcy in November 2011. Soon after, Friendly's was acquired by another Sun Capital-sponsored PE fund in a Section 363 bankruptcy sale, with its pension obligations offloaded onto the PBGC. Sun Capital was able to retain ownership of Friendly's, but neither the PE firm nor any of its funds had any responsibility for the pensions of Friendly's 6,000 employees and retirees. Oxford Automotive and Relizon, among other companies, also went bankrupt while in private equity hands and were also sold from one affiliate of a PE firm to another affiliate.

Private equity funds' strategies to avoid pension liabilities are particularly offensive given that pension funds represent over one-third of the investors in PE. These pension funds are in the contradictory position of hoping to benefit from activities that sometimes undermine the retirement security of beneficiaries in funds like their own. This raises troubling questions: are the actions of pension funds that invest in private equity consistent with the interests and values of their own members?

Finally, private equity firms have sought to avoid liability under the Workers Adjustment and Retraining Notification (WARN) Act, which requires companies that close down plants to give workers 60 days' notice and pay, whether or not they continue to work. In the recent case of PE-owned Golden Guernsey dairy, OpenGate Capital has argued that it is not liable under the WARN Act. In a surprising verdict in October 2015, the court ruled that OpenGate Capital was indeed responsible for back pay under the law.

---

without first putting in place a Plan for Reorganization for the distribution of proceeds. While the secured creditors get paid, there is no requirement to renegotiate pension obligations—typically the largest unsecured creditor in a bankruptcy case. As a result, pension liabilities typically get shifted to the PBGC, and employees receive only the basic guaranteed retirement benefits.

Section 363 sales were extremely rare in the 1990s (only 4% of large publicly traded companies), but they represent 21% of bankruptcies in the 2000s. According to the PBGC, employees and retirees lost more than $650 million in 363 sales of bankrupt companies owned or controlled by private equity firms from 2003 to 2012. Exploitation of the 363 loophole, in addition, has severely strained the financial stability of the PBGC in recent years.

How Should Private Equity Be Regulated?

Private equity partners act as managers and employers of the companies they take over, even though the law treats them as passive investors in the companies they own. Several legal and regulatory changes would curb the negative effects of private equity on companies and working people, while preserving the benefits of private pools of capital to stimulate growth and development in small and mid-sized companies.

A simple first step is greater transparency. With the exception of a few large publicly traded firms (including Blackstone, Apollo, and Carlyle), PE firms face far less stringent Securities and Exchange Commission (SEC) reporting requirements than public corporations, and very little of what they report can legally be made public. And privately owned PE portfolio companies have no reporting requirements at all.

Even the limited partners who invest in private equity have little information about, for example, how decisions are made or how fund performance is measured.

Limiting the amount of debt that can be loaded onto portfolio companies is critical to reduce the risk of bankruptcy by PE-owned companies. Federal bank regulators took a first step in 2013 by issuing guidelines effectively reducing the willingness of banks to make loans that raise a company's debt level above six times its earnings. This has had some effect on PE firms' ability to overleverage the companies they acquire. But KKR and other large PE firms have responded by making loans available to other PE funds for leveraged buyouts. More direct steps to limit excessive use of debt include limiting the tax deductibility of interest payments or simply capping the use of debt over a certain percentage of the purchase price.

Eliminating the "carried interest" loophole in the capital gains tax would make the tax code fairer. This loophole lets private equity general partners pay the capital gains tax rate on their share of PE fund profits. Profit-sharing income of other managers, meanwhile, is taxed at the higher rate applied to ordinary income. More broadly, the carried-interest tax loophole comes at the expense of other taxpayers, who must either pay higher taxes or receive fewer or lower-quality public services. Changing the tax code to eliminate the loophole would also have the positive effect of reducing the incentive to load acquired companies with excessive levels of debt.

Reforms are also needed to hold private equity partners accountable for their actions as managers and employers in the same way as public corporations are. Private equity general partners make decisions that affect a portfolio company's debt structure, operations, human resources management, staffing levels, and plant closures. The PE firm and its funds are not passive investors and should be viewed, along with the portfolio company, as the joint employer of the portfolio company's workers. Employment laws such as the WARN Act and Employee Retirement Income Security Act (ERISA) need to be updated to explicitly reflect this new reality. Loopholes in the bankruptcy code must be closed to prevent PE firms from offloading pension liabilities onto the PBGC.

In sum, a set of legal and regulatory changes are needed to ensure that PE firms are transparent and accountable for their actions, that they pay their fair share of taxes, and that they assume the same liability as publicly traded companies for any negative effects of their actions on the jobs, incomes, and pensions of the workers in the companies they own. ❏

Sources: Eileen Appelbaum and Rosemary Batt, *Private Equity at Work: When Wall Street Manages Main Street* (Russell Sage Foundation, 2014); Steven J. Davis, John C. Haltiwanger, Ron S. Jarmin, Josh Lerner, and Javier Miranda, "Private Equity and Employment," National Bureau of Economic Research, NBER Working Paper 17399, 2011 (nber.org); Matthew Goldstein, "As Banks Retreat, Private Equity Rushes to Buy Troubled Home Mortgages," *New York Times*, Sept. 28, 2015 (nytimes.com); Andrew McIntyre, "5 Firms Steer $690M Deal for Manhattan Rental Portfolio," *Law360*, Sept. 11, 2015 (law360.com); Private Equity Growth Capital Council, "Private Equity by the Numbers" (pegcc.org); Eileen Appelbaum, "CalPERS Releases Data on Performance Fees Paid to Private Equity," Center for Economic Policy Research blog, November 25, 2015 (cepr.net/blogs/cepr-blog).

Article 4.5

A CASE FOR PUBLIC OWNERSHIP

BY ARTHUR MacEWAN
September/October 2015

> Dear Dr. Dollar:
> *Would the U.S. economy work better if some industries were nationalized?*
> *Banks? Other industries? Which ones and why?*
> —Richard Hobbs, San Jose, Calif.

Even in a thoroughly capitalist economy, where most economic activity takes place in markets and firms are driven by profit-making, there are good reasons for some industries to be publicly owned. Indeed, a non-trivial amount of industry in the United States is already publicly owned.

For example, as Gar Alperovitz and Thomas Hanna pointed out in a July *New York Times* opinion piece, there are "more than 2,000 publicly owned electric utilities that, along with cooperatives, supply more than 25 percent of the country's electricity... In one of the most conservative states, Nebraska, every single resident and business receives electricity from publicly owned utilities, cooperatives or public power districts. Partly as a result, Nebraskans pay one of the lowest rates for electricity in the nation."

Electric utilities (and other utilities) are "natural monopolies," operating in realms of the economy which are not (or are hardly) open to multiple, competing firms. Roads, subway systems, and major water control systems are other examples of "natural monopolies." Another form of natural monopoly arises with unreproducible minerals (oil, copper, iron, etc.); public ownership could allow society in general, rather than private firms, to reap the profits from their scarce supply. Private ownership is, of course, possible in such cases, but, if it is to be socially acceptable, it must be heavily regulated or heavily taxed or both. Given the costs—and often the failures—of meaningful regulation and the ineffective taxation of large firms, public ownership can be a more effective way to go.

In other industries, where the operations of firms have large impacts beyond the firms' immediate actions, public ownership can also be the best economic option. Here is where banking provides the prime example. Because the actions of banks have such far-reaching impacts on the whole economy ("systemic impact"), they must be either publicly owned or thoroughly regulated—and, as experience of recent years has demonstrated, regulation has not worked. Also, firms outside the financial sector can have systemic impacts, and, indeed, during the Great Recession the federal government in effect nationalized large auto firms to prevent their failure from wreaking havoc throughout the economy. (However, the government played a minimal role in operating the firms and quickly moved to return them to private ownership.)

In other types of industry, firms can have large impacts beyond their immediate actions where positive "spill-over effects" ("externalities") are large. For example, the Tennessee Valley Authority and California's Water Resources Control Board (which operates as both a de facto enterprise and a regulatory agency), deliver essential services that have such large impacts. Private firms could not capture profits from all the immense social benefits that such enterprises can create. Thus the huge investments in water systems that these public agencies provide would not be undertaken by private firms.

Still another example where public operation makes economic sense is with so-called "public goods," where one individual can consume the product without reducing its availability to another individual and from which no one is excluded. Street lights are the classic example, and other municipal services—for example, fire-fighting and traffic-control systems—also fall in this category.

Clearly, it is possible for private firms to be engaged in some of these public activities. A private firm, for example, could operate the public lighting system under contract from a municipality. Garbage collection is privately operated in many locales, and road construction and repair are often contracted to private firms. Yet, when private firms are engaged, regulation and public oversight—more difficult in some realms than in others—has to be extensive.

Under present political conditions, moving to greater public ownership is not likely. Privatization, in fact, has been at the top of the agenda at many levels of government—for example, with schools, hospitals, the military, and prisons. In these cases, not only does it generally make more economic sense (in terms of costs) for the operations to be in the public sector; in addition, privatization undermines democratic control precisely in areas where it is most important. Public schools, hospitals, the military, and prisons all have their problems, sometimes severe, but placing these institutions in the private sector is neither economically nor politically beneficial.

"Public ownership" can have many forms, and certainly control of economic activity by a distant government authority does not assure democratic control. Yet, public ownership by both worker and consumer cooperatives, as well as by local governments, generally holds out more promise of democratic control as well as a greater likelihood of serving public interests. ❏

For information on public banking, see the Public Banking Institute, publicbankinginstitute.org.

Article 4.6

CO-OP ECONOMICS
What can economics teach us about the challenges and potential of cooperation?

BY NANCY FOLBRE
September/October 2013

I teach economics, a discipline largely inhabited by people skeptical of human potential for cooperation. But I live in a small New England town and work in a university environment that are, for the most part, cooperative. If I eat lunch on campus, I buy it from a student-managed, democratically run business that offers the tastiest, healthiest, cheapest provisions available. If I need to buy bread or milk on the way home, I pull into the Leverett Village Co-op. If my car needs attention, it goes to a worker-owned business, Pelham Auto, where I know both service managers by name. My money sits at the Five College Federal Credit Union, where it earns more interest and gains me better service than I've ever gotten at any other bank.

About four years ago, I began to weave economic theory more closely into my everyday life. The threads began coming together when Adam Trott and Michael Johnson, two members of the local Valley Alliance of Worker Cooperatives, reached out to tell me about their efforts to promote locally owned and democratically managed firms.

Although we lived in the same community, they found me as a result of a short post I wrote for the *New York Times'* "Economix" blog, describing a collaborative agreement between the United Steel Workers and the largest worker-owned business in the world, Mondragón Corporation. It seemed ironic, but also encouraging, that we first connected online, and that it might be possible to go from the global to the local and then back again.

Even in our cooperative-rich area of Western Massachusetts, Adam and Michael explained, most potential worker/owners knew virtually nothing about the principles involved (beyond liking the general idea). Why couldn't a public university provide better education and training for students potentially interested in starting up or joining a worker-owned business? Of course it could, and should. We decided to try to make that happen.

In a collaborative process that involved interested faculty and graduate students, as well as representatives from the Valley Alliance, we developed a new upper-division economics course and designed a Certificate Program for Applied Economic Research on Cooperative Enterprises centered on a summer research internship with a local cooperative.

Here, I want to share some of the ideas and opinions I've formed in the process of developing this program, which we believe could be a good model for other colleges and universities.

History Matters

Most people, including most college students, seem to think that cooperatives are a counter-cultural leftover from the 1960s, a niche phenomenon confined to hip neighborhoods and college towns. The economic history of the United States is typically portrayed as the steady march of corporate capitalism, trampling all other institutional forms. Many on the right see it as a march of progress; many on the left, as a march of doom.

Ironically, the traditional left preoccupation with corporate capitalism may simply feed the beast—overstating its hegemonic role, as though it can't be contained until the revolution comes. J.K. Gibson-Graham makes this point persuasively in *The End of Capitalism (As We Knew It)*: What we call "capitalism" involves many different creatures. Families, communities, non-profit organizations, and the state actually account for a larger share of economic activity—broadly defined—than capitalist firms.

Though standard economics texts hardly mention them, consumer cooperatives and worker-owned businesses have shaped our history. Their influence, however, has been uneven, greater in some industries and regions than others.

Marxist scholars have often associated cooperatives with the so-called "utopian socialists"—whom they have traditionally considered well-meaning but misguided. Efforts to establish alternative businesses have often been labeled a form of co-optation less politically virtuous than trade-union organizing or socialist political parties. Yet cooperative efforts have typically been closely linked to and complementary with larger anti-corporate organizing efforts. In a fascinating article entitled "Toward an Organizationally Diverse American Capitalism? Cooperative, Mutual, and Local, State-Owned Enterprise," sociologist Mark Schnaiberg traces the history of cooperative marketing efforts in the grain and dairy industries, originally dominated by large monopsonies that used their market power to pay farmers as little as possible. (A monopsony is a single buyer that dominates a market, just as a monopoly is a single seller.) When farmers successfully started up cooperatives, other members of the community also became more likely to organize on their own behalf.

Even when cooperative enterprises represent only a small proportion of market transactions in a local community, they often exercise a disproportionate influence, disciplining capitalist enterprises or pioneering innovations that are later adopted by them. Local food cooperatives were the first to begin marketing organic and local produce, and large supermarket chains gradually followed suit. Local credit unions have made it harder for large banking institutions to charge excessive fees. Worker-owned businesses have pulled the small-business community in a more progressive direction, serving as a counterweight to large, footloose firms.

By demonstrating the viability of businesses aimed to serve larger social goals, cooperatives have altered our economic ecology.

Culture Matters

As an economist, I was trained to emphasize the difference between for-profit and non-profit firms. But that difference may be less significant than the moral and cultural values central to the definition of cooperative enterprises.

Consumer cooperatives seek to provide high-quality products at minimal cost. Worker-owned businesses need to generate profits both to pay themselves and to finance investment. Both, however, are committed to seven "cooperative principles" (see box, next page) that include democracy and concern for community.

In this respect, cooperative enterprises can be seen as a subset of efforts to develop a solidarity economy, which also includes non-profit businesses and community organizations. They are also closely aligned with "buy local" efforts that urge consumers to shop in locally owned stores and build a local supply chain (for instance, by patronizing restaurants utilizing locally grown products).

Not that it's always clear how "concern for community" should be defined. Almost by their very nature as small, decentralized businesses, co-ops prioritize those with whom they are most likely to come into contact. But local solidarity is not automatically consistent with broader forms of solidarity. In fact, it risks a kind of parochialism that could lead to happy little enclaves embedded in a larger economy built on hierarchy and exploitation.

On the other hand, co-op culture can promote values that may lead people toward other forms of positive engagement, with the goal of steadily expanding the cooperative reach and linking many kinds of progressive efforts together. Co-op ventures also offer people the opportunity to build something new, rather than merely trying to tear down something old.

The Seven Cooperative Principles

Cooperatives around the world generally operate according to the same core principles and values, adopted by the International Co-operative Alliance (www.ica.coop) in 1995. Cooperatives trace the roots of these principles to the first modern cooperative, founded in Rochdale, England, in 1844.

1. **Voluntary and Open Membership**: Cooperatives are voluntary organizations, open to all people able to use its services and willing to accept the responsibilities of membership, without gender, social, racial, political or religious discrimination.
2. **Democratic Member Control**: Cooperatives are democratic organizations controlled by their members—those who buy the goods or use the services of the cooperative—who actively participate in setting policies and making decisions.
3. **Members' Economic Participation**: Members contribute equally to, and democratically control, the capital of the cooperative. This benefits members in proportion to the business they conduct with the cooperative rather than on the capital invested.
4. **Autonomy and Independence**: Cooperatives are autonomous, self-help organizations controlled by their members. If the co-op enters into agreements with other organizations or raises capital from external sources, it is done so based on terms that ensure democratic control by the members and maintains the cooperative's autonomy.
5. **Education, Training and Information**: Cooperatives provide education and training for members, elected representatives, managers and employees so they can contribute effectively to the development of their cooperative. Members also inform the general public about the nature and benefits of cooperatives.
6. **Cooperation among Cooperatives**: Cooperatives serve their members most effectively and strengthen the cooperative movement by working together through local, national, regional and international structures.
7. **Concern for Community**: While focusing on member needs, cooperatives work for the sustainable development of communities through policies and programs accepted by the members.

From the National Cooperative Business Association, International Year of Cooperatives (usa2012.coop).

The commitment to democratic decision-making distinguishes worker-owned businesses from other institutional forms that aim to enlarge economic goals (such as the new "social benefit" corporate charters) or to help incentivize workers (such as profit-sharing or employee-stock-ownership plans). This commitment reflects a cultural value—as well as a political principle. Other shared values encouraging respect and concern for others may help lubricate the democratic process by making collective decision-making less contentious.

Democratic values and skills may grow stronger in communities where they are consistently exercised, explaining why some regions of the world seem to foster more cooperative enterprises than others. The famous Mondragón cooperatives grew up in the Basque area of northern Spain, among people who felt embattled and impoverished by their minority status and strengthened by their progressive Catholic traditions. Many small cooperatives have prospered in northern Italy, an area with a long history of labor radicalism and a strong Communist Party. In Canada, the province of Quebec has successfully encouraged the cooperative provision of social services under the banner of the "social economy."

In the United States, cooperatives have often helped improve living standards in African-American communities, from a cooperative shipyard in 1860s Baltimore, to a co-op buying club in Depression-era Gary, Ind., to the Common Ground Collective in post-Katrina New Orleans. As Jessica Gordon-Nembhard and Ajowa Nzinga point out (see *Dollars & Sense*, July/August 2006), a common history of economic exclusion and hardship can foster cooperation.

Public policies have also played a role in developing these epicenters of cooperative development. But culture is surely one of the factors shaping the political alignments that generate such policies.

Efficiency Matters

Economists often overstate the value of efficiency, or define it in excessively narrow terms. But that doesn't mean it's not important. Efficiency is an important arbiter of success in competition and, in the world we live in, co-operators need to compete. Since competition between firms is, to some extent a "team sport," successful cooperation among team members can prove advantageous.

Democratically managed firms may be more efficient than others, even from the relatively narrow perspective of costs and benefits. The British economist John Stuart Mill made this argument in the mid-19th century, pointing out that workers who were also owners would be likely to work harder and smarter than those merely paid an hourly wage.

This issue never received much attention from early-twentieth-century Marxists convinced of the virtues of central planning. However, it came to the fore with Yugoslavian experiments in worker self-management in the mid-20th century and has since had a big impact on progressive economic thinking—in part because it helps frame a critique of both the traditional family firm and the modern corporation.

A long-standing favorite of neoclassical economists is an argument, developed by economists Armen Alchian and Harold Demsetz, that workers will have a tendency to shirk on the job unless they are overseen by an owner who can capture any profits (or "residual") left over after the workers are paid. This gives the "residual claimant" an incentive to crack the whip and make them work as hard as possible. Ownership in most modern corporations is highly fragmented, but owners presumably hire managers—from the chief executive officer or CEO down to supervisors and foremen—to fulfill this disciplinary role.

Radical economist Samuel Bowles effectively rebuts this argument, pointing out that it is difficult and costly to monitor effort. Workers seeking to resist capitalist exploitation may be especially likely to shirk unless managers can find a way to either secure their loyalty or threaten them with costly job loss.

Unfortunately, worker ownership alone doesn't necessarily solve this incentive problem. Workers either have to be really good at monitoring one another's efforts (so that no one can free ride without being sanctioned), or they have to feel such strong solidarity toward one another that no one even tries to free ride. (The latter is preferable, since it's often hard for a collective to fire someone who is slacking off.)

Other tensions among owner-workers can arise. For instance, young owner-workers have a stronger incentive to reinvest firm profits to increase their future earnings than older owner-workers, who would prefer to retain more earnings and/or fund their pensions. The success of a worker-owned enterprise depends on the ability of worker-owners to anticipate and creatively respond to such conflicts of interest. But the process of doing so—negotiating and resolving differences of opinion—can itself be quite costly, in two ways.

First, democratic decision-making can be quite time-consuming, especially if based on rules of consensus. Worker-owned firms generally treat time in meetings as part of their paid work, and the time they devote to it can cut down on directly productive activities.

Second, democratic decision-making can prove emotionally costly, as when good friends disagree about important matters and find it difficult to accommodate one another. On the other hand, conflict avoidance—such as a desire not to discipline a fellow worker who is also a friend—can also lower efficiency. This problem can be described as a "second order" free-rider problem—that is, a reluctance to openly point to or discourage free riding.

Representative democracy and delegation to a manager can help minimize these problems, but also at some cost. Majority rule can alienate the minority, and unstable factions can lead to lack of continuity in decision-making.

Worker-owned firms will be more likely to prosper if they cultivate an awareness of decision-making problems and develop the institutional structures and skills necessary to over-come them.

Here comes the Catch-22. Neither our educational system nor most employers do much to help people develop democratic management skills, so there's a big start-up problem. If we could just create more opportunities for people to develop and practice such skills, worker-owned businesses could enjoy more success.

Efficiency gains can also come at the macro level. Worker-owned businesses that get off the ground tend to be more stable than other small businesses, in part because workers have an incentive to hang in over the long haul, even if revenue slumps. This can buffer the effects of recession on the economy as a whole.

Most importantly, worker-owned businesses depend more on positive incentives than on the threat of job loss. Unlike employer-owned businesses, they don't rely on the labor discipline imposed by a high unemployment rate. And consistently high unemployment rates are among the most inefficient features of our current economic system.

Collaboration Matters

For all the reasons given above, the cooperative movement may need to reach a certain critical mass before it can really take off. More collaboration among cooperatives—and between cooperatives and other institutions such as public universities—could make a big difference.

Relatively few worker-owned businesses are started up in a given year, leading some to speculate that they are inherently less expansionary than capitalist firms (for the simple reason that worker-owners care about more than the rate of return on their capital investment). They also care about the quality of their work life and their place in the community. Some of the decision-making problems described above, moreover, may be more easily solved in small firms where everyone knows everyone else. Expansion can lead to complications.

However, collaboration and expansion could help worker-owned businesses in several ways. First, it could help them gain access to more and better financing. By definition, worker-owned firms can't sell equity shares in their business (because all owners must be workers). They can develop other forms of self-financing, including bonds that can be especially attractive to socially responsible investors. But they can also develop ways of pooling resources and helping to finance one another. Each firm belonging to the Valley Alliance of Worker Coops sets aside a percentage of its profits to promote local cooperative development. One can even imagine a kind of franchise model in which one firm could spin off smaller firms, which could become financially independent, but remain closely allied.

Second, vertical networking along the supply chain could increase efficiency and the ability to compete with large conglomerate capitalist enterprises. International networking among cooperatives holds particular promise, because it advances a larger fair-trade agenda, and also helps escape parochialism. Many examples of this kind of networking exist, such as the People's Market at UMass-Amherst buying only cooperatively produced coffee and actively seeking other cooperatively produced goods and services.

Third, more networking could help develop the distinctive managerial and decision-making skills described above. Indeed, the more worker-owners gain experience in different types of firms, the richer the skills they bring to the task of democratic management. And the more visible worker-owners become, the more young people are likely to become attracted to new prospects for more socially meaningful and economically rewarding work.

Finally, the more worker-owned businesses and other cooperative enterprises expand, the easier it becomes to build political coalitions and implement policies that promote their efforts. These synergies help explain how regional economies in the Basque area of Spain, northern Italy, and the Canadian province of Quebec have evolved.

A worker-owned business is what economists call a "microeconomic structure." But its ultimate success may depend on its ability to change the macroeconomic structure, which can, in turn, improve its microeconomic efficiency. Even a small cooperative firm can help a community enhance its standard of living and quality of life. More importantly, however, it can provide a catalyst for social and political changes that not only bring more and more worker-owned businesses into being, but also enable them to compete more effectively with capital-owned firms.

That's why worker-owned businesses fit the description of what the 20th-century Italian theorist and revolutionary Antonio Gramsci called a "non-reformist reform" and what sociologist Erik Olin Wright terms a "real utopia." Take another look at those seven cooperative principles. They offer a pretty good guide to running not just a business, but a whole society. ❏

Sources: J.K. Gibson-Graham, *The End of Capitalism (As We Knew It)* (University of Minnesota Press, 2006); Mark Schnaiberg, "Toward an Organizationally Diverse American Capitalism? Cooperative, Mutual, and Local, State-Owned Enterprise," *Seattle University Law Review*, Vol. 34, No. 4 (2011); Jessica Gordon-Nembhard and Ajowa Nzinga, "African-American Economic Solidarity," *Dollars & Sense*, July/August 2006; Erik Olin Wright, *Envisioning Real Utopias* (Verso, 2010).

Chapter 5

MARKET FAILURE I:
MARKET POWER

INTRODUCTION

With monopoly, we finally encounter a situation in which most economists, orthodox and otherwise, agree that unfettered markets lead to an undesirable outcome. If a firm is able to create a monopoly, it faces a downward-sloping demand curve—that is to say, if it reduces output, it can charge a higher price. Economists argue that competitive forces tend to undermine any monopoly, but failing this, they support antitrust policy as a backstop. The concept of monopoly not only points to an important failing of markets, but it opens the door to thinking about many possible market structures other than perfect competition, including oligopoly, in which a small group of producers dominates the market. Monopoly and oligopoly are examples of market structures in which firms wield "market power" (violating Tilly Assumption #1—see Article 1.2). That is, individual firms can affect the market-wide level of prices, profits, and wages. Market power alters how markets function from the ideal of perfect competition and delivers significantly less optimal results.

We begin this chapter with another seminal article by Chris Tilly, "Is Small Beautiful? Is Bigger Better? Small and Big Businesses Both Have Their Drawbacks" (Article 5.1). This article walks through the pluses and minuses of large and small businesses, and finds both wanting.

The current financial crisis has provided particularly egregious examples of what happens when we institute *laissez-faire* (hands-off) regulatory regimens, especially in the area of finance. In "A Brief History of Mergers and Antitrust Policy" (Article 5.2), Edward Herman provides a long-term context for the discussion, reviewing the history of U.S. antitrust law over the last century. He also criticizes economists for justifying a hands-off policy toward big business mergers over the last few decades.

Next, Arthur MacEwan discusses the relevance of the concept of "monopoly capital" in an age of globalized competition (Article 5.3). MacEwan finds that firm size and market concentration have continued to grow throughout the era of globalization and that large firms still exhibit extraordinary market power.

In "Want Free Trade? Open the Medical and Drug Industry to Competition" (Article 5.4), Dean Baker describes how companies in this sector are protected from market competition. Doctors are protected from international competition, even as "free trade" agreements have put blue-collar workers squarely in competition with workers all over the world. Meanwhile, pharmaceutical companies enjoy monopoly protections lasting decades, thanks to patents, without a significant counterweight from government price regulation.

The last two articles look at two examples of the exercise of market power today. Sasha Breger Bush focuses on the unequal relationship between farmers and the companies that dominate the food industry (Article 5.5). Breger Bush describes how, in the United States, poultry farmers find themselves under the thumb of giant "integrators" like Perdue, Tyson, and Pilgrim's Pride. In developing countries where coffee is widely grown, farmers face a similar relationship with coffee processors. In both cases, there is a fundamental relationship of "unequal exchange." Finally, Dean Baker focuses, in his article "The False Libertarianism of the Silicon Valley Billionaires" (Article 5.6), on revelations that tech companies illegally conspired to hold down wages (by agreeing not to compete with each other for employees). This arrangement, Baker argues, is revealing, in that it shows the "Silicon Valley billionaires" do not believe that they operate in truly competitive labor markets.

Discussion Questions

1. (Article 5.1) List the pros and cons of large and small businesses that Tilly discusses. How does this compare with the problems associated with market structure that your textbook mentions? Be sure to compare Tilly's list of small-business flaws with what your textbook has to say about small business.

2. (Articles 5.1 and 5.2) In what ways do these articles show that corporations control "the marketplace of ideas"? What are the possible consequences? What, if anything, should be done about it?

3. (Article 5.3) Mainstream economists view competition among many small firms as a prerequisite for "efficient" market outcomes. Some touted globalization as a way to increase competition and benefit consumers. What problems, if any, result from the large size and market dominance of a few global firms? Should this change our view of globalization in any way?

4. (Article 5.4) Baker argues that trade agreements have protected U.S. doctors and pharmaceutical companies from international competition. Why do you think this has been the case, when other kinds of workers and industries have borne the full brunt of global competition? Would policies to reduce the prices charged by the medical sector be desirable? What policies?

5. (Articles 5.5) Breger Bush notes that food producers (like chicken farmers or coffee farmers) occupy a highly competitive market segment, which food industry "integrators" occupy an much less competitive segment. What are the consequences of this set-up? Are they undesirable and, if so, what remedy would you propose?

6. (Article 5.6) Baker argues that, by their own behavior, Silicon Valley employers have shown that they do not believe they operate in competitive labor markets. What remedies might workers pursue when they are employed in an industry with a few dominant employers? Does the answer depend on whether those employers actively collude with each other or not?

Article 5.1

IS SMALL BEAUTIFUL? IS BIG BETTER?
Small and big businesses both have their drawbacks.

BY CHRIS TILLY
July/August 1989, revised April 2002

Beginning in the late 1980s, the United States has experienced a small, but significant boom in small business. While big businesses have downsized, small enterprises have proliferated. Should we be glad? Absolutely, declare the advocates of small business. Competition makes small businesses entrepreneurial, innovative, and responsive to customers.

Not so fast, reply big business's boosters. Big corporations grew big because they were efficient, and tend to stay efficient because they are big—and thus able to invest in research and upgrading of technology and workforce skills.

But each side in this debate omits crucial drawbacks. Small may be beautiful for consumers, but it's often oppressive for workers. And while big businesses wield the power to advance technology, they also often wield the market power to bash competitors and soak consumers. In the end, the choices are quite limited.

Big and Small

Is the United States a nation of big businesses, or of small ones? There are two conventional ways to measure business size. One is simply to count the number of employees per firm. By this measure, small businesses (say, business establishments with less than 20 employees) make up the vast majority of businesses (Table 1). But they provide only a small fraction of the total number of jobs.

The other approach gauges market share—each firm's share of total sales in a given industry. Industries range between two extremes: what economists call "perfect competition" (many firms selling a standardized product, each too tiny to affect the market price) and monopoly (one business controls all sales in an industry). Economy-wide, as with employment, small businesses are most numerous, but control only a small slice of total sales. Sole proprietorships account for 73% of established businesses, far outnumbering corporations, which are 20% of the total (the remainder are partnerships). But corporations ring up a hefty 90% of all sales, leaving sole proprietors with only 6%. It takes a lot of mom and pop stores to equal General Motors' 1999 total of $177 billion in sales.

Industry by industry, the degree of competition varies widely. Economists consider an industry concentrated when its top four companies account for more than 40% of total sales in the industry (Table 2). At the high end of the spectrum are the cigarette, beer, and aircraft industries, where four firms account for the bulk of U.S. production.

No market comes close to meeting the textbook specifications for perfect competition, but one can still find industries in which a large number of producers compete for sales. The clothing and restaurant industries, for example, remain relatively competitive. Overall, about one-third of U.S. goods are manufactured in concentrated industries, about one fifth are made in competitive industries, and the rest fall somewhere in between.

Beating the Competition

Those who tout the benefits of small, competitive business make a broad range of claims on its behalf. In addition to keeping prices low, they say the quality of the product is constantly improving, as companies seek a competitive edge. The same desire, they claim, drives firms toward technological innovations, leading to productivity increases.

The real story is not so simple. Competition does indeed keep prices low. Believe it or not, clothing costs us less—in real terms—than it cost our parents. Between 1960 and 1999, while the overall price level and hourly wages both increased nearly sixfold, apparel prices didn't even triple. And small businesses excel at offering variety, whether it is the ethnic restaurants that dot cities or the custom machine-tool work offered by small shops. Furthermore, however powerful small business lobbies may be in Washington, they do not influence the legislative process as blatantly as do corporate giants.

But those low prices often have an ugly underside. Our sportswear is cheap in part because the garment industry increasingly subcontracts work to sweatshops—whether they be export assembly plants in Haiti paying dollar-a-day wages, or the "underground" Los Angeles stitcheries that employ immigrant women in virtual slavery. Struggling to maintain razor-thin profit margins, small businesses cut costs any way they can—which usually translates into low wages and onerous working conditions.

"There is a rule of survival for small business," Bill Ryan, president of Ryan Transfer Corporation, commented some years ago. "There are certain things you want to have [in paying workers] and certain things you can afford. You had better go with what you can afford." Bottom line, workers in companies employing 500 or more people enjoy average wages 30% higher than their counterparts in small businesses.

Part of this wage gap results from differences other than size—unionization, the education of the workforce, the particular jobs and industries involved. But University of Michigan economist Charles Brown and his colleagues

TABLE 1:
SMALL BUSINESS NATION?

Most businesses are small, but most employees work for big businesses

Company size (number of employees)	Percent of all firms	Percent of all workers
1–4	54%	6%
5–9	20%	8%
10–19	13%	11%
20–49	8%	16%
50–99	3%	13%
100–249	2%	16%
250–499	0.4%	10%
500–999	0.2%	7%
1,000 or more	0.1%	13%

Note: "Businesses" refers to establishments, meaning business locations.

Source: County Business Patterns, 1998.

controlled for all these differences and more, and still found a 10% premium for big business's employees. A note of caution, however: Other recent research indicates that this wage bonus is linked to long-term employment and job ladders. To the extent that corporations dissolve these long-term ties—as they seem to be rapidly doing—the pay advantage may dissolve as well.

Small business gurus make extravagant claims about small businesses' job-generation capacity. An oft-quoted 1987 report by consultant David Birch claimed that businesses with fewer than 20 employees create 88% of new jobs. The reality is more mundane: over the long run, businesses with 19 or fewer workers account for about one quarter of net new jobs. One reason why Birch's statistics are misleading is that new small businesses are created in great numbers, but they also fail at a high rate. The result is that the *net* gain in jobs is much smaller than the number created in business start-ups.

For companies in very competitive markets, the same "whip of competition" that keeps prices down undermines many of competition's other supposed benefits. The flurry of competition in the airline industry following deregulation, for example, hardly resulted in a higher quality product. Flying became temporarily cheaper, but also less comfortable, reliable, and safe.

Technological innovation from competition is also more myth than reality. Small firms in competitive industries do very little research and development. They lack both the cash needed to make long-term investments and the market power to guarantee a return on that investment. In fact, many of them can't even count on surviving to reap the rewards: only one-third to one-half of small business startups survive for five years, and only about one in five makes it to ten years. A 1988 Census Bureau survey concluded that in manufacturing, "technology use is positively correlated with plant size." Agriculture may be the exception that proves the rule. That highly competitive industry has made marked productivity gains, but its research is supported by the taxpayer, and its risks are reduced by government price supports.

Of course, the biggest myth about competition is that it is in any way a "natural state" for capitalism. In fact, in most markets the very process of competing for high profits or a bigger market share tends to create a concentrated, rather than a competitive, market structure.

TABLE 2: WHO COMPETES, WHO DOESN'T

Industry	Percent of sales by top four firms
Light truck and utility vehicle manufacturing	96%
Breweries	91%
Home center stores	91%
Breakfast cereal manufacturing	78%
General book stores	77%
Credit card issuing	77%
Lawn equipment manufacturing	62%
Cable providers	63%
Computer and software stores	51%
Sock manufacturing	30%
Hotels and motels (excl. casinos)	22%
Gas stations	9%
Real estate	4%
Bars	2%

Source: 2002 Economic Census.

This process occurs in several ways. Big firms sometimes drive their smaller competitors out of business by selectively cutting prices to the bone. The smaller firms may lack the financial resources to last out the low prices. In the 1960s, several of IBM's smaller competitors sued it for cutting prices in a pattern that was designed to drive the smaller firms out of the market. Large corporations can also gain a lock on scarce resources: for example, large airlines like United and American operate the comprehensive, computerized information and reservation systems that travel agents tap into—and you can bet that each airline's system lists their own flights first. Or businesses may exploit an advantage in one market to dominate another, as Microsoft used its control of the computer operating system market to seize market share for its Internet browser.

Other firms eliminate competitors by buying them out—either in a hostile takeover or a friendly merger. Either way, a former competitor is neutralized. This strategy used to be severely limited by strict antitrust guidelines that prohibited most horizontal mergers—those between two firms that formerly competed in the same market. The Reagan administration's team at the Justice Department, however, loosened the merger guidelines significantly in the early 1980s. Since that time, many large mergers between former competitors have been allowed to go through, most notably in the airline industry.

The Power of Concentration

Concentration, then, is as natural to market economies as competition. And bigness, like smallness, is a mixed bag for us as consumers and workers. For workers, bigness is on the whole a plus. Whereas competition forces small businesses to be stingy, big firms are on average more generous, offering employees higher wages, greater job security, and more extensive fringe benefits. In 1993, 97% of businesses with 500 or more workers provided health insurance; only 43% of businesses with 25 or fewer employees did so. Large firms also provide much more employee training. The strongest unions, as well, have historically been in industries where a few firms control large shares of their markets, and can pass along increased costs to consumers—auto, steel, and tires, for example. When profits are threatened, though, firms in concentrated markets also have more resources with which to fight labor. They are better able to weather a strike, oppose unionization, and make agreements with rivals not to take advantage of each other's labor troubles. In addition, large companies, not surprisingly, score low on workplace autonomy.

What about consumers? Corporations in industries where there are few competitors may compete, but the competitive clash is seldom channeled into prolonged price wars. The soft drink industry is a classic example. David McFarland, a University of North Carolina economist, likens soft drink competition to professional wrestling. "They make a lot of sounds and groans and bounce on the mat, but they know who is going to win," he remarked.

Coke and Pepsi introduce new drinks and mount massive ad campaigns to win market share, but the net result is not lower prices. In fact, because competition between industry giants relies more on product differentiation than price, companies pass on their inflated advertising expenses to consumers. In the highly concentrated breakfast cereal market, the package frequently costs more than the contents. And of every dollar you pay for a box, nearly 20 cents goes for advertising.

It takes resources to develop and market a new idea, which gives large corporations distinct advantages in innovation. The original idea for the photocopier may have come from a patent lawyer who worked nights in his basement, but Xerox spent $16 million before it had a product it could sell. RCA invested $65 million developing the color television. RCA could take this gamble because its dominance in the television market ensured that it would not be immediately undercut by some other firm.

But market dominance can also translate into complacency. The steel industry illustrates the point. A few major producers earned steady profits through the 1950s and 1960s but were caught off-guard when new technologies vaulted foreign steel-makers to the top of the industry in the 1970s. Similarly, when IBM dominated the computer industry in the 1960s and early 1970s, innovation proceeded quite slowly, particularly compared to the frantic scramble in that industry today. With no competitors to worry about, it was more profitable for IBM to sit tight, since innovation would only have made its own machines obsolete.

And large corporations can also put their deep pockets and technical expertise to work to short-circuit public policy. In the 1980s, when Congress changed corporate liability laws to make corporate executives criminally liable for some kinds of offenses, General Electric's lobbyists and legal staff volunteered to help draft the final regulations, in order to minimize the damage.

Big businesses sometimes hide their lobbying behind a "citizen" smokescreen. The largest-spending lobby in Washington in 1986 was Citizens for the Control of Acid Rain. These good citizens had been organized by coal and electric utility companies to oppose tighter pollution controls. Along the same lines, the Coalition for Vehicle Choice (now, who could be against that?) was set up by Ford and General Motors in 1990 to fight higher fuel efficiency standards.

Concentration or Conglomeration

Over the last couple of decades, the mix of big and small businesses has changed, but the changes are small and—at first glance—contradictory. Over time, employment has shifted toward smaller firms, though the shift has been subtle, not revolutionary. Meanwhile, the overall level of industry-by-industry sales concentration in the economy has increased, but only slightly. As older industries become more concentrated, newer, more competitive ones crop up, leaving overall concentration relatively steady. In his book *Lean and Mean*, economist Bennett Harrison points out that there is actually no contradiction between the small business employment boomlet and big firms' continued grip on markets. Big businesses, it turns out, are orchestrating much of the flowering of small business, through a variety of outsourcing and subcontracting arrangements.

But if industry-by-industry concentration has changed little over the decades, conglomeration is a different matter. Corporate ownership of assets has become much more concentrated over time, reflecting the rise in conglomerates—corporations doing business in a variety of industries. Five decades ago, the top 200 manufacturing firms accounted for 48% of all sales in the U.S. economy. By 1993, the 200 biggest industrial businesses controlled 65% of sales.

Most mainstream economists see these groupings as irrelevant for the competitive structure of the economy. Antitrust laws place no restrictions on firms from different industries banding together under one corporate roof. But sheer size can easily affect competition in the markets of the individual firms involved. A parent company can use one especially profitable subsidiary to subsidize start-up costs for a new venture, giving it a competitive edge. And if one board of directors controls major interests in related industries, it can obviously influence any of those markets more forcefully.

A case in point is the mega-merger of Time Inc. and Warner, which will soon be joining with America Online. The resulting conglomerate will control massive sections of the home entertainment business, bringing together Time's journalists, film and television producers, and authors, Warner's entertainment machine, which includes Home Box Office, the nation's largest pay television channel, and AOL's huge share of the Internet access market. The conglomerate can influence the entertainment business from the initial point—the actors, writers, and directors—up to the point where the finished products appear on people's televisions or computers. Conglomeration also multiplies the political clout of large corportions. No wonder Disney and other entertainment giants have also hopped on the conglomeration bandwagon.

Choose Your Poison

Competition, concentration, or conglomeration: The choice is an unsavory one indeed. Opting for lots of tiny, competing firms leaves labor squeezed and sacrifices the potential technological advantages that come with concentrated resources. Yet the big monopolies tend to dominate their markets, charge high prices, and waste countless resources on glitzy ad campaigns and trivial product differentiation. And the big conglomerate firms, while not necessarily dominant in any single market, wield a frightening amount of political and economic power, with budgets larger than those of most countries.

Of course, we don't have much to say about the choice, no matter how much "shopping for a better world" we engage in. Market competition rolls on—sometimes cutthroat, other times genteel. Industries often start out as monopolies (based on new inventions), go through a competitive phase, but end up concentrating as they mature. As long as bigness remains profitable and the government maintains a hands-off attitude, companies in both competitive and concentrated industries will tend to merge with firms in other industries. This will feed a continuing trend toward conglomeration. Since bigness and smallness both have their drawbacks, the best we can do is to use public policies to minimize the disadvantages of each. ❑

Sources: Lean and Mean: The Changing Landscape of Corporate Power in the Age of Flexibility, Bennett Harrison, 1994; *Employers Large and Small,* Charles Brown, James Hamilton, and James Medoff, 1990.

Article 5.2

A BRIEF HISTORY OF MERGERS AND ANTITRUST POLICY

BY EDWARD HERMAN
May/June 1998

Government efforts to prevent or break up monopolies are called antitrust policy. They assume that when a few companies dominate an industry, this weakens competition and hurts the public by reducing production, raising prices, and slowing technical advance. Antitrust has gone through cycles during this century. In some years, strongly pro-business presidencies (usually Republican) have allowed businesses to merge at will. These have often been followed by "reform" administrations, which tend to restrain, but not to reverse, concentrations of corporate power.

The federal government first took on a strong antitrust role with the Sherman Act of 1890, which outlawed monopoly and efforts to obtain it. In 1914 the Clayton Act also put restrictions on stock purchases and interlocking directorates that would reduce competition. This legislation responded to public anger and fears about "trusts," which brought separate firms under common control. Most notorious were Rockefeller's Standard Oil Trust and James Duke's American Tobacco Company, which employed ruthless tactics to drive their competitors out of business.

Early on the antitrust laws also treated organized labor as a "monopoly," and were used in breaking the Pullman strike in 1892. In 1908, the Supreme Court awarded damages to an employer against whom unions had organized a secondary boycott. This led to the Clayton Act exempting unions from its restrictions.

Otherwise, the federal government only minimally enforced the Sherman Act until Theodore Roosevelt was elected in 1900. Then in 1911 the Supreme Court decided that both the Standard Oil and American Tobacco trusts were "bad trusts," and ordered their dismantling. But in 1920 the Court refused to condemn the U.S. Steel consolidation, because it was a "good trust" that didn't attack its smaller rivals. This began a long period when the Antitrust Division and the courts approved mergers that produced industries with a few dominant firms, but which were "well-behaved." And in the 1920s, Republicans virtually ended antitrust enforcement.

The Golden Age

Franklin Roosevelt revived antitrust during 1938 to 1941, and antitrust law had its golden age from 1945 to 1974, fueled by a liberal Supreme Court, anti-merger legislation passed in 1950, and mildly progressive enforcement (though less so in the Republican years). During this period Alcoa's monopoly over aluminum production was broken (1945), and the Court found the tobacco industry guilty of "group monopoly" (1946), although the companies were only assessed a modest fine.

During the 1960s, when antitrust law blocked mergers among companies in the same industry, businesses adapted by acquiring firms in unrelated industries. Many such "conglomerate" mergers took place during 1964-68, when Lyndon Johnson was president. Companies like International Telephone and Telegraph, Ling-Temco-Vought, Gulf & Western, Tenneco, and Litton Industries grew rapidly.

The Reagan-Bush Collapse

Antitrust policy went into recession around 1974, then plunged during the presidencies of Ronald Reagan and George H. W. Bush. They aggressively dismantled antitrust, imposing drastic cuts in budgets and manpower, installing officials hostile to the antitrust mission, and failing to enforce the laws. During 1981-89, the Antitrust Division of the Justice Dept. challenged only 16 of over 16,000 pre-merger notices filed with them.

Despite his high-profile contest with Microsoft, Bill Clinton largely accepted the conservative view that most mergers are harmless. During his two terms, federal authorities approved or ignored many giant mergers. These included Westinghouse's buyout of CBS, the joining of "Baby Bells" Bell Atlantic and Nynex, and the combination of Chemical Bank and Manufacturers Hanover. During 1997 alone, 156 mergers of $1 billion or more, and merger transactions totalling more than *$1 trillion*, passed antitrust muster.

Clinton's failure to attack giant mergers rests nominally on the alleged efficiency of large firms and the belief that globalized markets make for competition. FTC head Robert Pitofsky said, "this is an astonishing merger wave," but not to worry because these deals "should be judged on a global market scale, not just on national and local markets."

But the efficiency of large size—as opposed to the profit-making advantages that corporations gain from market power and cross-selling (pushing products through other divisions of the same company)—is eminently debatable. And many markets are not global—hospitals, for example, operate in local markets, yet only some 20 of 3,000 hospital mergers have been subjected to antitrust challenge. Even in global markets a few firms are often dominant, and a vast array of linkages such as joint ventures and licensing agreements increasingly mute global competition.

The Clinton administration's failure to contest many giant mergers did not rest only on intellectual arguments. It also reflected political weakness and an unwillingness to oppose powerful people who fund elections and own or dominate the media. This was conspicuously true of the great media combinations—Disney and Cap-Cities/ABC, and TimeWarner and Turner—and the merger of Boeing and McDonnell-Douglas, which involved institutions of enormous power, whose mergers the stock market greeted enthusiastically.

The Economists Sell Out

Since the early 1970s, powerful people and corporations have funded not only elections but conservative economists, who are frequently housed in think-tanks such as the American Enterprise, Hoover, and Cato Institutes, and serve as corporate consultants in regulatory and anti-trust cases. Most notable in hiring economic consultants have been AT&T and IBM, which together spent hundreds of millions of dollars on their antitrust defenses. AT&T hired some 30 economists from five leading economics departments during the 1970s and early 1980s.

Out of these investments came models and theories downgrading the "populist" idea that numerous sellers and decentralization were important for effective competition (and essential to a democratic society). They claimed instead that the market can do it all, and that regulation and antitrust actions are misconceived. First, theorists showed that efficiency gains from mergers might reduce prices even more than monopoly power would cause them to rise. Economists also stressed "entry," claiming that if mergers did not improve efficiency any price increases would be wiped out eventually by new companies entering the industry. Entry is also the heart of the theory of "contestable markets," developed by economic consultants to AT&T, who argued that the ease of entry in cases where resources (trucks, aircraft) can be shifted quickly at low cost, makes for effective competition.

Then there is the theory of a "market for corporate control," in which mergers allow better managers to displace the less efficient. In this view, poorly-managed firms have low stock prices, making them easy to buy. Finally, many economists justified conglomerate mergers on three grounds: that they function as "mini capital markets," with top managers allocating capital between divisions of a single firm so as to maximize efficiency; that they reduce transaction costs; and that they are a means of diversifying risk.

These theories, many coming out of the "Chicago School" (the economics department at the University of Chicago), suffer from over-simplification, a strong infusion of ideology, and lack of empirical support. Mergers often are motivated by factors other than enhancing efficiency—such as the desire for monopoly power, empire building, cutting taxes, improving stock values, and even as a cover for poor management (such as when the badly-run U.S. Steel bought control of Marathon Oil).

Several researchers have questioned the supposed benefits of mergers. In theory, a merger that improves efficiency should increase profits. But one study by Dennis Mueller, and another by F. W. Scherer and David Ravenscraft, showed that mergers more often than not have reduced returns to stockholders. A study by Michael Porter of Harvard University demonstrated that a staggering 74% of the conglomerate acquisitions of the 1960s were eventually sold off (divested)—a good indication that they were never based on improving efficiency. William Shepherd of the University of Massachusetts investigated the "contestable markets" model, finding that it is a hypothetical case with minimal applicability to the real world.

Despite their inadequacies, the new apologetic theories have profoundly affected policy, because they provide an intellectual rationale for the agenda of the powerful. ❏

Sources: "Competition Policy in America: The Anti-Antitrust Paradox," James Brock, *Antitrust Bulletin*, Summer 1997; "The Promotional-Financial Dynamic of Merger Movements: A Historical Perspective," Richard DuBoff and Edward Herman, *Journal of Economic Issues*, March 1989; "Antimerger Policy in the United States: History and Lessons," Dennis C. Mueller, *Empirica*, 1996; "Dim Prospects: effective competition in telecommunications, railroads and electricity," William Shepherd, *Antitrust Bulletin*, 1997.

Article 5.3

MONOPOLY CAPITAL AND GLOBAL COMPETITION

BY ARTHUR MacEWAN
September/October 2011

Dear Dr. Dollar:
Is the concept of monopoly capital relevant today, considering such things as global competition?

—Paul Tracy, Oceanside, Calif.

In 1960, the largest 100 firms on *Fortune* magazine's "annual ranking of America's largest corporations" accounted for 15% of corporate profits and had revenues that were 24% as large as GDP. By the early 2000s, each of these figures had roughly doubled: the top 100 firms accounted for about 30% of corporate profits and their revenues were over 40% as large as GDP.*

The banking industry is a prime example of what has been going on: In 2007 the top ten banks were holding over 50% of industry assets, compared with about 25% in 1985.

If by "monopoly capital" we mean that a relatively small number of huge firms play a disproportionately large role in our economic lives, then monopoly capital is a relevant concept today, even more so than a few decades ago.

Global competition has certainly played a role in reshaping aspects of the economy, but it has not altered the importance of very large firms. Even while, for example, Toyota and Honda have gained a substantial share of the U.S. and world auto markets, this does not change the fact that a small number of firms dominate the U.S. and world markets. Moreover, much of the rise in imports, which looks like competition, is not competition for the large U.S. firms themselves. General Motors, for example, has established parts suppliers in Mexico, allowing the company to pay lower wages and hire fewer workers in the states. And Wal-Mart, Target, and other large retailers obtain low-cost goods from subcontractors in China and elsewhere.

Economics textbooks tell us that in markets dominated by a few large firms, prices will be higher than would otherwise be the case. This has generally been true of the auto industry. Also, this appears to be the case in pharmaceuticals, telecommunications, and several other industries.

Wal-Mart and other "big box" stores, however, often do compete by offering very low prices. They are monopsonistic (few buyers) as well as monopolistic (few sellers). They use their power to force down both their payments to suppliers and the wages of their workers. In either case—high prices or low prices—large firms are exercising their market power to shift income to themselves from the rest of us.

Beyond their operation within markets, the very large firms shift income to themselves by shaping markets. Advertising is important in this regard, including, for example, the way pharmaceutical firms effectively create "needs" in pushing their products. Then there is the power of large firms in the political sphere. General

Electric, for example, maintains huge legal and lobbying departments that are able to affect and use tax laws to reduce the firm's tax liability to virtually nothing. Or consider the success of the large banks in shaping (or eliminating) financial regulation, or the accomplishments of the huge oil companies and the military contractors that establish government policies, sometimes as direct subsidies, and thus raise their profits. And the list goes on.

None of this is to say that everything was fine in earlier decades when large firms were less dominant. Yet, as monopoly capital has become more entrenched, it has generated increasingly negative outcomes for the rest of us. Most obvious are the stagnant wages and rising income inequality of recent years. The power of the large firms (e.g., Wal-Mart) to hold down wages is an important part of the story. Then there is the current crisis of the U.S. economy—directly a result of the way the very large financial firms were able to shape their industry (deregulation). Large firms in general have been prime movers over recent decades in generating deregulation and the free-market ideology that supports deregulation.

So, yes, monopoly capital is still quite relevant. Globalization does make differences in our lives, but globalization has in large part been constructed under the influence and in the interest of the very large firms. In many ways globalization makes the concept of monopoly capital even more relevant. ❑

* The profits of the top 100 firms (ranked by revenue) were quite low in 2010, back near the same 15% of total profits as in 1960, because of huge losses connected to the financial crisis incurred by some of the largest firms. Fannie Mae, Freddie Mac, and AIG accounted for combined losses of over $100 billion. Also, the revenues of all firms are not the same as GDP; much of the former is sales of intermediate products, but only sales of final products are included in GDP. Thus, the largest firms' revenues, while 40% as large as GDP, do not constitute 40% of GDP.

Article 5.4

WANT FREE TRADE? OPEN THE MEDICAL AND DRUG INDUSTRY TO COMPEITITON

BY DEAN BAKER
November 2013; The Guardian Unlimited

Free trade is like apple pie, everyone is supposed to like it. Economists have written thousands of books and articles showing how everyone can gain from reducing trade barriers. While there is much merit to this argument, little of it applies to the trade pacts that are sold as "free-trade" agreements.

These deals are about structuring trade to redistribute income upward. In addition, these agreements also provide a mechanism for over-riding the democratic process in the countries that are parties to the deals. They are a tool whereby corporate interests can block health, safety, and environmental regulations that might otherwise be implemented by democratically elected officials. This is the story with both the Trans-Pacific Partnership (TPP) now being negotiated by General Electric, Merck, and other major corporations who have been invited to the table, as well as the European Union-United States (EU-U.S.) trade agreement.

But trade agreements don't have to be designed to make the rich richer. It is possible to envision trade deals that actually would liberalize trade. NAFTA and it successors were designed to push down the wages of manufacturing workers by making it as easy as possible to set up operations overseas. This put U.S. steelworkers and autoworkers in direct competition with the low-wage workers in the developing world, pushing down wages of manufacturing workers in the United States, and by reducing the number of manufacturing jobs, the wages of less educated workers more generally.

This is all very simple and straightforward. But suppose that instead of designing trade deals to give us cheaper manufacturing workers we designed trade deals to give us cheaper doctors. In the United States, we pay our doctors almost twice as much as the average in other wealthy countries, and almost three times as much as in countries like Sweden or Norway. Suppose we structured a trade deal to get our doctors' pay in line with pay in other wealthy countries.

If we could save an average of $100,000 per doctor, this would translate to savings of roughly $85 billion a year, which would come to more than $1 trillion over the next decade. Throw in dentists and a few other highly paid professions and we would be talking real money. Just the savings on doctors' pay would come to more than $12,000 for an average family of four over ten years. This dwarfs the potential gains that are projected even by supporters of the trade agreements now being negotiated.

But we can be sure that freer trade in physicians' services will not be on the agenda in these trade deals. While the United States brings in Stem workers, nurses, and even teachers from other countries in order to keep their wages down in the United States, no one in a policy position will talk about doing the same with doctors.

The reason is very simple: doctors have lots of money and power. Roughly a third of them can be found in the top 1%, and nearly all would be in the top 3% of the income distribution.

Of course, trade can be used to bring down prices in other areas as well. The United States pays close to twice as much for its prescription drugs as people in other wealthy countries. This is the deliberate result of a patent policy that gives unchecked monopolies to drug companies for decades. In contrast, every other wealthy country couples patent monopolies with price controls, negotiated prices or some other policy that limits the extent to which drug companies can exploit their monopoly.

The United States could simply change its patent policy, but with that route being politically blocked, it could in principle use free trade to bring about the same result. With the country spending over $300 billion a year on drugs at present, the potential gains here also could be well over $1 trillion over the course of a decade.

The industry will claim that lower drug prices will hurt the incentive to develop new drugs, but we can switch to more modern and efficient methods for financing research. By raising prices by tens or even hundreds of times above their free market price, drug patents create the same sort of distortions and waste that we would expect from tariffs of several thousand percent. It's not hard to envision a system that leads to less waste and corruption.

There are many other areas where trade could, in principle, be used to bring about gains for large segments of the U.S. population as well as its trading partners. Unfortunately, we are not likely to see trade agreements that will produce such broad gains. This has nothing to do with trade per se, it has due to with the fact that these trade deals are developed and negotiated by corporate interests for corporate interests.

With the drug companies sitting at the negotiating table at the TPP, does anyone think the deal will actually lower drug prices? Do we expect good rules regulating fracking when the oil and gas industries are writing them? And will the big banks working on the financial section produce good rules for regulating finance?

Yes, free trade can benefit the country as a whole. But the trade deals we will see in the next year have nothing to do with free trade, they are just one more item on the agenda for redistributing wealth upward. ❑

Article 5.5

NO FRIENDSHIP IN TRADE
Farmers face modern-day robber barons, in the United States and worldwide.

BY SASHA BREGER-BUSH
Mach/April 2015

Presiding over monopolies in shipping and railroads, U.S. robber baron Cornelius Vanderbilt once said that "there is no friendship in trade." During the 19th century, railroad magnates like Vanderbilt used their concentrated power to increase the price of freight, creating financial hardships for farmers who needed to ship their produce. Likewise, bankers like J.P. Morgan squeezed farmers, who were reliant on credit to get through the growing season, with high interest rates. By the latter part of the century, farmers "found the prices for their produce going down, and the prices of transportation and loans going up," wrote historian Howard Zinn, "because the individual farmer could not control the price of his grain, while the monopolist railroad and the monopolist banker could charge what they liked." The market dynamics set in motion by the robber barons ushered in decades of conflict between farmers and the railroad magnates, motivating populist movements and calls for government regulation of monopolies.

Biographer T.J. Stiles notes that a "blood-chilling ruthlessness infused all [of Vanderbilt's] actions." He continues, "Although Vanderbilt habitually dressed in the simple black-and-white outfit of a Protestant clergyman, his only religion was economic power." This religion of economic power is alive and well in today's global food system and farmers trade with the new robber barons of the global food system at their peril.

The small farmers and laborers who grow and process most of the world's food—who provide one of the few things we cannot live without—are themselves often hungry and poor. That is the simple, central paradox of the global food system.

Much of the explanation for this state of affairs focuses on processes of "unequal exchange." Unequal exchange results from trading relationships between parties with unequal levels of power, between powerful monopolies on the one hand and people who struggle in more competitive markets on the other. Unequal exchange is a mechanism for *exploitation* in the food system; that is, it siphons wealth away from farmers and workers and enriches multinational food and finance corporations.

Power, Inequality, and Unequal Exchange

Beginning in the 16th century, colonization, industrialization, and globalization have worked to undermine locally self-sufficient systems of food production, gradually replacing them with a system of global food interdependence. In this new system, food production, processing, distribution, and consumption are divided up among lots of different people and communities performing different food-related tasks, often in different parts of the world. In other words, there is now a "global division of labor" in food, and the people within this division of labor (who, these days, represent most of the global population) are dependent upon one another for the food they need to survive.

This new system is hierarchically ordered, with large multinational food and agriculture corporations controlling many aspects of production, processing, distribution, and consumption. Multi-national corporations' (MNCs) dominance over the global food system owes in large part to their *market power*. "Market power" refers to a firm's ability to influence the terms of trade—such as prices, but also quality and production standards—in a given market.

Today's food monopolies have consolidated their power thanks both to changes in national and international laws and regulations and to the policies of international institutions like the World Trade Organization (WTO), World Bank, and International Monetary Fund (IMF), among others. Of course, the capital- and technology-intensive nature of food processing, distribution, and retail these days— a key part of the process of food industrialization—also results in high barriers to entry in these markets. These barriers reduce competition for companies in the food industry.

The global food system is riddled with monopolistic markets, markets in which, on one side, stand only one or a few multinational corporate juggernauts, while on the other side there are many people jockeying for position. Inequalities in market power are magnified by geographical inequalities (e.g., between the global North and the global South), gender inequalities, racial inequalities, and inequalities in standards of living.

The U.S. Poultry Economy

The U.S. poultry chain, depicted opposite, is a good example. In the United States, three companies—Tyson, Perdue, and Pilgrim's Pride—control more than 50% of the market in broiler chickens. These large, industrial poultry companies are called "integrators," a reference to the "vertically integrated" poultry chain where big companies own and control almost every stage of the poultry production process. One recent commentator notes: "In fundamental ways, the meat business has returned to the state where it was 100 years ago, a time when just four companies controlled the market with a shared monopoly."

Poultry producers working in Arkansas, Mississippi, Georgia, or Kentucky compete with one another like dogs for scraps from the integrator's table, and thus end up with low incomes, low standards of living, and large debts. Poultry producers are largely "contract growers," meaning that they produce at the behest of the integrators and must accept whatever price the integrators offer for their chickens. In fact, the chickens themselves are actually owned by the integrator, with the "integrated out growers" (poultry producers) owning only the expensive chicken houses that chicks are raised in. The chicken houses are often purchased from the integrators on credit, burdening producers with large debts. Poultry producers also risk injury on the job, income losses associated with dead birds, antibiotic resistance and allergy (stemming from their regular contact with the antibiotics used to treat sick birds), among other serious risks. While the most risky and costly stage of the process—growing out the birds—is left to poultry producers, the integrators enjoy absolute control, massive profits and minimal competition in virtually every other stage of production. The integrators even operate under a "gentlemen's agreement" of sorts, with each integrator agreeing not to employ the growers contracted by the others, limiting competition among integrators and constraining poultry producers even further.

This trading relationship—between monopolistic integrators on the one hand and poultry producers facing high competition, serious risk, and large production costs on the other—is a stark example of unequal exchange and has concrete implications for the well-being of producers.

In an interview with the *American Prospect* magazine, Mike Weaver, who heads up a West Virginia poultry producer association, describes the tenuous financial position of producers in the United States. Weaver notes that "chicken farmers in his area are settling for almost an entire cent less per pound of meat *than they did in 1975*—when the median household income [in the United States] was around

---

Held Up: The Life of a Poultry Farmer

By Craig Watts

In December 1991, I signed a contract to raise chickens for one to the country's largest integrators. I was three years out of business school, where I had been introduced to the term "economic holdup." Little did I know that when I signed that contract I would begin to live this concept each and every day.

The term refers to a situation where two parties (in my case a farmer and an integrator) may be able to work most efficiently by cooperating, but refrain from doing so due to concerns that they may give the other party increased bargaining power, and thereby reduce their own profits. In my contract with my integrator, I have no bargaining power.

To get started, I borrowed approximately $200,000 to construct two poultry houses, following the specifications required by the integrator. Initially, all went well and in 1994 I borrowed another $200,000 to build two more houses. At that time, I was also forced to borrow an additional $40,000 to bring my older houses up to the specs of the new houses. The industry term is "upgrades." Upgrades can be additional equipment and/or changes to the structures themselves, as required by the integrator.

In the initial recruitment pitch, the integrator presented a rosy picture: that the poultry houses would provide a steady and primary income. They said I'd have the chicken houses paid off in ten years. None of these claims have proven to be true. I see it time and again: farmers are constantly forced to upgrade their facilities, with no rhyme or reason or any cost-benefit documentation, just more and more debt.

The snag is that if you don't upgrade, the company will terminate your contract. The holdup problem rears its head. Debt eliminates any bargaining power for the farmer. When the first upgrades were pushed on my operation, I was $400,000 in debt with one choice: lose my contract or make the upgrades and take on more debt.

In the fall of 2004, I actually paid my farm off. I had no mortgage payment for two years. But relief was short-lived: in 2006, the company began a major push for upgrades. Rumor was they were giving their service techs bonuses based on how much a farmer spent for upgrades. I had to borrow another $100,000.

Twenty-two years after I began as a contract poultry producer, my income is less than it was 15 years ago. Adjust that for inflation and you quickly realize if your poultry operation is treading water, then you're one of the lucky ones. Meanwhile, consumers are paying more at the grocery store and the industry is enjoying windfall profits.

$11,800. ... The number of companies buying livestock from farmers has declined, and the surviving companies have grown bigger by acquiring the smaller firms. For growers, that often means doing business with only one firm. ..."

The inequalities and injustices apparent in the poultry chain are replicated within the corporate hierarchy of integrators like Tyson: there is a dangerous division of labor between those who must compete to survive and those who do not need to do so. Highly paid executives, who are engaged in management work and are secure in their positions, lord over low-paid, interchangeable employees who work with their hands capturing chickens one-by-one at night in the chicken houses or performing dangerous work in slaughterhouses. Most of these managers are white men, while many of the workers that actually capture and slaughter the chickens are people of color, often with insecure immigration status. The Food Empowerment Project notes that workers in meat processing are mostly people of color from low-income communities. Historically populated by African Americans, this workforce has recently witnessed an influx of Latin American workers, with some 38% of workers in meat processing today hailing from outside of the United States.

The Global Coffee Economy

The power dynamics, inequalities and unequal exchanges apparent in the U.S. poultry chain are replicated in a variety of global food production systems. Take, for example, the diagram below of the global coffee economy, a chain connecting different parts of the global division of coffee labor to one another, taking us downstream from the green coffees harvested in the field by farmers, through various traders and processors, to the cups of roasted coffee consumed by final consumers.

The diagram illustrates how the global coffee economy operates and the severe inequalities that characterize it. International traders and roasters operate in a very uncompetitive market setting—they are monopolists. The six largest coffee trading

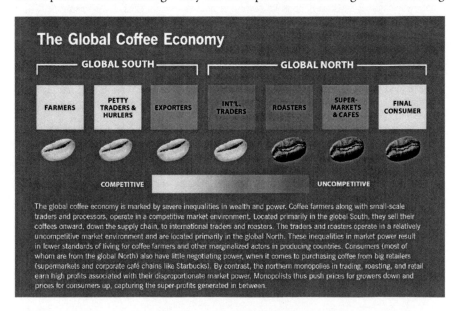

The Global Coffee Economy

GLOBAL SOUTH — GLOBAL NORTH

| FARMERS | PETTY TRADERS & HURLERS | EXPORTERS | INT'L. TRADERS | ROASTERS | SUPER-MARKETS & CAFES | FINAL CONSUMER |

COMPETITIVE — UNCOMPETITIVE

The global coffee economy is marked by severe inequalities in wealth and power. Coffee farmers along with small-scale traders and processors, operate in a competitive market environment. Located primarily in the global South, they sell their coffees onward, down the supply chain, to international traders and roasters. The traders and roasters operate in a relatively uncompetitive market environment and are located primarily in the global North. These inequalities in market power result in lower standards of living for coffee farmers and other marginalized actors in producing countries. Consumers (most of whom are from the global North) also have little negotiating power, when it comes to purchasing coffee from big retailers (supermarkets and corporate café chains like Starbucks). By contrast, the northern monopolies in trading, roasting, and retail earn high profits associated with their disproportionate market power. Monopolists thus push prices for growers down and prices for consumers up, capturing the super-profits generated in between.

DISTRIBUTION OF INCOME IN THE GLOBAL COFFEE ECONOMY (% OF INCOME)

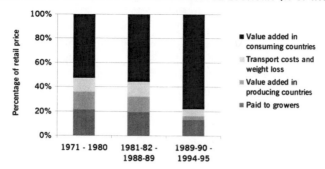

Source: John M. Talbot, "Where Does Your Coffee Dollar Go? The Division of Income and Surplus along the Coffee Commodity Chain," Studies in Comparative International Development, Vol. 32, No. 1 (1997), Tables 1 and 2.

Note: Data for 1971–1980 are for calendar years. Data for 1981–82 to 1988–89 and for 1989–90 to 1994–95 are for "coffee years" (Oct. 1–Sept. 30). Percentages of total retail price (reported by Talbot (1997)) for calendar years (1971–1980) or coffee years (1981–82 to 1988–89 and 1989–90 to 1994–95) were used to calculate means for intervals shown. Figures calculated did not add exactly to 100.0% due to rounding (in all cases between 99.9% and 100%). Bar graphs show each income category as percentage of sum of four income categories.

companies control over 50% of the marketplace at the trading step along the coffee chain (Neumann Kaffee Gruppe from Germany and ED&F Man based in London are the largest international traders). The roasting stage of coffee production is even more concentrated, with only two companies (Nestle and Phillip Morris) controlling almost 50% of the market. Market power gives these modern-day robber barons influence over prices and other terms of trade, allowing them to place downward pressure on prices they pay to farmers, and upward pressure on the prices they charge to consumers.

This inequality in market power introduces inequalities in incomes and standards of living between different actors in the coffee economy. Unsurprisingly, farmers operating in the shadow of the big traders and roasters have relatively low incomes and standards of living. By contrast, owners, managers, and some workers at the big coffee monopolies enjoy relatively high incomes and standards of living. There are also race and gender dimensions to consider: coffee farmers are disproportionately women of color, while owners and managers in the big coffee monopolies are generally white men. There is also a strong North-South dimension to this power inequality—coffee farmers from Latin America, Africa, and Asia compete fiercely with one another, their incomes undermined by the pricing power of monopolies headquartered in Europe and the United States.

Twenty-five million coffee farming families from Latin America, sub-Saharan Africa, South Asia, and Southeast Asia compete globally with one another to sell coffee to a handful of international coffee trading companies. Similar to the situation of poultry producers, there are in practice usually only one or two potential buyers for a farmer's coffee crop. Lacking the transport and information resources to effectively market their crops, many coffee farmers sell to whoever comes to the farm gate. Unsurprisingly, things do not usually go well for our coffee farmers.

The graph illustrates the distribution of income in the global coffee economy. Only a small percentage of total income is retained by those—growers, small-scale traders who transport coffee from the farm gate, and petty processors who transform dried coffee cherries into green beans in producing countries—who operate in competitive markets. Most of the income is appropriated in consuming countries, mainly by the coffee monopolists in trading and roasting, but also by large retailers (e.g., supermarkets and corporate café chains like Starbucks). The position of coffee growers deteriorated between the 1970s and 1990s. Expanded global trade in coffee since the late 1980s, with "free trade" increasing the market leverage of multinational traders and roasters over coffee farmers and final consumers, has led to decreasing relative income of growers.

Promoting Justice and Equity in the Global Food System

As the coffee and chicken examples suggest, unequal exchange is commonplace between farmers and producers on the one hand, and multinational, monopolistic middlemen (food traders, processors, and supermarkets) on the other. While larger corporate coffee farms may have some leverage in negotiating prices with these big middlemen, smaller and peasant farms have virtually no negotiating power. If a coffee farmer does not want to sell to the Neumann Kaffee Gruppe (NKG) at the price NKG offers, then NKG will simply move on until it finds a farmer who will. Similarly, if a poultry producer does not want to sell to Tyson at the company's offered price, the producer risks being cut out of the chain all together. Tyson will just move on to the next farm. In both cases, the market power of the monopolists also allows them to set conditions such as product quality and the specific technologies used in the production process. The same basic relationship holds for cattle ranchers and cocoa farmers selling to Cargill, pork producers selling to Smithfield (now owned by the China-headquartered WH Group), soy farmers selling to Archer Daniels Midland, vegetable producers selling to Walmart and Tesco, and orange producers selling to Coca-Cola Co. (to make Fanta Orange and Minute Maid juices), among many other global examples.

The Farmer and the Supplier

Unequal exchange is also common for farmers looking to purchase supplies for their businesses. In conventional farming systems, farmers and livestock growers regularly purchase seeds, young animals, feed, pesticides, or fertilizers from large multinational corporations like Tyson, Monsanto, and Cargill. In this unequal exchange, multinational giants charge farmers small fortunes for the supplies they need.

The farmers receive overpriced goods that often fail to work as advertised. In the case of expensive genetically modified seeds, farmers often end up with lower-than-promised yields and rising costs for fertilizers, pesticides, and water. Fertilizers and pesticides, for their part, erode the long-term health of the soil and increase irrigation requirements. Worse still, as farmers rack up these huge input costs, the prices that international traders offer them for their crop often fails to cover the rising costs of production. Farmers are thus "squeezed" between two monopolies, with unequal exchange ensuring that farmers pay too much for their inputs and receive too little for their crop. This trading mechanism thus works to rob especially small and peasant farmers of wealth and redistributes it to the monopolies.

The outcome for farmers is bleak and frequently results in rising debt. In India, the debts that result from this financial squeeze have led more than 200,000 peasant farmers to commit suicide, according to author Vandana Shiva. Agricultural laborers in rural areas also often suffer in this context, as temporary workers are laid off by small farmers experiencing hardship.

Unequal exchange helps to explain inequalities in wealth and power in the global food system, and how trade relationships work to facilitate exploitation—the unjust redistribution of wealth from people with less to people with more market power, from poor to rich, from black and brown to white, from women to men, from the global South to the global North. In answer to the question posed at the outset—how is it that the people who produce our food are themselves so often poor and hungry?—I answer simply: Because they engage in unequal exchange with powerful food monopolies, and there is no friendship in this trade.

A variety of policies, programs, and alternatives could help to make the global food system more equitable and fair. These include, but are certainly not limited to, anti-trust enforcement, public commodity price management, and producer unionization. In 1890, the U.S. Congress passed the Sherman Anti-Trust Act, a piece of legislation aimed at breaking up some of the large monopolies that dominated the U.S. economy at the time. Among the targets of the new anti-trust enforcers were the big meatpackers. The Supreme Court's 1905 decision in *Swift & Co. v. United States* found the Chicago "meat trust" to be engaging in price-fixing for meat and shipping rates. The case set the stage for more stringent government regulation of monopolies. Since the early 1980s, starting with the Reagan administration, anti-trust enforcement in the U.S. has waned. According to Barry Lynn, the author of *Cornered: The New Monopoly Capitalism and the Economics of Destruction*, this is partly due to increasingly pro-big business ideologies and political interests of public officials, like Reagan. Yet, the Sherman Act remains on the books and could be revived as a tool to break up the new meat trusts in the U.S. food system.

Historically, governments have also intervened in food markets to set and stabilize prices. While the system was not perfect, the International Coffee Agreement that regulated global coffee trading from 1962 to 1989 did indeed help many coffee farmers obtain better prices for their crops. A system of import and export quotas at the international level was complemented by public institutions at the national level that were responsible for purchasing coffee from producers at fixed prices and then exporting the coffee into the global market according to the quota arrangement. While the system was a mechanism for exploiting farmers in some cases (as in Uganda in the 1970s), in other cases (like in Mexico) public commodity price management helped farmers earn more money and stabilize their incomes. With the eruption of the global food crisis in 2006–7, global interest in such institutions has been revived, perhaps creating a political opening for new public price management programs.

As with most economic cases in which individuals are overpowered by large companies—be they integrators, coffee roasters, or employers—organization and unionization can help them increase their market leverage and bargaining power. In Colombia, some three quarters of the country's coffee farmers are organized under the umbrella of a single union. The union advocates for farmers in various political forums, and negotiates coffee prices with exporters and traders, often securing higher prices for farmers than they could obtain on their own. Support for such organizations, as well as related farmer cooperatives and producer associations, could help to empower and organize producers.

Such policies and programs are not mutually exclusive. Further, anti-trust enforcement, public price management, and producer unionization could be complemented by a wide variety of other mechanisms for promoting justice and equity in the global food system. For example, programs that support national and local food self-sufficiency, crop and income diversification, and organic farming techniques can potentially reduce producer reliance on global monopolists for income, financing and production inputs, among many other benefits. ❏

Sources: Oscar Farfan, "Understanding and Escaping Commodity Dependency: A Global Value Chain Perspective," World Bank, 2005; Food Empowerment Project, "Slaughterhouse Workers," Food Empowerment Project, 2015 (foodispower.org); Michael Kazin, "Ruthless in Manhattan," *New York Times*, May 7, 2009; Christopher Leonard, "How the Meat Industry Keeps Chicken Prices High," March 3, 2014 (slate.com); Barry Lynn, "Killing the Competition: How the New Monopolies are Destroying Open Markets," *Harper's Magazine*, February 2012; National Chicken Council, "Vertical Integration," 2015 (nationalchickencouncil.org); Stefano Ponte, "The Latte Revolution," *World Development*, 2002; Monica Potts, "The Serfs of Arkansas," *The American Prospect*, March 5, 2011; Vandana Shiva, "From Seeds of Suicide to Seeds of Hope," Huffington Post, May 29, 2009; Howard Zinn, *A People's History of the United States* (Harper, 2005).

Article 5.6

THE FALSE LIBERTARIANISM OF THE SILICON VALLEY BILLIONAIRES

BY DEAN BAKER

January 2014; The Guardian

Last week Mark Ames published an article that should forever destroy any connection between the Silicon Valley tech billionaires and libertarian worldviews. The article reports on a court case that alleges that Apple, Google, and other Silicon Valley powerhouses actively conspired to keep their workers' wages down. According to documents filed in the case, these companies agreed not to compete for each others' workers dating at least as far back as 2005. Workers in the industry have filed a class action suit that could lead to the payment of billions of dollars in lost wages.

This case is striking at many levels, the most obvious being the effective theft of large amounts of money by some of the richest people on the planet from their employees. This is pernicious, but not altogether surprising. After all, the boss stealing from the workers is as dog bites man as it gets. Few would be surprised that rich people were willing to break the law to get even richer.

The real news here is how the Silicon Valley barons allegedly broke the law. The charge is that they actively colluded to stifle market forces. They collectively acted to prevent their workers from receiving the market-clearing wage. This means not only that they broke the law, and that they acted to undermine the market, but that they really don't think about the market the way libertarians claim to think about the market.

The classic libertarian view of the market is that we have a huge number of people in the market actively competing to buy and sell goods and services. They acknowledge the obvious—some actors are much bigger than others—but there is so much competition that no individual or company can really hope to have much impact on market outcomes.

This point is central to their argument that the government should not interfere with corporate practices. For example, if we think our local cable company is charging too much for cable access, our libertarian friends will insist that the phone company, satellite television, or other competitors will step in to keep prices in line. They would tell the same story if the issue were regulating the airlines, banks, health insurance, or any other sector where there is reason to believe that competition might be limited.

They would tell the same story on the labor side. If we are concerned that workers are getting low wages then the answer is to improve their skills through education and training rather than raise the minimum wage. If workers were worth more than the minimum wage, then the market would already be paying them more than the minimum wage.

They have the same story when it comes to requiring family leave, sick days, or other benefits. Libertarians would say that if workers value these benefits they would negotiate for them and be willing to trade off wages. There is no reason for the government to get involved.

This story about the wonders of the free market is simple in its appeal and it has the great implication that nothing should be done to keep the rich from getting ever richer. However, the Silicon Valley non-compete agreements show that this is not how the tech billionaires believe the market really works. This is just a story they peddle to children and gullible reporters.

If they really believed the market had a deep sea of competitors in which no individual actor could count for much, then their non-compete agreements would serve no purpose. If Google, Apple, Intel, and the other biggies agreed not to hire each others' workers, it really wouldn't affect their pay since there would always be new upstarts ready to jump in and hire away underpaid engineers.

The fact the Silicon Valley honchos took the time to negotiate and presumably enforce these non-compete agreements was because they did not think that there were enough competitors to hire away their workers. They believed that they had enough weight on the buy-side of the market for software engineers that if they agreed to not to compete for workers, they could keep their wages down.

It shouldn't be surprising that the Silicon Valley billionaires really are not libertarians. After all, much of their fortunes rest on patents and copyrights, both of which are government granted monopolies: the opposite of a free market.

But for some reason, seeing the tech whiz-kids forming a cartel to keep down their workers' wages seems an even more direct violation of any belief in libertarian principles. This is the same sort of cartel behavior that we associate with the cigar-chomping robber barons of the late 19th century. It turns out that the biggest difference between the tech billionaires of the Internet Age and the high rollers of the railroad age is the cigars. ❑

Chapter 6

MARKET FAILURE II: EXTERNALITIES

INTRODUCTION

Markets sometimes fail. Mainstream economists typically focus on cases in which existing markets fail to facilitate exchanges that would make both parties better off. When a factory pollutes the air, people downwind suffer a cost. They might be willing to pay the polluter to curb emissions, but there is no market for clean air. In cases like this, one solution is for the government to step in with regulations that ban industries from imposing pollution costs on others. The same goes when private markets do not provide sufficient amounts of public goods, such as vaccines, from which everyone benefits whether they contribute to paying for them or not. Again, government must step in. But what percentage of pollution should industries be required to eliminate? How much should be spent on public health? To decide how much government should step in, economists propose cost-benefit analysis, suggesting that the government weigh costs against benefits, in much the same way a firm decides how many cars to produce.

Orthodox economists typically see market failures as fairly limited in scope. In fact, they deny that many negative consequences of markets are market failures at all. When workers are paid wages too low to meet their basic needs, economists do not usually call their poverty and overwork market failures, but "incentives" to get a higher-paying job. When economists do recognize market failures, most argue that they are best solved by markets themselves. So pollution, for example, should be reduced by allowing firms to trade for the right to pollute. Finally, orthodox economists worry about government failure—the possibility that government responses to market failures may cause more problems than they solve. They conclude that the "invisible hand" of the market works pretty well, and that the alternatives, especially the "visible hand" of the state, will only make matters worse.

In "Pricing the Priceless: Inside the Strange World of Cost-Benefit Analysis" (Article 8.1), Lisa Heinzerling and Frank Ackerman point out key flaws in the use of cost-benefit analysis to guide government action. While weighing the costs of a course of action (like pollution limits) against the benefits has a superficial plausibility, cost-benefit analysis fails to clarify the nature of public choices. It fails, for example, to account for all relevant costs or benefits, it downgrades the importance of the future, and it does not deal with the problem of how costs and benefits are distributed.

The most common complaint from industry and their legions of lobbyists is that there is a rigid trade-off between environmental protection and employment. In "The Phantom Menace: Environmental Regulations are Not 'Job Killers'" (Article 6.2), Heidi Garrett-Peltier shows this is a false dichotomy. Enforcing environmental rules and "going green" not only might not cost net jobs, but in fact might create significant new employment, especially in weaning ourselves off hydrocarbon fuels.

While environmental protection is a net job creator, Jeremy Brecher notes, it would still cause some job losses in fossil-fuel producing and using industries (Article 6.3). Any policy response to the environmental challenges of our time—especially climate change—must therefore mitigate any negative impact on workers. Protecting workers from the fallout is not only the right thing to do, he argues, but also the only way to head off divisive "jobs vs. the environment" rhetoric.

In his article "Frackonomics: The Science and Economics of the Gas Boom" (Article 6.4), economist Rob Larson looks at the environmental impacts of this controversial new form of natural-gas extraction. He finds harms including everything from toxic pollution to increased seismic instability. Moreover, he argues, these problems are not well dealt with by neoclassical economics' usual prescription of strengthened private-property rights.

James K. Boyce's "Climate Policy as Wealth Creation" (Article 6.5) notes that the atmosphere is currently treated as a free dumping ground for carbon pollution. The richest dump the most, and the fossil-fuel companies profit in the bargain. The vision Boyce proposes is clear and profound—the atmosphere belongs to us all "in equal and common measure," and the key to addressing the climate crisis is the development of a system of public property rights over it.

Finally, in their article "Mapping Environmental Injustice" (Article 6.6), authors Klara Zwickl, Michael Ash, and James K. Boyce remind us that issues of race, class, and the distribution of power in society are never far off, including on environmental issues. They describe how the impacts of toxic air pollution fall along the contours of the American social hierarchy. Poor people tend to have higher exposure than rich people, and people of color tend to have higher exposure than whites.

Discussion Questions

1. (Article 6.1) Heinzerling and Frank Ackerman point out a number of flaws in cost-benefit analysis. These weaknesses suggest that the cost-benefit approach will work better in some situations, worse in others. Describe when you would expect it to work better or worse, and explain.

2. (Article 6.1) Make a list of types of goods that are harder to put a price on (valuate) than others. Why is it so hard to price these types of goods?

3. (Article 6.2) What are the main harms, in Larson's view, from gas extraction by hydraulic fracturing ("fracking")? What are some possible solutions? Why does

Larson doubt the viability of solutions based purely on private property and private legal action?

4. (Article 6.3) Do environmental regulations "kill jobs"? Is the choice between jobs and environmental regulations a false dichotomy? If so, why? Why is the concept "net jobs" important here?

5. (Article 6.4) If the net employment effects of environmental regulation are positive, why does Brecher think it's so important to have a "superfund for workers"?

6. (Article 6.5) Some commentators argue that environmental regulations, such as a carbon tax or other carbon price, would reduce economic growth—and so be a form of wealth destruction. Boyce argues, on the contrary, that climate policy can be a form of "wealth creation." What does he mean by this? Do you agree?

7. (Article 6.6) Two possible explanations for disparities in environmental conditions along lines or income or race are "selection" and "move-in." "Selection" means that polluting industries make decisions to locate in predominantly low-income or non-white areas. "Move-in" means that people with less resources are more likely to move into areas where environmental quality is lower. What do you think of these two explanations? Would your views of "environmental injustice" differ depending on which factor is more important?

Article 6.1

PRICING THE PRICELESS
Inside the Strange World of Cost-Benefit Analysis

BY LISA HEINZERLING AND FRANK ACKERMAN
March/April 2003

How strictly should we regulate arsenic in drinking water? Or carbon dioxide in the atmosphere? Or pesticides in our food? Or oil drilling in scenic places? The list of environmental harms and potential regulatory remedies often appears to be endless. In evaluating a proposed new initiative, how do we know if it is worth doing or not? Is there an objective way to decide how to proceed? Cost-benefit analysis promises to provide the solution—to add up the benefits of a public policy and compare them to the costs.

The costs of protecting health and the environment through pollution control devices and other approaches are, by their very nature, measured in dollars. The other side of the balance—calculating the benefits of life, health, and nature in dollars and cents—is far more problematic. Since there are no natural prices for a healthy environment, cost-benefit analysis creates artificial ones. Researchers, for example, may ask a cross-section of the affected population how much they would pay to preserve or protect something that can't be bought in a store. The average American household is supposedly willing to pay $257 to prevent the extinction of bald eagles, $208 to protect humpback whales, and $80 to protect gray wolves.

Costs and benefits of a policy, however, frequently fall at different times. When the analysis spans a number of years, future costs and benefits are *discounted,* or treated as equivalent to smaller amounts of money in today's dollars. The case for discounting begins with the observation that money received today is worth a little more than money received in the future. (For example, if the interest rate is 3%, you only need to deposit about $97 today to get $100 next year. Economists would say that, at a *3% discount rate,* $100 next year has a *present value* of $97.) For longer periods of time, or higher discount rates, the effect is magnified. The important issue for environmental policy is whether this logic also applies to outcomes far in the future, and to opportunities—like long life and good health—that are not naturally stated in dollar terms.

Why Cost-Benefit Analysis Doesn't Work

The case for cost-benefit analysis of environmental protection is, at best, wildly optimistic and, at worst, demonstrably wrong. The method simply does not offer the policy-making panacea its adherents promise. In practice, cost-benefit analysis frequently produces false and misleading results. Moreover, there is no quick fix, because these failures are intrinsic to the methodology, appearing whenever it is applied to any complex environmental problem.

It puts dollar figures on values that are not commodities, and have no price.
Artificial prices have been estimated for many benefits of environmental regulation. Preventing retardation due to childhood lead poisoning comes in at about $9,000 per lost IQ point. Saving a life is ostensibly worth $6.3 million. But what can it mean to say that one life is worth $6.3 million? You cannot buy the right to kill someone for $6.3 million, nor for any other price. If analysts calculated the value of life itself by asking people what it is worth to them (the most common method of valuation of other environmental benefits), the answer would be infinite. The standard response is that a value like $6.3 million is not actually a price on an individual's life or death. Rather, it is a way of expressing the value of small risks of death. If people are willing to pay $6.30 to avoid a one in a million increase in the risk of death, then the "value of a statistical life" is $6.3 million.

It ignores the collective choice presented to society by most public health and environmental problems.
Under the cost-benefit approach, valuation of environmental benefits is based on individuals' private decisions as consumers or workers, not on their public values as citizens. However, policies that protect the environment are often public goods, and are not available for purchase in individual portions. In a classic example of this distinction, the philosopher Mark Sagoff found that his students, in their role as citizens, opposed commercial ski development in a nearby wilderness area, but, in their role as consumers, would plan to go skiing there if the development was built. There is no contradiction between these two views: as individual consumers, the students would have no way to express their collective preference for wilderness preservation. Their individual willingness to pay for skiing would send a misleading signal about their views as citizens.

It is often impossible to arrive at a meaningful social valuation by adding up the willingness to pay expressed by individuals. What could it mean to ask how much you personally are willing to pay to clean up a major oil spill? If no one else contributes, the clean-up won't happen regardless of your decision. As the Nobel Prize-winning economist Amartya Sen has pointed out, if your willingness to pay for a large-scale public initiative is independent of what others are paying, then you probably have not understood the nature of the problem.

It systematically downgrades the importance of the future.
One of the great triumphs of environmental law is that it seeks to avert harms to people and to natural resources in the future, and not only within this generation, but in future generations as well. Indeed, one of the primary objectives of the National Environmental Policy Act, which has been called our basic charter of environmental protection, is to nudge the nation into "fulfill[ing] the responsibilities of each generation as trustee of the environment for succeeding generations."

The time periods involved in protecting the environment are often enormous—even many centuries, in such cases as climate change, radioactive waste, etc. With time spans this long, any discounting will make even global catastrophes seem trivial. At a discount rate of 5%, for example, the deaths of a billion people 500 years from now become less serious than the death of one person today. Seen in this way, discounting looks like a fancy justification for foisting our problems off onto the people who come after us.

It ignores considerations of distribution and fairness.
Cost-benefit analysis adds up all the costs of a policy, adds up all the benefits, and compares the totals. Implicit in this innocuous-sounding procedure is the assumption that it doesn't matter who gets the benefits and who pays the costs. Yet isn't there an important difference between spending state tax revenues, say, to improve the parks in rich communities, and spending the same revenues to clean up pollution in poor communities?

The problem of equity runs even deeper. Benefits are typically measured by willingness to pay for environmental improvement, and the rich are able and willing to pay for more than the poor. Imagine a cost-benefit analysis of locating an undesirable facility, such as a landfill or incinerator. Wealthy communities are willing to pay more for the benefit of not having the facility in their backyards; thus, under the logic of cost-benefit analysis, the net benefits to society will be maximized by putting the facility in a low-income area. In reality, pollution is typically dumped on the poor without waiting for formal analysis. Still, cost-benefit analysis rationalizes and reinforces the problem, allowing environmental burdens to flow downhill along the income slopes of an unequal society.

Conclusion

There is nothing objective about the basic premises of cost-benefit analysis. Treating individuals solely as consumers, rather than as citizens with a sense of moral responsibility, represents a distinct and highly questionable worldview. Likewise, discounting reflects judgments about the nature of environmental risks and citizens' responsibilities toward future generations.

These assumptions beg fundamental questions about ethics and equity, and one cannot decide whether to embrace them without thinking through the whole range of moral issues they raise. Yet once one has thought through these issues, there is no need then to collapse the complex moral inquiry into a series of numbers. Pricing the priceless just translates our inquiry into a different language, one with a painfully impoverished vocabulary. ❑

This article is a condensed version of the report Pricing the Priceless, *published by the Georgetown Environmental Law and Policy Institute at Georgetown University Law Center. The full report is available on-line at www. ase.tufts.edu/gdae. See also Ackerman and Heinzerling's book on these and related issues,* Priceless: Human Health, the Environment, and the Limits of the Market, *The New Press, January 2004.*

Article 6.2

THE PHANTOM MENACE
Environmental regulations are not "job-killers."

BY HEIDI GARRETT-PELTIER
July/August 2011

Polluting industries, along with the legislators who are in their pockets, consistently claim that environmental regulation will be a "job killer." They counter efforts to control pollution and to protect the environment by claiming that any such measures would increase costs and destroy jobs. But these are empty threats. In fact, the bulk of the evidence shows that environmental regulations do not hinder economic growth or employment and may actually stimulate both.

One recent example of this, the Northeast Regional Greenhouse Gas Initiative (RGGI), is an emissions-allowance program that caps and reduces emissions in ten northeast and mid-Atlantic states. Under RGGI, allowances are auctioned to power companies and the majority of the revenues are used to offset increases in consumer energy bills and to invest in energy efficiency and renewable energy. A report released in February 2011 shows that RGGI has created an economic return of $3 to $4 for every $1 invested, and has created jobs throughout the region. Yet this successful program has come under attack by right-wing ideologues, including the Koch brothers-funded "Americans for Prosperity"; as a result, the state of New Hampshire recently pulled out of the program.

The allegation that environmental regulation is a job-killer is based on a mischaracterization of costs, both by firms and by economists. Firms often frame spending on environmental controls or energy-efficient machinery as a pure cost—wasted spending that reduces profitability. But such expenses should instead be seen as investments that enhance productivity and in turn promote economic development. Not only can these investments lead to lower costs for energy use and waste disposal, they may also direct innovations in the production process itself that could increase the firm's long-run profits. This is the Porter Hypothesis, named after Harvard Business School professor Michael Porter. According to studies conducted by Porter, properly and flexibly designed environmental regulation can trigger innovation that partly or completely offsets the costs of complying with the regulation.

The positive aspects of environmental regulation are overlooked not only by firms, but also by economists who model the costs of compliance without including its widespread benefits. These include reduced mortality, fewer sick days for workers and school children, reduced health-care costs, increased biodiversity, and mitigation of climate change. But most mainstream models leave these benefits out of their calculations. The Environmental Protection Agency, which recently released a study of the impacts of the Clean Air Act from 1990 to 2020, compared the effects of a "cost-only" model with those of a more complete model. In the version which only incorporated the costs of compliance, both GDP and overall economic welfare were expected to decline by 2020 due to Clean Air Act regulations. However, once the costs of compliance were coupled with the benefits, the model showed that both GDP and economic welfare would increase over time, and that by 2020 the economic benefits would outweigh the costs. Likewise, the Office of Management and Budget found that to date the benefits of the law have far exceeded the cost, with an economic return of between $4 and $8 for every $1 invested in compliance.

Environmental regulations do affect jobs. But contrary to claims by polluting industries and congressional Republicans, efforts to protect our environment can actually create jobs. In order to reduce harmful pollution from power plants, for example, an electric company would have to equip plants with scrubbers and other technologies. These technologies would need to be manufactured and installed, creating jobs for people in the manufacturing and construction industries.

The official unemployment rate in the United States is still quite high, hovering around 9%. In this economic climate, politicians are more sensitive than ever to claims that environmental regulation could be a job-killer. By framing investments as wasted costs and relying on incomplete economic models, polluting industries have consistently tried to fight environmental standards. It's time to change the terms of the debate. We need to move beyond fear-mongering about the costs and start capturing the benefits. ❏

Article 6.3

A SUPERFUND FOR WORKERS
How to Promote a Just Transition and Break Out of the
Jobs vs. Environment Trap

BY JEREMY BRECHER
November/December 2015

When the Dominion Corporation proposed, on April 1, 2013, to build a lique-fied natural gas export facility at Cove Point, Md., right on the Chesapeake Bay, seven hundred people demonstrated against it and many were arrested in a series of civil disobedience actions. But an open letter endorsing the project main-tained it would "create more than 3,000 construction jobs" most of which would go "to local union members." The letter—on Dominion letterhead—was signed not only by business leaders, but also by twenty local and national trade union leaders.

Similarly, in the struggle over the Keystone XL pipeline, pipeline propo-nents were quick to seize on the "jobs issue" and tout support from building trades unions and eventually the AFL-CIO. In a press release titled "U.S. Chamber Calls Politically-Charged Decision to Deny Keystone a Job Killer," the Chamber said President Obama's denial of the Keystone permit was "sacrificing tens of thousands of good-paying American jobs in the short term, and many more than that in the long term."

The media repeat the jobs vs. environment frame again and again: an NPR headline on Keystone was typical of many: "Pipeline Decision Pits Jobs Against Environment." A similar dynamic has marked the "beyond coal" campaign, the fracking battle, and the struggle for EPA regulation of greenhouse gases under the Clean Air Act.

Is there a persuasive answer to the charge that climate protection policies are job-killers? A common environmentalist response has been that environmental protection produces far more jobs than it eliminates. EPA Administrator Lisa P. Jackson explained, "environmental protection creates jobs—1.7 million of them as of 2008." It is true that, on balance, environmental policies usually create jobs (see box, "Jobs: Clean Energy vs. Fossil Fuels," next page); unfortunately, this is of little comfort to the small number of workers in fossil-fuel producing and using industries who are likely to lose their jobs as a result of climate protection policies, including coal miners, power-plant workers, and oil refinery workers. And such workers can rapidly become Fox News poster children for the threat posed to workers by climate protection.

Fortunately, a strategy has been emerging to protect workers and communities whose livelihoods may be threatened by climate protection policies. Protecting those who lose their jobs due to necessary environmental policies has often been referred to as a "just transition," a phrase popularized by labor and environmental leader Tony Mazzocchi of the Oil, Chemical, and Atomic Workers union (now merged with the Steelworkers) in the 1990s. (More recently, the term "just transition" is often being used in a broader way to include not only justice for workers and communities adversely affected by environmental policies, but the inclusion in broader social justice objectives within environmental policies.)

To provide a just transition for workers harmed by environmental policies, Mazzocchi proposed the idea of a "Superfund for workers." The fund would provide financial support and opportunities for higher education for workers displaced by environmental protection policies. As Mazzocchi put it in 1993, "There is a Superfund for dirt. There ought to be one for workers." He argued that "Paying people to make the transition from one kind of economy—from one kind of job—to another is not welfare. Those who work with toxic materials on a daily basis ... in order to provide the world with the energy and the materials it needs deserve a helping hand to make a new start in life."

It is a basic principle of fairness that the burden of policies that are necessary for society—like protecting the environment—shouldn't be borne by a small minority, who through no fault of their own happen to be victimized by their side effects. It would be unfair for workers, who happen to work in jobs that need to be eliminated in order to achieve some social good, to bear the burden of that change by being left om their own without a job. Just transition policies mean workers will not just be thrown on the trash heap.

Transition Assistance

The principle that workers should be compensated for the effects of public policies that affect them adversely was recognized in the Trade Act of 1974 and subsequent programs for "trade adjustment assistance," which provides compensatory benefits

---

Jobs: Clean Energy vs. Fossil Fuels

Numerous studies have found that renewable energy and conservation produce substantially more jobs than fossil fuels, although the precise numbers vary somewhat from study to study and each local situation is unique. Renewable energy and energy efficiency tend to be labor-intensive and local. They contribute to job growth in manufacturing, construction, operation, and maintenance. In addition, dollars saved through energy efficiency tend to be spent and re-spent locally, creating further jobs.

A 2014 study by the Political Economy Research Institute (PERI) at the University of Massachusetts-Amherst examined the number of jobs created by spending the same amount on different forms of energy. It found that fuels like coal and natural gas are the least job-intensive energy solutions. A dollar invested in energy efficiency and alternative energy creates more than twice as many jobs as the same amount invested in coal or gas. Energy efficiency and alternative energy also produce little or no environmental pollution or climate-changing greenhouse gases.

Natural gas produces less pollution than coal. Their relative effect on climate is still under debate. Coal is slightly more job-intensive than natural gas.

There are many kinds of biofuels. Some, like corn-based ethanol, cause serious environmental damage, do little to reduce greenhouse gases, and raise food prices by diverting crops from food production. Others, such as new algae-based fuels, offer promising alternatives.

The relative cost of different energy sources varies depending on location and the ups and downs of the markets. A 2012 study by the Michigan Public Service Commission found that new renewable energy generation is now cheaper than new coal generation in Michigan. Over time, renewable energy and energy efficiency will almost certainly become progressively cheaper relative to fossil fuels.

to working people who lose their jobs as a result of U.S. trade policies. The eligibility requirements, benefits, and administration of trade adjustment programs, however, have been inadequate to provide displaced workers with a new start in life.

Indeed, transition assistance in the past has often meant little more than an economic hospice for working people and communities threatened by the side effects of globalization, environmental protection, and other public policies. Without a clear program to protect working people from the effects of climate-protection related policies such as plant closures and drilling bans, the struggle for clean energy can all too easily come to be perceived as a struggle against American workers—even though climate protection, in contrast to neoliberal trade legislation, will benefit rather than harm American workers.

A similar but better program can be developed for workers affected by energy-transition policies. Specifically, people who lose their jobs because of transition to a climate-safe economy should be eligible for:

- full wages and benefits for at least three years
- up to four years of education or training, including tuition and living expenses
- decent pensions with healthcare for those ready to retire.

The opportunity for individuals to access higher education and advanced training will also mesh with the need to develop new labor-force capabilities for the emerging green economy.

Such a program would in many ways resemble the "GI Bill of Rights" that provided education and training, loan guarantees for homes, farms, and businesses, and unemployment pay for veterans returning from war. The program was first established in 1944 for returning veterans of World War II and has been revamped repeatedly since. It was critical for the economic boom that followed World War II and for the ability of returning veterans to integrate back into American society. A similar program is needed today for those who are displaced from their jobs through no fault of their own.

Protecting Communities

Job reductions often affect not just individual workers but whole communities, and a just transition needs to address those impacts. Such transitions can emulate the highly successful process that helped local communities adjust to the disruption and job shifting that resulted from the closing of military bases under the 2005 Base Realignment and Closing Commission (BRAC). Those communities were helped by a wide range of federal assistance programs, including planning and economic assistance, environmental cleanup, community development grants, and funding for community services.

Individual workers dislocated by base closings also received extensive support. The Department of Defense (DoD) itself provided advance notification of job cuts, counseling, a hiring preference system with federal agencies to re-employ qualified displaced DoD employees, and financial incentives to encourage early retirement of those eligible.

Workers affected by base closings were also eligible for help under a variety of financial support and retraining programs.

Communities and individuals affected by climate policy transitions could be similarly targeted for assistance from such existing programs as the Department of Labor's (DoL) Rapid Response Services and national emergency grants from the DoL's Employment and Training Administration. The latter provides funding assistance in response to large, unexpected economic events which cause significant job losses, as well as funding from the Departments of Energy and Commerce for economic development of communities and technological modernization for companies.

There has been at least one effort to apply such an approach. Starting in 1992, the Department of Energy (DoE) eliminated 47,700 contractor personnel at thirteen major sites as a result of downsizing the nation's nuclear weapons complex. The DoE conducted a Worker and Community Transition Program that provided grants and other assistance for communities affected by the shutdown of nuclear facilities. The goal was to assist displaced workers and provide economic recovery and diversification assistance to the

---

What Might "Superfund For Workers" Legislation Look Like?

Perhaps surprisingly, some of the best ideas for protecting workers and communities hit by the side effects of public policy decisions were embodied in legislation championed in 1988 by Sen. John McCain (R-Ariz.) to protect working people and farmers from tobacco control policy. McCain's Universal Tobacco Settlement bill, which passed out of committee 19-1 but was defeated on the Senate floor, would have created an industry-funded $28 billion trust fund to help tobacco growers, cigarette factory workers, their families, and their communities adjust to the reduced purchase of American tobacco.

Workers and farmers would have received transition assistance from the fund if "the implementation of the national tobacco settlement contributed importantly to such workers' separation" from their jobs. Several tobacco states subsequently developed their own programs to help with the transition away from tobacco, such as Kentucky's Bill 611, which allocates half of the state's tobacco settlement funds for agricultural diversification.

The McCain tobacco bill also provided transition support not just for individuals, but for hard-hit communities. It would have created a Tobacco Community Revitalization Trust Fund to offer economic development grants over a twenty-five-year period. They would have supported:

- Business development and employment-creating activities "to provide a more viable economic base and enhance opportunities for improved incomes, living standards, and contributions by rural individuals to the economic and social development of their communities."

- Activities that "expand existing infrastructure, facilities, and services to capitalize on opportunities to diversify economies in tobacco communities that support the development of new industries or commercial ventures."

- Initiatives and technical assistance designed to "create or expand locally owned value-added processing and marketing operations in tobacco communities."

- Preference in employment under the program would be given to former tobacco workers and members of tobacco worker communities.

affected communities. The program was budgeted for $200 million in 1994, declining to $25 million in 2001. A nuclear test site in Nevada, for example, was repurposed to demonstrate concentrated solar power technologies.

The Obama administration's new "Power+ plan" incorporated in its fiscal year 2016 budget represents a significant breakthrough in recognizing the need for a "just transition" for workers and communities affected by climate-protecting changes in public policy. It provides more than $55 million for job training, job creation, economic diversification, and other programs for communities that have experienced layoffs due to the declining coal industry. It has been greeted enthusiastically by Appalachian social justice groups like the Mountain Association for Community Economic Development and Kentuckians For the Commonwealth.

While not nearly what is needed, this proposal for the first time puts a just transition for workers in fossil fuel-related industries on the national political agenda. As the EPA institutes its Clean Power Plan to reduce greenhouse gas emissions by reducing fossil-fuel pollution from power plants, states and the Federal government can promote similar provisions for workers and communities adversely affected by the closing of coal-fired power plants.

What Would a Superfund for Workers Cost?

The recent study *Green Growth* by the Political Economy Research Institute at the University of Massachusetts and the Center for American Progress estimated the cost of a "Superfund for workers" based on a climate action plan that would reduce U.S. greenhouse gas (GHG) emissions by 40% over 20 years. The PERI-CAP plan would create 4.2 million new direct, indirect, and induced jobs. Direct jobs include solar installers and engineers designing more energy-efficient equipment. Indirect jobs include steelworkers making the steel for windmill blades. Induced jobs include the food service jobs made possible by clean energy workers' wages. But it would also entail a loss of 1.5 million fossil fuel-related jobs—a 34% contraction in employment in fossil fuels compared to "business as usual" expectations for 2030.

Approximately 212,000 workers are directly employed in oil and gas extraction and 79,000 in coal mining, with about the same number in support activities. (These figures do not include such workers as truck drivers, train crews, and power-plant workers whose jobs are indirect rather than direct parts of the fossil-fuel economy, and who might find work as a result of overall green job growth.) If oil and gas production fell by 20% and coal production fell by 50%, there would be a loss of 100,000 direct jobs. If the downsizing is spread over ten years, an average of 10,000 jobs a year would be lost.

Trade Adjustment Assistance (TAA) provides displaced workers—in addition to whatever they receive from unemployment compensation, health coverage, and other programs—an average of $10,000 over a two-year period. To provide this level of support for laid-off fossil fuel workers would cost $200 million per year. A Superfund designed to provide education, health benefits, income supplements, and job opportunities would clearly require far more, with the exact amount depending on the specific level of benefits. *Green Growth* calculates what the cost would be if such a Superfund provided an average of $40,000 over two years for the average displaced fossil fuel worker, four times the level of TAA; a total of $800 million per year, or about 1/50 of 1% of the current federal budget.

Just Transition on the Ground

The fight for a just transition for workers adversely affected by side effects of climate protection doesn't have to wait for national legislation—in fact, it must not. Local struggles around mountaintop-removal coal mining, coal-fired power plants, oil and gas pipelines, and other fossil-fuel infrastructure are occurring every day. Unless those advocating greenhouse gas reduction fight to protect affected workers from harm, the result will be to turn workers and unions against climate protection. Climate protection advocates should insist from the outset that part of any transition away from fossil fuels includes protection for the well-being of workers whose jobs may be threatened. They need to ally with unions and the broader labor movement to demand protection for affected workers and communities.

The labor and climate movements should propose their own plans for protecting workers and communities. For example, when the Healthy Connecticut Alliance campaigned to close the Bridgeport Station coal-fired power plant they included in their demands a series of protections for those who worked in the plant:

- Negotiate a jobs agreement with unions representing affected workers.
- Find jobs for affected workers who want them.
- Ensure job retraining for those who need it to fill new jobs.
- Provide decent pensions with healthcare for workers who are not provided other jobs and who do not opt for retraining.
- Create jobs restoring the site.
- Reutilize facilities to replace losses in the tax base.
- Fund job-creating community economic development.

Significant struggles are already brewing in many states over how to implement the EPA's Clean Power Plan for greenhouse gas reduction. Effective state plans are already facing opposition based on the fear that they will threaten jobs.

Making a just transition program for workers a central feature of such plans may make the difference between united support for effective plans and a never-ending battle over "jobs vs. the environment." It could provide a critical element for drawing together workers, unions, and allies around a broader program for protecting jobs by protecting the climate. And it could serve as the leading edge for a program to provide workers and communities with protection against the vast economic insecurities of life under neoliberal capitalism. ❑

Sources: Jeremy Brecher, "'Jobs vs. the Environment': How to Counter This Divisive Big Lie," *The Nation*, April 22, 2014; "U.S. Chamber Calls Politically-Charged Decision to Deny Keystone a Job Killer," Jan. 17, 2012. (ushamber.com); "Pipeline Decision Pits Jobs Against Environment," NPR Morning Edition, Nov. 3, 2011 (npr.org); "Administrator Lisa P. Jackson, Remarks at the 2011 Good Jobs Green Jobs Conference, As Prepared," Aug. 2, 2011 (yosemite.epa.gov); Tony Mazzocchi, "A Superfund for Workers," *Earth Island Journal*, 9(1); John Lynch and Seth Kirshenberg, "Economic

Transition by the Energy-Impacted Communities," Commentary, Fall, 2000 (energyca.org); "Planning Guidance for Contractor Work Force Restructuring," Office of Worker and Community Transition, U.S. Department of Energy, December 1998 (energy.gov); "The President's Budget Fiscal Year 2016 Investing in Coal Communities, Workers, and Technology" (whitehouse.gov); "MACED statement on announcement of President Obama's proposed budget plan to aid Central Appalachian communities," Feb. 2, 2015 (maced.org); Lisa Abbott, "President proposes major new investments in Appalachian transition," Kentuckians For the Commonwealth, Feb. 2, 2015 (ktfc.org); Robert Pollin, Heidi Garrett-Peltier, James Heintz, and Bracken Hendricks, *Green Growth: A U.S. Program for Controlling Climate Change and Expanding Job Opportunities*, Political Economy Research Institute (PERI) and Center for American Progress, September 2014; Jeremy Brecher, *Jobs Beyond Coal: A Manual for Communities, Workers, and Environmentalists*, Labor Network for Sustainability (report.labor4sustainability.org); Healthy CT Alliance (healthyctalliance.org); Robert Pollin, James Heintz, and Heidi Garrett-Peltier, "Clean Energy Investments for the U.S. Economy," discussion paper, Surdna Foundation Conference, March 22, 2010 (peri.umass.edu); Michigan Public Service Commission, "Report on the Implementation of the P.A. 295 Renewable Energy Standard and the Cost-Effectiveness of the Energy Standards," Michigan Public Service Commission, 2012 (michigan. gov); The Universal Tobacco Settlement Act, S. 1414, 105th Cong., 1997 (thomas.loc.gov).

Article 6.4

FRACKONOMICS
The Science and Economics of the Gas Boom

BY ROBERT LARSON
July/August 2013

Between 1868 and 1969, Cleveland's Cuyahoga River caught fire at least ten times, including one blaze that reached the Standard Oil refinery where storage tanks detonated. Ultimately, the seemingly impossible and unnatural phenomenon of burning water came to represent the dangers of unregulated industrial development and generated popular support for the environmental laws of the 1970s, including the Clean Water Act and the Safe Drinking Water Act.

Today the unsettling sight of burning water has returned, from a new industry that is exempt from both these laws. In homes near installations using the drilling technique known as hydraulic fracturing, or "fracking," the tap water has been known to ignite with the touch of a lighter. The industry is relatively new, so the scientific literature yields only tentative results and provisional research conclusions. But the early research suggests fracking has serious negative consequences for public health and local ecology, from flaming tap water to toxic chemicals to ground tremors. Industry spokesmen insist that the negative side-effects of fracking are insignificant. But there's one positive side-effect everyone should be able to agree upon: fracking is an ideal vehicle for explaining key economic concepts of market failure and market power, including *externalities, asymmetrical information,* and *regulatory capture,* along with brand-new ones, like *science capture.* Let's start with the firewater.

Liar Liar, Taps on Fire

In the fracking process, natural gas (methane) is released from shale rock strata up to a mile underground, by injecting millions of gallons of water, along with sand and a variety of synthetic chemicals. The huge pressure of the water makes new cracks in the rock, allowing the gas to dissolve and be extracted. Natural gas is now responsible for 30% of U.S. electricity production and for heating half of all U.S. homes. The national and business media have breathlessly reported huge growth in gas production, and the oil-and-gas industry projects that North America will return to exporting energy by 2025. Besides the sheer growth in production, the *Wall Street Journal* reported earlier this year, the fracking boom has brought other economic benefits, "improving employment in some regions and a rebound in U.S.-based manufacturing," and "greater defense against overseas turmoil that can disrupt energy supplies."

As made notorious by the documentary *Gasland*, water supplies are a major focus of concern about fracking, especially since the emergence of dramatic footage of a number of Pennsylvania homes, near fracking pads above the Marcellus Shale formation, producing fireballs from the kitchen tap. Duke University earth scientists conducted a more rigorous exploration of this phenomenon, published in the *Proceedings of the National Academy of the Sciences*. They surveyed rural Pennsylvanian water wells for residential use, measuring concentrations of methane, the main chemical component of natural gas. Concentrations rose far above natural levels closer to drill pads, spiking within one kilometer of active gas development sites to a level that "represents a potential explosion hazard." It was also found that the specific gas chemistry in the wells matched those produced through drilling, rather than through naturally occurring compounds. As the gas boom goes "boom," the cautious scientists conclude: "Greater stewardship, knowledge, and—possibly— regulation are needed to ensure the sustainable future of shale-gas extraction."

In parts of the country where water is scarcer, the issue is more ominous. The Environmental Protection Agency (EPA) and U.S. Geological Survey have found toxic alcohols, glycols, and carcinogenic benzene in underground aquifers in Wyoming, evidence that fracking has tainted precious underground water supplies. In press accounts, local residents who requested the study "expressed gratitude to the EPA, and perhaps a bit of veiled doubt about the zeal of local and state regulators." In parched Texas, the volume of water adequate for irrigating $200,000 worth of crops can be used to frack $2.5 billion-worth of gas or oil. The *Wall Street Journal* reports that "companies have been on a buying spree, snapping up rights to scarce river water—easily outbidding traditional users such as farmers and cities." A Texan rancher relates: "They're just so much bigger and more powerful than we are…We're just kind of the little ant that gets squashed."

Top-Secret Ingredients

The heavy use of often-secret synthetic chemicals has also cast a shadow over the fracking debate. Bloomberg News reported in 2012 that energy companies and well operators were refusing to disclose the chemical formulas of thousands of substances used in the fracking process, enough to "keep [the] U.S. clueless on wells." Many states have instituted a self-reporting law, modeled on one first developed in Texas, allowing drillers to withhold the ingredients used in their chemical mixes. Bloomberg reports that drillers "claimed similar exemptions about 19,000 times" in the first eight months of 2012 alone. The congressional exemption of the industry from federal water requirements (discussed below) makes this non-disclosure possible, so that "neighbors of fracked wells … can't use the disclosures to watch for frack fluids migrating into creeks, rivers and aquifers, because they don't know what to look for."

This development is a perfect example of what economists call *asymmetric information*, where one participant in a transaction knows relevant information that is unknown to the other party. The lack of information on one side can put the other party at an advantage, like the seller of a used car who knows more about the car's problems than the prospective buyer. For example, a team of Colorado endocrinologists set out to catalogue these synthetic compounds used in wells across the country, based on regulatory filings. The survey was limited due to the "void of environmental authority" to compel chemical disclosure, and thus the data sheets and reports are "fraught with gaps in information about the formulation of the products." Many of these reports only specify the general chemical class or use the label "proprietary," providing no additional information. Ultimately, the scientists found that over 75% of the chemicals were harmful for the sensory organs, nearly half could affect the nervous and immune systems, and 25% could cause "cancer and mutations."

Another report by Colorado scientists observed that fracking development is increasingly located "near where people live, work, and play." The study used air sampling to find strongly elevated health risks within a radius of about half a mile from fracking sites. The effects ranged from "headaches and eye irritation" up to "tremors, temporary limb paralysis, and unconsciousness at higher exposures." A larger review by Pennsylvania scientists reached similar conclusions, based on local resident reporting and finding a match of over two-thirds "between known health effects of chemicals detected and symptoms reported."

The scientists caution that their findings "do not constitute definitive proof of cause and effect," but they do "indicate the strong likelihood that the health of people living in proximity to gas facilities is being affected by exposure to pollutants from those facilities." They frequently advocate the *precautionary principle*—that careful study showing that a product or process is *not* harmful should precede its use—as when they recommend "health impact assessments before permitting begins," and note that "scientific knowledge about the health and environmental impacts of shale gas development … are proceeding at a far slower pace than the development itself." These conclusions contradict the industry's claim that fracking is both safe for public health and not in need of any further study. Especially considering the earthquakes.

Tectonic Economics

Perhaps more alarming than the burning water and secret chemicals is the association of fracking with earthquakes. An early report of this development came from the Oklahoma Geological Survey, which surveyed the timing of tremors and their proximity to fracking sites and found a "strong correlation in time and space" and thus "a possibility these earthquakes were induced by hydraulic fracturing." Earthquake epicenters were mostly within two miles of wells, and any earthquake disruption or damage caused by fracking-related activities represents an *externality*, a side effect of an economic transaction that affects parties outside the transaction.

These findings are backed up by a review in the prestigious research journal *Science*, in which cautious scientists note that fracking *itself* is not responsible for "the earthquakes that have been shaking previously calm regions." Yet they find that the induced earthquakes do arise from "all manner of other energy-related fluid injection—including deep disposal of fracking's wastewater, extraction of methane from coal beds, and creation of geothermal energy reservoirs." A surveyed area in Arkansas typically had about two quakes a year, before the beginning of fracking-water disposal. The year water disposal began, the number rose to ten. The next year, to 54. After water injection was halted, the quakes tapered off. The *Science* authors observe the "strongly suggestive" correlation between water disposal and seismic activity: "The quakes began only after injection began, surged when the rate of injection surged, were limited to the vicinity of the wells, and trailed off after injection was stopped." The scientists' main conclusion is the adoption of the precautionary principle: "look before you leap … Stopping injection has stopped significant earthquakes within days to a year. … The new regulations in Ohio and Arkansas at least move in the direction of such a learn-as-you-go approach."

Fracknapping

You might wonder why the EPA has not limited or regulated fracking operations, in light of the combustible water, cancer-causing chemicals, and earthquake clusters. The EPA might well have adopted significant national policies on fracking by now, had the practice not been made exempt from the main national environmental laws in the Energy Policy Act of 2005, an offspring of Dick Cheney's secretive energy committee. The exemptions from the Clean Water Act, the Safe Drinking Water Act, the Clean Air Act, and the Superfund law drastically limit the agency's authority to act on fracking.

The drive to limit even EPA *research* into fracking is decades old. An extensive *New York Times* report, based on interviews with scientists and reviews of confidential files, found that "more than a quarter-century of efforts by some lawmakers and regulators to force the federal government to police the industry better have been thwarted, as EPA studies have been repeatedly narrowed in scope and important findings have been removed." When Congress first directed the EPA to investigate fracking in the 1980s, the *Times* reported, EPA scientists found that some fracking waste was "hazardous and should be tightly controlled." But the final report sent to Congress eliminated these conclusions. An agency scientist relates, "It was like science didn't matter. … The industry was going to get what it wanted, and we were not supposed to stand in the way."

Similarly, when an EPA public-advisory letter to the state of New York called for a moratorium on drilling, the advice was stripped from the released version. A staff scientist said the redaction was due to "politics," but could as well have said "business power." More importantly, the first major EPA review of fracking found "little or no threat to drinking water." This was an eyebrow-raising claim, given that five of seven members of the peer review panel had current or former energy industry affiliations, a detail noted by agency whistle-blower Weston Wilson. Other studies have been narrowed in scope or colored by similar conflicts of interest. More recently, the agency announced that its study finding contamination of Wyoming groundwater will not be subjected to outside peer review, and that further work instead will be funded directly by industry. As the EPA is presently drafting a brand-new report on the subject, these past embarrassments should be kept in mind.

This brings up the problem of *regulatory capture*, where an industry to be monitored gains major influence over regulators' policies. As mentioned above, fracking is very loosely regulated by the states, which is always a favorite outcome for corporate America since the regulatory resources of state governments are far smaller and the regulators are even more easily dominated than those of the federal government. The industry-sponsored FracFocus website is the state-sanctioned chemical-information clearing house, and a masterpiece of smooth PR design, suggesting clear water and full transparency. But Bloomberg News reports that "more than 40 percent of wells fracked in eight major drilling states last year had been omitted from the voluntary site."

Other state reactions have varied. In 2010, the New York State legislature voted to ban fracking, but then-Governor Paterson vetoed the bill and instead issued a temporary moratorium on the practice, though fracking remains illegal in the New York City watershed. Finally, while the EPA's main study is still pending, the agency has taken some steps, as in 2012 when it required well operators to reduce methane gas emissions from wells and storage pits to limit air pollution. But even here the regulation wears kid gloves: The new moves do not cut into industry profits. In fact, capturing the "fugitive" methane, the agency estimates, will *save* the industry $11 to $19 million annually. Also, the regulation won't take effect until 2015.

Neoclassical Gas

Mainstream, or "neoclassical," economic theory considers itself to have solutions to these problems—solutions centered as always on "free markets." The idea is that if firms create chronic health problems or combustible tap water, market forces should drive up their costs, as landowners learn of these firms' practices and demand higher payment for drilling. But as seen above, even households that have already leased their land for gas development remain unaware of the identities and effects of the obscure synthetic chemicals to which they are exposed. This *informational asymmetry*—the firms know things the landowners don't—significantly attenuates the ability of landowners to make informed choices.

On the other hand, households that are located near a drill pad but uninvolved in licensing the drilling will experience the ill effects as externalities. Neoclassicals suggest these can be fixed through a better property-rights system, where surrounding individuals can sue drillers for injuring their health. But this solution runs up against another problem: proving cause-and-effect from a drilling pad to a particular individual's health problems is extremely difficult. The tobacco industry notoriously made this point in court for many years, arguing that it was impossible to prove if a man's lung cancer was caused by a four-pack-a-day cigarette habit, as opposed to, say, local auto exhaust. If cause-and-effect is hard to prove in court for cigarettes, doing so for air-delivered volatile organic compounds will be almost impossible.

This problem is aggravated by the use of corporate resources to influence research. The showcase example is a study produced by the University of Texas, "Fact-Based Regulation for Environmental Protection in Shale Gas Development." The study gave fracking a guardedly positive bill of health, finding no evidence of negative health impacts. The commercial media gave the study a good deal of favorable attention, until the revelation that the lead researcher, Dr. Charles G. Groat, formerly of USGS, sits on the board of the Plains Exploration & Production Company, a Houston-based energy firm heavily invested in gas development. His compensation from the board was several times his academic salary, and he also held 40,000 shares of its stock. An in-house review by the university was outspoken, saying "the term 'fact-based' would not apply" to the paper, which was "inappropriately selective ... such that they seemed to suggest that public concerns were without scientific basis and largely resulted from media bias." Groat retired from the university the day the review was released, but this practice has become increasingly common from industries under fire for environmental or public-health impacts. Bloomberg News flatly stated that "producers are taking a page from the tobacco industry playbook: funding research at established universities that arrives at conclusions that counter concerns raised by critics." This raises the ugly possibility of *science capture.*

No Frackin' Way

Not that Americans are taking it lying down. A diverse popular coalition successfully fought to block a Gulf Coast gas terminal that stood to inflict major damage on local wildlife. The *Oil & Gas Journal* reports on the "firestorm" of activism: "In an unlikely but massive undertaking, environmental activists, sports fishermen, local politicians, media groups, and other citizens formed a coalition known as the 'Gumbo Alliance' that united opposition to the technology." The Louisiana governor vetoed the project "under considerable public pressure." Elsewhere, local residents have taken action to keep fracking and its negative externalities out of their communities. New York State "fractivists" have won an impressive 55 municipal bans and 105 local moratoriums against fracking, to date. The state's Court of Appeals—New York's highest court—recently upheld the bans against an industry lawsuit. These activist successes are an early challenge to what the *Wall Street Journal* called the new "shale barons."

American job markets remain highly depressed and state budgets are strained. What we need, instead of dogged extraction of every particle of fossil fuels from the ground, is a public employment program geared toward the construction of a new sustainable energy system. This would be a far superior alternative to fracking—on grounds of health, ecology, and employment. It could also serve as a springboard for a broader questioning of the suitability of capitalism for the challenges of the 21st century. That kind of radical approach would see the glass of water as half full, not half on fire. ❑

Sources: Russel Gold, "Gas Boom Projected to Grow for Decades," *Wall Street Journal*, February 28, 2013; Tom Fowler, "US Oil Sector Notches Historic Annual Gusher," *Wall Street Journal*, January 19, 2013; Stephen Osborn, Avner Vengosh, Nathaniel Warner, and Robert Jackson, "Methane contamination of drinking water accompanying gas-well drilling and hydraulic fracturing," *Proceedings of the National Academy of the Sciences*, Vol. 108, No. 20, May 17, 2011; Kirk Johnson, "EPA Links Tainted Water in Wyoming to Hydraulic Fracturing for Natural Gas," *New York Times*, December 8, 2011; Tennille Tracy, "New EPA Findings Test Fracking Site," *Wall Street Journal*, October 11, 2012; Felicity Barringer, "Spread of Hydrofracking Could Strain Water Resources in West, Study Finds," *New York Times*, May 2, 2013; Russel Gold and Ana Campoy, "Oil's Growing Thirst for Water," *Wall Street Journal*, December 6, 2011; Ben Elgin, Benjamin Haas and Phil Kuntz, "Fracking Secrets by Thousands Keep US Clueless on Wells," *Bloomberg News*, November 30, 2012; Theo Colborn, Carol Kwiatkowski, Kim Schultz and Mary Bachran, "Natural Gas Operations form a Public Health Perspective," *Human and Ecological Risk Assessment: An International Journal*, Vol. 17, No. 5, September 20, 2011; Lisa McKenzie,

Roxana Witter, Lee Newman, John Adgate, "Human health risk assessment of air emissions from development of unconventional natural gas resources," *Science of the Total Environment*, Vol. 424, May 1 2012; Nadia Steinzor, Wilma Subra, and Lisa Sumi, "Investigating Links between Shale Gas Development and Health Impacts Through a Community Survey Project in Pennsylvania," *New Solutions*, Vol. 23, No. 1, 2013; Austin Holland, Oklahoma Geological Survey, "Examination of Possibly Induced Seismicity from Hydraulic Fracturing in the Eolga Field, Garvin County, Oklahoma, August 2011; Richard Kerr, "Learning How NOT to Make Your Own Earthquakes," *Science*, Vol. 335, No. 6075, March 23 2012; Zoe Corbyn, "Method predicts size of fracking earthquakes," *Nature* News, December 9, 2011; Ian Urbina, "Pressure Limits Efforts to Police Drilling for Gas," *New York Times*, March 3, 2011; Devlin Barrett and Ryan Dezember, "Regulators Back 'Fracking' in New York," *Wall Street Journal*, July 1, 2011; John Broder, "US Caps Emissions in Drilling for Fuel," *New York Times*, February 4, 2012; Norman Augustine, Rita Colwell, and James Duderstadt, "A Review of the Processes of Preparation and Distribution of the report 'Fact-Based Regulation for Environmental Protection in Shale Gas Development,'" University of Texas at Austin, November 30, 2012; Jim Efsthathiou, "Frackers Fund University Research That Proves Their Case," Bloomberg News, July 23, 2012; Daron Threet, "US offshore LNG terminals face technical, legal maze," *Oil & Gas Journal*, December 24, 2007; Ellen Cantarow, "New York's Zoning Ban Movement Fracks Big Gas," Truthout, May 9, 2013 (Truthout.org); Alyssa Abkowitz, "The New Texas Land Rush," *Wall Street Journal*, April 25, 2013; Daron Threet, "US offshore LNG terminals face technical, legal maze," *Oil & Gas Journal*, December 24, 2007.

Article 6.5

CLIMATE POLICY AS WEALTH CREATION
The right policy would embody the principle that
we all own the earth's resources in equal and common measure.

BY JAMES K. BOYCE
July/August 2014

We know that climate change poses a grave threat to the earth and all who live on it. We also know, in the broadest sense, what we need to do to preserve a habitable planet: severely curtail greenhouse gas emissions from fossil fuels. The question of how to cure ourselves of our fossil-fuel dependence, however, has so far proven devilishly difficult. Possibilities like carbon taxes or carbon caps (and limited emissions permits) are widely discussed, but have so far run into political roadblocks: the power of vested interests like oil and coal companies, the attachment to fossil-fuel based ways of life, the fear of the economic costs involved, and the problem of coordinating national policies (and dividing up costs) to address a global problem. Economist James Boyce offers a policy proposal, based on the development of public-property rights over the atmosphere and the sharing of the proceeds from its use, which is both politically feasible and philosophically profound. This article is adapted from a lecture Boyce delivered, on March 31, as part of the "Climate Change Series" at the University of Pittsburgh Honors College. —Eds.*

Why Climate Policies That Operate on the Supply Side?

Broadly speaking, there are two types of policies to reduce carbon emissions from fossil-fuel combustion. One set operates on the demand side of the picture, on the need for fossil fuels. These policies include investments in energy efficiency, alternative sources of energy, mass transit, etc.—investments that reduce our demand for fossil fuels at any given price.

I'm going to focus on the complementary set of policies that operate not on the demand side of the equation, but the supply side—policies that raise the prices of fossil fuels, resulting in lower use. Those policies raise prices either by instituting a tax on carbon emissions or, alternatively, by putting a cap on emissions and thereby restricting supply. In the same way that OPEC restricts supply when it wishes to increase the price of oil, a cap works to raise the price, too.

The policies that involve shifts in demand—investments in mass transit, clean and renewable energy, or energy efficiency— take time, possibly decades, to be fully implemented. In the short run, if we want to see immediate reductions in fossil-fuel consumption, we need policies in the mix that operate on the price today, and reduce consumption today. That's one reason I think that price-based policies can and should be part of the policy mix.

In addition, price-based policies themselves are critical to the reduction in demand. If consumers, households, firms, and public-sector institutions know that, over the next decade or two, the price of fossil fuels will inexorably rise due to policies purposely making that happen, they will have an incentive to make investments in energy efficiency and renewable energy sources. They will face price signals to push that investment along.

The easiest way to put a price on carbon emissions is through an "upstream" pricing system, which means that you apply the price where the carbon enters the economy, not where it comes out the tailpipe. So that would mean at the tanker terminals, the pipelines, the coal-mine heads, where fossil fuels are entering the economy. The Congressional Budget Office (CBO) estimates than an upstream system in a cap-and-trade or carbon tax regime would involve 2,000 "compliance entities"—that's the name for the folks who have to either pay the tax or surrender a permit for each ton of carbon they bring into the economy. If you tax carbon or price carbon upstream, those price increases become part of the price of the fuel and are passed along to business and consumers, thereby creating incentives for investments that reduce emissions over the longer haul.

There are two instruments that one can use to price carbon—one is a tax and the other is a cap. A tax sets the price and allows the quantity of emissions to fluctuate. A cap sets the quantity and allows the price of emissions to fluctuate. Other than that, they're basically the same thing. You can think of them both as involving permits. A tax says, "Here are permits, as long as you pay the price for them, you can have as many permits as you want." A cap says, "Here is the fixed number of permits, and we're going to let their price be determined at an auction or in a market."

If we had a tax to put a price on carbon emissions, I'd be all for it. But since the main policy objective is to hit the quantity target—to reduce the quantity of emissions—it seems to me that targeting the quantity rather than the price makes a lot of sense. We don't know for sure exactly what the relationship is between quantity and price. We know that a 10% increase in prices results in roughly

---

Is Climate Change a "Tragedy of the Commons"?

Ecologist Garret Hardin coined the now-familiar phrase "the tragedy of the commons" in a 1968 article in the journal *Science*. Hardin argued that people inevitably deplete commonly held resources because they do not pay the full cost of using them. For example, livestock herders have an incentive to overgraze their own animals on common pasture— maximizing the benefits to themselves, while inflicting the costs of the overgrazing on others. Similar arguments have been made about the depletion of fisheries and many other environmental problems, among them climate change: each person enjoys the private benefits of fossil-fuel use, depleting the finite capacity of the atmosphere to absorb and recycle greenhouse gases, and inflicting damages on others. Mainstream economists have often seized upon this reasoning to argue that the solution to environmental problems is the division and enclosure of commons into private property, which would mean that each owner would bear the full cost of using his or her own property.

What economists are describing as "the tragedy of the commons," Boyce argues, would be better described as the "the tragedy of open access." Open access allows individuals to appropriate resources at no cost, and when these resources are scarce, to inflict the costs of depletion on others. Understanding that a commons, however, can be "regulated through a system of common-property resource management," recasts the problem—and the solution. Protecting and preserving these resources does not require privatization: it can be achieved thought the development of public-property rights and regulations over their use. —*Eds.*

a 3% reduction in demand in the short run, but that relationship isn't precise. Moreover, it can change over time, particularly as more technologies are discovered. So if you want to hit the quantity target, it seems to me that setting a cap has advantages over setting a tax.

One way or another, however, what's important is to get a price on carbon. When we put a price on carbon, what we're doing is we're moving from an open-access regime, which is a situation where there are no property rights, to creating a set of property rights (see box). Regulations already assert a certain type of property right, the right of the public acting through the government to make rules about how the resource is used. Putting a price on emissions takes that process one step further. It not only sets rules about using the resource, but also charges a price for using that resource. So it moves along the spectrum from a complete absence of property rights towards a more full specification of property rights.

Just How Much Would It Cost?

Back in 2009, the Speaker of the House of Representatives, John Boehner (R-Ohio), claimed in the debate running up to the vote on the American Clean Energy and Security Act— known as the Waxman-Markey bill, after its main sponsors, Henry Waxman (D-Calif.) and Ed Markey (D-Mass.)—that if this bill were passed, it would be the biggest tax increase on working families in American history. Now, that was probably political hyperbole, but Boehner wasn't entirely wrong. It would be like a tax increase, and it would be substantial. It has to be substantial if it's going to bring about the changes in consumption of fossil fuels that are needed to push forward the clean-energy transition. We're talking about big changes: an 80% reduction in our emissions by the year 2050. We're talking about an energy revolution, and the kinds of price increases that would be ultimately needed to drive that forward are not inconsequential.

What was the Democratic response? "No, no, it's not a tax, it's not a big price increase, and it's really not going to hurt people all that much. It's equivalent to a postage stamp a day." Now, that postage-stamp-a-day figure is an estimate of something quite different from the price increases that households would face. This is the estimated cost of abatement: how much it would cost to invest in energy-efficiency improvements to reduce fossil fuel consumption to 75% of the current level. That's not a huge cost because, in fact, there's a lot of low-hanging fruit out there in terms of investment opportunities.

The consulting firm McKinsey & Company produced a study a few years back that showed there are even investments that would have a negative cost. In other words, if you make that investment to reduce carbon emissions, you actually get money back because it's so efficient to make those investments. So overall, you can achieve reductions at a fairly modest cost.

But what I want to draw your attention to is the price of the emissions we're not reducing—the 75% that we're not cutting. That's the higher price consumers will be paying for their use of fossil fuels, and that's the primary reason for the price increases you will see at every gas pump, on every electric bill, and that you will see trickling through into the prices of other commodities in proportion to the use of fossil fuels in their production and distribution.

Let me remind you that gasoline prices are the most politically visible prices in the United States. They're advertised in twelve-inch-high numbers on street corners across America. During the 2008 Presidential campaign, when all the major candidates— including Hillary Clinton and John McCain—were talking about global warming and said they were in favor of limiting carbon emissions with a cap-and-trade policy, gas prices went up. And both Clinton and McCain said this was a terrible burden on the American people, that we needed to have a federal gas tax holiday for the summer to relieve this burden. Well, the federal gas tax is about 18 cents a gallon—it's really not that much. Compared to the price increases that we're going to see if we have a serious climate policy, I hate to tell it to you folks, but 18 cents rounds to about zero.

We're going to see gas prices going well above $5 a gallon in the first few years of the policy, and ultimately higher than that. How are you going to have a policy that squares the circle between, on the one hand, the need to price those emissions to address the problem of climate change and, on the other hand, even those politicians who see climate change as a problem saying, "We can't let the price of gas go up because it's going to hurt the American family"?

Who Gets the Money?

How much money are we talking about when we put a cap on carbon emissions? What I want to share here are some "back of the envelope" calculations. Don't take these to the bank, but they'll give you some idea of the ballpark we're talking about.

These figures trace the trajectory if we're going to achieve an 80% cut in emissions by the year 2050. In the first six years of the policy, if we were to have such a policy in 2015, we'd be emitting on average about 6 billion tons of carbon dioxide per year, a little bit less than in the absence of a policy. The price associated with that reduction would probably be in the neighborhood of $15 a ton, so we'd be talking about $90 billion a year, or about $540 billion over those first six years. In the next decade, we'd be ratcheting those emissions down further to about 4.5 billion tons. To do so, the price would have to be about $30 a ton, generating a total cost to consumers and therefore a pot of money of about $135 billion a year, or $1.35 trillion over the decade. In the next decade, the 2030s, getting down to about 3 billion tons of carbon, we'd be raising the price to about $60 a ton, generating about $1.8 trillion over the decade. And the last decade, the 2040s, ratcheting down further to 1.5 billion tons, perhaps somewhat optimistically assuming here that the price needed would be only $120 a ton—this assumes that a lot of R&D has happened, a lot of new technologies come online, investments in public mass transit are online, etc., so you don't have to push the price through the roof—that would generate another $1.8 trillion.

You add it up and over that 35-year period, we're talking about something to the order of $5.5 trillion. Economists have a technical term for it—"a hell of a lot of money." The question is: Who owns the atmosphere and, therefore, who will get the money?

One possible answer is the fossil-fuel corporations. You could give them the money that consumers pay in higher prices. If you give the permits to the firms for free, on the basis of some allocation formula, then those permits have to be tradable,

---

What Should We Make of the New EPA Rules?

This June, the U.S. Environmental Protection Agency (EPA) announced a new "Clean Power Plan" targeting a 30% reduction of carbon emissions from fossil-fuel-fired electrical power plants, relative to the 2005 level, by the year 2030. While we may think first of motor vehicles when we think about fossil-fuel use, electrical power generation actually accounts for more of our carbon emissions—over 2 billion metric tons, or nearly one-third of the U.S. total, each year. The EPA policy is not a new law (as climate legislation has been blocked in Congress), but a new set of rules that the Obama administration proposes to implement under the authority of the Clean Air Act.

The Clean Power Plan allows states to each develop their own paths to emissions-reduction targets. The EPA describes four ways to achieve reductions: increased efficiency of coal-fired power plants, a shift towards natural gasfired (away from coal-fired) plants, a shift toward renewables like wind and solar (away from fossil-fuel-based power generation), and increased energy efficiency in consumption. "States can meet their goal using any measures that make sense to them," the official EPA blog states. "They do not have to use all the measures EPA identified, and they can use other approaches that will work to bring down that carbon intensity rate."

One approach is to cap power plant emissions and auction the permits to the power companies. Nine northeastern states are already doing this under the Regional Greenhouse Gas Initiative (RGGI), and last year California began doing so under its Global Warming Solutions Act. Auction revenue can be returned to the people as dividends, or used to fund public investments, or some mix of the two as California is now doing.

"The Clean Power Plan offers every state the opportunity to institute cap-and-dividend climate policies," Boyce observes. "Earmarking some fraction of the auction revenue for public investment can make sense, too, but folks should understand that once we've capped emissions from the power sector, those emissions won't be reduced any further by public investments since the level has already been set by the cap. The biggest chunk of carbon revenue, I think, can and should be returned to the people as the rightful owners of our atmosphere." —Eds.

Sources: Carol Davenport, "Obama to Take Action to Slash Coal Pollution," New York Times, June 1, 2014 (nytimes.com); EPA News Release, June 2, 2014 (yosemite.epa.gov); EPA, National Greenhouse Gas Emissions Data (epa.gov); EPA, "Understanding State Goals under the Clean Power Plan," June 4, 2014 (blog.epa.gov).

---

because some firms end up being able to reduce emissions more cheaply while for others it's more expensive, so they need to be able to trade permits with each other. This is where the phrase "cap and trade" comes from. Cap and trade is really "cap and giveaway and trade." If you don't give away the permits, there's no need to make them tradable.

Who ultimately gets the resulting windfall profits? Well, they're distributed to whoever owns the firms, in proportion to stock ownership. Since stock ownership is very unequal and it's concentrated at the top of the wealth pyramid, most of the returns would go to those households. And some of the money would flow abroad to foreign owners.

A second possibility is cap and spend. It's analogous to tax and spend. In this case, the government doesn't give away the permits, but auctions them. There's an auction held monthly or quarterly. Only so many permits are on the table, and the firms bid for them. If they want to bring carbon into the economy, they need to have enough permits for the next month or the next quarter. The auction revenue is retained by the government, and it can be used to increase government spending on anything you want to imagine: on public education, on environmental improvements, on foreign wars, you name it. It could be used to cut taxes. It could be used to reduce the deficit. All of those are possible uses of the revenue that comes from a cap-and-spend type policy.

The third possibility is what I'm going to call "cap and dividend." In this case, the money is recycled to the people on an equal per capita basis. In this case, too, permits are auctioned, but a week after the auction—every month or every quarter— you get your share of the money as your dividend. The result is that it protects the purchasing power of working families. The strongest instrumental appeal of a cap-and-dividend policy is that it would make working families whole. It would protect the middle class and working families from impacts of higher fuel prices and thus build in durable support for the climate policy for the decades it will take to achieve the clean-energy transition.

How Would Cap and Dividend Work?

A carbon price is a regressive tax, one that hits the poor harder than the rich, as a proportion of their incomes. Because fuels are a necessity, not a luxury, they account for a bigger share of the family budget for low-income families than they do for middle-income families, and a bigger share for middle-income families than for high-income families. As you go up the income scale, however, you actually have a bigger carbon footprint—you tend to consume more fuels and more things that are produced and distributed using fuels. You consume more of just about everything— that's what being affluent is all about. So in absolute amounts, if you price carbon, high-income folks are going to pay more than low-income folks.

Under a policy with a carbon price, households' purchasing power is being eroded by that big price increase. But with cap and dividend, money is coming back to them in the form of the dividend. Because income and expenditures are so skewed towards the wealthy, the mean—the average amount of money coming in from the carbon price and being paid back out in equal dividends—is above the median, the amount that the "middle" person pays. So more than 50% of the people would get back more than they pay in under such a policy. As those fuel prices are going up, then, people will say, "I don't mind because I'm getting my share back in a very visible and concrete fashion." It's politically fantastical, I think, to imagine that widespread and durable public support for a climate policy that increases energy prices will succeed in any other way.

There are precedents for doing this kind of thing. The best known is the Alaska Permanent Fund. In the 1970s, the Republican governor of Alaska, Jay Hammond, instituted this policy when North Slope oil production was starting up. What they did in Alaska was impose a royalty payment on every barrel of oil being pumped out. They said that this oil belongs to every Alaskan in equal and common measure—current Alaskans and future generations, too. So what we're going to do is charge a royalty for extracting our oil, put it in what we'll call the Permanent Fund, and use that money in three ways: Part will go for long-term investment. Part will be put into financial assets, so that it will always be there, even after the oil is gone, for future Alaskans. And part of it will be paid out in equal per-person dividends to every man, woman, and child in the state of Alaska. That payment has been as much as about $2,000 a year. This way of providing dividends is not a complicated thing to do. It's not rocket science, folks. It's dead easy.

Apart from helping to support family incomes, I think that this policy has deep philosophical appeal, because it's founded on the principle that we all own the earth's resources, the gifts of creation, in equal and common measure. The planet's limited carbon absorptive capacity does not belong to corporations. It does not belong to governments. It belongs to all of us. Cap and dividend is a way of implementing that sense of common ownership, rather than abdicating ownership—giving it away for free—which we currently have under the open access regime.

Ask people, not only in this country but around the world, "Who owns the air? Who owns the gifts of creation?" The answer you will hear most often is that we all own them in equal and common measure. I think our challenge in addressing climate change is to translate this very widely held philosophical principle into actual policy by which we, as the owners of these gifts, use them responsibly. In the case of the atmosphere's ability to absorb carbon dioxide emissions, that means limiting the amount of carbon we put in the atmosphere. That's what we need to do. ❏

Article 6.6

MAPPING ENVIRONMENTAL INJUSTICE
Race, Class, and Industrial Air Pollution

BY KLARA ZWICKL, MICHAEL ASH, AND JAMES K. BOYCE
November/December 2015

East St. Louis, Ill., just across the Mississippi River from St. Louis, Mo., is not your typical American town. It has a hazardous waste incinerator, numerous chemical plants, and multiple "national priority" toxic waste sites. It's also home to 26,000 residents, 98% of them African-American. The median household income is about $21,000—meaning that half the households in the city have annual incomes even lower. The rate of childhood asthma is among the highest in the nation.

America's polluters are not color-blind. Nor are they oblivious to distinctions of class. Studies of environmental inequality have found that minorities and low-income communities often bear disproportionate pollution burdens. One of the reasons was revealed in a consultant report to the California Waste Management Board that surfaced in the 1980s: "A great deal of time, resources, and planning could be saved and political problems avoided if people who are resentful and people who are amenable to Waste-to-Energy projects [a.k.a. incinerators] could be identified before selecting a site," the report observed. It recommended that "middle and higher-socioeconomic strata neighborhoods should not fall at least within the one-mile and five-mile radii of the proposed site."

Rather than being distributed randomly across the U.S. population, pollution mirrors the distribution of power and wealth. Pollution disparities reflect conscious

FIGURE 1: INDUSTRIAL AIR TOXICS EXPOSURE BY EPA REGION

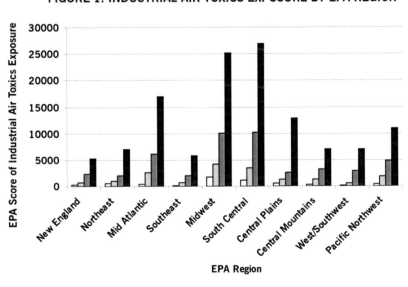

EPA Score of Industrial Air Toxics Exposure

EPA Region

□ 25th percentile   □ median   ▨ 75th percentile   ■ 90th percentile

decisions—decisions by companies to locate hazardous facilities in vulnerable communities, and decisions by government regulators to give less priority to environmental enforcement in these communities. They can also reflect neighborhood changes driven by environmental degradation: pollution pushes out the affluent and lowers property values, while poorer people seeking low-cost housing move in, either unaware of the health risks or unable to afford alternatives. Even after accounting for differences related to income, however, studies find that racial and ethnic minorities often face higher pollution burdens—implying that disparities are the result of differences in political power as well as purchasing power.

The United States is a big, heterogeneous country. Electoral politics, social movements, industrial structure, residential segregation, and environmental policies differ across regions. So patterns of pollution may vary, too. Our recent study "Regional variation in environmental inequality: Industrial air toxics exposure in U.S. cities" examines these patterns to ask two key questions. First, is minority status or income more important in explaining environmental disparities? Second, does income protect minorities from pollution as much as it protects whites?

To tackle these questions, we used data on industrial air pollution from the U.S. Environmental Protection Agency (EPA). In the 1980s, in the wake of the deadly toxic gas release at a plant owned by the U.S.-based company Union Carbide in Bhopal, India, in which thousands of nearby residents were killed, environmental advocates in the U.S. demanded disclosure of information on hazards faced by communities near industrial facilities. In response, Congress passed the Emergency Planning and Community Right-to-Know Act of 1986, requiring corporations to disclose their releases of dangerous chemicals into our air, water, and lands. These are reported annually in the EPA's Toxics Release Inventory. The EPA has combined

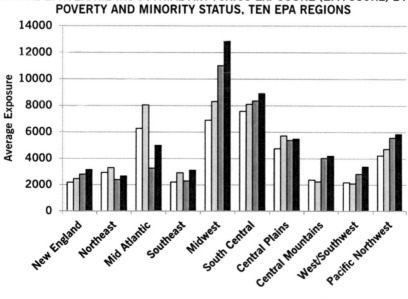

FIGURE 2: AVERAGE INDUSTRIAL AIR TOXICS EXPOSURE (EPA SCORE) BY POVERTY AND MINORITY STATUS, TEN EPA REGIONS

□ Non-poor white   □ Poor white   ▨ Non-poor minorities   ■ Poor minorities these data with information on the toxicity and dispersion of hazardous chemical releases to create the Risk-Screening Environmental Indicators (RSEI), the database we use, that estimates the total human health risks in neighborhoods across the country from multiple industrial pollution sources and chemicals.

Industrial air pollution varies greatly across regions of the country. Figure 1 shows the level of health risk faced by the median resident (in the middle of the region's exposure distribution) as well as by more highly impacted residents (in the 75th and 90th percentiles of exposure). The Midwest and South Central regions have the highest levels, reflecting historical patterns of both industrial and residential development.

Figure 2 shows average pollution exposure by region for four groups: non-poor whites, poor whites, non-poor minorities and poor minorities. Poor minorities consistently face higher average exposure than non-poor minorities, and in most regions poor whites face higher average exposure than non-poor whites. In general, poor minorities also face higher exposure than poor whites, and non-poor minorities face higher exposure than non-poor whites. But in mapping environmental injustice we do find some noteworthy inter-regional differences—for example, in the contrast between racial disparities in the Midwest and Mid-Atlantic regions—that point to the need for location-specific analyses.

Finally, Figure 3 depicts the average pollution exposure for four racial/ethnic groups across income strata at the national level. The most striking finding here is that racial disparities in exposure are much wider among people who live in lower-income neighborhoods. At the lower-income end of the scale, the average exposures of African Americans are substantially greater than those of whites. The lower average exposures for Hispanics in low-income neighborhoods are largely explained by their concentration in western and southwestern cities with

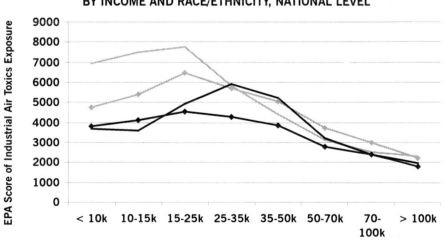

FIGURE 3: AVERAGE INDUSTRIAL AIR TOXICS EXPOSURE BY INCOME AND RACE/ETHNICITY, NATIONAL LEVEL

below-average pollution. Statistical analysis shows, however, that within these cities Hispanics also tend to live in the more polluted neighborhoods.

Pollution risk increases with average neighborhood income for all groups up to a turning point at around $25,000 per year. This can be explained by the positive association between industrialization and economic development. After that point, however, income becomes protective, and rising neighborhood income is associated with lower pollution exposure. Among these higher-income neighborhoods, racial and ethnic disparities in exposure are almost non-existent. But because of the correlation between minority status and income, minorities are more concentrated in lower-income communities whereas whites are more concentrated in upper-income communities. Based on where they live, whites may be more likely to see income as the main factor explaining disparities in pollution exposure, whereas African Americans are more likely to see the racial composition of neighborhoods as what matters most.

Environmental protection is not just about protecting nature from people: it's also about protecting people from other people. Those who benefit from industrial air pollution are the corporations that reap higher profits and their consumers, insofar as avoided pollution-control costs are passed on in the form of lower prices. Those who bear the greatest harm are the residents of nearby communities. Safeguarding the environment requires remedying this injustice and the imbalances of power that lie behind it. ❑

Sources: Michael Ash and T. Robert Fetter, "Who Lives on the Wrong Side of the Environmental Tracks?" *Social Science Quarterly*, 85(2), 2004; H. Spencer Banzhaf and Randall B. Walsh, "Do People Vote with Their Feet?" *American Economic Review*, 98(3), 2008; Vicki Been and Francis Gupta, "Coming to the nuisance or going to the barrios?" *Ecology Law Quarterly*, 24(1), 1997; James K. Boyce, "Inequality and Environmental Protection," in Jean-Marie Baland, Pranab K. Bardhan, and Samuel Bowles, eds., *Inequality, Cooperation, and Environmental Sustainability* (Princeton University Press, 2007); James K. Boyce, *The Political Economy of the Environment* (Edward Elgar, 2002); Paul Mohai and Robin Saha, "Reassessing Racial and Socioeconomic Disparities in Environmental Justice Research," *Demography*, 43(2), 2006; Rachel Morello-Frosch, et al., "Environmental Justice and Regional Inequality in Southern California: Implications for Future Research," *Environmental Health Perspectives*, 110(S2), 2002; Manuel Pastor, Jim Sadd, and John Hipp, "Which Came First? Toxic Facilities, Minority Move-In, and Environmental Justice," *Journal of Urban Affairs*, 23(1), 2001; Evan J. Ringquist, "Assessing Evidence of Environmental Inequities: A Meta-Analysis," *Journal of Policy Analysis and Management*, 24(2), 2005; Klara Zwickl, Michael Ash, and James K. Boyce, "Regional Variation in Environmental Inequality: Industrial Air Toxics exposure in U.S. Cities," *Ecological Economics*, (107), 2014.

Chapter 7

LABOR MARKETS

INTRODUCTION

Mainstream economics textbooks emphasize the ways that labor markets are similar to other markets. In the standard model, labor suppliers (workers) decide how
much to work in the same way that producers decide how much to supply, by weighing
the revenues against the costs—in this case, the opportunity costs of foregone leisure,
and other potential costs of having a job, like physical injury. Workers are paid their
marginal product, the extra output the firm gets from employing one extra unit (e.g.,
hour) of labor. Workers earn different wages because they contribute different marginal products to output. Of course, economists of every stripe acknowledge that, in
reality, many non-market factors, such as government assistance programs, unionization, and discrimination, affect labor markets. But in most economics textbooks, these
produce only limited deviations from the basic laws of supply and demand.

In the first article, Alejandro Reuss addresses the reasons behind union decline
in the United States (Article 7.1). While mainstream economists often attribute this
trend to the inexorable forces of globalization, Reuss points out that unions have not
declined to the same extent in other countries (including the United States' more
globalized neighbor to the north). He emphasizes, instead, the differences between
institutions and policies in different countries and their effects on the balance of power
between workers and employers.

John Miller and Jeannette Wicks-Lim take apart the argument, increasingly
heard in policy circles, that a large share of unemployment today is a result not of the
generalized lack of demand caused by the recession, but of workers not having the
skills that employers desire (Article 7.2). In this article, Miller and Wicks-Lim show
that this argument has little empirical support and that it shifts the blame for unemployment onto workers themselves.

Next, Dean Baker looks at the so-called "sharing economy," exemplified by the
likes of the driving services Uber and Lyft. Baker argues that these services could use
some competition—in the form of a "public option." That is, the government could
provide a platform connecting willing drivers and consumers seeking rides, just like
these private, for-profit services, but without skimming a large portion of the revenues.
(Article 7.3)

Gerald Friedman continues the discussion of insecure "contingent labor,"
or what he calls the "gig economy" in the United States. In "Dog Walking and
College Teaching" (Article 7.4), Friedman shows how labor contracts with little

job security have been on the rise in everything from construction and office work to higher education.

Next, Zoe Sherman (Article 7.6) turns our attention to the nail-care industry, the subject of a recent major exposé in the *New York Times*. Sherman notes that it is not so surprising—when goods are provided by anonymous (to the consumer) people living and working far away—that the end consumer not give much though to the labor conditions under which those goods were produced. She then asks how the same is possible when services are provided my people in close, direct contact with the recipient.

Nancy Folbre follows with another article on labor that is often "invisible," in this case to official government economic accounts—unpaid household labor. As Folbre notes, the exclusion of this labor, largely done by women, from government estimates of employment and GDP is "pretty crazy, since we know that these services contribute to our living standards and also to the development of human capabilities."

Finally, Sirisha Naidu looks at conditions for women in India's labor market today. Naidu shows, that even as India's economy has been growing fast, millions of women have been pushed out of the wage labor force. She argues for a new development program prioritizing job creation, living-wage and labor-conditions regulation, and essential public services. Government action against gender discrimination and sexual harassment, too, is necessary for inclusive development. (Article 7.7).

Discussion Questions

1. (Article 7.1) Why has the number of workers represented by unions fallen in the United States over the last few decades? Is globalization, by itself, a plausible explanation?

2. (Article 7.2) What data support the case that today's high unemployment rates can be attributed to a mismatch between job openings and workers' skills? How do Miller and Wicks-Lim respond to these arguments?

3. (Article 7.3) Baker argues for the introduction of a "public option" to sharing-economy sectors like driving services. What do you think that mainstream economists, who tout the positive effects of market competition, would say about this?

4. (Article 7.4) Why have "contingent" labor arrangements increased so much in recent decades? How do employers benefit from these arrangements? If workers, on balance, are harmed by reduced job security, why do employers not have a hard time finding people willing to work under such contracts?

5. (Article 7.5) What is "commodity fetishism"? Do you think the concept is useful in explaining the social distance between consumers and workers, even when the two are in close physical proximity?

6. (Article 7.6) In Folbre's view, how has the "invisibility" of household labor and production from official economic data had negative consequences, both on our economic understanding and economic policies?

7. (Article 7.7) According to Naidu, why has there been such a large decline in women's labor force participation in India?

Article 7.1

WHAT'S BEHIND UNION DECLINE?

It's not just globalization, as a U.S.-Canada comparison shows.

BY ALEJANDRO REUSS
May 2015

The total number of union members in the United States peaked between the late 1970s and early 1980s, at over 20 million. As of 2010, it remained near 15 million. The story of union decline in the United States, however, does not begin in the 1980s, nor is it as modest as these figures would suggest. Union density (or the "unionization rate"), the number of workers who are members of unions as a percentage of all employed workers, has been declining in the United States for over half a century. The share of U.S. workers in unions peaked in 1954, at just over 25%. For nonagricultural workers, the high-water mark—at more than one third of employed workers—came even earlier, in 1945. It would reach nearly the same percentage again in the early 1950s, before beginning a long and virtually uninterrupted decline.

By 2010, the U.S. unionization rate was less than 12%. It would be even lower were it not for the growth of public-sector unions since the 1960s. For private-sector workers, the unionization rate is now less than 7%.

There are multiple reasons for union decline, including shrinking employment in highly unionized industries, falling unionization rates within these traditional bastions of unionism, and failures to unionize in new, growing sectors.

Employers' determination to rid themselves of unions has certainly played a major role in declining unionization rates. Where employers could not break unions, they were determined to find ways around them—even during the period of the so-called "capital-labor accord," from the 1940s to the 1970s. In reality, this was less a friendly relationship than a transition, on the part of employers, to low-intensity warfare when a frontal assault was not possible. Unionized companies established parallel non-union operations, a practice sometimes known as "double breasting," gradually shifting production and employment away from their unionized facilities. Some employers began contracting out work formerly done by union employees to non-union subcontractors (the original meaning of "outsourcing"). Some established new operations far from their traditional production centers, especially in less unionized and lower-wage areas. Many companies based in the Northeast and Upper Midwest, for example, set up new production sites in the South and West, and eventually in other countries. Finally, new employers entering highly unionized sectors usually remained non-union. The auto industry is a good example. So-called "transplants" (factories owned by non-U.S. headquartered companies) have accounted for an increasing share of the industry's shrinking labor force, and have remained overwhelmingly non-union.

Historically, union growth has come primarily in short spurts when unions expand into new industries. Since the 1940s, however, U.S. unions have failed to organize in growing industries to compensate for the declines in employment and unionization rates in traditional union strongholds. The public sector represents the one major exception. Since the early 1970s, union density for public-sector workers has increased from about 20% to over 35%. This has not been nearly enough, however, to counteract the decline among private-sector workers. To maintain the overall unionization rates of the 1950s or 1960s, unions would have had to enlist millions more workers in the private sector, especially in services.

The Employers' Offensive

Since the 1970s, employers have fought unions and unionization drives with increasing aggressiveness, as part of what labor historian Michael Goldfield calls the "employer offensive." Many employers facing unionization drives fire vocal union supporters, both eliminating pro-union campaigners and spreading fear among the other workers. Researchers at the Center for Economic and Policy Research (CEPR) have found that, between 2001 and 2005, pro-union workers were illegally fired in around one-fourth of all union election campaigns. Meanwhile, during many unionization campaigns, employers threaten to shut down the facility (at least in part) if the union wins. Labor researcher Kate Bronfenbrenner reports, in a study from the mid 1990s, that employers threatened plant closings in more than half of all unionization campaigns, and that such threats cut the union victory rate (compared to those in which no such threat was made) by about 30%.

The employer offensive has unfolded, especially since the 1980s, against a backdrop of government hostility towards unions. The federal government has often turned a blind eye to illegal tactics (or "unfair labor practices") routinely used by employers to fight unionization drives. Employer retaliation against workers (by firing or otherwise) for union membership, union activity, or support for unionization is illegal. So is an employer threatening to close a specific plant in response to a unionization drive. However, since the 1980s, union supporters argue, the government agencies tasked with enforcing labor law have increasingly ignored such

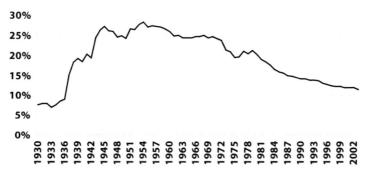

FIGURE 1: UNION MEMBERS AS A PERCENTAGE OF EMPLOYED WORKERS UNITED STATES, 1930-2003

Source: Gerald Mayer, Union Membership Trends in the United States, CRS Report for Congress, August 31, 2004, Table A1, Union Membership in the United States, 1930-2003 (digitalcommons.ilr.cornell.edu/key_workplace/174).

FIGURE 2: WORK STOPPAGES INVOLVING 1,000 OR MORE WORKERS UNITED STATES, 1947-2010

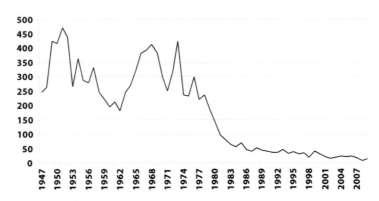

Source: Bureau of Labor Statistics, Work Stoppages Involving 1,000 or More Workers, 1947-2008 (bls.gov/news.release/ wkstp.t01.htm).

practices, imposed only "slap on the wrist" punishments, or delayed judgment, sometimes for years, long after the unionization drive is over and done with.

Before the 1980s, it was relatively rare for employers to fire striking workers and hire "permanent replacements." (Sometimes, employers would bring in replacements during a strike, but striking workers would get their jobs back after a settlement was reached.) During the 1980s, private employers increasingly responded to strikes by firing the strikers and bringing in permanent replacements—a practice that is illegal in many countries, but not in the United States. Some labor historians point to the Reagan administration's mass firing of striking air-traffic controllers (members of the Professional Air Traffic Controllers Organization, or PATCO) in 1981 as a deliberate signal to private employers that the government approved their use of permanent replacements (as well as other union-busting tactics). The number of large strikes, already in sharp decline during the preceding few years (possibly due to the employers' offensive, rising unemployment, and other factors), has since declined to microscopic proportions. People do not go out on strike if they feel that they are not only likely to lose, but to lose their jobs in the bargain.

At this point, union density in the United States—less than a tenth of all private-sector workers—is almost back down to its level on the eve of the Great Depression. An optimistic union supporter might note that the 1930s turned out to be the greatest period of union growth in U.S. history, with substantial additional growth in the 1940s and 1950s largely an aftershock of that earlier explosion. There is no guarantee, however, that history will repeat itself, and that the weakness of organized labor today will give way to a new burst of energy. In the midst of a deep recession, and now more than five years of a feeble recovery, there have been few signs of a labor revival. Ironically, only the recent attacks on public-sector workers and unions have provoked a mass-movement fight-back. Labor supporters, however, should understand this, soberly, as coming from a very defensive position.

Is it Globalization?

Union size and strength have declined not only in the United States, but also in most other high-income countries. The reasons are complex, but globalization has surely played a role. Along with changing patterns of demand and increasing mechanization, global sourcing of production has contributed to employment declines in traditionally high-unionization industries. It has also provided employers with a stronger trump card when workers try to form new unions—the threat to relocate, especially to low-wage countries. To a greater or lesser extent, these effects are probably felt in all high-income countries.

Unionization rates, however, have declined in some countries much more than in others. According to data compiled by economist Gerald Friedman, the unionization rate for the United States peaked earlier, peaked at a lower percentage, and has declined to a lower percentage today, compared to those of most other high-income countries. Today, fourteen high-income countries (out of 15 listed by Friedman) currently have unionization rates higher than the United States' 14%. Ten have rates higher than the U.S. peak of about 26% (reached in 1956). Six have rates above 50%; three, above 80% (Gerald Friedman, "Is Labor Dead?" International Labor and Working Class History, Vol. 75, Issue 1, Table One: The Decline of the Labor Movement). (The declines in the unionization rates for ten of these countries, since each one's peak-unionization year, are shown in Figure 3.)

Let's compare, in more detail, the trajectories of unionization in the United States and its neighbor to the north, Canada (shown in Figure 4). Until the 1960s, the trends in the two countries were similar—declining in the 1920s, bottoming out in the early 1930s, growing dramatically through the rest of the 1930s, the 1940s, and into the 1950s. Since then, however, the two have diverged. The U.S. unionization rate has traced a long and nearly uninterrupted path of decline for the last half century. Meanwhile, the Canadian rate, which had gone into decline

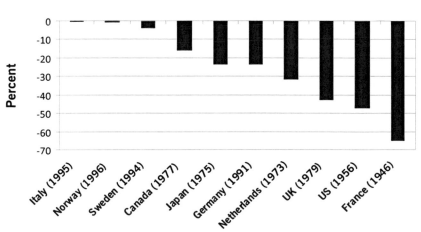

FIGURE 3: PERCENTAGE DECLINE FROM PEAK UNIONZATION RATE, SELECTED COUNTRIES (PEAK YEAR IN PARENTHESES

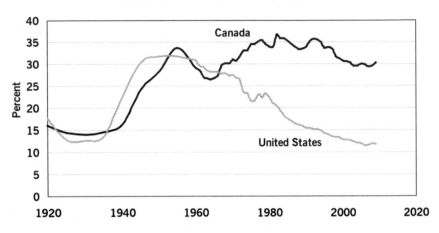

FIGURE 4: UNIONZATION RATES,
CANADA AND UNITED STATES, 1920-2009

in the 1950s and 1960s, recovered between the 1970s and 1990s. It has declined somewhat since then, but remains nearly three times the U.S. rate (almost 30%, compared to just over 10% for the United States). It would be difficult, even ignoring the Canadian data, to attribute U.S. union decline just to international factors, such as import competition (which became a major factor in the 1970s) or global sourcing (which has been a major factor since the 1990s). These factors simply come too late to fully explain trends going back to the 1950s. Looking at the comparison with Canada, however, drives the point home: "globalization" is simply not the irresistible tidal wave, wiping out unions across the globe, that many commentators claim.

There are a couple of possible explanations for the divergence of U.S. and Canadian unionization rates (or, more generally, the divergence of the unionization rates in any two capitalist economies in the era of globalization).

First, perhaps it is possible for a country to effectively insulate itself from the global economy. That is, it may use controls on international trade and investment to prevent its economy from becoming "globalized" or, more likely, to regulate the ways that it is integrated into the world capitalist economy. That is, however, definitely not what is going on with Canada. It is a member of NAFTA; its economy is highly integrated with that of the United States, both in terms of trade and investment; its imports and exports, as a percentage of GDP, are actually much larger than those of the United States. By any standard Canada has a more globalized economy than the United States.

Second, even if a country's economy is highly integrated into the world capitalist economy, the political and legal environments for labor relations—as well as the history and culture of its labor movement—have tremendous effects on the ability of unions to survive in the age of globalization. A recent report from the Center for Economic and Policy Research (CEPR) attributes the much sharper decline of U.S. unions primarily to "employer opposition to unions—together with relatively weak labor law" in the United States compared to Canada, rather than "structural changes to the economy ... related to globalization or technological progress."

The report, "Protecting Fundamental Labor Rights: Lessons from Canada for the United States," focuses in particular on two differences in labor law: In Canada, workers have card-check unionization, the right to form a union once most of the workers in a bargaining unit have signed a union card. This prevents employers from fighting unionization—including by firing union supporters or threatening shut downs, as are common in the United States—during a long, drawn-out period before a union election. (U.S. unions have proposed a similar legislation at the national level, but employers have so far prevented such a bill from passing.) Also, Canadian law requires, in the event that a union and employer cannot arrive at a first collective bargaining agreement, that the two parties enter arbitration. As the CEPR report put it, this "ensure[s] that workers who voted to unionize [are] able to negotiate a contract despite continued employer opposition." In the United States, in contrast, employers often stonewall in initial negotiations, and many new unions never actually achieve a signed union contract.

A third factor, not discussed in the CEPR report, is the difference between the United States and Canada in laws governing the right to strike. In the United States, it is legal for employers to fire striking workers and hire permanent replacements. Since the late 1970s, when U.S. employers started routinely using permanent replacements, strikes have become much harder for workers to win and, as a result, much less frequent. This has deprived U.S. workers of their main form of bargaining power, the ability to withdraw their labor and shut down production, cutting off the source of the employer's profits. In contrast, most Canadian provinces ban employers from using permanent replacements.

Finally, the CEPR report does note the possibility that weaknesses of the U.S. labor movement itself—especially the "lack of focus on organizing new members" —accounts for at least part of the divergence. Indeed, the labor movements in most capitalist countries have faced changes in employment patterns, and the relative decline of traditional high-unionization industries. As Friedman notes, however, some have been able to make up for declining employment in their traditional strongholds by organizing workers in growing-employment sectors (Friedman, Reigniting the Labor Movement (Routledge, 2008)). The U.S. labor movement—mostly, to be sure, due to the hostile environment for new organizing—has not been able to do so. The Canadian labor movement also differs from U.S. labor in having created an explicitly labor-oriented political party, the New Democratic Party. (Most western European countries also have strong labor, social democratic, or socialist parties with institutional and historical ties to unions.) In many countries, such parties have played an important role in gaining favorable labor legislation, and more generally blunting attacks on labor by employers and governments.

Global economic forces affecting all countries cannot, by themselves, explain the various patterns of union decline across different capitalist countries (or the patterns would be more similar). The differing political environments in different countries—such as the laws protecting workers' rights to form unions, to go on strike, and so on—likely explain most of the differences in the degree of union decline in different high-income countries. ❏

Sources: Michael Goldfield, "Labor in American Politics—Its Current Weakness," *The Journal of Politics*, Vol. 48, No. 1. (Feb., 1986), pp. 2-29; Kate Bronfenbrenner, "Final Report: The Effects of Plant Closing or Threat of Plant Closing on the Right of Workers to Organize," *International Publications*, Paper 1, 1996 (digitalcommons.ilr.cornell.edu/intl/1); Gerald Friedman, *Reigniting the Labor Movement: Restoring Means to Ends in a Democratic Labor Movement* (New York: Routledge, 2008); Gerald Mayer, "Union Membership Trends in the United States," CRS Report for Congress, August 31, 2004, Table A1, Union Membership in the United States, 1930-2003 (digitalcommons.ilr.cornell.edu/key_workplace/174); Bureau of Labor Statistics, "Work Stoppages Involving 1,000 or More Workers," 1947-2008 (www.bls.gov/news.release/wkstp.t01.htm); John Schmitt and Ben Zipperer, "Dropping the Ax: Illegal Firings During Union Election Campaigns," Center for Economic and Policy Research, January 2007 (www.cepr.net/documents/publications/unions_2007_01.pdf); Kris Warner, "Protecting Fundamental Labor Rights: Lessons from Canada for the United States," Center for Economic and Policy Research, August 2012 (http://cepr.net/documents/publications/canada-2012-08.pdf).

Article 7.2

UNEMPLOYMENT: A JOBS DEFICIT OR A SKILLS DEFICIT?

BY JOHN MILLER AND JEANNETTE WICKS-LIM
January/February 2011

Millions of Americans remain unemployed nearly a year and a half after the official end-date of the Great Recession, and the nation's official unemployment rate continues at nearly 10%.

Why? We are being told that it is because—wait for it—workers are not qualified for the jobs that employers are offering.

Yes, it's true. In the aftermath of the deepest downturn since the Great Depression, some pundits and policymakers—and economists—have begun to pin persistently high unemployment on workers' inadequate skills.

The problem, in this view, is a mismatch between job openings and the skills of those looking for work. In economics jargon, this is termed a problem of "structural unemployment," in contrast to the "cyclical unemployment" caused by a downturn in the business cycle.

The skills-gap message is coming from many quarters. Policymaker-in-chief Obama told Congress in February 2009: "Right now, three-quarters of the fastest-growing occupations require more than a high school diploma. And yet, just over half of our citizens have that level of education." His message: workers need to go back to school if they want a place in tomorrow's job market.

The last Democrat in the White House has caught the bug too. Bill Clinton explained in a September 2010 interview, "The last unemployment report said that for the first time in my lifetime, and I'm not young ... we are coming out of a recession but job openings are going up twice as fast as new hires. And yet we can all cite cases that we know about where somebody opened a job and 400 people showed up. How could this be? Because people don't have the job skills for the jobs that are open."

Economists and other "experts" are most likely the source of the skills-gap story. Last August, for instance, Narayana Kocherlakota, president of the Federal Reserve Bank of Minneapolis, wrote in a Fed newsletter: "How much of the current unemployment rate is really due to mismatch, as opposed to conditions that the Fed can readily ameliorate? The answer seems to be a lot." Kocherlakota's point was that the Fed's monetary policy tools may be able to spur economic growth, but that won't help if workers have few or the wrong skills. "The Fed does not have a means to transform construction workers into manufacturing workers," he explained.

The skills-mismatch explanation has a lot to recommend it if you're a federal or Fed policymaker: it puts the blame for the economic suffering experienced by the 17% of the U.S. workforce that is unemployed or underemployed on the workers themselves. Even if the Fed or the government did its darndest to boost overall spending, unemployment would be unlikely to subside unless workers upgraded their own skills.

The only problem is that this explanation is basically wrong. The weight of the evidence shows that it is not a mismatch of skills but a lack of demand that lies at the heart of today's severe unemployment problem.

High-Skill Jobs?

President Obama's claim that new jobs are requiring higher and higher skill levels would tend to support the skills-gap thesis. His interpretation of job-market trends, however, misses the mark. The figure that Obama cited comes from the U.S. Department of Labor's employment projections for 2006 to 2016. Specifically, the DOL reports that among the 30 fastest growing occupations, 22 of them (75%) will typically require more than a high school degree. These occupations include network systems and data communications analysts, computer software engineers, and financial advisors. What he fails to say, however, is that these 22 occupations are projected to represent less than 3% of all U.S. jobs.

What would seem more relevant to the 27 million unemployed and underemployed workers are the occupations with the *largest* growth. These are the occupations that will offer workers the greatest number of new job opportunities. Among the 30 occupations with the largest growth, 70%—21 out of 30—typically do not require more than a high school degree. To become fully qualified for these jobs, workers will only need on-the-job training. The DOL projects that one-quarter of all jobs in 2016 will be in these 21 occupations, which include retail salespeople, food-preparation and food-service workers, and personal and home care aides.

In fact, the DOL employment projections estimate that more than two-thirds (68%) of the jobs in 2016 will be accessible to workers with a high school degree

---

Labor Market Musical Chairs

To understand the data discussed here, try picturing the U.S. labor market as a game of musical chairs, with a few twists. At any time, chairs (job openings) can be added to the circle and players can sit down (get hired). When the music stops at the end of the month, not all the chairs are filled. Still, many people—far more people than the number of empty chairs—are left standing.

Each month, the Bureau of Labor Statistics reports on what happened in that month's game of labor market musical chairs in its various measures of unemployment and in the Job Openings and Labor Turnover Survey (JOLTS). Here's how the BLS scorecard for labor market musical chairs works.

- Job openings is a snapshot of the number of jobs available on the last day of the month—the number of empty chairs when the music stops.
- Hires are all the new additions to payroll during the month—the number of people who found a chair to sit in while the music was playing. Because many chairs are added to the circle and filled within the same month, the number of hires over a month is typically greater than the number of openings available on the last day of that month.
- Unemployed persons are those who looked for a job that month but couldn't find one—the number of people who played the game but were left standing when the music stopped at the end of the month.

or less. Couple this with the fact that today, nearly two-thirds (62%) of the adult labor force has at least some college experience, and an alleged skills gap fails to be convincing as a driving force behind persistent high unemployment.

Low-Skill Workers?

If employers were having a hard time finding qualified workers to fill job openings, you'd think that any workers who are qualified would be snapped right up. But what the unemployment data show is that there remains a substantial backlog of experienced workers looking for jobs or for more hours in their existing part-time jobs in those major industries that have begun hiring—including education, healthcare, durable goods manufacturing, and mining.

Most telling are the *underemployed*—those with part-time jobs who want to work full-time. Today there are more underemployed workers in each of the major industries of the private economy than during the period from 2000 to 2007, as Arjun Jayadev and Mike Konczal document in a 2010 paper published by the Roosevelt Institute. Even in the major industries with the highest number of job openings— education and health services, professional and business services, transportation and utilities, leisure and hospitality, and manufacturing—underemployment in 2010 remains at levels twice as high or nearly twice as high as during the earlier period (measured as a percentage of employed workers).

Purveyors of the mismatch theory would have a hard time explaining how it is that underemployed workers who want full-time work do not possess the skills to do the jobs full time that they are already doing, say, 20 hours a week.

More broadly, workers with a diverse set of skills—not just construction workers—lost jobs during the Great Recession. Workers in manufacturing, professional and business services, leisure and hospitality, transportation and utilities, and a host of other industries were turned out of their jobs. And many of these experienced workers are still looking for work. In each of the 16 major industries of the economy unemployment rates in September 2010 were still far higher than they had been at the onset of the Great Recession in December 2007. In the industries with a large number of (cumulative) job openings during the recovery—education and health services, professional and business services, and manufacturing—experienced workers face unemployment rates twice what they were back in December 2007.

There are plenty of experienced workers still looking for work in the industries with job openings. To be faithful to the data, Kocherlakota and the other mismatch proponents would need to show that experienced workers no longer possess the skills to work in their industry, even though that industry employed them no more than three years ago. That seems implausible.

Statistical Errors

Still, the statistical oddity that Bill Clinton and many economists have pointed to does seem to complicate the picture. If the number of job openings is rising at a good clip yet the number of new hires is growing more slowly and the unemployment rate is stagnant, then maybe employers *are* having trouble finding qualified folks to hire. Once you take a closer looks at the numbers, though, there is less here than meets the eye.

First, the *rate* at which job openings and new hires numbers change over time is not the right place to look. What we really need to know is how the number of unfilled job posts compares to the number of qualified workers employers hire over the same month. If employers in today's recovery are having a hard time finding workers, then the job openings left unfilled at the end of the month should be relatively high compared to the number of newly hired workers that month. In other words, if the number of positions left unfilled at the end of the month relative to the number of new hires rises *above* what we've seen during past recoveries, this would mean that employers are finding it harder to fill their positions with the right workers this time around.

But it turns out that the ratio of unfilled job openings to new hires is approximately the same during this recovery as in the recovery from the 2001 recession. In September 2010, fifteen months into the current economic recovery, the ratio of job posts left unoccupied at the end of the month to the number of monthly new hires stood at 69%—very close to its 67% level in February 2003, fifteen months into the

---

Where Mismatches May Matter

The skills-mismatch theory does not go very far toward explaining stubbornly high U.S. unemployment. Still, there are unquestionably some unemployed and underemployed workers whose job prospects are limited by "structural" factors.

One kind of structural unemployment that does seem to fit the contours of the Great Recession to at least some degree is that caused by a mismatch of geography: the workers are in one part of the country while the jobs they could get are in another. The housing crisis surely has compromised the ability of unemployed workers to unload their single largest asset, a house, and move to another part of the country. Plus, job losses have been particularly heavy in regions where the housing crisis hit hardest.

But at the same time, lost jobs have been widespread across industries and there is little real evidence of geographic mismatch between job openings and unemployed workers. As labor economist Michael Reich reports, "economic decline and the growth of unemployment have been more widespread than ever before, making it unclear where the unemployed should migrate for greater job opportunities."

Even where there is a skills mismatch, that doesn't mean the government shouldn't get involved. On the contrary, government policies to boost economic demand can help significantly. When demand is high, labor markets become very tight and there are few available workers to hire. Workers previously viewed as "unemployable" get hired, get experience and on-the-job training, and see their overall career prospects brighten.

And, of course, government can fund expanded job-training programs. If the economy continues to slog along with low growth rates and persistent unemployment, the ranks of the long-term unemployed will rise. As they go longer and longer without work, their skills will atrophy or become obsolete and they will face a genuine skills-mismatch problem that will make job-training programs more and more necessary.

last recovery. In other words, today's employers are filling their job openings with the same rate of success as yesterday's employers.

Comparisons that focus on the unemployment rate rather than on the number of new hires are even less meaningful. As hiring picks up at the beginning of an economic recovery, workers who had given up the job search start looking again. This brings them back into the official count of the unemployed, keeping the unemployment rate from dropping even as both job openings and new hires rise.

Not Enough Jobs

The reality of the situation—the widespread job losses and the long, fruitless job searches of experienced workers—make it clear that today's employment problem is a jobs deficit across the economy, not a skills deficit among those looking for work.

While it's true that any given month ends with some number of unfilled job openings, the total number of jobs added to the economy during this recovery has simply been inadequate to put the unemployed back to work. In fact, if every job that stood open at the end of September 2010 had been filled, 11.7 million officially unemployed workers would still have been jobless.

This recovery has seen far fewer job openings than even the so-called "jobless" recovery following the 2001 recession. Economists Lawrence Mishel, Heidi Shierholz, and Kathryn Edwards of the Economic Policy Institute report that cumulative job openings during the first year of this recovery were roughly 25% lower than during the first year of the recovery following the 2001 recession—that's 10 million fewer jobs. Even in the industries generating the most job openings in the current recovery—education and health services, professional and business services, leisure and hospitality, and manufacturing—the cumulative number of job openings has lagged well behind the figure for those industries during the first year of the recovery from the 2001 recession. (Only the mining and logging category, which accounted for just 0.5% of employment in 2007, has had more job openings during the first year of this recovery than during the first year of the 2001 recovery.)

Why has the pick-up in jobs following the Great Recession been worse than usual? The simple answer is that the recession was worse than usual. The sharp and extreme decline of output and employment in the Great Recession has severely dampened demand—that is, people have not had money to buy things. With the resulting lack of sales, businesses were not willing to either invest or hire; and this in turn has meant a continuing lack of demand.

If businesses have barely resumed hiring, it has not been for lack of profits. By the middle of 2010, corporate profits (adjusted for inflation) were about 60% above their low point at the end of 2008, well on their way back to the peak level of mid-2006. Also, in early 2010 non-financial firms were sitting on almost $2 trillion in cash. There was no lack of ability to invest and hire, but there was a lack of incentive to invest and hire, that is, a lack of an expectation that demand (sales) would rise. As is well known, small businesses have generally accounted for a disproportionately large share of job growth. Yet, since the onset of the Great Recession, small business owners have consistently identified poor sales as their single most important problem—and thus, presumably, what has prevented them from expanding employment.

The Role of Demand

Regardless of the lack of evidence to support it, the skills-mismatch story has seeped into media coverage of the economy. Take, for example, National Public Radio's recent Morning Edition series titled "Skills gap: holding back the labor market." In one segment, reporter Wendy Kaufman presents anecdotes about employers turning down record numbers of applicants and leaving job openings unfilled. Economist Peter Capelli then comes on and remarks, "You know, a generation ago you'd never expect that somebody could come into a reasonably skilled, sophisticated position in your organization and immediately make a contribution. That's a brand new demand." Now, that comment does not point to today's workers possessing fewer skills or qualifications. Rather, it suggests that employers have raised the bar: they are pickier than in the past.

That makes sense. We've seen that employers are successfully filling positions at about the same rate as in the recent past. What's different this time around is that employers have had up to six unemployed workers competing for every job opening left vacant at the close of the month. This is by far the highest ratio on record with data back to 2000. During the 2001 recession, that ratio rose to just over two unemployed workers for each opening. (In the first years of the "jobless recovery" following the 2001 recession, the ratio continued to rise, but it remained below three to one.) Clearly, these numbers favor the alternative explanation. Unfortunately, Kaufman doesn't even consider it.

That's too bad. Recognizing that a lack of demand for goods and services is to blame for the severe crisis of unemployment puts the focus squarely back on the federal government and on the Fed, which could help to remedy the problem —*if* they had the political will to do so. Millions of unemployed workers, organized and armed with an accurate diagnosis of the problem, could create that political will— unless they are distracted by a wrong-headed diagnosis that tries to blame them for the problem. ❑

Sources: Bureau of Labor Statistics Table A-14, Unemployed persons by industry and class of workers, not seasonally adjusted, historical data (bls.gov); Lawrence Mishel, Heidi Shierholz, and Kathryn Anne Edwards, "Reasons for Skepticism About Structural Unemployment," Economic Policy Institute, Briefing Paper #279, September 22, 2010 (epi.org); Arjun Jayadev and Mike Konczal, "The Stagnating Labor Market," The Roosevelt Institute, September 19, 2010 (rooseveltinstitute. org); Bureau of Labor Statistics, Job Openings and Labor Turnover (JOLTS) Highlights, September 2010 (bls.gov); Michael Reich, "High Unemployment after the Great Recession: Why? What Can We Do?," Policy Brief from the Center on Wage and Employment Dynamics, Institute for Research on Labor and Employment, University of California, Berkeley, June 2010 (irle.berkeley.edu/cwed); Narayana Kocherlakota, President Federal Reserve Bank of Minneapolis, "Inside the FOMC," Marquette, Michigan, August 17, 2010 (minneapolisfed.org); Lawrence Mishel and Katherine Anne Edwards, "Bill Clinton Gets It Wrong," Economic Policy Institute, Economic Snapshot, September 27, 2010 (epi.org); "Remarks of President Barack Obama—Address to Joint Session of Congress," February 24, 2009 (whitehouse.gov); "The Skills Gap: Holding Back the Labor Market," Morning Edition, National Public Radio, November 15, 2010 (npr.org).

Article 7.3

THE SHARING ECONOMY NEEDS A PUBLIC OPTION

BY DEAN BAKER

March 2015, Al Jazeera America

So-called "sharing economy" companies such as Uber, Airbnb, and Task Rabbit are posing policy headaches for governments around the world. Their argument that they should be exempt from existing regulations because their services are ordered over the web does not make much sense, but it provides an adequate fig leaf for politicians seeking campaign contributions from these highly capitalized newcomers.

For those who have missed the hype, "sharing economy" refers to a wide variety of companies that use the web to connect consumers and providers. While there is not reliable data on its size, in part because it is not well-defined, Airbnb now boasts far more room listings than Hilton or Marriott, and Uber has quickly grown to be the largest taxi service in the world.

Part of the response to the innovations associated with these sharing economy companies should be to modernize regulations. It is reasonable to regulate taxi services in ways that ensure that cars are safe and drivers are competent and responsible. It is also reasonable to regulate rented rooms to ensure they are not fire traps. Similarly, both should be regulated in ways that ensure access to the handicapped and prevents discrimination. In addition, employees in these companies should be covered by workers' compensation and protected by minimum wage and overtime rules.

These efforts will require a rewriting of existing regulations, many of which were put in place to protect the existing companies in the industry rather than serve a legitimate public purpose. This sort of modernization is clearly a doable task from a technical standpoint, although sharing economy companies will undoubtedly use their money to try to block the imposition of rules that put them on an equal footing with their old-fashioned competitors.

In addition to a level-the-playing-field approach, we can also treat the sharing economy companies to some new competition: a public option. The idea is that governments can set up public sites that would provide the same services as the sharing economy companies. The difference would be that the public sites would cut out the middle man. They would be set up to benefit customers and service providers with the government only charging the fees necessary to cover costs.

For example, a taxi service could allow for drivers to register in the same way as they do for Uber and Lyft. Customers could use an app to order their services just as they do with Uber and Lyft. The difference would be that the public service would likely take out a lower share of the fare than its for-profit competitors. If its design was effective, only drivers who felt like being ripped off would work for Uber and Lyft.

In addition, a public service could directly apply standards to providers as a condition of participating. Cab drivers would have to meet licensing standards and their cars would have to pass inspection. And they would have to arrange insurance for both car and driver. A public version of Airbnb could require that potential renters had their rooms inspected for fire safety and also provide copies of leases or condo agreements to ensure that these were not being violated by renting out rooms or whole units.

A non-profit in England (with the unfortunate name Beyond Jobs) has established an open-source program for many of these purposes. This system may not be fully up to the job, but it should provide a basis from which to work.

In addition to cutting out the middle man and ensuring that necessary standards are met, a public service could provide other important benefits. Most notably, it could ensure that customer reviews are the property of the service provider. As it stands now, the reviews are typically the property of the company.

This means if an Uber driver has established himself as a safe and reliable driver, he can't use his recommendations with another service. The same would be the case with someone renting out a room or apartment through Airbnb. This issue is perhaps most important with labor-service providers such as Task Rabbit. If a worker has established herself as a reliable electrician, plumber, or child-care provider, she should be able to carry this record with her. While Task Rabbit and comparable services may not allow such transfers, a public system could assure workers of transferable recommendations.

Another great feature to the public option route is that it can be implemented at the local level. There is no need to worry about an intransigent Congress or even hostile state legislators. Any city with a substantial progressive base should be able to take the initiative to set up its own public-sharing economy system. Such systems can also be linked between cities, which could be especially helpful in the case of competing with Airbnb.

Naturally, there will be problems in setting up such systems, as is always the case in establishing something new. But there is no reason that a public system cannot be at least as efficient as the private networks now operating. After all, the administrative costs of the public Social Security system are less than one tenth as high as the costs of private retirement accounts.

Rather than trying to squash sharing economy companies, which would almost certainly not be possible in any case, a far better strategy for progressives is to take advantage of the innovations they offer and restructure them in ways that ensure the public and service providers both benefit. This can be done, if we are prepared to try some new tactics. ❑

Article 7.4

DOG WALKING AND COLLEGE TEACHING
The Rise of the Gig Economy

BY GERALD FRIEDMAN
March/April 2014

G rowing numbers of Americans no longer hold a regular "job" with a long-term connection to a particular business. Instead, they work "gigs" where they are employed on a particular task or for a defined time, with little more connection to their employer than a consumer has with a particular brand of chips. Borrowed from the music industry, the word "gig" has been applied to all sorts of flexible employment (otherwise referred to as "contingent labor," "temp labor," or the "precariat"). Some have praised the rise of the gig economy for freeing workers from the grip of employers' "internal labor markets," where career advancement is tied to a particular business instead of competitive bidding between employers. Rather than being driven by worker preferences, however, the rise of the gig economy comes from employers' drive to lower costs, especially during business downturns. Gig workers experience greater insecurity than workers in traditional jobs and suffer from lack of access to established systems of social insurance.

FIGURE 1: EMPLOYED WORKERS BY CONTRACT TYPE, 1999

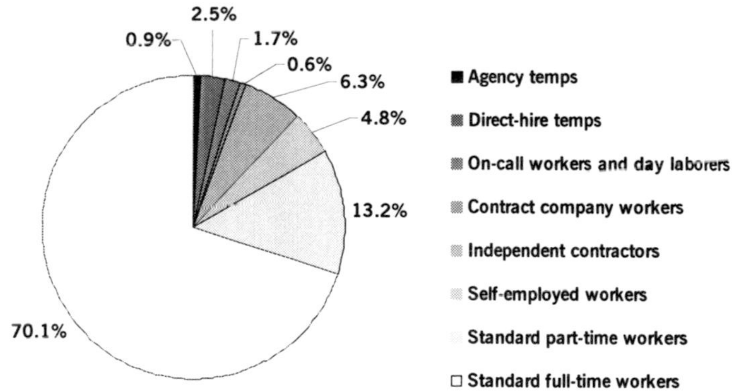

- 2.5%
- 0.9%
- 1.7%
- 0.6%
- 6.3%
- 4.8%
- 13.2%
- 70.1%

■ Agency temps

▨ Direct-hire temps

▨ On-call workers and day laborers

▨ Contract company workers

▨ Independent contractors

▨ Self-employed workers

Standard part-time workers

☐ Standard full-time workers

Special surveys by the Bureau of Labor Statistics in 1995, 2001, and 2005, and by the General Accounting Office in 1999, yielded widely varying estimates of the scale of the gig economy. The GAO estimated that as many as 30% of workers were on some type of contingent labor contract, including some categories of workers (self-employed and part-time workers) who are not counted as contingent workers by the BLS. According to BLS, 12% of workers were in "alternative work arrangements" (which includes independent contractors, temporary workers, on-call workers, and workers provided by contract firms) in 1999, similar to the number estimated from more recent surveys.

FIGURE 2: SHARE OF WORKERS IN ALTERNATIVE WORK ARRANGEMENTS, BY INDUSTRY, 2005

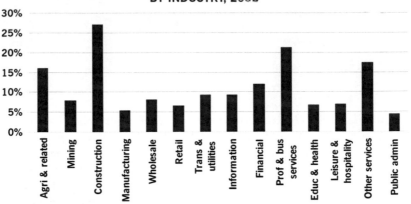

Contingent workers are employed throughout the economy, in all industries and in virtually all occupations. Workers in what the BLS terms "alternative work arrangements" made up over 11% of employed workers in 2005, according to BLS. Some workers in such arrangements do low-wage work in agriculture, construction, manufacturing, retail trade, and services; others are employed as highly paid financial analysts, lawyers, accountants, and physicians..

FIGURE 3: CONTINGENT LABOR, COLLEGE AND UNIVERSITY FACULTY

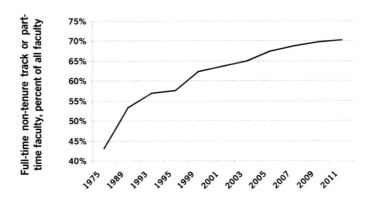

While many people may think of "day laborers" in construction or office "temps" when they think of contingent workers, few occupations have seen as sharp an increase in contingent labor as teaching in higher education. Full-time non-tenure track or part-time professors now account for the great majority of college faculty nationwide. Tenured and tenure-track faculty now comprise less than a third of the teaching staff, and teach barely half of all classes. Colleges and universities hire adjunct faculty because they make it possible to more precisely match faculty to the demand for classes, and because adjuncts are paid substantially less.

FIGURE 4: AVERAGE COMPENSATION, TRADITIONAL VS. CONTINGENT EMPLOYMENT

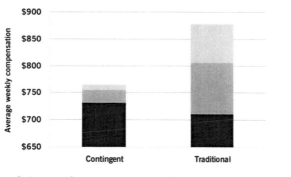

Note: Vertical axis begins at $650, to show detail.

■ Cash wages ▨ Government mandated benefits ▨ Employer-provided benefits

Employers prefer contingent labor because it is more "flexible." Workers can be laid off at any time in response to a decline in sales. Employers can also pay contingent workers less by not offering benefits. By treating many contingent workers as independent contractors, employers avoid paying for government-mandated benefits (the employer's half of Social Security, unemployment insurance, workers' compensation, etc.). They also usually exclude contingent workers from employer-provided benefits such as health insurance and pensions. Counting wages and benefits, contingent workers are paid substantially less than workers in traditional jobs and are left much more vulnerable to illness or economic downturns.

FIGURE 5: NET JOB GROWTH, TRADITIONAL VS. CONTINGENT, 1995-2013

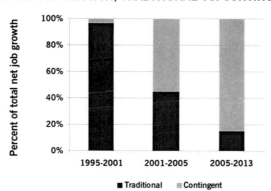

■ Traditional ▨ Contingent

While a solid majority of workers is still employed under traditional arrangements, most new net job growth since 2001 has been under "alternative" arrangements. This is in sharp contrast to the late 1990s, when unemployment rates were low and employers had to offer workers more desirable long-term contracts. With the early 2000s recession, followed by the Great Recession and the anemic recovery (2007 to the present), however, employers have shunned long-term employment contracts and workers have had to settle. ❑

Sources: General Accounting Office (GAO), Contingent Workers: Incomes and Benefits Lag Behind Those of Rest of Workforce (gao.gov); Bureau of Labor Statistics (BLS), Contingent and Alternative Employment Arrangements, February 2005 and February 2001 (bls.gov); Sharon Cohany, "Workers in Alternative Employment Arrangements." *Monthly Labor Review* (October): 31–46; U.S. Department of Education, National Center for Education Statistics, National Study of Postsecondary Faculty; John Curtis, "Trends in Faculty Employment Status, 1975-2011" (aaup.org).

Article 7.5

MANICURES, PEDICURES, AND COMMODITY FETISHISM

BY ZOE SHERMAN
September/October 2015

Almost everything costs more in the New York metropolitan area. But there is one notable exception: nail salon services. The price of a manicure or pedicure in New York is surprisingly low. A series of articles published in the *New York Times* in May of this year brought attention to the shocking abuses endured by many of the women providing those services. The manicure costs the customer $10 or $15. It costs the manicurist her freedom, dignity, and health. (This is true even if we leave aside the business of coerced prostitution for which some nail salons are a front.) Manicurists are most often immigrants, very often recently arrived. With immediate need for income and limited knowledge of local labor markets and labor rights, they are vulnerable.

We are used to hearing about labor abuses in sweatshops, both domestically and abroad. We are sometimes asked to attend to the frighteningly harsh conditions endured by farm workers—migrant workers picking strawberries in California, children on cocoa plantations in West Africa. That happens far from the point of purchase. We don't hear the din of the sewing machines when we browse the clothing rack, feel the blaze of the sun and the ache of a stooped back when we peruse the produce aisle. We may regret the abuses we hear about, but we can understand why most don't see them clearly: the goods are produced by the combined labor of hundreds of people and shipped thousands of miles from the hands of the makers to those of the consumers. In the nail salon, the others, whose labor provides for us, cradle our hands and feet in their hands. They work in brightly illuminated spaces, often behind plate glass windows clearly visible to passersby. Why didn't we know how desperate and dangerous their situations were?

"It's a beautiful industry, it makes people feel better," said Eugenia Colón, who worked as a self-employed manicurist in Brooklyn until suffering lung damage that prompted her to leave the business. "But if a lot of people knew the truth behind it, it wouldn't happen. They wouldn't go."

"The Truth Behind It"

Only about a quarter of manicurists make the legally mandated minimum wage; the rest make less. Virtually all, even that minority whose compensation meets the legal minimum, have been victims of wage theft, working hours for which they are not paid. Indeed, it is common for new workers to pay the salon owner a fee to secure a position and work for months without receiving pay. Even after manicurists gain months or years of on-the-job experience, salon owners may insist on more payments for promotions to better-paid positions within the salon. Manicurists' days in the salon are long. They have little protection from abusive treatment by customers or oppressive supervisors. The industry operates on a rigid racial caste system with Latinas on the lowest rung and Koreans on the highest (though there remains a sharp divide between Korean employees and owners). Nationality largely determines job assignments and pay scales.

Dangers come, too, from the physical conditions of work, not just the socio-economic conditions. The materials used in nail care are toxic. The level of exposure experienced by customers is small enough that most will not suffer obvious health consequences. Even a regular customer may only be in the salon for 30 to 60 minutes at a stretch every few weeks. The workers are in the salon ten or twelve hours at a stretch, six or seven days a week, potentially for years on end. Common health consequences include respiratory disease, constant headaches, and reproductive problems. Many miscarry, and even those children of manicurists who are born full term seem to suffer developmental delays with higher frequency than the general population. (Limited data availability makes it impossible to calculate the increased risk for any of these health outcomes with great precision, but there are enough data to strongly suggest that manicurists suffer these harms at higher rates than the general population.) In addition to the toxin exposure, close contact with dozens of customers a day exposes manicurists to every contagious bacterium, virus, and fungus customers carry with them. Extended exposure to some of the chemicals in nail products causes a distinctive skin discoloration; manicurists with enough years in the industry say they can spot one another on the street.

The revelations were so appalling that New York Governor Andrew Cuomo responded immediately with a proposal for stricter oversight and more vigorous protection for those vulnerable to being caught in an abusive workplace in the nail care industry.

Hidden in Plain Sight—But with a Price Tag

Why couldn't we see what was happening? There is a long tradition of economic thinking that explains how the working conditions for those who produce goods are obscured from those who buy the goods. Our ignorance of a product's origins is a component of the phenomenon Karl Marx called *commodity fetishism* (see box, next page). But the concept of commodity fetishism is most familiarly applied to objects that travel a great distance from the worker to the buyer. It is perhaps more surprising that commodity fetishism can operate at close range. Yet with a combination of intentional veiling by salon owners and coerced role playing by manicurists—the name on her smock is often not actually her name—we were able to not see what the manicure costs the manicurist.

We did, however, have one big clue that could have tipped us off to the labor abuses in the salons: the surprisingly low price. In the translation from a complex web of human interdependence to a market price, a great deal of information is lost. What clues do prices give us about the human relations veiled by the market transaction? Marx began his exploration of this question with a first, highly simplified approximation, adapted from the work of earlier political economists such as Adam Smith and David Ricardo, and proceeded to allow more and more real-world complications into the analysis.

As a first approximation, Marx supposed that goods trade in proportion to the typical amount of labor required to produce them. If it normally takes ten hours to make a barrel and five hours to make a basket, barrels will cost twice as much as baskets. This is not just the labor of the final assembly, but also the labor that went into materials and tools. The value of a cabinet is proportional not just to the labor of the cabinetmaker but also to the labor of the lumberjack and the machinist. Keep in mind, too, that the value must be in proportion to the hours of labor that *typically* go into making a good of that kind, what Marx called the "socially necessary labor," not the exact number of hours that went into one specific example of that good. If the products are the same, producers who take longer get the same price

---

Commodity Fetishism: The Paradox of Market Interdependence

In nail salons, the market—the exchange of a service for money—seems to have acted as a veil. This is true for most everything we buy: the market brings goods to our attention and makes them available for us to buy, but hides their histories from us. They arrive stripped of association with those whose labor produced them. (Stripped, too, of association with the environmental source of the materials those workers labored to transform.) It leaves us profoundly ignorant of the human interdependencies we are all a part of. As consumers, we don't know where the objects with which we furnish our lives come from. As workers, we are invisible to those who buy what we make ... unless some investigative reporting brings workers' stories to light.

In the nineteenth century, Karl Marx named the veiling effect of the market "commodity fetishism." It is, then, an old idea, but an idea that is as potent and relevant as ever. Many of the concerns roused by the nail salon story are not particular to this specific personal service industry, but a general feature of a market economy.

By "commodity," we mean any good produced for sale and exchanged for money. (Not only the narrower definition of commodity as indistinguishable raw materials traded on a large-scale market, like crude oil or grain.) The word "commodity" shares an etymological root with commodious and accommodate—suggesting that commodities are things that bring comfort to life. Marx adopted the word "fetishism" from its use in the anthropology of his day. Anthropologists used the word to describe the practice in many religious traditions of ascribing sacred powers to physical objects. The anthropologists observing these practices were pretty certain that the objects, though sacred to believers, did not in fact have any special powers prior to the believers' faith. Put the two together and what on earth did Marx mean?

He meant that when we encounter commodities in the market, they have a price and that price appears to us as a characteristic of the commodity itself, just as sacred powers appear, to the believer, to be inherent features of the sacred object. We ascribe the price to the qualities of the object. But this, he explained, is a fetishistic delusion. Just as the powers of the sacred object originate with the believer and do not arise independently in the object, a commodity's price comes from market relations that we create and do not really reflect the qualities of the object as object. Instead, a market price is a reflection of the social relations in which the object was produced and exchanged. But it all happens in such a complex way that our own participation in making it so is hard for us to see. The market looks like it mediates relationships among goods; really it mediates relationships among people.

Our interdependencies are, as the economy becomes globally integrated, more intricate, more profound, and more invisible. Most of us don't have the faintest idea how to survive without the flow of commodities that sustain us, but we most often perceive our consumer choices as a relationship between ourselves and things, rather than, as they really are, a relationship between ourselves and other people.

as producers who churn things out faster. So relative prices give us a clue about the labor required for production.

A manicure requires a half hour of the manicurists' labor plus a little additional labor for the polish that is used up and small sliver of labor time for the table, chair, and brush that are reused for many manicures before needing replacement. Even at low New York manicure prices and high New York grocery store prices, the manicure costs more than a pint of ice cream. Ice cream production is largely automated and takes very little human labor time. Even the labor that went into making the machines that automated the production process is divided up across so many pints of ice cream that the labor per pint is small. In contrast, a manicure costs far less than a men's three-piece suit. Even with mechanized spinning and weaving of fabric and sewing machines for assembly, a suit requires much more than half an hour of human labor to produce.

This might look at first like a technical matter, like the characteristics of the object determine the price after all. But the choice of production method is largely a matter of human relationships. Characteristics of the object and the state of technical knowledge are relevant to the choice of production methods, certainly, but the relations in which production methods are chosen matter a heck of a lot, too. When do labor-saving machines pay for themselves? That depends in part on how much power workers have to bargain for higher wages. Machines may also be chosen for control of the workforce. If you have watched Charlie Chaplin's classic movie *Modern Times*, you can imagine here Chaplin haplessly attempting to keep up with the speed-up of the assembly-line machinery until he is finally sucked into the gears.

We know that relative prices track the quantity of labor embodied in goods only very loosely so there is more we must add to the story. As a next detail, we can recognize that not every work hour is equal. Some work requires special training or skill; a surgeon, for example, puts in many hours of training before she performs her first surgery. The value of an hour of her work time reflects the hours she spent in preparation for her job and so is worth more than an hour of work that can be done with less prior training. And some training is more recognized and rewarded than others: providing excellent childcare also requires many hours of experience, for example, but does not get the same respect or remuneration as surgery. The combination of formal training (if any) and on-the-job experience typical for manicurists is less extensive and less rewarded than many other professions.

Marx began his analysis with production, but markets matter, too. Market competition in New York is fierce; there are many more nail salons per capita than in most of the rest of the country. Salon owners made some attempts to mute price competition, but there were too many and they were too disorganized to sustain any agreement on pricing. (Also, for perfectly good reasons, there are laws against price fixing.)

The markets for inputs also matter. (The inputs are all the components needed to make the final product: materials, tools, workspace, labor, etc.) The most important input into a manicure is the labor of the manicurist and manicurists are drawn from a profoundly disempowered pool of workers operating under a rigid and divisive racial caste system. As a result, half an hour of a manicurist's time costs significantly less than a schoolteacher's or a secretary's time and costs orders of magnitude less than half an hour of a doctor's or a lawyer's time. So the low price results from the relatively small amount of labor needed to produce the good, the fierce price competition among salons, and the extreme exploitation of the workforce. All of these factors describe relationships among people.

What Can We Do?

Governor Cuomo called for consumer action, asking customers to spend conscientiously. If you see abuses, he urged, "walk out the door, go down the block, patronize another business. … Nobody can do it faster than the consumer can do it," he said. "Nobody can do it faster than the marketplace can do it." But ethical, informed consumerism can only take us so far. Information is difficult and time consuming to get. As *New York Times* reporter Sarah Maslin Nir wrote, "much of how salons operate and how workers are treated is kept deliberately opaque to the outside world." What information an individual consumer can get is hard to interpret, and whatever ethical judgments we can make are uncertain. Even when we turn to supposedly independent certifiers of a business's labor and environmental records, we can be misled.

There are a few notable success stories for consumer action, but they involved *collective* consumer actions: college students pressuring their colleges as large-scale, institutional buyers. Students on several college campuses were involved in the Justice for Janitors campaign, for example. Also, student activists used their colleges' leverage as large buyers of licensed apparel to force Adidas to do better by workers who produced the gear. (See Sarah Blaskey and Phil Gasper "Campus Struggles Against Sweatshops Continue," Article 3.5.) Individual consumers cannot do as much. From patriots in the late 18th-century colonies boycotting English textiles in favor of homespun, to abolitionists in the mid-19th century boycotting slave-produced sugar, to conscientious 20th-century grocery shoppers boycotting grapes in support of agricultural workers, consumer action has more often brought attention to a cause and contributed to mobilizing other forms of action (up to and including war) than it has directly applied market discipline to achieve just ends. The marketplace cannot do it as fast as Cuomo claims and probably can't do it at all. An unorganized smattering of nail salon customers finding a more responsible business to patronize or choosing to go without will not be enough.

Nor is a return to a mythical past of personalized face-to-face economic interdependence a solution. People have a long track record of exploiting and abusing others at close range, especially when there are differences of race, gender, or other markers of social status that can be called on as justification. There is no mystifying market intermediation between the slaveowner and the products of the slave's labor.

Instead, as the *New York Times* editorial board noted, the best thing we can do is to empower workers to act collectively in defense of their own rights. In our roles as consumers we will never know in detail the production history of every item we handle. Our lives will always be furnished with the embodied labor of those we will never know and cannot see. As workers and as citizens we can, however, support workers' rights for ourselves and for others.

With real worker protections, some items would end up costing more, as they probably should. Not many—and perhaps no one with substantive freedom of choice—would pay for a manicure, or even a thousand manicures, with a miscarriage or lung disease. We can't expect anyone else to pay that price on our behalf.

Sources: Sarah Maslin Nir, "The Price of Nice Nails," *New York Times*, May 7, 2015; Sarah Maslin Nir, "Perfect Nails, Poisoned Workers," *New York Times*, May 8, 2015; Michael M. Brynbaum, "New York Nail Salons Now Required to Post Workers' Bill of Rights," *New York Times*, May 29, 2015; Karl Marx, "The Fetishism of Commodities and the Secret Thereof," *Capital*, Vol. 1, Ch. 1.

Article 7.6

HOUSEHOLD LABOR, CARING LABOR, UNPAID LABOR

AN INTERVIEW WITH NANCY FOLBRE

September/October 2015

Nancy Folbre is a professor emerita of economics at the University of Massachusetts-Amherst. She is the author of numerous books, including Who Pays for the Kids? Gender and the Structures of Constraint (1994), The Invisible Heart: Economics and Family Values (2001), and Valuing Children: Rethinking the Economics of the Family (2008), related to household and caring labor.

Dollars & Sense: You've written about the tendency in economics to view household labor (and especially women's labor) as "unproductive." Can you explain how this is reflected in conventional macroeconomic measures?

Nancy Folbre: Non-market household services such as meal preparation and childcare are not considered part of what we call "the economy." This means they literally don't count as part of Gross Domestic Product, household income, or household consumption.

This is pretty crazy, since we know that these services contribute to our living standards and also to the development of human capabilities. They are all at least partially fungible: time and money may not be perfect substitutes, but there is clearly a trade-off. You can, in principle, pay someone to prepare your meals (as you do in a restaurant), or to look after your kids.

If you or someone else in your household provides these services for no charge (even if they expect something in return, such as a share of household earnings) that leaves more earnings available to buy other things. In fact, you could think of household income after taxes and after needs for domestic services have been met as a more meaningful definition of "disposable income" than the conventional definition, which is simply market income after taxes.

D&S: What is the practical consequence of not measuring household labor and production? Are economic policies and institutions different, especially in their impact on women, than what they would be if household labor were fully reflected in statistics on total employment or output?

NF: One macroeconomic consequence is a tendency to overstate economic growth when activities shift from an arena in which they are unpaid to one in which they are paid (all else equal). When mothers of young children enter paid employment, for instance, they reduce the amount of time they engage in unpaid work, but that reduction goes unmeasured. All that is counted is the increase in earnings that results, along with the increase in expenditures on services such as paid childcare.

As a result, rapid increases in women's labor force participation, such as those typical in the United States between about 1960 and the mid-1990s, tend to boost the rate of growth of GDP. When women's labor force participation levels out, as it has in the United States since the mid 1990s, the rate of growth of GDP slows down. At least some part of the difference in growth rates over these two periods simply reflects the increased "countability" of women's work.

Consideration of the microeconomic consequences helps explain this phenomenon. When households collectively supply more labor hours to the market, their market incomes go up. But they have to use a substantial portion of those incomes to purchase substitutes for services they once provided on their own—spending more money on meals away from home (or pre-prepared foods), and child care. So, the increase in their money incomes overstates the improvement in their genuinely disposable income.

A disturbing example of policy relevance emerges from consideration of the changes in public assistance to single mothers implemented in the United States in 1996, which put increased pressure on these mothers to engage in paid employment. Many studies proclaimed the success because market income in many of these families went up. But much of that market income had to be spent paying for services such as child care, because public provision and subsidies fell short.

D&S: You've also written extensively about "caring labor"? What is caring labor? To what extent is this labor (and the output of services associated with it) directly or indirectly captured by conventional measures like GDP?

NF: Everything I've discussed above is about quantity. But quality is also important. I define caring labor as labor where the quality of the services provided is likely to be affected by concern for the well-being of the care recipient. Love, affection, and commitment almost always enhance the care of dependents, and this is a big reason why market-provided services are not always perfect substitutes for those provided by family members and friends.

On the other hand, many people—especially women—work in occupations like child care, elder care, education, medicine, or social services where they genuinely care about their clients or "consumers." The market value of this work is counted as part of Gross Domestic Product and household income. But in many cases, the wage paid is considerably less than the value of the services provided. Workers in these jobs often give more in the way of quality than they are actually paid for.

D&S: As a practical matter, how could one go about measuring the value of services currently provided by unpaid household labor? In your estimation, how would our picture of economic life change if we did?

NF: It is pretty easy to estimate a lower-bound for the value of unpaid work by counting the number of hours that people spend engaging in it (which in the United States adds up to almost exactly the same total as hours of market work), and multiplying those hours times the hourly wage one would pay for a replacement.

Measures of hours worked in different activities such as meal preparation, child care, cleaning, shopping, and so on are typically based on a nationally representative survey of individuals who report all of their activities on the preceding day. The American Time Use Survey, administered since 2003 on an annual basis as a supplement to the Current Population Survey, provides reliable, high-quality data on time use.

Several studies have used these data to assign a dollar value to non-market work in what is called a "satellite" national income account (because it revolves around, rather than replacing the conventional account). Obviously, including this value in a measure of "extended GDP" makes the economy look bigger. More importantly, it revises estimates of how the economy has grown over time—in the downward direction.

Counting the value of non-market work has an equalizing effect on measures of household income, not because low-income households do a lot more of it, but because most households of similar size and composition do about the same amount. Here again, the trends are more interesting than the levels: since the relative importance of non-market work has declined over time, its equalizing effect has probably also declined. ❑

Article 7.7

MISSING WOMEN WORKERS

Explaining the decline in women's labor-force participation in India.

BY SIRISHA C. NAIDU
September/October 2015

Between 2005 and 20012, nearly 25 million women—roughly the size of the population of Australia—withdrew from the Indian wage-labor market. Imagine the frenzied reaction of news media, researchers, and policymakers if the entire population of Australia pulled out of the labor market in less than a decade! This decline in Indian women's labor force participation rate—which counts women who are employed in regular or casual wage work, self-employed or working in family-owned businesses, plus those who are seeking work, as a percentage of all working-age women—is part of a longer-term trend. The labor force participation rate for rural women declined from 42.5% in 1988 to 18% in 2012, and for urban women from 24.5% to 13.4% over the same span.

Development scholars and policymakers often assume that economic growth is a panacea that will unshackle women from the confines of the domestic sphere, increase their social status, and allow them to participate in economic and political decision-making as equals. It is puzzling, then, that the decline in women's participation in the labor market has continued into the current period, during which India has experienced robust economic growth—the World Bank expects India to overtake China as the world's fastest-growing economy by 2017.

No Cause for Alarm?

The most common understanding of women's labor force participation rate is as a "U-shaped" curve—high for countries with very low or very high levels of development, and low for countries at middling levels of development. At low levels of economic development, countries are more likely to be labor-intensive agrarian economies using low levels of technology and high inputs of female labor. Poverty compels women to contribute to household income. These factors lead to a high participation rate. As countries begin to develop and achieve moderate levels of development, they make the transition from agricultural to industrial production. Agriculture begins to employ more "advanced" technology, which reduces the demand for labor, particularly women's labor. Meanwhile, the increase in non-agricultural jobs increases household incomes and reduces the need for women to participate in the labor market. (Economists call this the "income effect.") The overall result of the demand and supply factors is a lower proportion of women in the labor force. Finally, as these countries continue to develop, there is increased demand for highly skilled labor which, as women secure higher levels of education, they are able to fulfill. The net result is an increase in women's participation in the labor force once again.

Applying this hypothesis to India, some researchers argue that the declining proportion of women in the Indian labor force is no cause for alarm. Rather, it is just a reflection of the downward portion of the U-shaped relationship. Women, according to this argument, can afford the luxury of not working for pay due to higher household income. Indeed, India has some of the trappings of a middle-development country. Per capita income has increased from about $1,100 in 1990 to over $5,000 in 2012. Meanwhile, the contribution of the agricultural sector to GDP has declined from 29% to 18%, as the economy transitions toward higher-value sectors.

Demand Deficiency

To test the plausibility of the assertion that "there is no cause for alarm," let's explore some features associated with the demand and supply of women's labor in India. We start with the demand-side. Even though agriculture's contribution to *GDP* has declined, it still accounted for 47% of total *employment* in India by 2012. The rural female labor force, which is almost four times the size of the urban female labor force, derived 75% of its total employment from agriculture. Therefore, the sectors that create jobs for women are suffering from low growth in a period of overall high economic growth. Between 2005 and 2010, women workers suffered a net loss of 21.5 million agricultural and 3.1 million manufacturing jobs; meanwhile, more than 80% of the 22.3 million non-agricultural jobs created in this period went to male workers. The decline in agricultural employment, while perhaps desirable in the process of economic development, has not been sufficiently compensated by an increase in jobs in other sectors. The biggest losers of this phase of "jobless economic growth" in India have been women workers.

A second undesirable trend in the process of Indian economic development is that there is a far greater demand for contingent or informal workers than regular workers. Informal employment is contractual or insecure in nature and, according to a recent report from the Indian government, is characterized by lower wages, little or no benefits, lower job security, and higher instances of sexual harassment, compared to regular employment. Thus, along with jobless growth, women workers have to contend with poor quality, insecure jobs with a higher risk of harassment. These, along with some other factors, suggest that conditions on the demand side of the labor market are very undesirable for women workers.

Now let's look at the supply side. As stated earlier, according the "U-shaped" explanation, women reduce their labor market participation because of the *income effect*. While Indian per capita income has indeed increased, it has been accompanied by lower overall calorie consumption and poorer nutrition. It is thus possible, as research by economists Amit Basole and Deepankar Basu suggests, that despite higher incomes, many Indian households are suffering from increased expenditures on other essentials such as education and health, thus leading to a food-budget squeeze. Further, there is evidence of increased income inequality, which indicates that the benefits of economic development have not been widely shared. The latest data released by the Indian government's Socio Economic and Caste Census reveals that 75% of Indian households live on less than 5,000 rupees ($78.74) per month. Thus, it seems overly optimistic to claim that women, especially in the poorest households, are withdrawing from the labor market due to higher household incomes.

Women's reduced participation in the labor force coincides with an increase in working-age women's participation in "domestic and other allied activities." These consist of production for household consumption—such as processing one's own food or caring for animals that produce milk and meat for the household. It also includes cooking, cleaning, and caring for one's own family. These activities increase the consumption of total goods and services by the household, but do not show up in official GDP or labor-force statistics because they do not pass through the market. (See the interview with Nancy Folbre, "Household Labor, Caring Labor, Unpaid Labor," Article 7.6) Under the current system, if the very same work performed for the family is offered in the market, it increases GDP without actually increasing the value of goods and services in the economy. At the household level, if a family member earns just enough to purchase goods and services that she was previously producing for household consumption, she would add to household income but not household consumption. As feminist economists have argued, the exclusion of domestic and other allied work from the calculation of labor force participation rate underestimates the economically active population.

Indian women's increased participation in household production—at a time of high poverty and inequality, and low demand for women's labor—fails to square with the argument that women's labor force participation has declined due to the income effect. Rather, it suggests that women and their households are scrambling to ensure a minimum level of consumption for survival. Withdrawal from the labor market does not allow women to engage in leisure activities; it has instead pushed them back into the undervalued and invisible domestic sphere. This condition is exacerbated by the Indian government's dismal role in providing essentials such as education, healthcare, and well-paying decent jobs.

A Development Program

Thus, it is imperative that the Indian government take the following steps that dovetail with higher economic development:

- Include domestic and other allied activities in the calculation of women's labor force participation rate so that adequate policies can be formulated.

- Direct economic growth toward

- employment-generating sectors so that women workers can secure jobs.

- Regulate the labor market to ensure a living wage and better working conditions

- Provide basic services essential for survival and a healthy workforce, and free women from the drudgery of housework.

- Pass and enforce laws against gender discrimination in the workplace and enforce existing laws against sexual harassment.

Such intervention is necessary for two reasons. First, countries in North America and Western Europe that experienced an upturn in women's labor force participation, after an initial decline, often put in place deliberate policy measures—such as implementing anti-discrimination laws and investing in public education. Second, these countries faced different global economic conditions at the same stage of development as India presently. In today's economic environment, in which public sector jobs have declined, workers increasingly depend on employment in the private sector, which can relocate to almost any part of the world. This threatens workers' ability to negotiate higher wages, better working conditions, and a higher standard of living. It also reduces the promise of higher investment and jobs in the domestic economy by high-performing businesses. All of this negatively affects women's participation in the labor market. Rather than accepting the decline in women's participation rate as a necessary but temporary fallout of the development process, it is essential that the Indian government take corrective measures, so the Indian economy can fully employ its vast working age population, both male and female. ❏

Sources: Vinoj Abraham, "Missing labour or consistent 'de-feminisation'?" Economic and Political Weekly, Vol. 48, No. 31, 2013; Deepankar Basu and Amit Basole, "The calorie consumption puzzle in India: an empirical investigation," PERI Working Paper Series No. 285, University of Massachusetts-Amherst, 2013; Indrani Mazumdar and Neetha N., "Gender dimensions: employment trends in India, 1993-94 to 2009-10," Occasional Paper No. 56, Centre for Women's Development Studies, 2011; MRD, Socio Economic and Caste Census 2011, Ministry of Rural Development, Government of India, 2015; National Commission for Enterprises in the Unorganised Sector, *The Challenge of Employment in India: An Informal Economy Perspective*, Volume I, 2014; NSSO, Employment and Unemployment Situation in India, 68th Round July 2011-June 2012, Ministry of Statistics and Programme Implementation, Government of India, 2014; NSSO, *Participation of Women in Specified Activities along with Domestic Duties*, 68th Round, July 2011-June 2012, Ministry of Statistics and Programme Implementation, Government of India, 2014; Jayan Jose Thomas, "India's labour market during the 2000s: Surveying the Changes," *Economic & Political Weekly*, Vol. 48, No. 51, 2012; Jayan Jose Thomas, "The demographic challenge and employment growth in India," *Economic and Political Weekly*, Vol. 49, No. 6; The World Bank World Development Indicators (data.worldbank.org), 2014.

Chapter 8

THE DISTRIBUTION OF INCOME AND WEALTH

INTRODUCTION

For many mainstream economists, inequality in the distribution of income is a natural outcome of the functioning of markets. If workers get paid based on productivity, wage differences simply reflect underlying differences in productivity.

People who supply other inputs—investors or lenders supplying capital, landowners supplying land—are similarly rewarded according to the marginal products of those inputs. Even poverty is largely seen as a result of low productivity, which can be interpreted more compassionately as the consequence of a lack of education and training, or, at an extreme, as a result of shirking and a whole host of moral failings. President Reagan's deliberate use of the term "welfare queen" to cast poor, black women as undeserving of society's support is perhaps the most famous example of the latter. Indeed, in this view, a high degree of equality (or measures aimed at reducing inequality) would reduce the incentives for increasing productivity, slowing overall growth. Economists also argue that because the rich tend to save more (thus swelling the pool of resources available for investment), the larger the share of the economic pie that goes to them, the better the entire economy does. Trickle on down!

Chris Tilly, in his remarkable essay "Geese, Golden Eggs, and Traps" (Article 8.1), lays out the arguments for and against income equality and then takes down the rosy view of the economic benefits of inequality. His analysis shows how economies such as the United States' can end up in an "inequality trap" where high inequality leads to low growth, which in turn can lead to even higher inequality.

Dean Baker ("Inequality: The Silly Tales Economists Like to Tell," Article 8.2) rebuts mainstream economists' claims that globalization and technological change are the causes of rising inequality (and their implicit view that there is, therefore, nothing that can be done about it). Technological change, he argues, affects both lower-income and higher-income individuals. Meanwhile, the only reason that lower-income workers have borne the brunt of globalization is that, unlike high-income professionals, they lack the political power to secure protection from global competition.

The next two articles look at patterns of inequality along lines of gender and race. In his article "The Wages of Gender" (Article 8.3), Gerald Friedman reports that the gender income gap has narrowed in recent decades, owing to increased educational and work opportunities for women. There is still, however, a long way to go to achieve full equality. Meanwhile, Jeannette Wicks-Lim discusses how "It Pays to Be White" (Article 8.4) whether we're talking about education, job opportunities, policing, or just about any other aspect of life in the United States today. Wicks-Lim argues that the "social environment in the United States, steeped in race-based haves and have-nots" causes deep-rooted racial biases throughout the society. She ends the article by discussing possible policies to uproot these biases. The next two articles return to the underlying causes of income inequality. For anyone who wants to explore questions of inequality and fairness, Gar Alperovitz and Lew Daly's article "The Undeserving Rich" (Article 8.6) provides some fascinating grist for the mill. They argue that growth is built on a base of collectively produced knowledge that each generation inherits—not merely on the efforts of individuals. Therfore, they argue, those who appropriate a disproportionate share are "undeserving" of their fortunes.

This leads nicely into the next article, Arthur MacEwan's "Unions and Income Inequality" (Article 8.7). If the concentration of income at the very top is "unde-served," what can be done about it? MacEwan points out that the income share of the richest 1% declined when the share of workers who were union members rose, and has risen as union membership has fallen. To MacEwan it seems clear that restoring union size and strength would go a long way toward reducing inequal-ity (Article 8.5).

Gerald Friedman (Article 8.7) describes one of the most extreme manifes-tations of inequality and poverty in the United States today, widespread food insecurity. He notes that government nutrition programs have positive impacts both in terms of short-term alleviation of hunger and long-term health and eco-nomic benefits for recipients—but are just not extensive enough.

Finally, in "Inequality in the World," Arthur MacEwan looks at the complexi-ties involved in answering a seemingly simple question: Is global income inequality rising or falling? MawcEwan notes that, because some lower-income economies have grown faster than the high-income economies, inequality between countries has declined somewhat in recent years, Wait before you start celebrating. At the same time, income inequality within most large economies has increased sharply over the same period.

Discussion Questions

1. (Article 8.1) According to Tilly, many of the mechanisms linking equality and growth are political. Should economic models incorporate political behavior as well as economic behavior? What are some ways they could do that?

2. (Article 8.1) Explain Tilly's metaphor about the "Goose That Laid the Golden Eggs." How is equality the goose?

3. (Article 8.2) Why does Baker think that increasing inequality is not simply due to unavoidable processes of globalization and technological change? How is eco-nomic inequality, in Baker's analysis, related to inequalities in political power?

4. (Article 8.3) What are the key factors explaining the decline of the wage gap between men and women? Has this always been because women's compensation has grown spectacularly?

5. (Article 8.3) According to Friedman, what have been the wider social consequences of the increase in women's educational and work opportunities, and in turn their increasing role as household "breadwinners"?

6. (Article 8.4) It is common for people to view racial disparities in society (like job discrimination or racial profiling) as a consequence of racial biases. Wicks-Lim argues that biases are a consequence of racial disparities. Explain.

7. (Article 8.5) MacEwan shows that union strength and economic inequality are negatively associated (when one is high, the other is low). What possible explanations does MacEwan offer? Is there good reason to believe that higher unionization was the cause of greater equality in the past, and the decline of unions explains increased inequality in recent years?

8. (Article 8.6) Consider the following quotation:

   "I think we've been through a period where too many people have been given to understand that if they have a problem, it's the government's job to cope with it. ... They're casting their problem on society. And, you know, there is no such thing as society. There are individual men and women, and there are families."

   —British Prime Minister Margaret Thatcher, talking to *Women's Own* magazine, October 31, 1987

   After reading Alperovitz and Daly's article "The Undeserving Rich," how do you think the authors would respond to Thatcher? How would you respond?

9. (Article 8.7) If, as Friedman says, the United States is "wealthy enough that everyone could have enough to eat," why do people go hungry anyway? In your view, what could and should be done to remedy this situation?

10. (Article 8.8) If inequalities between countries are decreasing, how can inequality in the world be increasing?

Article 8.1

GEESE, GOLDEN EGGS, AND TRAPS
Why inequality is bad for the economy.

BY CHRIS TILLY
July/August 2004

Whenever progressives propose ways to redistribute wealth from the rich to those with low and moderate incomes, conservative politicians and economists accuse them of trying to kill the goose that lays the golden egg. The advocates of unfettered capitalism proclaim that inequality is good for the economy because it promotes economic growth. Unequal incomes, they say, provide the incentives necessary to guide productive economic decisions by businesses and individuals. Try to reduce inequality, and you'll sap growth. Furthermore, the conservatives argue, growth actually promotes equality by boosting the have-nots more than the haves. So instead of fiddling with who gets how much, the best way to help those at the bottom is to pump up growth.

But these conservative prescriptions are absolutely, dangerously wrong. Instead of the goose-killer, equality turns out to be the goose. Inequality stifles growth; equality gooses it up. Moreover, economic expansion does not necessarily promote equality—instead, it is the types of jobs and the rules of the economic game that matter most.

Inequality: Goose or Goose-Killer?

The conservative argument may be wrong, but it's straightforward. Inequality is good for the economy, conservatives say, because it provides the right incentives for innovation and economic growth. First of all, people will only have the motivation to work hard, innovate, and invest wisely if the economic system rewards them for good economic choices and penalizes bad ones. Robin Hood-style policies that collect from the wealthy and help those who are worse off violate this principle. They reduce the payoff to smart decisions and lessen the sting of dumb ones. The result: people and companies are bound to make less efficient decisions. "We must allow [individuals] to fail, as well as succeed, and we must replace the nanny state with a regime of self-reliance and self-respect," writes conservative lawyer Stephen Kinsella in *The Freeman: Ideas on Liberty* (not clear how the free woman fits in). To prove their point, conservatives point to the former state socialist countries, whose economies had become stagnant and inefficient by the time they fell at the end of the 1980s.

If you don't buy this incentive story, there's always the well-worn trickle-down theory. To grow, the economy needs productive investments: new offices, factories, computers, and machines. To finance such investments takes a pool of savings. The rich save a larger fraction of their incomes than those less well-off. So to spur growth, give more to the well-heeled (or at least take less away from them in the form of taxes), and give less to the down-and-out. The rich will save their money and then invest it, promoting growth that's good for everyone.

Unfortunately for trickle-down, the brilliant economist John Maynard Keynes debunked the theory in his *General Theory of Employment, Interest, and*

Money in 1936. Keynes, whose precepts guided liberal U.S. economic policy from the 1940s through the 1970s, agreed that investments must be financed out of savings. But he showed that most often it's changes in investment that drive savings, rather than the other way around. When businesses are optimistic about the future and invest in building and retooling, the economy booms, all of us make more money, and we put some of it in banks, 401(k)s, stocks, and so on. That is, saving grows to match investment. When companies are glum, the process runs in reverse, and savings shrink to equal investment. This leads to the "paradox of thrift": if people try to save too much, businesses will see less consumer spending, will invest less, and total savings will end up diminishing rather than growing as the economy spirals downward. A number of Keynes's followers added the next logical step: shifting money from the high-saving rich to the high-spending rest of us, and not the other way around, will spur investment and growth.

Of the two conservative arguments in favor of inequality, the incentive argument is a little weightier. Keynes himself agreed that people needed financial consequences to steer their actions, but questioned whether the differences in payoffs needed to be so huge. Certainly state socialist countries' attempts to replace material incentives with moral exhortation have often fallen short. In 1970, the Cuban government launched the Gran Zafra (Great Harvest), an attempt to reap 10 million tons of sugar cane with (strongly encouraged) volunteer labor. Originally inspired by Che Guevara's ideal of the New Socialist Man (not clear how the New Socialist Woman fit in), the effort ended with Fidel Castro tearfully apologizing to the Cuban people in a nationally broadcast speech for letting wishful thinking guide economic policy.

But before conceding this point to the conservatives, let's look at the evidence about the connection between equality and growth. Economists William Easterly of New York University and Gary Fields of Cornell University have recently summarized this evidence:

- Countries, and regions within countries, with more equal incomes grow faster. (These growth figures do not include environmental destruction or improvement. If they knocked off points for environmental destruction and added points for environmental improvement, the correlation between equality and growth would be even stronger, since desperation drives poor people to adopt environmentally destructive practices such as rapid deforestation.)
- Countries with more equally distributed land grow faster.
- Somewhat disturbingly, more ethnically homogeneous countries and regions grow faster—presumably because there are fewer ethnically based inequalities.
- In addition, more worker rights are associated with higher rates of economic growth, according to Josh Bivens and Christian Weller, economists at two Washington think tanks, the Economic Policy Institute and the Center for American Progress.

These patterns recommend a second look at the incentive question. In fact, more equality can actually strengthen incentives and opportunities to produce.

Equality as the Goose

Equality can boost growth in several ways. Perhaps the simplest is that study after study has shown that farmland is more productive when cultivated in small plots. So organizations promoting more equal distribution of land, like Brazil's Landless Workers' Movement, are not just helping the landless poor—they're contributing to agricultural productivity!

Another reason for the link between equality and growth is what Easterly calls "match effects," which have been highlighted in research by Stanford's Paul Roemer and others in recent years. One example of a match effect is the fact that well-educated people are most productive when working with others who have lots of schooling. Likewise, people working with computers are more productive when many others have computers (so that, for example, email communication is widespread, and know-how about computer repair and software is easy to come by). In very unequal societies, highly educated, computer-using elites are surrounded by majorities with little education and no computer access, dragging down their productivity. This decreases young people's incentive to get more education and businesses' incentive to invest in computers, since the pay-off will be smaller.

Match effects can even matter at the level of a metropolitan area. Urban economist Larry Ledebur looked at income and employment growth in 85 U.S. cities and their neighboring suburbs. He found that where the income gap between those in the suburbs and those in the city was largest, income and job growth was slower for everyone.

"Pressure effects" also help explain why equality sparks growth. Policies that close off the low-road strategy of exploiting poor and working people create pressure effects, driving economic elites to search for investment opportunities that pay off by boosting productivity rather than squeezing the have-nots harder. For example, where workers have more rights, they will place greater demands on businesses. Business owners will respond by trying to increase productivity, both to remain profitable even after paying higher wages, and to find ways to produce with fewer workers. The CIO union drives in U.S. mass production industries in the 1930s and 1940s provide much of the explanation for the superb productivity growth of the 1950s and 1960s. (The absence of pressure effects may help explain why many past and present state socialist countries have seen slow growth, since they tend to offer numerous protections for workers but no right to organize independent unions.) Similarly, if a government buys out large land-holdings in order to break them up, wealthy families who simply kept their fortunes tied up in land for generations will look for new, productive investments. Industrialization in Asian "tigers" South Korea and Taiwan took off in the 1950s on the wings of funds freed up in exactly this way.

Inequality, Conflict, and Growth

Inequality hinders growth in another important way: it fuels social conflict. Stark inequality in countries such as Bolivia and Haiti has led to chronic conflict that hobbles economic growth. Moreover, inequality ties up resources in unproductive uses such as paying for large numbers of police and security guards—attempts to prevent individuals from redistributing resources through theft.

Ethnic variety is connected to slower growth because, on the average, more ethnically diverse countries are also more likely to be ethnically divided. In other words, the problem isn't ethnic variety itself, but racism and ethnic conflict that can exist among diverse populations. In nations like Guatemala, Congo, and Nigeria, ethnic strife has crippled growth—a problem alien to ethnically uniform Japan and South Korea. The reasons are similar to some of the reasons that large class divides hurt growth. Where ethnic divisions (which can take tribal, language, religious, racial, or regional forms) loom large, dominant ethnic groups seek to use government power to better themselves at the expense of other groups, rather than making broad-based investments in education and infrastructure. This can involve keeping down the underdogs—slower growth in the U.S. South for much of the country's history was linked to the Southern system of white supremacy. Or it can involve seizing the surplus of ethnic groups perceived as better off—in the extreme, Nazi Germany's expropriation and genocide of the Jews, who often held professional and commercial jobs.

Of course, the solution to such divisions is not "ethnic cleansing" so that each country has only one ethnic group—in addition to being morally abhorrent, this is simply impossible in a world with 191 countries and 5,000 ethnic groups. Rather, the solution is to diminish ethnic inequalities. Once the 1964 Civil Rights Act forced the South to drop racist laws, the New South's economic growth spurt began. Easterly reports that in countries with strong rule of law, professional bureaucracies, protection of contracts, and freedom from expropriation—all rules that make it harder for one ethnic group to economically oppress another—ethnic diversity has no negative impact on growth.

If more equality leads to faster growth so everybody benefits, why do the rich typically resist redistribution? Looking at the ways that equity seeds growth helps us understand why. The importance of pressure effects tells us that the wealthy often don't think about more productive ways to invest or reorganize their businesses until they are forced to. But also, if a country becomes very unequal, it can get stuck in an "inequality trap." Any redistribution involves a tradeoff for the rich. They lose by giving up part of their wealth, but they gain a share in increased economic growth. The bigger the disparity between the rich and the rest, the more the rich have to lose, and the less likely that the equal share of boosted growth they'll get will make up for their loss. Once the gap goes beyond a certain point, the wealthy have a strong incentive to restrict democracy, and to block spending on education which might lead the poor to challenge economic injustice—making reform that much harder.

Does Economic Growth Reduce Inequality?

If inequality isn't actually good for the economy, what about the second part of the conservatives' argument—that growth itself promotes equality? According to the conservatives, those who care about equality should simply pursue growth and wait for equality to follow.

"A rising tide lifts all boats," President John F. Kennedy famously declared. But he said nothing about which boats will rise fastest when the economic tide comes in. Growth does typically reduce poverty, according to studies reviewed by economist Gary Fields, though some "boats"—especially families with strong barriers to participating in the labor force—stay "stuck in the mud." But inequality can increase at the same time that poverty falls, if the rich gain even faster than the poor do. True, sustained periods of low unemployment, like that in the late 1990s United States, do tend to raise wages at the bottom even faster than salaries at the top. But growth after the recessions of 1991 and 2001 began with years of "jobless recoveries"— growth with inequality.

For decades the prevailing view about growth and inequality within countries was that expressed by Simon Kuznets in his 1955 presidential address to the American Economic Association. Kuznets argued that as countries grew, inequality would first increase, then decrease. The reason is that people will gradually move from the low-income agricultural sector to higher-income industrial jobs—with inequality peaking when the workforce is equally divided between low- and high-income sectors. For mature industrial economies, Kuznets's proposition counsels focusing on growth, assuming that it will bring equity. In developing countries, it calls for enduring current inequality for the sake of future equity and prosperity.

But economic growth doesn't automatically fuel equality. In 1998, economists Klaus Deininger and Lyn Squire traced inequality and growth over time in 48 countries. Five followed the Kuznets pattern, four followed the reverse pattern (decreasing inequality followed by an increase), and the rest showed no systematic pattern. In the United States, for example:

- incomes became more equal during the 1930s through 1940s New Deal period (a time that included economic decline followed by growth);
- from the 1950s through the 1970s, income gaps lessened during booms and expanded during slumps;
- from the late 1970s forward, income inequality worsened fairly consistently, whether the economy was stagnating or growing.

The reasons are not hard to guess. The New Deal introduced widespread unionization, a minimum wage, social security, unemployment insurance, and welfare. Since the late 1970s, unions have declined, the inflation-adjusted value of the minimum wage has fallen, and the social safety net has been shredded. In the United States, as elsewhere, growth only promotes equality if policies and institutions to support equity are in place.

Trapped?

Let's revisit the idea of an inequality trap. The notion is that as the gap between the rich and everybody else grows wider, the wealthy become more willing to give up overall growth in return for the larger share they're getting for themselves. The "haves" back policies to control the "have-nots," instead of devoting social resources to educating the poor so they'll be more productive.

Sound familiar? It should. After two decades of widening inequality, the last few years have brought us massive tax cuts that primarily benefit the wealthiest, at the expense of investment in infrastructure and the education, child care, and income supports that would help raise less well-off kids to be productive adults. Federal and state governments have cranked up expenditures on prisons, police, and "homeland security," and Republican campaign organizations have devoted major resources to keeping blacks and the poor away from the polls. If the economic patterns of the past are any indication, we're going to pay for these policies in slower growth and stagnation unless we can find our way out of this inequality trap. ❑

Article 8.2

INEQUALITY: THE SILLY TALES ECONOMISTS LIKE TO TELL

BY DEAN BAKER
October 2012; Al Jazeera English

There is no serious dispute that the United States has seen a massive increase in inequality over the last three decades. However there is a major dispute over the causes of this rise in inequality.

The explanation most popular in elite and policy circles is that the rise in inequality was simply the natural working of the economy. Their story is that the explosion of information technology and globalization have increased demand for highly-skilled workers while sharply reducing the demand for less-educated workers.

While the first part of this story is at best questionable, the second part should invite ridicule and derision. It doesn't pass the laugh test.

As far as the technology story, yes information technologies have displaced large amounts of less-skilled labor. So did the technologies that preceded them. There are hundreds of books and articles from the 1950s and 1960s that expressed grave concerns that automation would leave much of the workforce unemployed. Is there evidence that the displacement is taking place more rapidly today than in that era? If so, it is not showing up on our productivity data.

More germane to the issue at hand, unlike the earlier wave of technology, computerization offers the potential for displacing vast amounts of highly skilled labor. Legal research that might have previously required a highly skilled lawyer can now be done by an intelligent college grad and a good search engine. Medical diagnosis and the interpretation of test results that may have previously required a physician, and quite possibly a highly paid specialist, can now be done by technical specialists who may not even have a college education.

There is no reason to believe that current technologies are replacing comparatively more less-educated workers than highly educated workers. The fact that lawyers and doctors largely control how their professions are practiced almost certainly has much more to do with the demand for their services.

If the technology explanation for inequality is weak, the globalization part of the story is positively pernicious. The basic story is that globalization has integrated a huge labor force of billions of workers in developing countries into the world economy. These workers are able to fill many of the jobs that used to provide middle class living standards to workers in the United States and will accept a fraction of the wage. This makes many formerly middle class jobs uncompetitive in the world economy given current wages and currency values.

This part of the story is true. The part that our elite leave out is that there are tens of millions of bright and highly educated workers in the developing world who could fill most of the top paying jobs in the U.S. economy: Doctors, lawyers, accountants, etc. These workers are also willing to work for a small fraction of the wages of their U.S. counterparts since they come from poor countries with much lower standards of living.

The reason why the manufacturing workers, construction workers, and restaurant workers lose their jobs to low-paid workers from the developing world, and doctors and lawyers don't, is that doctors and lawyers use their political power to limit the extent to which they are exposed to competition from their low-paid counterparts in the developing world. Our trade policy has been explicitly designed to remove barriers that prevent General Electric and other companies from moving their manufacturing operations to Mexico, China or other developing countries. By contrast, many of the barriers that make it difficult for foreign professionals to work in the United States have actually been strengthened in the last two decades.

If economics was an honest profession, economists would focus their efforts on documenting the waste associated with protectionist barriers for professionals. They devoted endless research studies to estimating the cost to consumers of tariffs on products like shoes and tires. It speaks to the incredible corruption of the economics profession that there are not hundreds of studies showing the loss to consumers from the barriers to trade in physicians' services. If trade could bring down the wages of physicians in the United States just to European levels, it would save consumers close to $100 billion a year.

But economists are not rewarded for studying the economy. That is why almost everyone in the profession missed the $8 trillion housing bubble, the collapse of which stands to cost the country more than $7 trillion in lost output according to the Congressional Budget Office (that comes to around $60,000 per household).

Few if any economists lost their six-figure paychecks for this disastrous mistake. But most economists are not paid for knowing about the economy. They are paid for telling stories that justify giving more money to rich people. Hence we can look forward to many more people telling us that all the money going to the rich was just the natural workings of the economy. When it comes to all the government rules and regulations that shifted income upward, they just don't know what you're talking about. ❏

Article 8.3

THE WAGES OF GENDER

BY GERALD FRIEDMAN
September/October 2013 and November/December 2013

Fifty years ago, in June 1963, President John F. Kennedy signed the Equal Pay Act, forbidding what he called the "unconscionable practice of paying female employees less wages than male employees for the same job." While acknowledging that "much remains to be done to achieve full equality of economic opportunity," he pronounced the law a "significant step forward."

Women have made much progress since then because of anti-discrimination leg-islation and the work of millions of activists to open occupations previously closed to women. The gap between men's and women's wages has narrowed significantly, and women have gained access to a broad range of professional and managerial occupations. With these economic gains, the balance of power between the genders and within families has changed because women can support themselves and their families even without a husband.

A great deal, however, still remains to be done. Women still earn less than men for reasons tied to gender—including outright discrimination in many occupations as well as the continued expectation that women will bear the primary responsibility for childcare and other household responsibilities. The great progress made in reduc-ing gender disparities over the past decades shows the importance of maintaining political and social movements to eliminate remaining gender inequities.

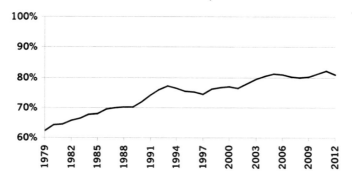

FIGURE 1: WOMEN'S MEDIAN WEEKLY EARNINGS VS. MEN'S, FULL-TIME EMPLOYEES, 1979-2012

The median weekly wage for women employed full time is 81% of the figure for men. While this is a significant shortfall, it is also a significant improvement over the 1979 figure of 62%. While there has been progress in most years, improvement may have slowed. The ratio of women's earnings to men's increased by nearly eight percentage points in the 1980s, five points in the 1990s, and only four points since 2000.

FIGURE 2: WOMENS MEDIAN WEEKLY EARNINGS VS. MEN'S, BY AGE AND YEAR

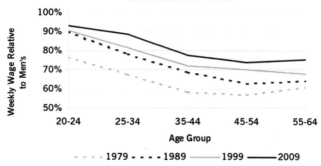

This graph shows median earnings for women compared to men, across different age groups, in 1979, 1989, 1999, and 2009. At least in part because of gender discrimination and the unequal burdens of family care work, women's wages grow more slowly with age than do those of men (reflected in the downward slope of each curve). This pattern has persisted even while women's wages have increased relative to men's for all age groups (reflected in the curve's consistent rise from one decade to the next).

FIGURE 3: PERCENTAGE CHANGE IN INFLATION-ADJUSTED MEDIAN WEEKLY EARNINGS, BY GENDER AND EDUCATION, 1979-2011

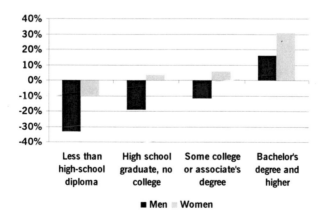

Rising relative earnings for women reflect both the entry of women into higher-paid occupations and rising earnings for women relative to men within occupations. Women's wages have risen relative to men's for all levels of education. For less-educated workers, however, much of the narrowing of the gender wage gap has come because women's wages have fallen less than men's have. Only among college graduates has the gender gap narrowed because wages have risen for both women and men, but have risen faster for women.

FIGURE 4: WOMEN'S MEDIAN WEEKLY EARNINGS VS. MEN'S, BY POSITION IN FEMALE AND MALE INCOME RANKINGS

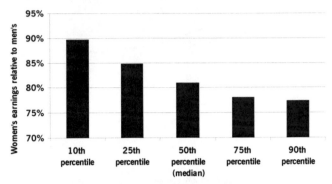

The gender pay gap is greater for higher-income workers. At low-paying jobs, women earn almost as much as men. (Women who are low in the female income ranking make almost 90% as much as men who are low in the male income ranking.) At higher income levels, however, women's pay lags further behind men's. This reflects the continuing exclusion of women from many of the highest-paid occupations and the top positions within occupations—the so-called "glass ceiling."

FIGURE 5: MARRIED WOMEN WHO EARN MORE THAN THEIR HUSBANDS, 1947-2011

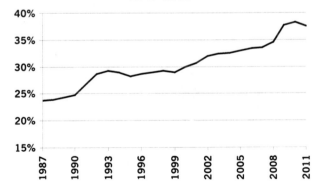

Women earn more than their husbands in a growing share of opposite-sex marriages. This increase is due not only to rising relative wages for women but also to an increase in the proportion of married women working outside the home. In addition, there has been a decline, especially since the beginning of the Great Recession, in the share of married men working outside the home—due both to higher male unemployment and more men dropping out of the labor force altogether.

FIGURE 6: BA DEGREES BY GENDER, UNITED STATES, 1964-2006

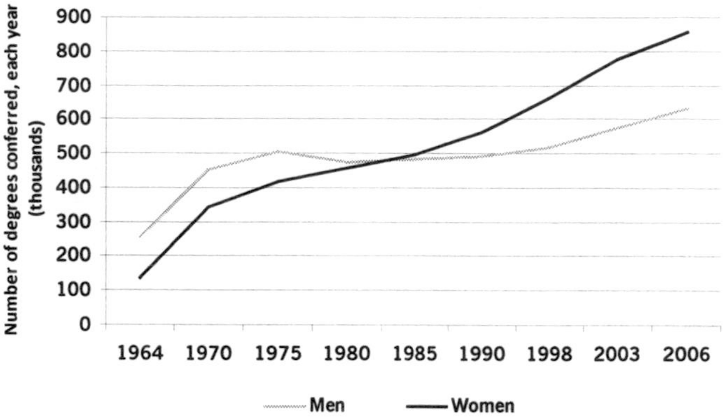

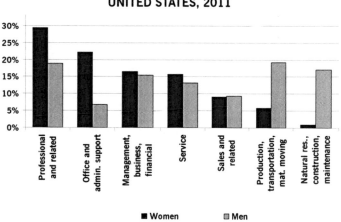

While barely a third of college degrees went to women in the early 1960s, the number of women earning BAs passed the number of men in the 1980s. Since then, college graduation numbers for women have continued to outpace the figures for men. With improvements in their educational attainment, women have gained access to more highly paid professions, like medicine and law, and their incomes have increased accordingly.

FIGURE 7: OCCUPATIONAL DISTRIBUTION, BY GENDER, UNITED STATES, 2011

Compared to men, there are relatively few women employed in many traditional blue-collar occupations, including construction, manufacturing, mining, and transportation. To the extent that these jobs were relatively well-paid, the exclusion of women lowered their relative earnings. Over the past 40 years, however, more women have moved into higher paid professional and managerial occupations while wages for production workers have fallen relative to earnings in traditionally female service and office occupations.

FIGURE 8: HOUSEWORK TIME, BY GENDER AND MARITAL STATUS, 1976-2005

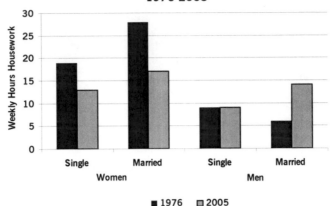

In the 1970s, marriage dramatically increased women's housework time while reducing men's. Since then, increasing women's economic equality has been associated with a change in the impact of marriage on housework. As of 2005, married men did more housework than unmarried men, rather than less. While married women still do more housework than men, marriage now causes a relatively small increase in the housework done by women, compared to what it did in the 1970s.

FIGURE 9: WOMEN'S LABOR FORCE PARTICIPATION RATE, BY FAMILY STATUS

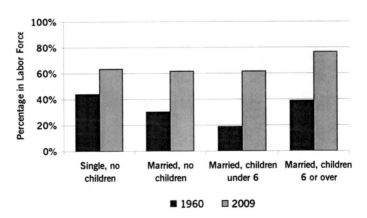

In 1960, fewer women were in the paid labor force, many left the labor force when they married, and most left when they had children. Family status has had much less effect on labor-force participation in more recent years. By 2009, few women left the labor force to marry and care for children. By continuing their paid employment, women are able to continue accumulating on-the-job training, remain part of work teams, and generally maintain their careers

FIGURE 10: PERCENTAGE OF TOTAL EMPLOYEES, BY GENDER

Caring Occupations   **Other Occupations**

☷ Men ■ Women

Women remain in a vulnerable economic position because their employment is concentrated in a particular subset of the economy. Women are disproportionately employed in "caring" occupations, including elementary school teachers (82% female), nurses (90%), housekeepers (90%), childcare workers (94%), and personal care attendants (87%). Cutbacks in government funding and social support for these occupations could undermine many of the economic gains made by women over the past decades. ❏

Sources: Bureau of Labor Statistics (BLS), Weekly and hourly earnings data from the Current Population Survey; BLS, "Highlights of Women's Earnings in 2011," October 2012; BLS, 1988–2012 Annual Social and Economic Supplements to the Current Population Survey (CPS); BLS, Current Population Survey, Labor Force Participation, Bulletin 2307; Department of Education, National Council of Education Statistics at (nces.ed.gov); Panel Study of Income Dynamics at University of Michigan, Institute for Social Research (www.nsf.gov).

Article 8.4

IT PAYS TO BE WHITE

Assessing how White people benefit from race-based economic inequality.

BY JEANNETTE WICKS-LIM
May/June 2016

By every major socioeconomic measure, there is an undeniable race-based hierarchy in the United States—with Black Americans sitting at or near the bot-tom. In 2014, the share of Black adults (at least 25 years old) with bachelor's or advanced degrees (22%) is notably lower than their White counterparts (32%). The official unemployment rate for Black workers is persistently double that of White workers: in 2015, 9.7% vs. 4.3%. Also in 2015, the African-American poverty rate (26.2%) stood at more than double that among White Americans (10.1%). Black Americans account for 38% of the prison population, nearly three times their share of the U.S. population. White Americans, in contrast, account for 59% of U.S. prisoners, under-representing their 77% population share.

These lopsided outcomes have, of course, two sides: by every major socioeconomic measure, White Americans sit at or near the top of the race-based hierarchy. This is an obvious point. Here's another one: if the economic odds are stacked against African Americans, the flipside is that White Americans have the odds stacked in their favor. We need to even these odds to achieve racial justice.

Current policy debates largely focus on reducing potential hurdles set in the way of African Americans. These same debates, however, overlook how race-based advantages put White Americans on an easier life path. To eliminate the United States' race-based hierarchy, we need to redirect economic resources that currently operate as a premium for being White into creating equal opportunities for African Americans and other communities of color.

Unfortunately, two policies specifically created to do so—affirmative action and reparations—only exist on the outer fringes of current policy debates.

It Pays to Be White at School

According to a 2012 study, about one-third of the nation's students attend hyper-segregated schools: schools that are 90% White or 90% non-White. Students in the nearly all-White schools benefit from $4,985 in local and state education spending per student (adjusted for regional differences in living costs), an $810 premium over the $4,176 spent on their counterparts in the nearly all-non-White schools. (All figures are inflation-adjusted to 2015 dollars.)

Over a 13-year K-12 public-school education, this White-school premium adds up to nearly $10,000 more spending on each student in nearly all-White schools compared to students in nearly all-non-White schools ($810 premium x 13 years of schooling = $10,530).

This White advantage is even more impressive when pooled together under one school's roof. Given the average school size of 500 students, this White premium scales up to an extra $2.8 million dollar investment into the elementary education in a nearly all-White school ($810 per student x 500 students x 7 years of elementary education = $2.8 million). This White school premium can translate into White students learning in better physical facilities, having access to more curriculum offerings with more and higher-quality materials, and served by greater numbers of teachers and support staff.

It Pays to Be White on the Streets

City police departments' pro-active "stop and frisk" policing techniques have come under scrutiny in recent years. The term "stop and frisk" refers to when a police officer stops and detains a person if the officer believes he or she has a reasonable suspicion that criminal activity is taking place. Controversy over "stop and frisk" policing is due to charges that officers apply the tactics unevenly— surveying and interrupting the daily routines of White Americans much less frequently than those of Black Americans.

Take, for example, the practices of the Boston Police Department (BPD). In 2010, the American Civil Liberties Union of Massachusetts and the BPD co-sponsored a study of the BPD's "Field Interrogating Observation Frisk and/or Search" (FIOS) practices. Researchers approved by both organizations examined the BPD's database of FIOS incidents from 2007–2010. The study, released in 2015, concluded that the BPD treated White neighborhoods more favorably—initiated fewer FIOS incidents, compared to Black neighborhoods, even after taking into account differences in neighborhood crime rates. In fact, the figures in the study indicate that White neighborhoods (defined here as 85% White) accumulated 2,500 fewer FIOS incidents annually compared to Boston neighborhoods with a high concentration of Black residents (85% Black).

This difference implies that if you're living in an 85% White neighborhood, chances are that you would be subject to police surveillance about once every decade. So, for example, by the age 30, such a resident might be surveyed, stopped and/or frisked twice: once at age 15 and then again at age 25. This resident's life is minimally disrupted by the BPD. If you're living in a Black neighborhood, chances are you'd have a FIOS incident every three years. In other words, by age 30, you can expect to have already had six unsolicited police encounters: at age 15, then at age 18, again at 21, again at 24, again at 27, and again at 30 years old. The situation for Whites is even better than these numbers suggest. If you're White, the police are 11% more likely to only stop and ask you questions, not frisk or search you and your belongings compared to if you're Black. This difference in frisking rates of Whites versus Blacks is the same as the BPD's differential frisking rate of non-gang members versus gang members.

What's it worth to be White on Boston's streets? It's hard to put a price tag on the ability to move around freely.

It Pays to Be White at Work

How much more do White workers benefit from paid employment than their Black counterparts? That is, what is the bonus for being White in the workplace? One way to get a handle on this is to calculate how much more the average White worker earns, over a working lifetime, compared to their Black counterpart. Note that in this exercise I do not "net out" differences in educational credentials, or any other type of possible measures of skill. This is in order to take account of how, for example, any White premium in schooling builds up into an additional White bonus at work in the form of job market preparation. In other words, the premium I calculate for being White at work includes the White bonus of better-funded educational opportunities, as well as increased access to better job opportunities, and higher rewards for work.

Take the situation of an average White male fulltime worker and compare his experience in the labor force to his Black counterpart: In 2014, the average White male full-time worker earned $10,900 more than his Black counterpart: $44,900 vs. $34,000. This average male White worker also has access to a paid job more consistently compared to his Black counterpart; the employment rate for White males is much higher than for Black males (95.7% vs. 90.3%). Their annual earnings equal $42,900 and $30,700, after accounting for their average unemployment spells. The gap is now $12,200. At this rate, this White worker could work three months less per year, and still earn more money.

What does this mean over their entire work careers? To keep things simple, let's say each continues to work until the end of his or her life. Because White men live longer than Black men, this means that the average male White worker could potentially work from 25 to 77 years old, or 52 years. Black men die, on average, five years sooner at 72 years, for a work career of 47 years. Therefore, over an entire working career, White workers get a work bonus of $790,000—$2.2 million vs. $1.4 million. It really does pay to be White at work.

It Pays to Be White When You Stumble

In 2011, the average White household held $23,000 in liquid wealth, like deposits in a checking account or a retirement account. This is more than 100 times the average amount of $200 held by African-American households. Considering all assets, including equity in a home, the average White American had more than ten times that of the average Black American, $111,740 vs. $7,113.

White people's access to wealth gives them a boost when they're down on their luck. Chances are much better that, if you're White, you can draw on some inherited asset or the assets of a family member when the proverbial chips are down. Hit with a large, unexpected medical bill? If you're White, your chances of managing this as just a bump in the road are much better than if you are Black.

Likewise, White people's greater access to wealth gives them a leg up when trying to get ahead. Starting a small business or trying to buy a house where there are good neighborhood schools? Trying to get a college degree without paying for tuition with your credit card? If you're White, your likelihood of being able to make that initial business investment, home down payment, or to cover that college bill, is far better than if you're Black. These, of course, are key steps to anyone's larger effort to enter and stay in America's middle class—by improving one's own educational and employment prospects, as well as those of one's children.

White households' outsized share of wealth is deeply tied to the country's history of racist social institutions. Public policy has built up wealth for White citizens, at the expense of any social group considered non-White, for nearly the United States' entire history. Exemplars of such public policies include, of course, enslaving Africans and African Americans and expropriating land from Native Americans.

But public policies that build up wealth for White citizens, at the expense of other social groups extend through to more recent times. Take Pres. Franklin Delano Roosevelt's New Deal programs starting in the 1930s, such as the Home Owners' Loan Corporation (HOLC) and the Federal Housing Administration (FHA), or the 1944 Servicemen's Readjustment Act (GI Bill) that provided aid to World War II veterans. These programs intervened massively in the housing market by providing federally subsidized home mortgages. From 1935 to 1953, FHA and the Veteran's Administration backed, on average, 45% of the mortgages for new construction. This support, however, focused specifically on subsidizing home ownership for Whites. White families benefited from the programs' use of restrictive covenants that required White homeowners to only sell to White buyers and from redlining that designated Black neighborhoods as undesirable areas for mortgage lending. These practices did not officially end until the 1968 passage of the Fair Housing Act. These policies effectively represented large-scale federal affirmative action programs for White Americans.

It Pays to Be White Nearly Everywhere

Growing evidence from the field of social psychology over roughly the past 20 years demonstrate how living and breathing in a world defined by an economic racial hierarchy appears to shape our most basic intuitions about the world—what is good or bad, what is dangerous or safe, what has value and what is valueless. This is the basic conclusion of social psychologists researching the phenomenon of implicit racial bias—a person's unconscious favorable or unfavorable action toward, or thoughts and feelings about, another person based on the person's race. Crucially, this bias occurs even in the absence of any consciously identified racial bias (see sidebar, next page).

Implicit racial bias helps to make sense of what economists Marianne Bertrand and Sendhil Mullainathan observed in their 2004 study, "Are Emily and Greg More Employable than Lakisha and Jamal?" They found that the answer is: yes, across a wide range of occupations and industries. For their study they sent out thousands of essentially identical resumes, with the exception of the name of the applicant. Those with stereotypically White names got callbacks for interviews 50% more frequently than resumes sent with stereotypically Black names.

Hard-pressed to find any economic rationale for this racial bias, the researchers speculate, "Employers receive so many resumes that they may use quick heuristics in reading these resumes. One such heuristic could be to simply read no further when they see an African-American name." Moreover, the shock expressed by human resource managers over Bertrand and Mullainathan's findings suggests that this heuristic operates through an implicit—rather than explicit—racial bias. That is, employers don't consciously discard resumes with Black-sounding names. More likely, employers' hold an implicit racial bias that causes them, at a glance, to consider more favorably resumes with White-sounding names.

The social environment in the United States, steeped in race-based haves and have-nots, appears to train people's gut feelings to turn positive towards White people and negative towards Black people, unconsciously and automatically. As a result, it pays to be White nearly everywhere.

Policy Implications of White Privilege

All this leads to the conclusion that if African Americans have the deck stacked against them in every major life activity, White Americans have the deck stacked in their favor. Current policy debates need to focus on the question of how to eliminate White privilege. Two examples of public policies designed to do this include affirmative action and reparations.

The explicit goal of affirmative action policies is to increase the number of people of socially stigmatized groups into positions of prestige. Affirmative action is not just a policy about diversifying the classroom or the workplace. These types of policies aim to change the make-up of who holds high-ranking positions by decreasing the over-representation of members of advantaged groups.

Reparations, in the U.S. context, typically refers to a policy of providing compensation to descendants of Africans and African Americans who were enslaved in the United States. It can also refer to compensation for the damage generated by any other systematically racist public policy. Whatever the form and amount of compensation, the basic aim of reparations is to use government funds to transfer wealth to African-American households in order to correct for past government practices that transferred wealth from Black households to White households.

How to Detect Implicit Racial Bias

Social psychologists have come up with clever experimental designs to detect implicit racial bias. They do this with what's called an "Implicit Association Test" (IAT). To detect implicit racial bias, the IAT measures whether a person associates, without conscious deliberation, the concept or feeling of "good" with a White person compared to a Black person.

One version of this test has a participant sit in front of a computer. Words and names alternately appear on the screen. First, the person is instructed to hit the "I" key with their right hand to indicate if a word is "good" (e.g., "joy") and the "E" key with their left hand if the word is "bad" (e.g., "pain"). When a name appears on the screen, the person is instructed to hit the "I" key if the name is typically White ("Brad") and the "E" key if the name is typically Black ("Jamal"). This set-up associates "good" with "White"— the "I" key is hit for both, and "bad" with "Black"— the "E" key is hit for both. Then the exercise is repeated but with the association reversed: the participant is instructed to hit the "I" key if the name is typically Black ("Lakisha") and the "E" key if the name is typically White ("Allison"), while the words are sorted in the same way as before. Now, the set-up associates "good" with "Black" and "bad" with "White."

Researchers have found that people sort with greater ease when the key for Black and negative are the same, and the key for White and positive words are the same— evidence of an implicit racial bias. Studies using an IAT test like this one have found evidence of implicit racial bias regardless of whether participants express any type of explicit racial bias.

Implicit racial bias, however, is a major pernicious obstacle to public policies aimed at correcting for White privilege. Implicit racial bias supports the existing racial hierarchy with a gut feeling that people get what they get because that's what they deserve—in particular, that White people tend to get more because they deserve more, while Black people get less because they deserve less. This is one factor explaining the often- vitriolic political resistance to calls for reparations. Even affirmative action is currently treated as a policy debate non-starter.

Policies that require White people to give something valuable up—privileged access to a well-funded neighborhood school, an apartment or house, admission to a university, a high-paying or high-status job, a seat in Congress—become politically toxic when combined with implicit racial bias. This is the ultimate upside of race-based inequality for White Americans: it encourages White Americans to feel entitled to rebuke the policies that would end their White privilege.

What about tackling the issue of economic inequality more broadly? A flatter social hierarchy would, at minimum, limit the size of race-based gaps. Take for example, raising the federal minimum from today's $7.25 to $15.00. This policy would result in raises to 54% of Black workers and 59% of Latino workers compared to 38% of White workers.

At the same time, to uphold the moral integrity of such a political movement, and its potential broad-based political appeal, depends on coming honestly to the unifying call that "we're all in this together." This requires explicitly addressing the reality that yes, we're all in this together, but even among the 99% some get—and feel entitled to— more than their fair share.

In other words, policies that address inequality more broadly must not be used as a way to sidestep the truth about the racial hierarchy that exists in the United States. To be sure, we need social policies that address inequality more generally to build a more just economy. The United States has about 20 million poor White Americans to show for that. Still, White people—up and down the economic scale—benefit from a race-based advantage that simply does not exist for African Americans.

Promoting race-based policies, such as affirmative action or reparations, does present a political risk: it could critically weaken class-based solidarity by exacerbating race-based tensions. Such racial division can thwart efforts to hold together the needed political coalitions to fight for a more broadly just economy. In a forceful critique against calls for reparations, Black American political scientist Adolph Reed states plainly that "there's nothing (less) solidaristic than demanding a designer type policy that will redistribute only to one's own group."

At the same time, the continuing success of Donald Trump's 2016 presidential bid (as of this writing) suggests that this view may be shortsighted. Trump's racist innuendos—his "dog-whistle" politics—clearly tap into deeply felt, race-based resentments among White workers frustrated by their four-decades-long experience of economic stagnation. His stump speeches might not have such an electrifying appeal if this country ever had an honest reckoning of past and existing racist policies and practices—an honest reckoning that would reasonably call for policies such as affirmative action and reparations.

Such a reconciliation process may represent the best chance of removing Black Americans from the go-to list of scapegoats for why America is no longer great, and must be made "great again," to paraphrase Trump's slogan. In the long run, challenging White privilege head-on may open the way to secure a cross-racial, class-based, political alliance resistant to cleaving under the pressure of economic hard times.

The sobering reality is that the odds that this type of reconciliation would lead to such a positive outcome, while greater than zero, are still slim, given the country's long-standing history of racial division. However, it could very well be the only path to building a solidarity movement among the 99% resilient enough to address inequality more broadly. ❑

Sources: Marianne Bertrand and Sendhil Mullainathan, "Are Emily and Greg More Employable than Lakisha and Jamal? A Field Experiment on Labor Market Discrimination," *The American Economic Review*, September 2004; Carmen DeNavas-Walt and Bernadette D. Proctor, "Income and Poverty in the United States: 2014," *Population Reports*, September 2015; Jeffrey Fagan, Anthony A. Braga, Rod K. Brunson, April Pattavina, "Final Report: An Analysis of Race and Ethnicity, Patterns in Boston Police Department Field Interrogation, Observation, Frisk, and/or Search Reports," June 15, 2015; Federal Bureau of Prisons, March 26, 2016 (bop.gov); Leo Grebler, David M. Blank, and Louis Winnick, "The Role of Federal Aids in Mortgage Finance," in Leo Grebler, David M. Blank, and Louis Winnick, eds., *Capital Formation in Residential Real Estate: Trends and Prospects* (Princeton University Press, 1956); Anthony G. Greenwald, Debbie E. McGhee, and Jordan L. K. Schwartz, "Measuring Individual Differences in Implicit Cognition: The Implicit Association Test," *Journal of Personality and Social Psychology*, 1998; Anthony Greenwald and Mahzarin R. Banaji, "Implicit Social Cognition: Attitudes, Self-esteem, and Stereotypes," *Journal of Personality and Social Psychology*, 995; National Center for Education Statistics, "Numbers and Types of Public Elementary and Secondary Schools From the Common Core of Data: School Year 2009-10," September 2012 (nces. ed.gov); Adolph Reed, Jr., "The Case Against Reparations," *The Progressive*, December 2000; Ary Spatig-Amerikaner, "Unequal Education: Federal Loophole Enables Lower Spending on Students of Color," Center for American Progress, August 2012; Rebecca Tippett, Avis Jones-DeWeever, May Rockeymoore, Darrick Hamilton, and William Darity, "Beyond Broke: Why Closing the Racial Wealth Gap is a Priority for National Economic Security," Center for Global Policy Solutions, 2014; United States Bureau of Labor Statistics, "Labor Force Characteristics by Race and Ethnicity," November 2015 (bls.gov); United States Census Bureau, "QuickFacts," 2015 (census. gov); United States Census Bureau, "Educational Attainment in the United States: 2014," 2015 (census.gov); Jeannette Wicks-Lim, "A $15 Federal Minimum Wage: Who Would Benefit?" PERI Research Brief, March 2016; Jiaquan Xu, Sherry L. Murphy, Kenneth D. Kochanek and Brigham A. Bastian, "Deaths: Final Data for 2013," Division of Vital Statistics, Feb. 6, 2016

Article 8.5

UNIONS AND INCOME INEQUALITY

BY ARTHUR MacEWAN
November/December 2011

Dear Dr. Dollar:

I know unions have shrunk in the United States, but by how much? And how best to respond to my right-wing friends who claim that unions are bad for the economy?
—Rich Sanford, Hardwick, Mass.

Take a look at the graph below. The two lines on the graph show for the period 1917 through 2007 (1) labor union membership as a percentage of the total U.S. work force and (2) the percentage of all income obtained by the highest 1% of income recipients. So the lines show, roughly, the strength of unions and the distribution of income for the past century. (John Miller and I developed this graph for our book *Economic Collapse, Economic Change.*)

The picture is pretty clear. In periods when unions have been strong, income distribution has been less unequal. In periods when unions have been weak, income distribution has been more unequal. In the post-World War II era, union members were about 25% of the labor force; today the figure is about 10%. In those postwar years, the highest-income 1% got 10% to 12% of all income; today they get about 25%.

UNION MEMBERSHIP AND INCOME INEQUALITY, 1917-2007

Source: Arthur MacEwan and John A. Miller, *Economic Collapse, Economic Change: Getting to the Root of the Crisis* (M.E. Sharpe, 2011).

The causation between union strength and income distribution is not simple. Nonetheless, there are some fairly direct connections. For example, when unions are strong, they can push for higher wages and thus we see a more equal distribution of income. Also, strong unions can have an impact on the political process, bringing about policies that are more favorable to workers.

But causation can work in the other direction as well. Great income inequality puts more power in the hands of the rich, and they can use that power to get policies put in place that weaken unions—for example, getting people who are hostile to unions appointed to the National Labor Relations Board.

And then there are other factors that affect both union strength and income distribution—for example, the changing structure of the global economy, which places U.S. workers in competition with poorly paid workers elsewhere. Yet the structure of the global economy is itself affected by the distribution of political power. For example, the "free trade" agreements that the United States has established with other countries generally ignore workers' rights (to say nothing of the environment) and go to great lengths to protect the rights of corporations. So, again, causation works in complex ways, and there are certainly other factors that need to be taken account of to explain the relationship shown in the graph.

However one explains the relationship, it is hard to imagine that we can return to a more equal distribution of income while unions remain weak. This means, at the very least, that the interests of unions and of people at the bottom of the income distribution are bound up with one another. Building stronger unions is an important part of fighting poverty—and the hunger and homelessness that are the clear manifestations of poverty.

One important thing to notice in the graph: In the post-World War II years, economic growth was the best we have seen. Certainly no one can claim that it is impossible for strong unions and a more equal distribution of income to co-exist with fairly rapid economic growth. Indeed, we might even argue that strong unions and a more equal distribution of income create favorable conditions for economic growth!

Stronger unions, it turns out, could be good preventive medicine for much of what ails our economy. ❑

Article 8.6

THE UNDESERVING RICH

Collectively produced and inherited knowledge and the (re)distribution of income and wealth.

BY GAR ALPEROVITZ AND LEW DALY

March/April 2010

Warren Buffett, one of the wealthiest men in the nation, is worth nearly $50 billion. Does he "deserve" all this money? Why? Did he work so much harder than everyone else? Did he create something so extraordinary that no one else could have created it? Ask Buffett himself and he will tell you that he thinks "society is responsible for a very significant percentage of what I've earned." But if that's true, doesn't society deserve a very significant share of what he has earned?

When asked why he is so successful, Buffett commonly replies that this is the wrong question. The more important question, he stresses, is why he has *so much to work with* compared to other people in the world, or compared to previous generations of Americans. Buffett asks: how much money would he have if he had been born in Bangladesh, or in the United States in 1700?

Buffett may or may not deserve something more than another person working with what a given historical or collective context provides. As he observes, however, it is simply not possible to argue in any serious way that he deserves *all* of the benefits that are clearly attributable to living in a highly developed society.

Buffett has put his finger on one of the most explosive issues developing just beneath the surface of public awareness. Over the last several decades, economic research has done a great deal of solid work pinpointing much more precisely than in the past what share of what we call "wealth" society creates versus what share any individual can be said to have earned and thus deserved. This research raises profound moral—and ultimately political—questions.

Through No Effort of Our Own

Recent estimates suggest that U.S. economic output per capita has increased more than twenty-fold since 1800. Output per hour worked has increased an estimated fifteen-fold since 1870 alone. Yet the average modern person likely works with no greater commitment, risk, or intelligence than his or her counterpart from the past. What is the primary cause of such vast gains if individuals do not really "improve"? Clearly, it is largely that the scientific, technical, and cultural knowledge available to us, and the efficiency of our means of storing and retrieving this knowledge, have grown at a scale and pace that far outstrip any other factor in the nation's economic development.

A half century ago, in 1957, economist Robert Solow calculated that nearly 90% of productivity growth in the first half of the 20th century (from 1909 to 1949) could only be attributed to "technical change in the broadest sense." The supply of labor and capital—what workers and employers contribute—appeared almost incidental to this massive technological "residual." Subsequent research inspired by

Solow and others continued to point to "advances in knowledge" as the main source of growth. Economist William Baumol calculates that "nearly 90 percent . . . of current GDP was contributed by innovation carried out since 1870." Baumol judges that his estimate, in fact, understates the cumulative influence of past advances: Even "the steam engine, the railroad, and many other inventions of an earlier era, still add to today's GDP."

Related research on the sources of invention bolsters the new view, posing a powerful challenge to conventional, heroic views of technology that characterize progress as a sequence of extraordinary contributions by "Great Men" (occasionally "Great Women") and their "Great Inventions." In contrast to this popular view, historians of technology have carefully delineated the incremental and cumulative way most technologies actually develop. In general, a specific field of knowledge builds up slowly through diverse contributions over time until—at a particular moment when enough has been established—the next so-called "breakthrough" becomes all but inevitable.

Often many people reach the same point at virtually the same time, for the simple reason that they all are working from the same developing information and research base. The next step commonly becomes obvious (or if not obvious, very likely to be taken within a few months or years). We tend to give credit to the person who gets there first—or rather, who gets the first public attention, since often the real originator is not as good at public relations as the one who jumps to the front of the line and claims credit. Thus, we remember Alexander Graham Bell as the inventor of the telephone even though, among others, Elisha Gray and Antonio Meucci got there at the same time or even before him. Newton and Leibniz hit upon the calculus at roughly the same time in the 1670s; Darwin and Alfred Russel Wallace produced essentially the same theory of evolution at roughly the same time in the late 1850s.

Less important than who gets the credit is the simple fact that most breakthroughs occur not so much thanks to one "genius," but because of the longer historical unfolding of knowledge. All of this knowledge—the overwhelming source of all modern wealth—comes to us today *through no effort of our own*. It is the generous and unearned gift of the past. In the words of Northwestern economist Joel Mokyr, it is a "free lunch."

Collective knowledge is often created by formal public efforts as well, a point progressives often stress. Many of the advances which propelled our high-tech economy in the early 1990s grew directly out of research programs and technical systems financed and often collaboratively developed by the federal government. The Internet, to take the most obvious example, began as a government defense project, the ARPANET, in the early 1960s. Up through the 1980s there was little private investment or interest in developing computer networks. Today's vast software industry also rests on a foundation of computer language and operating hardware developed in large part with public support. The Bill Gateses of the world—the heroes of the "New Economy"—might still be working with vacuum tubes and punch cards were it not for critical research and technology programs created or financed by the federal government after World War II. Other illustrations range from jet airplanes and radar to the basic life science research undergirding many pharmaceutical industry advances. Yet the truth is that the role of collectively inherited knowledge is far, far greater than just the contributions made by direct public support, important as they are.

Earned Income?

A straightforward but rarely confronted question arises from these facts: If most of what we have today is attributable to advances we inherit in common, then why should this gift of our collective history not more generously benefit all members of society?

The top 1% of U.S. households now receives more income than the bottom 120 million Americans combined. The richest 1% of households owns nearly half of all investment assets (stocks and mutual funds, financial securities, business equity, trusts, non-home real estate). The bottom 90% of the population owns less than 15%; the bottom half—150 million Americans—owns less than 1%. If America's vast wealth is mainly a gift of our common past, what justifies such disparities?

Robert Dahl, one of America's leading political scientists—and one of the few to have confronted these facts—put it this way after reading economist Edward Denison's pioneering work on growth accounting: "It is immediately obvious that little growth in the American economy can be attributed to the actions of particular individuals." He concluded straightforwardly that, accordingly, "the control and ownership of the economy rightfully belongs to 'society.'"

Contrast Dahl's view with that of Joe the Plumber, who famously inserted himself into the 2008 presidential campaign with his repeated claim that he has "earned" everything he gets and so any attempt to tax his earnings is totally unjustified. Likewise, "we didn't rely on somebody else to build what we built," banking titan Sanford Weill tells us in a *New York Times* front-page story on the "New Gilded Age." "I think there are people," another executive tells the *Times*, "who because of their uniqueness warrant whatever the market will bear."

A direct confrontation with the role of knowledge—and especially inherited knowledge—goes to the root of a profound challenge to such arguments. One way to think about all this is by focusing on the concept of "earned" versus "unearned" income. Today this distinction can be found in conservative attacks on welfare "cheats" who refuse to work to earn their keep, as well as in calls even by some Republican senators to tax the windfall oil-company profits occasioned by the Iraq war and Hurricane Katrina.

The concept of unearned income first came into clear focus during the era of rapidly rising land values caused by grain shortages in early 19th-century England. Wealth derived *simply* from owning land whose price was escalating appeared illegitimate because no individual truly "earned" such wealth. Land values—and especially explosively high values—were largely the product of factors such as fertility, location, and population pressures. The huge profits (unearned "rents," in the technical language of economics) landowners reaped when there were food shortages were viewed as particularly egregious. David Ricardo's influential theory of "differential rent"—i.e., that land values are determined by differences in fertility and location between different plots of land—along with religious perspectives reaching back to the Book of Genesis played a central role in sharpening this critical moral distinction.

John Stuart Mill, among others, developed the distinction between "earned" and "unearned" in the middle decades of the 19th century and applied it to other forms of "external wealth," or what he called "wealth created by circumstances." Mill's approach fed into a growing sense of the importance of societal inputs which produce economic gains beyond what can be ascribed to one person working alone in nature without benefit of civilization's many contributions. Here a second element of what appears, historically, as a slowly evolving understanding also becomes clear: If contribution is important in determining rewards, then, Mill and others urged, since society at large makes major contributions to economic achievement, it too has "earned" and deserves a share of what has been created. Mill believed strongly in personal contribution and individual reward, but he held that in principle wealth "created by circumstances" should be reclaimed for social purposes. Karl Marx, of course, tapped the distinction between earned and unearned in his much broader attack on capitalism and its exploitation of workers' labor.

The American republican writer Thomas Paine was among the first to articulate a societal theory of wealth based directly on the earned/unearned distinction. Paine argued that everything "beyond what a man's own hands produce" was a gift which came to him simply by living in society, and hence "he owes on every principle of justice, of gratitude, and of civilization, a part of that accumulation back again to society from whence the whole came." A later American reformer, Henry George, focused on urban land rather than the agricultural land at the heart of Ricardo's concern. George challenged what he called "the unearned increment" which is created when population growth and other societal factors increase land values. In Britain, J. A. Hobson argued that the unearned value created by the industrial system in general was much larger than just the part which accrued to landowners, and that it should be treated in a similar (if not more radical and comprehensive) fashion. In a similar vein, Hobson's early 20th-century contemporary Leonard Trelawny Hobhouse declared that the "prosperous business man" should consider "what single step he could have taken" without the "sum of intelligence which civilization has placed at his disposal." More recently, the famed American social scientist Herbert Simon judged that if "we are very generous with ourselves, I suppose we might claim that we 'earned' as much as one fifth of [our income]."

The distinction between earned and unearned gains is central to most of these thinkers, as is the notion that societal contributions—including everything an industrial economy requires, from the creation of laws, police, and courts to the development of schools, trade restrictions, and patents—must be recognized and rewarded. The understanding that such societal contributions are both contemporary and have made a huge and cumulative contribution over all of history is also widely accepted. Much of the income they permit and confer now appears broadly analogous to the unearned rent a landlord claims. What is new and significant here is the further clarification that by far the most important element in all this is the accumulated *knowledge* which society contributes over time.

All of this, as sociologist Daniel Bell has suggested, requires a new "knowledge theory of value"—especially as we move deeper into the high-tech era through computerization, the Internet, cybernetics, and cutting-edge fields such as gene therapy and nanotechnology. One way to grasp what is at stake is the following: A person today working the same number of hours as a similar person in 1870—working just as hard but no harder—will produce perhaps 15 times as much economic output. It is clear that the contemporary person can hardly be said to have "earned" his much greater productivity.

Consider further that if we project forward the past century's rate of growth, a person working a century from now would be able to produce—and potentially receive as "income"—up to seven times today's average income. By far the greatest part of this gain will also come to this person as a free gift of the past—the gift of the new knowledge created, passed on, and inherited from our own time forward.

She and her descendents, in fact, will inevitably contribute less, relative to the huge and now expanded contribution of the past, than we do today. The obvious question, again, is simply this: to what degree is it meaningful to say that this person will have "earned" all that may come her way? These and other realities suggest that the quiet revolution in our understanding of how wealth is created has ramifications for a much more profound and far-reaching challenge to today's untenable distribution of income and wealth. ❑

Article 8.7

HUNGER IN AFFLUENT AMERICA

BY GERALD FRIEDMAN
March/April 2015

T he United States is wealthy enough that everyone could have enough to eat. Nonetheless, millions of Americans go hungry each day, subsist on an unhealthy diet because they cannot afford healthier foods, or would go hungry except for social assistance, notably the Food Stamp program, now known as the Supplemental Nutritional Assistance Program (SNAP). Rising average income has done little to reduce the problem of food insecurity, and cutbacks in effective social welfare programs have added to the problems of hunger and malnutrition. SNAP and other safety-net programs are far too small to end hunger in America.

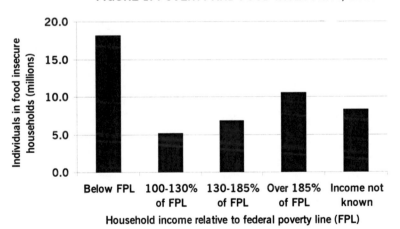

FIGURE 1: POVERTY AND FOOD INSECURITY, 2013

Millions of Americans cannot afford adequate nutrition. Nearly 50 million Americans are in "food insecure" households, which lack access to enough food for an active, healthy life for all household members. Food insecurity is most common in households under the federal poverty line. Insecurity is also more common in households with many children. While the urban poor dominate our images of hunger, rural residents actually have a slightly higher rate of food insecurity. (Data on food insecurity are based on an annual survey by the Current Population Survey. U.S. Department of Agriculture studies based on these data distinguish between low food security households ("reduced quality, variety, or desirability of diet") and very low food security households ("disrupted eating patterns and reduced food intake").)

FIGURE 2: ECONOMIC GROWTH AND FOOD INSECURITY

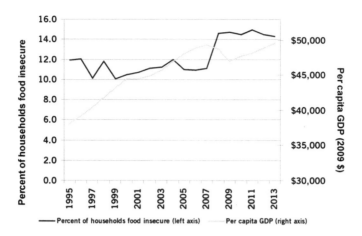

Economic growth does not solve the problem of food insecurity. Food insecurity has increased since the 1990s despite rising average income. A small decline in food insecurity during the boom of the late 1990s was largely reversed even before the Great Recession. Insecurity then soared with the economic crisis, beginning in 2007. High unemployment rates and stagnant or falling wages for working Americans have left illions hungry; cutbacks in social welfare programs have added to the burden of poverty. A dramatic increase in the size of the SNAP program, however, has helped prevent the problem from growing worse since 2009.

FIGURE 3: PEOPLE IN FOOD INSECURE HOUSEHOLDS, 2013

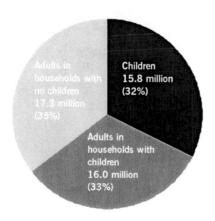

Children and their care-givers account for the majority of people in food-insecure households. Of the 49 million people in food-insecure households, nearly 16 million are children. Another 16 million are their caregivers, including 4 million single mothers. The remaining 17 million people in food-insecure households—adults in households without children—include not only many who are unemployed or working sporadically, but also many full-time workers whose wages are too low for them to afford adequate food.

FIGURE 4: VERY LOW FOOD SECURITY HOUSEHOLDS, 2013

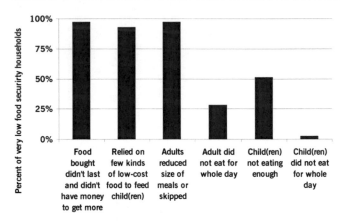

Food-insecure people go hungry, eat badly, and try to save food for their children. Food insecurity means anxiety, stress, sacrifice, and real hunger for millions of Americans. Almost all "very low food security households"—including more than 17 million people—run out of food sometimes, even though they rely on low-cost foods, skimp on portion size, or skip meals. Adults in these households sacrifice so their children can eat. Almost all reported skipping meals, and over a quarter skipped eating for a whole day. Despite these sacrifices, children in over half the households at least sometimes did not get enough to eat. In over 400,000 very low food security households, at least one child did not eat at all for at least one day in the previous month.

FIGURE 5: DIFFERENCES IN ADULT OUTCOMES, CHILDREN WHO RECEIVED SNAP COMPARED TO THOSE WHO DID NOT

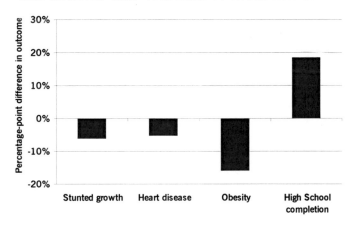

Note: From sample of individuals born 1956-1981 into "disadvantaged families" (household head had less than a high-school education).

SNAP (Food Stamps) increases food security and has lasting beneficial effects. While 26% of food-insecure households report using food pantries and 3% use soup kitchens, the federal Supplemental Nutrition Assistance Program (SNAP) is the largest source of food assistance. Even SNAP's $70 billion is only enough to provide $125 in food assistance per person per month, barely $1.30 per meal. SNAP reduces the incidence of food insecurity, but it still leaves 49 million people in food-insecure households. Despite these limitations, SNAP has both immediate and lasting benefits. Households that receive SNAP benefits eat better and have better health than similar households that do not. When aid is provided to households with young children, these benefits persist throughout the lifetimes of recipients. Those who receive assistance are healthier as adults and are more likely to finish high school, compared to those who do not. ❏

Sources: United States Department of Agriculture, Household Food Security in the United States (ers.usda.gov); Bureau of Economic Analysis (bea.gov); Federal Reserve Bank of St. Louis (FRED) (research.stlouisfed.org); Hilary W. Hoynes, Diane Whitmore Schanzenbach, and Douglas Almond, "Long Run Impacts of Childhood Access to the Safety Net," National Bureau for Economic Research (NBER), November 2012.

Article 8.8

INEQUALITY IN THE WORLD

BY ARTHUR MacEWAN
November/December 2014

> Dear Dr. Dollar:
> *I had thought that neoliberal globalization was making the world more unequal. But recently I have seen claims that the distribution of income in the world has become more equal. Is this true?*
> —Evan Swinerton, Brookline, Mass.

The answer to these questions depends on what you mean by "in the world." In many countries in the world—including most of the high-income countries and the most populous lower-income countries—the distribution of income has become more unequal. If we look at the income differences among countries, however, the situation has become more equal because per capita income has generally increased more rapidly in lower-income countries than in higher-income countries—though with important exceptions. And if we look at income distribution among all the people in the world—accounting for inequality both within and between countries—it seems that in recent decades the very high degree of inequality has remained about the same. (Before proceeding, please see the warning in the box below.)

Distribution Within Countries

Take a look at Figures 1 and 2, which show the changes in the distribution of income within selected countries, several high-income and several low- or middle-income, over roughly the last two decades. The measure of income distribution used in these graphs is the ratio of the total income of the highest-income tenth of the population to the total income of the lowest-income tenth of the population.

Warning!

There are many problems in determining the extent of income inequality. The results can differ depending on which measure of inequality we use. Also, there are data difficulties. While some of these difficulties arise from poor reporting, plenty arise from the complexity of the issues. Also, different countries collect income data in different ways and do so in different years. With one exception (explained below), I will not detail the difficulties here, but readers should keep in mind that such difficulties exist.

How we compare incomes in different countries, where relative prices differ, currencies differ, and exchange rates (e.g., the number of Mexican pesos it takes to buy a dollar) often do not tell us accurately the buying power of income in different countries. The income data here are reported in terms of purchasing power parity (PPP) and reported in relation to the U.S. dollar. Comparing incomes in different countries using the PPP method gives us a comparison of the real buying power of income in the different countries. Calculating PPP data is complex and not precise, but the PPP figures are the best we have.

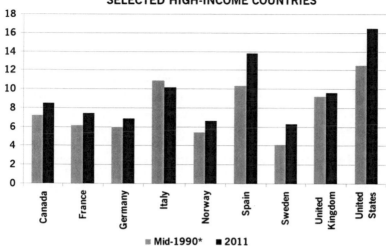

FIGURE 1: INCOME RATIO, TOP 10% TO BOTTOM 10%,
SELECTED HIGH-INCOME COUNTRIES

■ Mid-1990*   ■ 2011

Source: OECD. *For the U.K. the figure is for 1999; for Spain the figure is for 2004; for France the figure is for 1996. For all others the earlier figures are for 1995. The later U.S. figure is for 2012.

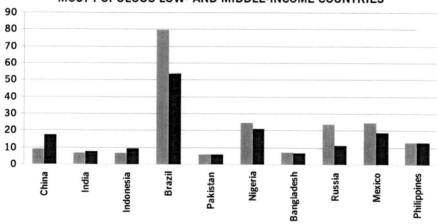

FIGURE 2: INCOME RATIO, TOP 10% TO BOTTOM 10%,
MOST POPULOUS LOW- AND MIDDLE-INCOME COUNTRIES

Source: World Bank. *Note:* These countries along with the United States and Japan are the twelve most populous countries in the world. The combined population of these ten accounts for 55% of the world's population in 2014.

The first thing that stands out in Figure 1 is that the U.S. income distribution is substantially more unequal than those of any of the other countries. Also, the absolute increase by this measure of inequality is greatest in the United States. However, with the sole exception of Italy, all the countries in Figure 1 experienced rising income inequality.

Things are different in Figure 2, which includes the ten most populous lower-income countries (ten of the twelve most populous countries in the world, the United States and Japan being the other two). The degree of inequality is quite high in some of the countries in the graph. Brazil is the extreme case. However, Brazil and most of the other countries in Figure 2 experienced a reduction of inequality in this period—though several are still highly unequal. The most populous countries in Figure 2—China, India, and Indonesia—though, experienced rising inequality. These countries are the first, second, and fourth most populous countries in the world (with the United States third).

The data in Figures 1 and 2 illustrate the widespread rise of income inequality within countries, especially among high-income countries. Among lower-income countries, the picture is mixed. Although Brazil remains highly unequal, the reduction of inequality in Brazil is important because it has been achieved, at least in part, by policies directed at reducing poverty. Brazil's redistributive policies represent a trend in many Latin American countries—a backlash against the neoliberal policies of preceding decades.

Distribution Among Countries

Figure 3 illustrates what has been happening to income distribution among countries and indicates that the situation has become more equal because, in general, lower-income countries have grown more rapidly during the last two decades than have higher-income countries. For 1994 and 2013, the two columns in Figure 3 show Gross Domestic Product (GDP) per capita in the ten most populous low- and middle-income countries (listed by population) compared to GDP per capita in the United States. The comparison is in terms of purchasing power parity (PPP).

For nine of these ten countries—Mexico is the exception—GDP per capita rose more rapidly than in the United States. Taken as a group and using an average weighted by population, these ten countries in 1994 had an average GDP per capita 9% of that in the United States, but by 2013 this figure had risen to 17%. The basic result is not due simply to the remarkably rapid economic growth in China. When China is removed from the group, the weighted average still increases over this time

FIGURE 3: PER CAPITA GDP, MOST POPULOUS LOW- AND MIDDLE-INCOME COUNTRIES, AS PERCENTAGE OF U.S. GDP (PPP)

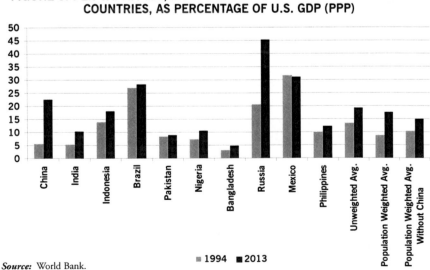

Source: World Bank.

■ 1994 ■ 2013

period, from 10% to 15%. (This general phenomenon is certainly not a universal phenomenon; several very low-income countries have fallen further and further behind.)

So, if countries are our units of observation, Figure 3 illustrates how things have become more equal since the early 1990s. Going back further in time, comparing countries' incomes weighted by population shows inequality dropping pretty much continuously since 1960, and especially sharply since the early 1990s. But if the average is not weighted by population—thus removing the dominance of China, India, and some other very populous countries—the situation among countries only started to become more equal from 2000. Nonetheless, many low-income countries have been left behind in this period, most notably several countries of Africa. The dominant trend is not the exclusive trend.

Global Distribution Among People

To obtain a truly global estimate of the distribution of income, it is necessary to compare the incomes of people (or families or households) in the world. Availability of data (as well as other data problems) makes such an estimate rough, but useful nonetheless. Branko Milanovic, perhaps the leading expert on these issues, has shown that, from the mid-1980s to 2011, global inequality remained roughly constant, with a slight decline toward the end of this period—likely explained by the greater slowdown of high-income countries compared to low-income countries in the Great Recession. The relative stability of income distribution would seem to result from a rough balance between the reduction of inequality among countries (Figure 3) and the rise of inequality within countries (Figure 1 and the most populous countries of Figure 2).

Milanovic's estimate uses the Gini coefficient, a standard measure of income inequality. The Gini takes account of incomes of the whole population, unlike the measure used in Figures 1 and 2, which focuses on extremes. The Gini can vary from 0 (everyone has the same income) to 1 (all the income goes to one person). For income distribution in almost all countries, the Gini ranges from about 0.27 (Norway) to about 0.65 (South Africa).

For the global population, over the period of Milanovic's estimates, the Gini varies around 0.70—a higher figure, showing a more unequal distribution, than for any single country. However, if inequality were measured by a comparison of extremes, it is likely that inequality would be rising. There remains a large share of the world's population that continues to live in extreme poverty, while incomes at the very top have sky-rocketed in recent years. But whether the measure is the Gini or a comparison of extremes, the distribution among people in the world is very unequal.

What Matters?

Each of these measures of income inequality "in the world" matters in one way or another. For example, to understand political conflicts within countries, the changes in the distribution within countries is probably most important. To understand how the changing structures of the global economy have affected people's lives in various parts of the world, it is useful to consider all of these measures. And to understand the dynamics of international politics, the measures that focus on inequalities among countries are probably paramount.

The measurements show both some positive and negative changes in the world. On the one hand, the rapid growth of several low-income and middle-income countries has, in spite of the high (and sometimes rising) level of inequality in these countries, pulled many people out of abject poverty. On the other hand, we know that rising inequality within a country tends to undermine social cohesion and generate stress at virtually all levels of society—with damaging effects on health, education, the natural environment, and crime. Even in this era of increased globalization, it is in the national context that inequality has the primary impact on people's behavior and how they judge their well-being.

And no matter how we look at the situation, the world has long been and remains a very unequal place. ❑

Sources: Branko Milanovic, *Worlds Apart: Measuring International and Global Inequality*, Princeton University Press, 2005; Branko Milanovic, *Global Income Inequality by the Numbers: in History and Now—An Overview*, The World Bank, Development Research Group, Poverty and Inequality Team, November 2012; Christoph Lakner and Branko Milanovic, *Global Income Distribution: From the Fall of the Berlin Wall to the Great Recession*, The World Bank, Development Research Group, Poverty and Inequality Team, December 2013, WPS6719; Richard Wilkinson and Kate Pickett, *The Spirit Level: Why Greater Equality Makes Societies Stronger*, Bloomsbury Press, 2009.

Chapter 9

TAXATION

INTRODUCTION

"Only the little people pay taxes." —*Leona Helmsley*

"Taxes are the price we pay for civilization." —*Oliver Wendell Holmes, Jr.*

Taxation is a fascinating subject. It is perhaps the clearest manifestation of class struggle one can find. How a modern government funds itself in order to provide services is an elaborate study in power. The contentious tango of taxes and their inverse, subsidies, plays out daily at all three levels of government—federal, state and local. Who pays taxes and at what rates? What is taxed? Who bears the burden of taxation? And how are tax revenues collected? These are questions that this chapter will address.

In the Reagan era, "supply-side" economist Arthur Laffer famously claimed that high marginal tax rates discourage work and saving, and that cutting tax rates on the rich would spur investment and economic growth. We start the chapter with two articles on the subject: In "Can Tax Cuts Really Increase Government Revenue?" (Article 9.1), economist Ellen Frank reviews the basic arguments made by Laffer and the other supply-siders, and why there is reason to be skeptical. Gerald Friedman puts these arguments to the test, and finds that cutting taxes on the very rich, as the U.S. government has been doing for decades, has not led to the promised investment or economic growth (Article 9.2).

Next, Roger Bybee critiques the growing phenomenon of "corporate inversions." Already, U.S. corporations stash trillions in profits in fictitious overseas accounts, as a way to minimize their taxes. That's still not enough for some of them, Bybee points out, so they engage in "inversions"—their legal takeover by companies headquartered in lower-tax countries.(Article 9.3)

Economist Arthur MacEwan answers the question "What's Wrong with a Flat Tax?" (Article 9.4). As MacEwan points out, an income tax that takes the same percentage from everyone may sound even-handed. However, it would eliminate the main "progressive" federal tax (which takes a larger percentage from those with higher incomes), while leaving in place "regressive" taxes (that take a larger share of income from those with lower incomes) such as sales or payroll taxes. That, MacEwan argues, would just shift the tax burden from rich to poor.

Gerald Friedman (Article 9.5) argues that a focus on federal taxes creates the mistaken impression that the U.S. tax system is quite progressive, falling more heavily on high-income people than low-income people. In fact, he notes, the heavy reliance of state and local governments on regressive taxes and fees greatly reduces this progressivity.

In "Transaction Tax: Sand in the Wheels, Not in the Face" (Article 9.6), economist John Miller makes the case for a tax on stock and other securities trades. This kind of tax, he argues, will not only raise revenue, but also reduce speculation in financial markets and help restore a focus on longer-term planning and job creation in the economy.

Steven Pressman (Article 9.7) analyzes the celebrated work of French economist Thomas Piketty on the growth of income inequality over the history of capitalism. Pressman summarizes Piketty's arguments that rising inequality is not a short-term anomaly, but a deep long-term trend in capitalist societies, then turns to a thoughtful discussion of Piketty's proposed policy responses.

Discussion Questions

1. (Articles 9.1 and 9.2) What is the basis of supply-siders' claim that lowering the highest marginal tax rate will generate more tax revenue? What are the main arguments against this view?

2. (Article 9.2) In what way have tax policies contributed to growing inequality in the United States? Do you think there is a case for remaking tax policy to be more progressive?

3. (Article 9.3) Do you think corporations should be able to change their legal headquarters to whatever country they want, as a way of avoiding taxes? If not, what should be done to prevent "inversions"?

4. (Article 9.3) Why do corporations complain about a corporate marginal tax rate of 35% when in fact hardly any companies actually pay that rate?

5. (Article 9.4) In MacEwan's view, why is a "flat" income tax not desirable? What are some arguments in favor of progressive taxation?

6. (Article 9.5) Are state and local tax systems inherently more regressive than the federal system? Could state and local governments raise revenue in more progressive ways?

7. (Article 9.6) What is a "Tobin Tax"? Why is this a "two birds with one stone" form of taxation?

8. (Article 9.7) Economist Thomas Piketty proposes a global tax on wealth as a response to rising inequality. Do you think that his solution is feasible? Is it desirable?

Article 9.1

CAN TAX CUTS REALLY INCREASE GOVERNMENT REVENUE?

BY ELLEN FRANK
November/December 2003

Dear Dr. Dollar:

A Republican friend tells me that the huge new tax cuts will actually produce more revenue than the government would have collected before the cut, because once rich beneficiaries invest the money, they will pay taxes on every transaction. He suggested that the increase could be as much as 50% more than the originally scheduled revenues. Is this possible?
—Judith Walker, New York, N.Y.

Back in the 1970s, conservative economist Arthur Laffer proposed that high marginal tax rates discouraged people from earning additional income. By cutting taxes, especially on those with the highest incomes, Laffer argued, governments would spur individuals to work harder and invest more, stoking economic growth. Though the government would get a smaller bite from every dollar the economy generated, there would be so many more dollars to tax that government revenues would actually rise. Ronald Reagan invoked the "Laffer curve" in the 1980s, insisting he could cut taxes, hike defense spending, and still balance the budget.

Bush's 2001 and 2003 tax packages are eerily reminiscent of the Reagan cuts. They reduce rates levied on ordinary income, with the largest rate cut going to the wealthiest taxpayers. They extend business tax write-offs and increase the child tax credit (though only for two years and only for families who earn enough to pay federal income taxes). They cut the tax on capital gains from 28% to 15%; dividend income, previously taxed at the same rate as ordinary income, now faces a top rate of 15%.

Citizens for Tax Justice estimates that two-thirds of the 2003 tax cut will accrue to the richest 10% of taxpayers. By 2006, the increased child credit will be phased out and nine out of ten taxpayers will find their taxes cut by less than $100. The top 1%, in contrast, will save an average $24,000 annually over the next four years, thanks to the 2003 cut alone.

Though inspired by the same "supply-side" vision that guided Reagan, Bush officials have not explicitly cited Laffer's arguments in defense of their tax packages. Probably, they wish to avoid ridicule. After the Reagan tax cut, the U.S. economy sank into recession and federal tax collections dropped nearly 10%. The deficit soared and economic growth was tepid through much of Reagan's presidency, despite sharp hikes in military spending. Some of the Republican faithful continue to argue that tax cuts will unleash enough growth to pay for themselves, but most are embarrassed to raise the now discredited Laffer curve.

The problem with your friend's assertion is fairly simple. If the government cuts projected taxes by $1.5 trillion over the next decade, those dollars will recirculate through the economy. The $1.5 trillion tax cut becomes $1.5 trillion in taxable income and is itself taxed, as your friend suggests. But this would be just as true if, instead of cutting taxes, the government spent $1.5 trillion on highways or national defense or schools or, for that matter, if it trimmed $1.5 trillion from the tax liability of low- and middle-income households. All tax cuts become income, are re-spent, and taxed. That reality is already factored into everyone's economic projections. But the new income, taxed at a lower rate, will generate lower overall tax collections.

To conclude that revenues will rise rather than fall following a tax cut, one must maintain that the tax cut causes the economy to grow faster than it would have otherwise—that cutting taxes on the upper crust stimulates enough additional growth to offset the lower tax rates, more growth than would be propelled by, say, building roads or reducing payroll taxes. Free-marketeers insist that this is indeed the case. Spend $1.5 trillion on highways and you get $1.5 trillion worth of highways. Give it to Wall Street and investors will develop new technologies, improve productivity, and spur the economy to new heights.

Critics of the Bush cuts contend, however, that faster growth arises from robust demand for goods and from solid, well-maintained public infrastructure. Give $1.5 to Wall Street and you get inflated stock prices and real estate bubbles. Give it to working families or state governments and you get crowded malls, ringing cash registers, and businesses busily investing to keep up with their customers.

Who is right? Die-hard supply-siders insist that the Reagan tax cuts worked as planned—the payoff just didn't arrive until the mid-1990s! But the Bush administration's own budget office is predicting sizable deficits for the next several years. Maybe, like your friend, they believe the tax cuts will pay for themselves—but they're not banking on it. ❑

Article 9.2

THE GREAT TAX-CUT EXPERIMENT
Has cutting tax rates for the rich helped the economy?

BY GERALD FRIEDMAN
January/February 2013

S ince the late 1970s, during the Carter Administration, conservative economists have been warning that high taxes retard economic growth by discouraging productive work and investment. These arguments have resonated with politicians, who have steadily cut income taxes, especially those borne by the richest Americans. The highest marginal tax rate, which stood at 70% by the end of the 1970s, was cut to less than 30% in less than a decade. (The "marginal" rate for a person is the one applied to his or her last dollar of income. A marginal rate that applies to, say, the bracket above $250,000, then, is paid only on that portion of income. The portion of a person's income below that threshold is taxed at the lower rates applying to lower tax brackets.) Despite increases in the early 1990s, the top marginal rate remained below 40%, when it was cut further during the administration of George W. Bush. These dramatic cuts in tax rates, however, have not led to an acceleration in economic growth, investment, or productivity.

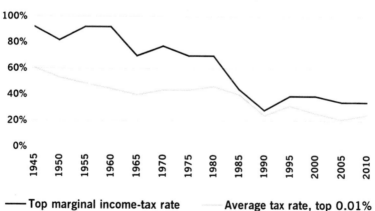

FIGURE 1: FEDERAL TAXES ON RICHEST AMERICANS, MARGINAL AND AVERAGE RATES, 1945-2010

—— Top marginal income-tax rate   Average tax rate, top 0.01%

The federal government has been cutting taxes on the richest Americans since the end of World War II. The average tax paid by the richest taxpayers, as a percentage of income, is typically less than the top marginal rate. Some of their income (the portion below the threshold for the top marginal rate, any capital-gains income, etc.) is taxed at lower rates. Some is not subject to federal income tax because of deductions for state and local taxes, health-care costs, and other expenses. The decline in the average tax rate for the richest, however, does follow the cuts in the top marginal income-tax rate.

FIGURE 2: TAX REVENUE AS A PERCENTAGE OF GDP, 2008

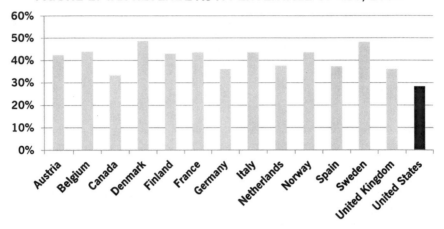

Americans pay a smaller proportion of total income in taxes than do people in any other advanced capitalist economy. As recently as the late 1960s, taxes accounted for as high a share of national income in the United States as in Western European countries. After decades of tax cuts, however, the United States now stands out for its low taxes and small government sector.

FIGURE 3: AVERAGE TAX RATES ON RICHEST AND REAL GDP GROWTH, BY PRESIDENT, 1947-2010

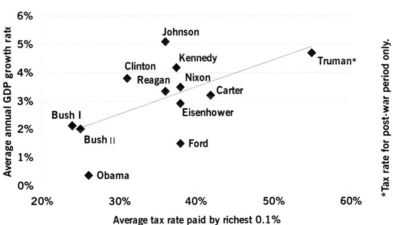

On average, the economy has grown faster during presidential administrations with higher tax rates on the richest Americans. Growth was unusually slow during George W. Bush's two terms (Bush II) and during Obama's first term, when the Bush tax cuts remained in effect. On average, every 10 percentage-point rise in the average tax rate on the richest has been associated with an increase in annual GDP growth of almost one percentage point.

FIGURE 4: TOP MARGINAL TAX RATE AND INVESTMENT, 1963-2011

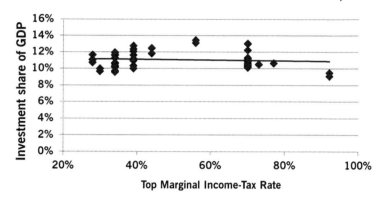

Cutting taxes on the richest Americans has not led them to invest more in plant and equipment. Over the past 50 years, as tax rates have declined, there has been no increase in investment spending as a percentage of GDP. (The flat trend line shows that changes in the highest marginal income-tax rate have not affected investment much, one way or the other.) Instead, the investment share of the economy has been determined by other factors, such as aggregate demand, rather than tax policy.

FIGURE 5: TAX SHARE OF GDP AND PRODUCTIVITY GROWTH

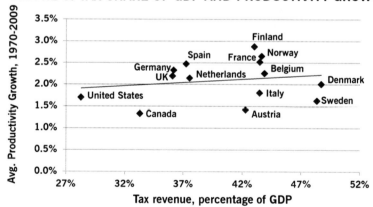

Despite lower and declining tax rates, especially on the rich, the United States has had slower productivity growth over the last several decades than other advanced economies. Overall, lower taxes are associated with slower growth in GDP per hour worked. A 10 percentage point increase in taxes as a share of GDP is associated with an increase in the productivity growth rate of 0.2 percentage points. ❑

Sources: Tom Petska and Mike Strudler, "Income, Taxes, and Tax Progressivity: An Examination of Recent Trends in the Distribution of Individual Income and Taxes" (Statistics of Income Division, Internal Revenue Service, 1997); Thomas Hungerford, "Taxes and the Economy: An Economic Analysis of the Top Tax Rates Since 1945" (Congressional Research Service, 2012); Economic Report of the President, 2012; Bureau of Economic Analysis (bea.gov); Organization of Economic Cooperation and Development, OECD STAT.

Article 9.3

INVERSION ACCELERATION
More and more U.S. corporations are sending their headquarters offshore to reap immense tax savings.

BY ROGER BYBEE
May/June 2016

Corporate "inversions"—the fast-accelerating phenomenon of major U.S. firms moving their official headquarters to low-tax nations through complex legal maneuvers—are causing an annual loss of about $100 billion in federal tax revenues.

But new rules imposed in early April by the U.S. Treasury Department scuttled the mammoth $162 billion deal between pharmaceutical giant Pfizer and Allergan, based on relocating the official headquarters to low-tax Ireland. The Treasury rules are designed to inhibit "serial inverters"—corporations that repeatedly shift their official headquarters to cut U.S. taxes—and to discourage "earnings stripping," where firms use loans between their American units and foreign partners to reduce U.S. profits subject to federal taxation. The collapse of the Pfizer-Allergan inversion suggests that the Treasury regulations may constitute a major barrier to some future inversions. However, with firms like Johnson Controls and Tyco moving ahead with their inversion plans, stronger measures will clearly be needed to halt the tide.

U.S. corporations have pulled off about 60 inversions over the last two decades, according to *Fortune*. In the last five years alone, corporations have executed 40 inversions, the *New York Times* stated.

This fast-rising dimension of corporate globalization has immense implications for Americans. The industrial powerhouse Eaton Corp. (#163 on the Fortune 500), Medtronic, Accenture (formerly the consulting wing of Arthur Andersen), Burger King, and AbbVie (the world's 11th-largest drug maker) are among the firms that have repudiated their U.S. nationality and shifted their official headquarters to low-tax nations. The annual toll to the U.S. Treasury from corporate inversions is about $100 billion, based on the studies of Reed College economist Kimberly Clausing. This impact is likely to worsen significantly in the near future. Another dozen or more inversions are currently under consideration, according to conservative *New York Times* business columnist Andrew Ross Sorkin.

Fortune senior writer Allan Sloan, who has been outraged by inversions despite his overall pro-corporate stance, points to powerful vested interests who stand to gain: "There's a critical mass of hedge funds, corporate raiders, consultants, investment bankers, and others who benefit from inversions." (The collapse of the Pfizer-Allergan deal could cost just the major banks as much as $200 million, the *New York Times* reported.) These interests and their political allies have incessantly claimed that American-based multinational corporations are driven to repudiate their U.S. nationality in order to escape "burdensome" U.S. corporate tax rates that they call "the world's highest."

In reality, actual federal corporate taxes on 288 profitable corporations —as distinguished from the official 35% rate almost all firms easily avoid—were actually only 19.4% in the 2008-2012 period, a 2014 Citizens for Tax Justice (CTJ) report revealed. This placed the United States 8th lowest among the advanced nations in the Organization for Economic Cooperation and Development (OECD), the CTJ found (see sidebar).

A just-released CTJ study went further in its scope and included state and local taxes as well as federal levies in comparing the United States with other OECD countries. It found combined U.S. corporate taxes at 25.7%, ranking 4th lowest in the OECD, based on U.S. Treasury figures. The OECD average is 34.1%. Only Chile, Mexico, and South Korea had a lower total burden as a share of GDP.

Incessant Talk of 35% Tax "Burden" Diverts Focus from Minimal Taxes

Elite debate about corporate taxes is dominated by the notion that U.S. corporations are afflicted by the highest official corporate tax rate in the world. In fact, the 35% official rate is easily avoided by almost all corporations. *Effective* U.S. corporate taxes—what corporations actually end up paying—are among the lowest in the advanced world. This represents a huge drain on the U.S. Treasury's revenues needed for public services.

- A 2014 study by Citizens for Tax Justice found an *effective* average tax rate of only 19.4% for major, consistently profitable corporations. This places the United States at 8th-lowest among the 34 OECD nations in terms of the effective federal tax rate.

- The most recent study on corporate taxes by the CTJ, released in April 2016, went further in its scope and included state and local taxes as well as federal levies. It found combined U.S. corporate taxes at 25.7%, ranking 4th-lowest in the OECD (above only Chile, Mexico, and South Korea). The OECD average is 34.1%.

- Strategies for tax avoidance have been particularly effective for the very largest members of the Fortune 500. Corporations studied by CTJ included 26—such as Boeing, General Electric, Priceline.com, and Verizon—that paid no federal income tax whatsoever over the five-year period.

- Boeing, which depends heavily on federal contracts, had an effective federal tax rate of negative 2%, despite earning $26.4 billion in profits 2008-2013. It also collected a record $13.2 billion in state-level tax breaks and subsidies in 2013. About one-third of the corporations—93 of the 288 studied by CTJ—paid an effective tax rate of less than 10% between 2008 and 2013. And contrary to claims that U.S. corporate taxes are far higher than those facing their foreign competitors, two-thirds of those corporations with significant offshore profits paid higher corporate tax rates to foreign governments for their overseas operations than they paid in the United States on their U.S. profits.

Source: Citizens for Tax Justice, "The Sorry State of Corporate Taxes," 2014 (ctj.org).

270 | REAL WORLD MICRO

Despite this reality of low corporate taxes, a growing number of large multinational firms have concluded that repudiating their U.S. "citizenship" and inverting is the most effective means of cutting their tax burdens, avoiding possible reforms that could potentially hike their tax bills, and most importantly, gaining direct and unregulated access to untaxed "offshore" funds.

The 35% Myth

The fundamental realities of U.S. taxes on multinational corporations are obscured by an elite debate fixated on the official statutory rate of 35%, which is relentlessly cited as a barrier to U.S. competitiveness.

House Republican James Sensenbrenner (R-Wisc.), for example, wrote in a recent *Milwaukee Journal Sentinel* opinion piece, "The current rate paid by American companies is 35 percent—the highest corporate tax rate among developed countries."

This narrative—endlessly recited by leading corporate and media elites, along with virtually all Republicans and a number of Democrats, has come to dominate much of the national dialogue. Robert Pozen, a senior fellow at the liberal Brookings Foundation, urgently called for a sharp cut in the 35% statutory rate, claiming broad bi-partisan support in Congress. "If there's one policy agreement between Republicans and Democrats, it's that the 35% corporate tax rate in the United States should be reduced to 28% or 25%," he asserted. "The current rate, highest in the advanced industrial world, disincentivizes investment and encourages corporations to relocate overseas."

Even President Barack Obama, while an outspoken foe of inversions, perversely weakened his own case against them by speaking of "companies that are doing the right thing and choosing to stay here, [and] they get hit with one of the highest tax rates in the world. That doesn't make sense," as he told a Milwaukee audience in a typical comment.

Obama has thus inadvertently reinforced the conventional wisdom among U.S. elites that is used to justify inversions, as outlined by John Samuels of the International Tax Foundation. "Today, with most of their income and almost all of their growth outside the United States, U.S. companies have a lot more to gain by relocating their headquarters to a foreign country with a more hospitable tax regime," declares Samuels. "And conversely they have a lot more to lose by remaining in the United States and having their growing global income swept into the worldwide U.S. tax net and taxed at a 35% rate."

Why Inversions?

The crucial motive in transferring corporations' "nationality" and official headquarters to low-tax nations is that inversions shield the "foreign" profits of U.S. corporations from federal taxation and ease access to these assets. This protects total U.S. corporate profits held outside the United States—a stunning $2.1 trillion—from any U.S. corporate taxes until they are "repatriated" back to the United States.

Major corporations benefit hugely from the infinite deferral of taxes purportedly generated by their foreign subsidiaries. "If you are a multinational corporation, the federal government turns your tax bill into an interest-free loan," wrote David Cay Johnston, Pulitzer-Prize winning writer and author of two books on corporate tax avoidance. Thanks to this deferral, he explained, "Apple and General Electric owe at least $36 billion in taxes on profits being held tax-free offshore, Microsoft nearly $27 billion, and Pfizer $24 billion."

Nonetheless, top CEOs and their political allies constantly reiterate the claim that the U.S. tax system "traps" U.S. corporate profits overseas and thereby block domestic investment of these funds. But these "offshore" corporate funds are anything but trapped outside the United States. "The [typical multinational] firm … chooses to keep the earnings offshore simply *because it does not want to pay the U.S. income taxes it owes*," explains Thomas Hungerford of the Economic Policy Institute. "This is a very strange definition of 'trapped'."

In fact, these offshore profits can be, and are, routed back into the United States through the use of tax havens. (Tax havens, where corporations and super-rich individuals place an estimated $7.6 trillion, were thrust into the international spotlight with the recent release of the Panama Papers. See William K. Black, "Business Press Spins Elite Tax Fraud as 'Good News'," p. 5.) "'Overseas' profits are neither overseas nor trapped," explained Kitty Rogers and John Craig. "It is true that for accounting purposes, multinational corporations keep these dollars off of their U.S. books. But in the real world, the money is often deposited in U.S. banks, circulating in the U.S."

However, the "overseas" profits come with some significant constraints on their use, pointed out David Cay Johnston. "The funds can only be accessed for short-term loans back to the U.S., and are not useful for major investments like new factories or long term R&D, or for investment outside the U.S.," said Johnston. But inversions eliminate these restrictions on how such funds can be used. "By inverting and then using a variety of tax avoidance schemes, the firms can have access to these earnings virtually free of U.S. taxes," notes Hungerford. "This is undoubtedly the primary motivation to invert."

The inversion route is not the only means for U.S. corporations to radically slash their U.S. taxes and gain access to offshore earnings. Any particular company's tax-avoidance strategy is dependent on the specific conditions it faces. As tax expert Johnston notes, "Every company has its own unique issues so it will decide what works for it."

Some giant multinational corporations, like Apple, Microsoft, and Google, have chosen to bypass inverting. Instead, they utilize immensely complex shifts of their revenue to minimize their taxes and maintain access to their offshore earnings. These maneuvers have gained exotic names like "Double Dutch Irish Sandwich," reflecting the multiple transfers of capital that they employ. The corporations involved are able to avoid the public backlash brought on by jettisoning their U.S. nationality. On the other hand, such ploys require careful planning and execution, compared to the simple, direct step of inverting.

Corporate inversions also head off the possibility of higher rates being imposed in the United States, an idea with very broad public support as shown by polling. But in addition to the vast political resources that corporations bring to any fight in Congress on corporate taxes, inversions remind U.S. public officials that their policies can be undermined by CEOs' unilateral decisions to relocate anywhere on the globe. Companies use this trump card to weaken the push for increases in corporate taxes and instead build momentum for further federal concessions.

Johnson Controls: The Ugly Truth

The most recent inversion deal, orchestrated by Johnson Controls—called the "latest and quite possibly the most brazen tax-dodger" in a *New York Times* editorial—explodes the myths underlying the standard rationale for inversions. Johnson Controls, which has been based in the Milwaukee area for 131 years, is the 66th largest firm in the United States.

Much media coverage has focused on the $149 million in annual tax savings that Johnson Controls will purportedly reap by jettisoning its U.S. identity and moving its official "domicile" to Ireland, where the tax rate is 12.5%. This is a tidy sum, but not because Johnson Controls was victimized by paying the statutory rate of 35%.

On the contrary, Johnson Controls has already been benefitting handsomely from a U.S. tax system that is remarkably generous to major corporations. As Matthew Gardner of the Institute on Tax and Economic Policy pointed out, "Between 2010 and 2014, Johnson Controls reported just over $6 billion in U.S. pretax income, and it paid a federal income tax rate averaging just 12.2 percent over this period." Significantly, "This is actually *lower* than the 12.5 percent tax rate Ireland applies to most corporate profits."

Far more central to Johnson Controls' inversion is the virtually tax-free status that it will gain over its vast pile of profits accumulated offshore, Gardner argues. Digging beneath the surface, Gardner found, "At the end of 2014, Johnson Controls disclosed holding $8.1 billion of its profits as permanently reinvested foreign income, profits it has declared it intends to keep offshore indefinitely."

The tax stakes for Johnson Controls are therefore much higher than the annual savings so often cited. "Reincorporating abroad would allow Johnson Controls to avoid ever paying a dime in U.S. income tax on profits currently stashed in tax havens," Gardner stated.

Johnson Controls is using the common inversion strategy of arranging for a smaller corporation based in a low-tax nation to purchase a much larger firm operating in the United States. In this case, the Ireland-based Tyco International (itself an inverted firm which had long been based in the United States) is buying Johnson Controls. Tax expert Edward Kleinbard describes this as a "minnow swallowing a whale" scenario that characterizes many inversions.

The Johnson Controls-Tyco deal qualifies as a so-called "super inversion," as *Fortune* put it, because it evades a number of new ownership regulations set by the U.S. Treasury Department to discourage inversions. "Tyco shareholders will own 44% of the deal after it is done, avoiding any penalties the Treasury Department has tried to impose on these deals," *Fortune* reported. "The Treasury Department had set an ownership requirement in 2014 of 40% for foreign firms involved in inversion deals with U.S. corporations, in an effort to discourage inversions."

The deal with Tyco will change virtually nothing for Johnson Controls International except for its slightly modified name—"Johnson Controls plc."—and its ability to manipulate the U.S. tax system. The company's new domicile will officially be Cork, Ireland, but it will retain its real operating headquarters in its present site near Milwaukee. It will continue to be listed on the S&P 500 stock index. Johnson Controls will still be protected by the vast legal architecture safeguarding U.S. firms, like those on securities, intellectual property, and patents.

The corporation's CEO Alex Molinaroli insists that the firm is simply acting to best serve its shareholders: "It would be irresponsible for us as a company to not take advantage of the opportunities that come along." The inversion will also provide some advantages to the CEO himself, with *Fortune* observing, "Molinaroli will receive at least $20.5 million and as much as $79.6 million for doing the deal over the next 18 months."

Johnson Controls also stands to retain other advantages. It will remain eligible for U.S. government and state contracts under current law, as have Accenture and other firms which have staged inversions. Between 2010 and 2014, Johnson and its subsidiaries received more than $1 billion in federal contracts—more than $210 million a year, according to ITEP's Gardner. Furthermore, Johnson Controls' ability to gain federal and state tax incentives for job creation will apparently continue.

The Pushback

In an age of fast-eroding economic security, corporate inversions have stirred vast public anxieties and outrage over corporations that seem both rootless and ruthless. Public anger over inversions is mounting, as household incomes continue to fall for tens of millions of Americans and worry about the offshoring of capital and jobs becomes more widespread. An August 2014 poll by Americans for Tax Fairness revealed that more than two-thirds of likely voters disapprove of corporate inversions—86% of Democrats, 80% of independents, and 69% of Republicans.

Surprisingly, one of the loudest voices to emerge against inversions has been *Fortune*'s Allan Sloan. Sloan penned a cover story titled "Positively Un-American," warning, "We have an emergency, folks, with inversions begetting inversions." Even though Sloan advocates long-term changes that would tilt the tax system further in a pro-corporate direction, he called for immediate action by the Congress and President Obama to stem the tide of inversions. "I still think we need to stop inversions cold right now," he wrote, "to keep our tax base from eroding beyond repair."

Besides the drain to the U.S. tax base, Sloan expressed concern about the impact of inversions on Americans' view of corporate America: "It also threatens to undermine the American public's already shrinking respect for big corporations."

The recently announced Johnson Controls inversion dealt a major blow to public trust in America's largest corporations, reflected in calls by Democratic presidential candidates Bernie Sanders and Hillary Clinton for stiff regulation on inversions.

Johnson Controls' announcement gave Sanders and Clinton a chance to tap a strong vein of public sentiment. Lashing out at the company in a January 25 media release, Sanders called it and its new partner Tyco "corporate deserters." Sanders declared, "Profitable companies that have received corporate welfare from American taxpayers should not be allowed to renounce their U.S. citizenship to avoid paying U.S. taxes."

Clinton blasted Johnson Controls on January 27 at an Iowa campaign stop, stating "I will do everything I can to prevent this from happening, because I don't want to see companies that thrive, use the tax code, the gimmicks, the shenanigans ... to evade their responsibility to support our country." She also began using a TV commercial aired in Michigan and elsewhere, showing her speaking in front of the Johnson Controls headquarters to denounce the corporation's inversion.

A Cure Worse Than the Disease

Up until now, conservative Republicans' control of the House of Representatives has blocked even modest legislation from gaining any traction, despite public outrage against inversions. Using the standard Republican soundbite about the high corporate tax rate driving U.S. firms and jobs overseas, Sensenbrenner, wrote in an op-ed in the *Milwaukee Journal Sentinel*: "Despite the negative effects the departures of these companies are having on the American economy, it is difficult to blame corporate leaders when you crunch the numbers."

Similarly, influential hedge-fund tycoon Carl Icahn, although acknowledging the dislocation and insecurity generated by inversions, exempted corporations from any obligation to the United States and laid the blame at the feet of Congress for failing to cut corporate taxes. "Chief executives have a fiduciary duty to enhance value for their shareholders," he argued in a *New York Times* opinion piece. "The fault does not lie with them but with our uncompetitive international tax code and with our dysfunctional Congress for not changing it."

Icahn expressed hope that the public's sense of urgency about stopping inversions could be shunted away from its current anti-corporate trajectory and instead stampede Congress into lowering corporate tax rates this year. He wrote in the *New York Times*, "How will representatives and senators, with an election year approaching, explain to their constituents why they are out of work because their employers left the country, when it could so easily have been avoided?"

In pressing for lower corporate taxes in the name of heading off more inversions, corporate and financial figures like Icahn and Republicans are backed by some influential Democrats and self-described liberals who share an elite consensus on corporations' absolute "right" to switch their nationalities and to offshore jobs and capital. *New York Times* business columnist Jeffrey Sommer summarized this consensus in 2014, inadvertently illustrating the vast gulf between elite opinion and majority sentiment. "At this stage of globalization," Sommer declared, "... most American consumers, investors and politicians have tacitly accepted that if a company is profitable, doesn't violate the law and produces appealing products and services, it can operate wherever and however it likes."

Treating corporate investment decisions as sacrosanct regardless of their impact on the public welfare, key Democratic figures like Sen. Charles Schumer (D-N.Y.) and Senate Minority Leader Harry Reid (D-Nev.) are calling for a "tax holiday" on the foreign profits of U.S. corporations. They essentially seek to replicate the holiday declared in 2004 to encourage corporations to "repatriate" foreign profits to the United States by giving them a radically discounted tax rate.

The "tax holiday" idea is a particularly counter-productive measure. First, tax holidays reinforce corporations' use of tax deferrals as they create an incentive for the companies to wait for Congress to capitulate and offer discounted tax rates. Second, these top Democrats' backing of a new corporate-tax holiday is particularly indefensible given the disastrous outcome of the 2004 holiday. "Advocates said it would create 660,000 new jobs," pointed out David Cay Johnston. "Didn't happen. Pfizer brought home the most, $37 billion, escaping $11 billion in taxes. Then Pfizer fired 41,000 workers."

A Real Solution

If corporate tax avoidance is to be stopped, the most immediate step is ending corporations' ability to endlessly defer taxes on income which they claim to have generated overseas.

Offshore tax havens enable corporations to routinely engage in a practice called "profit-stripping." With this practice, taxable earnings in the United States are stripped—with costs allocated to the U.S. units and earnings attributed to firms' foreign subsidiaries. "This kind of accounting alchemy actually works, turning the black tax ink of profit into red ink of debt," Johnston explained. "You appear as a pauper to government but valuable to investors."

"Most of America's largest corporations maintain subsidiaries in offshore tax havens," reported Citizens for Tax Justice. "At least 358 companies, nearly 72 percent of the Fortune 500, operate subsidiaries in tax haven jurisdictions as of the end of 2014."

This means a loss of an additional $90 billion to the Treasury, according to Citizens for Tax Justice, apart from the cost of inversions.

It is relatively easy to envision reforms that would give the U.S. tax code a badly needed updating—suited to the current era dominated by the global operations of multinational corporations—to foreclose maneuvers like inversions and the deferral of taxes on foreign earnings.

But serious action on inversions and major loopholes will likely prove impossible as long as our political democracy continues to be eroded by a torrent of campaign contributions from the multinational corporations exploiting the existing tax system.

Until that link—between those who write the big campaign checks and those who write our laws and tax code—is irrevocably broken, our political system will remain impervious to majority sentiment for stiffer taxes and restrictions on corporations' inversions and the offshoring of capital and jobs. ❏

Sources: Matt Gardner, "Johnson Controls Attempts a Snow Job," Tax Justice Blog, Jan. 26, 2016 (taxjusticeblog.org); Citizens for Tax Justice "The Sorry State of Corporate Taxes," 2014 (ctj.org); Citizens for Tax Justice, "Offshore Shell Games," Oct. 5, 2015 (ctj.org); Jesse Drucker and Zachary R. Mider, "Tax Inversion: How U.S. Companies Buy Tax Breaks," BloombergView QuickTake, Nov 23, 2015 (bloombergview.com); David Cay Johnston, "Corporate Deadbeats: How Companies Get Rich Off Of Taxes," *Newsweek*, Sept. 4, 2014; Andrew Ross Sorkin, "A Tidal Wave of Corporate Migrants Seeking (Tax) Shelter," Dealbook, *New York Times*, Jan. 26, 2016; David Cay Johnston, "The Shocking Numbers Behind Corporate Welfare: Boeing and Its Stockholders Fly High on Tax Dollars,"

Al Jazeera America, Feb. 25, 2014 (america.aljazeera.com); Kimberly Clausing, "3 Myths About Inversions and U.S. Corporate Taxes," Fortune, Jan. 30, 2016; Carl Icahn, "How to Stop Turning U.S. Corporations Into Tax Exiles," *New York Times*, Dec. 14, 2015; Allen Sloan, "How to Stop Companies from Deserting America before It's Too Late," *Fortune*, Aug. 11, 2014; Thomas Hungerford, "Policy Responses to Corporate Inversions: Close the Barn Door Before the Horse Bolts," Economic Policy Institute Issue Brief #386, Sept. 8, 2014 (epi.org); James Sensenbrenner, "Tax Reform Is Critical For American Economic Prosperity," *Milwaukee Journal Sentinel*, Feb. 8, 2016; Philip Mattera, "Subsidizing the Corporate One Percent: Subsidy Tracker 2.0 Reveals Big-Business Dominance of State and Local Development Incentives," Good Jobs First Subsidy Tracker, February 2014 (goodjobsfirst.org/subsidy-tracker); Roger Bybee, "Corporate 'Consensus' on Offshoring, Inversions," *Progressive Populist*, Nov. 1, 2014 (populist.com); Chris Matthews, "Why Washington is Tackling the Tax Inversion Problem All Wrong," *Fortune*, Nov. 25, 2015; Thomas Content and Cary Spivak, "After getting taxpayers' help, Johnson Controls packs its bags," *Milwaukee Journal Sentinel*, Jan. 30, 2016; Stephen Gandel, "You Won't Believe How Much Johnson Controls' CEO Is Making on the Tyco Deal," *Fortune*, Jan. 25, 2016; Roger Bybee, "Manufacturing Revival a Worthy Goal, but Obama's Timid Plans Won't Get Job Done," Working in These Times blog, Feb. 20, 2012 (inthesetimes.com); "The Corporate Tax Dodge Continues," *New York Times*, Jan. 29, 2016; Eileen Applebaum, "No Tax Holiday for Multinational Corporations," Truthout, June 11, 2011 (truthout.org); Geoff Colvin, "Tyco-Johnson Controls Gives Us a Window into the Business World's Hardest Challenge," *Fortune*, Jan. 27, 2015; Allan Sloan, "Positively Un-American," Fortune, July 7, 2014; Allan Sloan, "Corporate Tax Dodgers Leave the Rest of Us to Foot the Bill," *Washington Post*, July 12, 2014; "U.S. Polling Shows Strong Opposition to More of the Same U.S. Trade Deals from Independents, Republicans and Democrats Alike," Public Citizen, July 2015 (citizen.org); James O'Toole, "GAO: U.S. corporations pay average effective tax rate of 12.6%," CNN, July 1, 2013 (cnn.com); Jesse Drucker and Zachary R. Mider, "Tax Inversion: How U.S. Companies Buy Tax Breaks," BloombergView, updated Nov. 23, 2015 (bloombergview.com); Michael Henigan, "IMF explains 'Double Irish Dutch Sandwich' Tax Avoidance," FinFacts Ireland, Oct. 11, 2013 (finfacts.ie); Elizabeth Warren, "Enough Is Enough: The President's Latest Wall Street Nominee," Huffington Post, Nov. 19, 2014 (huffingtonpost.com); David Sell, "Here and in New York, CEOs Talk Tax Inversion—or Don't," *Philadelphia Inquirer*, Sept. 3, 2014 (philly.com); Cliff Taylor, "Explained: The Upside Down World of Corporate Tax Inversions," *Irish Times*, Nov. 23, 2015 (irishtimes.com); Orsolya Kun, "A Broader View of Corporate Inversions: The Interplay of Tax, Corporate and Economic Implications," Bepress Legal Series, Sept. 26, 2003 (law.bepress.com); Americans for Tax Fairness, "Tax Fairness Coalition Sees Poll Results on Corporate Inversions as a Sign that the Issue Will Be Hot this Election Season," Aug. 5, 2014 (americansfortaxfairness.org); Citizens for Tax Justice, "Memo to Senate Permanent Subcommittee on Investigations: US Corporations Already Pay a Low Tax Rate," July 30, 2015 (ctj.org); Citizens for Tax Justice, "The U.S. Is One of the Least Taxed Developed Countries," April 2016 (ctj.org);Robert C. Pozen, "35 Percent Is Way Too High For Corporate Taxes," Brookings Institution," Jan. 29, 2016 (Brookings.edu); Leslie Picker, "Pfizer And Allergan Advisers Lose Out On $200 Million In Fees," *New York Times* Dealbook, April 6, 206; Diana Furchtgott-Roth, "Free Pfizer!: Why Inversions are Good for the U.S.," *New York Times*, April 7, 2016; Oxfam, "An Economy for the 1%,", Jan. 18, 2016.

Article 9.4

WHAT'S WRONG WITH A FLAT TAX?

BY ARTHUR MacEWAN
September/October 2012

> Dear Dr. Dollar:
> *Today a minister asked me why a flat tax, where "everybody pays their fair share," is not the best idea. I did not have a short, convincing explanation. Can you help?* —Arthur Milholland, Silver Springs, MD

Although flat tax proposals differ, they have one basic thing in common: they would all reduce the tax rates for people with high incomes. Thus they would either shift the tax burden to people with lower incomes or lead to a reduction in government services or both.

Currently, the federal personal income tax is quite progressive on paper and somewhat progressive in fact. A "progressive" income tax system is one where people with higher incomes pay a larger percentage of their income as taxes than do people with lower incomes. (A "regressive" system is one where people with lower incomes pay a higher share of their income as taxes; a "proportional" system is one where everyone pays the same proportion of their income as taxes. A flat tax and a proportional tax are the same.)

The justification for a progressive tax system is fairness: people with higher incomes have a greater ability to pay taxes and therefore should be subject to a higher tax rate. For example (to take an extreme case), a family with an income of $2 million can pay $200,000 in taxes more easily (i.e., with less impact on their circumstances) than a family with an income of $20,000 can pay $2,000 in taxes. Also, the principle of fairness suggests that high-income families should pay higher rates to support a system that provides so well for them. These concepts of fairness have been long established in the U.S. personal income-tax system.

Even today, with rates for high-income people lowered from earlier years, the system still has a significant element of progressivity. For example, a family with taxable income of $20,000 would supposedly pay $2,150 (10.75%), while a family with taxable income of $1 million would supposedly pay $320,000 (32%). Of course many people, especially those with high-incomes, find various "loopholes," and do not end up paying as much in taxes as they otherwise would. Many loopholes are in the deductions that allow people to keep their taxable income—and therefore their taxes—down. At the same time, many people with low incomes have their taxes greatly reduced—sometimes resulting in payments *from* the government rather than tax payments *to* the government.

The Tax Policy Center has estimated that in 2010 people in the lowest 40% of the income distribution on average got money back from the government (because of the Earned Income Tax Credit and the Child Tax Credit), while people in the highest-income 20% on average paid taxes at a rate of 13.6%. People at the very top, the highest-income 1%, paid on average 18.6%.

Conservative ideologues like to jump on the fact that many low-income people pay no federal income tax at all. Yet federal income taxes are only part of the tax story. Low-income people still pay Social Security and Medicare taxes, sales taxes at the state level, and various other taxes. Overall, the U.S. tax system is hardly progressive at all, and may even be regressive.

Advocates of a flat tax claim it would be better to get rid of all the complications in the federal income tax—the adjustments, the credits, the deductions, etc.—and just charge everyone the same rate. Also, they argue that a flat tax would boost the economy because the current high rates on people with high incomes harm the incentive to invest and to work. Yet there is no way around the simple arithmetic: to lower the top rate and to obtain the same amount of revenue from a flat tax as from the current system, people below the top would have to have their tax rates increased. (While advocates of a flat tax generally reject the principles of fairness on which the progressivity of the U.S. tax code has long been based, it would be possible to introduce an element of progressivity into a flat tax by exempting all income below a certain level. Still, except for those people near the bottom, tax rates would have to be raised for most people—though not for those at the top.)

Furthermore, the claim that with a flat tax all the adjustments, credits, deductions, etc. would be eliminated is not credible. Indeed, since a flat tax would increase the after-tax income of those at the top, it would increase the amount of money they would have to buy influence to get their favorite "complications" reinstated (as if they didn't have enough influence already!). As to the argument that reducing the tax rate on people with high incomes would boost the economy, well, we have seen how well that has worked since the Bush tax cuts for the wealthy were put in place in 2001.

So a flat tax would be one more break for the rich, increasing their income on the backs of the great majority of the populace. Not fair at all. That's what's wrong with a flat tax. ❑

Article 9.5

THE BURDENS OF AMERICAN FEDERALISM
Income Redistribution Through Taxation

BY GERALD FRIEDMAN
September/October 2015

Because of increasing economic inequality, many scholars and activists have looked at tax policy both for changes that may explain widening income gaps and for reforms that might reduce inequality of market incomes. While it is appropriate to study the role of federal taxes, state and local governments take in nearly half of all government revenue. Non-tax revenues from fees and service charges account for nearly 15% of government revenue (all levels).

Americans are accustomed to thinking of the tax system as progressive, requiring higher-income people to pay a higher percentage of their incomes in taxes than lower-income people. Because the burden of state and local taxes and non-tax revenues is much heavier on poor people and the working class than it is on the rich, however, the fiscal system as a whole is much less progressive than it seems from looking only at federal-level taxation. While all states have regressive tax systems, requiring lower-income people to pay a higher percentage of their incomes than higher-income people, some states are more regressive than others. States that rely on sales taxes and user fees impose a heavier burden on poor and working people; states that rely more on income taxes do less to widen the income gap.

FIGURE 1: TOTAL GOVERNMENT REVENUE BY LEVEL, 2012

The federal government collects only a little more than half of government revenues. The federal government and its taxes—totaling just over $2.5 trillion (or 56% of government revenue)—have often been the focus of political attention and controversy. State and local governments, however, collect nearly $2 trillion in taxes and other types of revenue. (Non-tax revenue includes charges for services (such as water, the lottery, or college tuition) as well as fees (such as motor vehicle registration or licenses).) States and localities collect 44% of total government revenues. Therefore, to understand the distributional impact of government revenue policies in the United States, we have to consider all levels of government, not just the federal.

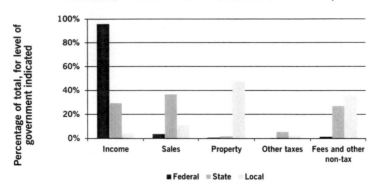

FIGURE 2: GOVERNMENT REVENUE BY SOURCE, 2012

Federal revenues are collected largely from income and payroll taxes; states and localities collect sales and property taxes, and charge fees. There are three distinct tax systems in the United States, corresponding to the three levels of government. The federal government draws the vast majority of its revenue from taxes on income, including corporate and personal income taxes as well as Social Security and Medicare payroll taxes. In contrast, income taxes account for less than 30% of state tax revenue and virtually no local tax revenue. States are more likely to collect revenue from fees and from sales taxes, especially on material goods. (Business and consumer services usually go untaxed.) For their part, local governments rely little on sales taxes but draw most of their revenue from fees and from property taxes, mostly on real estate.

FIGURE 3: DISTRIBUTION OF FISCAL BURDEN, 2011-2012

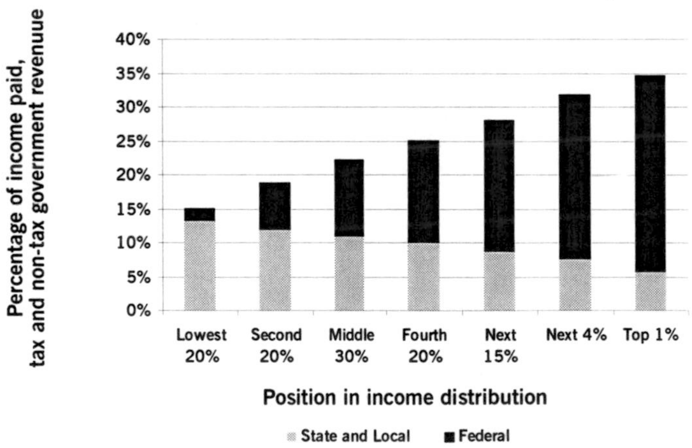

The economic burden of state and local government falls most heavily on poor and working people. Most Americans pay more in state and local government taxes and fees than they do in federal taxes. Because federal taxes fall more heavily on the rich than on the poor, they redistribute income "downwards." In contrast, state and local taxes and fees fall more heavily on the poor and the working class, while the richest Americans pay relatively little. (Property taxes, significant at the local level, are actually *regressive* on balance: While it depends somewhat on how one apportions the burden of property taxes between landlords and renters, the Intstitute for Taxation and Economic Policy calculates the bottom 20% pay 3.7% of their incomes in property taxes while the richest 1% pay only 1.6%.) The balance between state and local revenues, on the one hand, and federal revenues, on the other, is therefore important for understanding the impact of taxation on income distribution. The larger the share of state and local taxes and fees—apart from state and local income taxes—the less government redistributes income downward; and the larger the share of national taxation, the more the government does to equalize after-tax incomes.

FIGURE 4A: DISTRIBUTION OF INCOME TAX BURDEN, 2011-2012

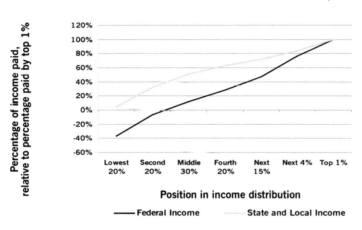

FIGURE 4B: DISTRIBUTION OF SALES TAX BURDEN, 2011-2012

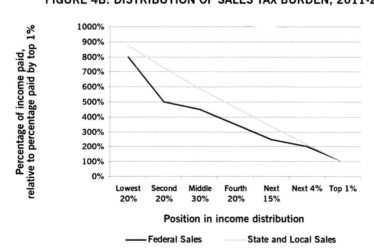

Differences in the burdens of taxation between the federal government and states and localities result from the type of tax assessed. Whether assessed on the state or on the national level, income taxes fall more heavily on the rich than on the poor.

Because of federal and state earned-income tax credits (tax exemptions on labor income that favor low-income people) and progressive income-tax rates, high-income people pay a much higher percentage of their incomes in income taxes than do lower-income people. This is true on both the state and federal levels. By contrast, sales taxes fall more heavily on lower-income people. This is because poor and working people spend higher proportions of their incomes on consumption than rich people do, and are more likely to consume material goods subject to sales taxes. Rich people spend more of their incomes on sales-tax-exempt services, such as legal services and personal care.

FIGURE 5: PROGRESSIVITY OF STATE TAX SYSTEMS, 2012

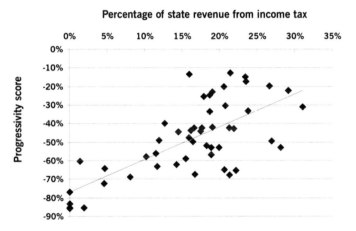

Note: Progressivity score = (percentage of income paid by top 1% - percentage of income paid by bottom 20%)/(percentage of income paid by bottom 20%). Only for state taxes (excludes local taxes and all fees).

States that rely on income taxes have more equitable tax systems; those that rely on sales taxes and fees widen the gap between rich and poor. While every state has a regressive tax system, some states are much more regressive than others. Regionally, southern states have more regressive tax systems, with the richest 1% paying only half as much of their incomes (in percentage terms) as do the poorest 20%; in northeastern states, by contrast, the richest 1% pay two-thirds as much as do the poor. The regressive effect of state and local revenue collection is not just a matter of region, but of policy. As with the federal government, progressivity in state and local taxation comes from reliance on income taxes. Whether in the North or the South, states without an income tax, like Texas, Washington, and Wyoming, or states where relatively little revenue comes from the income tax, have the most regressive revenue systems. By contrast, the states with the least regressive systems tend to rely more on income taxation and draw less of their revenue from sales taxes and fees. ❑

Sources: Internal Revenue Service (irs.gov); The White House, Budget for Fiscal Year 2016 (whitehouse.gov); U.S. Bureau of the Census (census.gov); Institute for Taxation and Economic Policy (itep.org); Congressional Budget Office, The Distribution of Household Income and Federal Taxes(cbo.gov).

Article 9.6

TRANSACTION TAX: SAND IN THE WHEELS, NOT IN THE FACE

Why a transaction tax is a really good idea.

BY JOHN MILLER
March/April 2010

WHY TAXING STOCK TRADES IS A REALLY BAD IDEA

[S]urely it is "socially useful" to let free people transact freely, without regulators and legislators micromanaging them. ... It's Economics 101 that the free actions of market participants cause supply and demand to reach equilibrium. And isn't that what investors—indeed even speculators—do? Can they do it as well when facing the dead-weight costs of a transaction tax?

If not, then trading volume in our stock markets will fall. Beyond the tax, everyone—investors and speculator, great and small—who buys or sells stocks will pay more to transact in markets that are less liquid. In such a world, markets would necessarily be more risky, and the cost of capital for business would necessarily rise. The consequence of that is that innovation, growth, and jobs would necessarily fall. That would be the full and true cost of the trading tax.

—Donald L. Luskin and Chris Hynes, "Why Taxing Stock Trades Is a Really Bad Idea," *Wall Street Journal*, Jan. 5, 2010

"Some financial activities which proliferated over the last 10 years were socially useless," Britain's Finance Service Authority Chairman Adiar Turner told a black-tie gathering of financial executives in London in September 2009. That is why he had proposed a transaction tax for the United Kingdom and why British Prime Minister Gordon Brown would propose an international transaction tax at the November G-20 summit.

The gathered bankers "saw red," as one report described their reaction. Investment bankers Donald L. Luskin and Chris Hynes are still irate.

In some ways their reaction is surprising. A financial transaction tax is nothing other than a sales tax on trading stocks and other securities. Transaction taxes are already in place in about 30 countries, and a transaction tax applied to the sale of stock in the United States from 1914 to 1964.

In addition, the transaction tax rates on a single trade are typically quite low. For instance, the "Let Wall Street Pay for the Restoration of Main Street Act of 2009," proposed by U.S. Representative Peter DeFazio (D-Ore.), would assess a one quarter of one percent (.25%) tax on the value of stock transactions, and two one hundredths of one percent (.02%) tax on the sale on a variety of derivative assets—including credit default swaps, which played such a large role in the mortgage crisis. To target speculators, the bill exempts retirement accounts, mutual funds, education and health savings accounts, and the first $100,000 of transactions annually.

In other ways, Luskin's and Hynes's reaction is not surprising at all. At its heart, a transaction tax is a radical measure. Its premise is that faster-acting financial markets driven by speculation don't bring relief to the economy—instead, they loot the economy. Its purpose, as Nobel Prize-winning economist James Tobin put it when he proposed his original transaction tax on international money markets during the 1970s, is to "throw sand in the wheels" of our financial markets.

Also, while its tax rate is low, the burden of a transaction tax adds up as securities are repeatedly traded, as is the practice on Wall Street today. For instance, even after accounting for its exemptions and allowing for a sizable decline in trading, the DeFazio bill would still raise $63.5 billion annually, according to the estimates of Dean Baker, co-director of the Center for Economic Policy Research.

Luskin and Hynes have two main objections to the transaction tax. The first is that a transaction tax would affect every single person who owns and invests in stocks, not just speculators. Customers would not have to pay a tax to buy or sell mutual funds, but, as Luskin and Hynes emphasize, the mutual funds themselves would have to pay a tax every time they trade stocks. So everyone holding mutual funds would still end up paying the tax.

What Luskin and Hynes don't say is this: Mutual funds that actively trade stocks would pay three times the transaction taxes of an average fund, as the Investment Company Institute, the fund industry trade group, reports. And stock index funds, which hold a sample of all stocks but seldom trade them, are taxed the least. Those funds have historically outperformed other mutual funds. So a transaction tax would work to push mutual fund customers to invest their savings more wisely, providing some with higher rates of return with a transaction tax than their previous funds provided without it. And that would mean fewer broker fees and lower profits for the fund industry.

But what really sticks in Luskin's and Hynes's craw is the assertion that financial trading is not socially useful. That claim flies in face of the long-held contention, buttressed by much of finance theory, that the equilibrium outcomes of financial markets are efficient. And if financial markets are efficient, there is no need for a tax that will reduce trading.

But much of what Luskin and Hynes have to say is not right. First, as anyone who *paid attention* in Economics 101 would know, reaching an equilibrium is not in and of itself desirable. To endorse the outcomes of today's speculative financial markets as desirable because they reach an equilibrium is the equivalent of describing a gambler in a poker game raking in a big pot as desirable because it clears the table. And the gamblers in our financial markets did rake in some awfully big pots betting that subprime borrowers would default on their loans. The last few years show us just how undesirable that equilibrium turned out to be.

Second, speculation dwarfs financing investment in U.S. stock markets. During the 1970s, for every dollar of new investment in plants and equipment, $1.30 in stocks were traded on the U.S. exchanges, reports Robert Pollin, co-director of the Political Economy Research Institute. But from 1998 to 2007, $27 in stocks were traded on the U.S. exchanges for every dollar of corporate investment in plant equipment. Such a rapid stock turnover has diverted the attention of managers of enterprises from long-term planning. Whatever damage that churning caused on Main Street, it paid off handsomely on Wall Street. From 1973 to 2007, the size of the financial (and insurance) sector relative to the economy doubled, financial sector profits went from one-quarter to two-fifths of domestic profits, and compensation in the finance industry went from just about average to 180% of the private industry average.

By counteracting these trends, a transactions tax can actually enhance, not diminish, the efficiency of financial markets. If it forces the financial sector to fulfill its function of transferring savings to investment with less short-term churning, then the tax will have freed up resources for more productive uses.

A transaction tax would surely be a step in the right direction toward reducing the bloat of the finance industry, righting the balance of speculation over enterprise, and restoring the focus on long-term planning and job-creation in the economy.

None of that will happen unless every last grain of the decades' worth of sand the bullies on Wall Street have kicked in our faces gets thrown into the wheels of finance. That is a tall order. But as DeFazio's and Turner's example shows, some of today's policymakers are up to the task. ❑

Sources: Dean Baker, "The Benefits of a Financial Transaction Tax," Center For Economic and Policy Research, December 2008 (cepr.net); Robert Pollin and Dean Baker, "Public Investment, Industrial Policy, and U.S. Economic Renewal," Political Economy Research Institute, December 2009; Caroline Binham, "Turner Plan on 'Socially Useless' Trades Make Bankers See Red" (Bloomberg.com); Yaiman Onaran, "Taxing Wall Street Today Wins Support for Keynes Idea (Update 1)" (Bloomberg.com); Dean Baker, Robert Pollin, Travis McArthur, and Matt Sherman, "The Potential Revenue from Financial Transactions Taxes, Political Economy Research Institute, Working paper no. 212, December 2009; Donald L. Luskin and Chris Hynes, "Why Taxing Stock Trades Is a Really Bad Idea," *Wall Street Journal*, Jan. 5, 2010; John McKinnon, "Lawmakers Weigh A Wall Street Tax," *Wall Street Journal*, Dec. 19, 2009; Tobin Tax (freerisk.org/wiki/index.php/Tobin_tax); text of HR 4191—"Let Wall Street Pay for the Restoration of Main Street Act of 2009" (www.govtrack.us).

Article 9.7

WEALTH INEQUALITY AND WEALTH TAXATION
A Primer on Piketty

BY STEVEN PRESSMAN
May 2014

Great works in economics address important issues head-on, adopt a broad per-spective, and change our views regarding how economies work. Make no mistake about it: Thomas Piketty's *Capital in the Twenty-First Century* is a great work. As an added bonus, it is extremely well written (and translated).

Given decades of rising inequality and its negative consequences and public concern about a disappearing middle class, this book is particularly timely. It relies on a wide array of data, collected by the author, showing long-term trends in income and wealth distribution. It explains the causes of these trends and ends by setting forth some bold policy solutions.

Still, the most important aspect of *Capital in the Twenty-First Century* is that it changes how we view the world. The following parallel might provide some historical perspective on the book, and help understand its importance and the emotional reaction it has elicited.

Thomas Malthus became one of the most controversial figures in economics following the publication of his *Essay on Population* in 1798. Despite much optimism at the time that ordinary people's lives could be improved, for Malthus poverty was inevitable due to the relationship between population growth and the growth of the food supply. His *Essay* argued (based on some empirical data) that population growth would outstrip food supply growth, resulting in famine and misery.

Piketty can best be understood as a sort of modern-day Malthus. Both doubting Thomases sought to refute popular beliefs that life could easily be improved for most people, both used simple growth rates to do this, and both were criticized for their pessimistic conclusions.

Optimism regarding the future distribution of income stems from the work of Nobel laureate Simon Kuznets. In the 1950s, Kuznets examined U.S. income-tax data and saw income inequality improving over several decades. According to the standard interpretation of his work, he hypothesized that as capitalist economies developed, inequality first increases and then decreases. This message fit America's economic experience during the post-war years and its geo-political needs during the Cold War. Most economists came to accept this message of hope.

But times have changed. Inequality is rising in the United States and other high-income capitalist countries. Piketty explains why economists got it wrong. He argues that greater equality between World War I and the 1960s was not part of some positive long-term trend; rather, it stemmed from a unique set of factors—two wars (that destroyed much wealth), the very high marginal tax rates implemented to pay for these wars, plus a stock-market crash and Great Depression. Starting in the 1970s or 1980s (dates differ by country) the moneyed class revolted and began to influence policy. Top income-tax rates fell; income and wealth inequality rose rapidly. As a result, we seem headed toward another Gilded Age, similar to the late 19th century, where the fabulously wealthy live charmed lives and everyone else struggles to survive.

Piketty, like Malthus, draws his dismal conclusion from the relationship between two growth rates. In Piketty's case, they are the rate of return to wealth or capital (r) and the growth rate of the economy (g). When r exceeds g, more money flows to those at the top and inequality increases; when r is less than g, more benefits of economic growth flow to workers, making income and wealth distribution more equal.

One great virtue of Piketty's book is that it explains why income inequality has grown of late. First, the ratio of wealth to GDP declined in Europe from 6:1 or 7:1 around World War I to 2:1 in the 1960s. It has since rebounded to nearly 6:1. The United States experienced a smaller decline, since its factories were not destroyed by the two wars, but has also experienced a growing wealth-to-GDP ratio of late. Second, r has averaged around 5% over long periods of time in many different countries, while g cannot be expected to grow by much more than 1%.

Together these results create a distribution problem, which may be easiest to comprehend in personal terms.

Suppose you receive a $200,000 inheritance (your wealth) and you make $100,000 a year. If your wealth grows at 5% per year and your wages grow by 1%, after 35 years (a typical working life) your wages would be around $140,000 and your wealth (assuming no spending down of this wealth) over $1 million. After several generations, around 100 years, your great grandchild would have labor income of $268,000 and have $25 million in capital assets. With a 5% return, their capital income ($1.25 million) would dwarf their labor income. If some income from wealth gets consumed, which is likely, this process just takes a little longer to work out. At some point income from wealth will far exceed income from labor.

The problem is that we don't all begin with equal amounts of capital. Some start with large inheritances; most people begin with nothing. As a result, the incomes of the haves grow much more rapidly than those of the have-nots and wealth inequality soars.

Piketty's story is far superior to standard economic explanations of rising inequality, such as technological change and globalization. He rightly rejects these theories because they cannot explain national differences in rising inequality—technological change and globalization should have similar impacts on all developed nations.

Compiling the data to make this case has been a heroic endeavor. Piketty uses income tax returns to get data on the share of national income going to the top 10%, the top 1%, and the top 0.1% of households. Estate tax returns enable him to estimate wealth inequality. Substantial evidence supports Piketty's conclusion that income and wealth inequality have risen in the United States and elsewhere since the late 20th century.

Similar to Malthus's *Essay*, Piketty's *Capital* contains virtually no economic theory. It does not address what determines economic growth or the return to wealth. Its dismal conclusion stems from historic trends and Piketty's explanation of why high rates of return to wealth increase inequality.

So Where Do We Go From Here?

The last part of Piketty's book discusses how to deal with rising inequality. Piketty is skeptical that institutional policies such as raising the minimum wage, or more generous government spending programs, will help much. It is not that he opposes such efforts. Rather, he thinks they are inadequate when wealth is so unevenly distributed and grows so rapidly. Government spending programs can help, but they cannot increase labor income by 5% annually over the long run.

Tax policy is all that is left (no pun intended). Piketty favors a more progressive individual income tax, with a 70% top rate. Corporations, he argues, also need to be taxed based on where they pay wages so they cannot book profits to subsidiaries in low-tax countries.

These policies would reduce income inequality and slow down, but not reverse, the more pressing issue of greater wealth inequality. To deal with this latter problem, Piketty advocates an annual wealth tax, imposed at very low rates—one or two percent on wealth in excess of 1 million euros (nearly $1.4 million). And it must be a global tax, so that it cannot be escaped by moving wealth abroad.

Those on the right objected to the tax rates that Piketty proposes as excessively high. The worst of these objections engaged in name-calling, deeming anyone a socialist who proposes higher taxes for whatever reason. Almost as bad have been the objections that higher taxes would give the government more money to waste—as if businesses never, ever wasted money and consumers always spent their money cautiously and rationally (e.g., they would never buy homes or be able to obtain mortgages that they couldn't possibly afford to repay). The more thoughtful and reasonable objections from the right have focused on the bad incentives to work hard, earn money, accumulate wealth, and provide for one's children and grandchildren as a result of higher taxes.

Those on the left and toward the center of the political spectrum have been fairly consistent in maintaining that the main policy proposal of Piketty was impractical because a global wealth tax would never get enacted. After making this point, the next sentence of these critiques typically push other policies (invariably the personal favorites of those criticizing Piketty), which are just as unlikely to get enacted given the current political situation in the United States and elsewhere.

I find all these criticisms both disturbing and a little bit off the mark. But before looking at his wealth tax proposals in greater detail, it is worth examining what Piketty has to say regarding monetary policy and fiscal policy, something which was not discussed in most of the prominent reviews of his book. Piketty downplays monetary policy in favor of fiscal policy. Monetary policy, he contends, cannot deal with the problem of rising inequality. In fact, he contends that we cannot know the impact of monetary policy on income and wealth distribution, although there is no argument for this. My gut instinct is that this is true, but I would have liked to see some data that supports this contention—say, looking at how income and wealth distribution vary based on interest rates. Such a study would make for a great thesis or doctoral dissertation, to say nothing about a nice professional paper.

Regarding fiscal policy, Piketty is fairly critical of government deficits. He spends a good deal of time focusing on the need to tax wealth so that we can repay existing government debt, but he fails to address the issue of whether government deficits and debt may be necessary at times. He also doesn't address the issue of whether government debt does any actual harm to overall macroeconomic performance. Rather, the focus is mainly (Surprise! Surprise!) on the impact of debt on income distribution. Piketty's main point is that the large majority of government bonds created when the government goes into debt is owned by the very wealthy. They benefit greatly from government debt. With little risk, they receive positive returns on their money. This income generates part of their 5% rate of return on wealth or capital.

Unfortunately, the passages on fiscal policy and distribution are too brief. There are two key reasons I wish Piketty had written a good deal more on the relationship between fiscal policy and inequality. First, he argues throughout Capital that one main reason inequality declined from World War I through the 1950s was that there were high marginal tax rates on top incomes. This reduced the after-tax gains from owning wealth. Second, fiscal policy is central to Piketty's major policy proposals.

Writing more on fiscal policy and distribution would not have been all that difficult to do. Moreover, his entire case for changes in tax policy would have been considerably stronger had Piketty spent more time on this topic and then related it to the beginnings of the revolt of the rentiers in the United Kingdom and the United States when Margaret Thatcher and Ronald Reagan were elected heads of government.

The story in both cases is rather similar and involved several policy changes. There was a sharp cut in government spending (that hurt the poor and middle class more than wealthy households, which can provide their own benefits) and a sharp cut in taxes focused at the top of the income distribution. Overall, the cuts in government expenditures were less than the tax cuts, and the government had to borrow money by selling bonds. Abstracting a little from the overall process, the Reagan and Thatcher governments gave large tax breaks to the wealthy, and then borrowed the money back from them to pay for the tax cuts. Everyone else got small tax cuts that were funded by cutting the government benefits they received. Or in slightly bolder and simpler terms, the Reagan and Thatcher governments decided to fund a good deal of government spending by borrowing money from the wealthy rather than taxing the wealthy.

As Piketty's data demonstrate, these changes led to sharply rising inequality in the UK and the United States over the past several decades. And it is no wonder why this occurred. Those earning high incomes got to keep a lot more of their income. Yet they had to do something with all this additional money. It could not be kept under the mattress, earning nothing. Bank deposits were insured, but not for balances of the sort that the very wealthy possessed. The result could only be that all this additional disposable income fueled rising asset prices, which also primarily benefited the wealthy.

According to the gospel of "supply-side" economics, which was used to justify these policy changes, the whole process should have resulted in much greater economic growth and enormous tax collections by the government so that there would be no deficit. However, this claim ignored the "balanced-budget multiplier" described by the great 20th-century U.S. economist Paul Samuelson. Samuelson showed that an equal cut in taxes and in government spending would slow economic growth or reduce GDP by an amount equal to the tax cut (or cut in government spending). The reason for this is very simple. A dollar less in government spending is a dollar less spending while a dollar tax cut was not an additional dollar in spending since some of the spending will be saved. Overall, this will reduce spending and economic growth. Yet ideology triumphed over economic knowledge. The U.S. government and the UK government gave huge tax cuts to the wealthy, and then borrowed the money back from them in order to fund the tax cut. Economic growth slowed as the balanced budget multiplier predicted it would. This made distributional matters even worse because it increased the gap between r and g by lowering g.

One last thing is worth some additional comments before getting to the issue of income and wealth taxes, especially since this has been one of the most frequent criticisms of Piketty. Many commentators complained that Piketty ignored alternative policies such as supporting unions and raising the minimum wage—but Piketty actually does discuss these policies. Chapter 9 of the book includes an extensive discussion of the minimum wage. The data Piketty presents and the written text both make it very clear that the distribution of wages has remained relatively equal in France because the French have continually increased the minimum wage and that the French minimum wage is rather high compared to average wages. Piketty even discusses why this happened—French President Charles de Gaulle (in office 1958-1969) was worried about the crisis of May 1968 and used higher minimum wages to deal with a problem that was more cultural and social than economic. Moreover, Piketty clearly supports raising the minimum wage and even provides several justifications for raising the minimum wage. So it is puzzling that so many people would criticize Piketty for not supporting higher minimum wages.

The real problem Piketty has with raising the minimum wage is not that it won't help equalize wage income, but that it won't deal with the problem of rising capital income in the long run. He is also skeptical that the minimum wage can be increased enough (5% per year in real terms) over the long haul without generating substantial unemployment. To try to make Piketty's point as simple and clear as possible, even if wages (and we can add rising union power here) were made completely equal across the board, inequality would be high and would continue to increase because of the immense wealth that is possessed by a few people.

It is wealth inequality for Piketty that is the main force driving inequality to rise under capitalism. A higher minimum wage can slow the process down. So too can stronger unions. So too can government spending policies that equalize after-tax incomes, such as paid parental leave, child allowances, generous unemployment insurance programs, and a large and sturdy social safety net. These are all policies that Piketty, I imagine, would support. But the key insight of Capital is this: the driving force of inequality is that we start with great wealth inequality and the high returns to wealth make things worse over time. Policies that equalize income distribution will help a little, but they ignore the main problem.

Still, Piketty does focus on tax policy to reduce the distribution of wage income. He argues first for a progressive income tax because this (along with inheritance taxes) is the only progressive form of taxation that governments have. Sales or indirect taxes are regressive in nature and social-insurance taxes (for retirement and for unemployment) tend to be proportional or regressive. Again, Piketty does not make either a strong or forceful case for this policy. I wish he had put a little more emphasis on the fact that high marginal tax rates during the war years and in the decade or so after World War II contributed to the falling inequality in this era. Historically, he contends that high marginal income tax rates have led to lower (before-tax) inequality. It is in the data; it should have been stressed more in the policy section of the book.

On the other hand, Piketty does worry about current trends in individual income taxation. In particular, by exempting capital income from the income tax (or taxing it at lower rates) the income tax becomes regressive at the very top (because that is where they get most of their income) and tends to make the entire tax system regressive in developed countries. But, again, the big issue for Piketty is that progressive income taxes cannot solve the wealth inequality problem. Like progressive spending programs, a progressive income tax would help reduce income inequality, but it does not solve the problem that wealth inequality tends to rise because of the high returns to wealth—much of it, such as stocks and homes that are not sold, are not taxed at all.

In a couple of pages that were pretty much ignored in the reviews of Capital, Piketty calls for a reform of corporate taxation. He proposes that corporate income taxes be assessed based on wages paid in different countries rather than on where in the world the multi-national firm declares its profits to come from (typically the country that has the lowest corporate income tax rate). This is not headline grabbing, and tax reform is never as exciting as proposing a new type of tax (this is why there are so many articles on the flat tax and the Tobin Tax and why reviews of this book focused on the global wealth tax), but it is something that needs to receive serious consideration and should be pushed more.

Again, the fact that Piketty does not focus a lot of attention on this proposal probably stems from the fact that (like higher marginal income tax rates) it will affect income distribution but not wealth distribution. When corporations pay higher taxes to governments there is less profit to distribute to the owners as dividends. This will reduce current incomes. However, higher corporate income taxes also reduce future profits after-taxes, which should affect the value of corporate stock. This will lower the price of shares of stock. Since it is mainly the very wealthy who own large amounts of stock, and whose wealth portfolio contains a higher percentage of stock compared to middle-income households, this policy should have significant and substantial effect on wealth inequality.

Piketty and the Global Tax on Wealth

At last, we come to Piketty's main policy conclusion, his claim that the way to keep more and more income from going to those at the very top of the distribution is a global wealth tax. The tax needs to be global in order to keep wealth from moving to tax havens where it is not subject to the tax. Piketty also wants to keep the tax rate low (1-2%) in order to mitigate negative disincentives. His particular plan is that net assets worth between 1 million Euros ($1.35 million) and 5 million Euros

($6.75 million) be taxed at 1% and net assets worth more than 5 million Euros be taxed at 2%. The goal in all this, Piketty makes clear, is not to raise money for social programs but to tame the inequality that inevitably results under capitalism.

Piketty provides several different arguments for his progressive and global wealth tax.

First, he resorts to an appeal to authority. He invokes the 1918 American Economic Association Presidential address by Irving Fisher, in which Fisher worries about the fact that only 2% of the U.S. population owned more than 50% of the nation's wealth while two-thirds of the population had no net wealth. Fisher then went on to suggest a steeply progressive wealth tax to remedy this situation.

Second, Piketty argues that the rewards going to the very top are not justified by traditional economic arguments (that they depend on the marginal productivity of the worker). Instead, Piketty makes the case that CEO pay is due to luck to a large degree and that a bargaining model fits the data better than marginal productivity theory. He argues that when the government takes a very large chunk of any extra income, it is not worth it for a CEO to bargain with a compensation committee or shareholders to get higher pay. And he points to empirical evidence that high marginal tax rates keep down CEO pay while not hurting the economic performance of the firm.

Finally there is the main argument—that a global wealth tax is the only way to limit the growth of wealth accumulation and a return to 19th-century levels of inequality. Or, this is the only way we can avoid all the negative economic, social, and political consequences of great inequality. A tax on income will not achieve this end because much income is tied up in stocks and bonds and real estate that generally do not get taxed. The gains from these investments are taxed when assets are sold. This allows the gains to accumulate at the top and to keep doing so. Only a wealth tax can stop this process.

Finally, while his many critics fault Piketty for making such an unrealistic proposal, Piketty himself recognizes that a global wealth tax (or even higher taxes on income from capital in the United States) is not likely to happen anytime soon and perhaps will never happen. He has no unrealistic illusions about this policy being passed in the United States or Europe.

The alternative policy proposals made by critics of Piketty, as noted above, are probably as unrealistic as a global wealth tax. But the strong case against them, as Piketty points out, is that only a progressive wealth tax deals with the problem of rising inequality in income and wealth under capitalism. A higher minimum wage and greater support for labor unions cannot reduce the concentration of capital. Nor can progressive government programs such as paid parental leave and generous unemployment insurance. Even reforming individual and corporate income taxes will be of limited help (although, as I argue above, global corporate tax reform can do a lot of good). We are left with few options if we want to halt a return to the Gilded Age. ❑

Chapter 10

TRADE AND DEVELOPMENT

INTRODUCTION

Given the economic turmoil of the last decade in high-income countries, it is ironic that the developing world is still being urged to adopt free markets and increased privatization as the keys to catching up with the West. These neoliberal policy prescriptions have been applied across the developing world, over the last few decades, as a one-size-fits-all solution to problems such as poverty, malnutrition, and political conflict. While spiking unemployment in the United States led to a (temporary) surge in government spending, developing countries with double-digit unemployment were routinely told that macroeconomic crises could only be dealt with by "tightening their belts." And while the West, having experienced a financial crisis, now embraced some new financial regulations, similar calls for more regulation from developing countries have been dismissed as misguided.

The contributors to this section take on different aspects of the neoliberal (or "free market") policy mix, raising questions that recur through this entire volume. Where do the limits of the market lie? At what point do we decide that markets are no longer serving the general public, whose well-being economists claim to champion? And to what extent should communities, via politically representative bodies of all kinds, be able to regulate and control markets?

The first tenet of the neoliberal faith is the belief that openness to international trade is the key to growth and development. Ramaa Vasudevan, in her primer "Comparative Advantage" (Article 10.1), starts off this chapter with a critique of the Ricardian theory of comparative advantage that is central to the neoclassical argument for free trade.

Thomas Palley offers a concise and useful metaphor for the effects of globalization and outsourcing on productive industry in the United States. "The Globalization Clock" (Article 10.2) describes how globalization and outsourcing pick off domestic industries one by one, based on the relative exportability of the goods or services and the skill level of the workers. This metaphor also illustrates why, at any given period of time, there has not been a majority consensus against outsourcing: The majority of people (consumers) benefit through lower prices from the outsourced industry; only those acutely affected through the loss of their jobs are against it. But as the clock ticks forward, more and more industries at higher and higher levels of skill become outsourced.

Next, Arthur MacEwan considers whether economic globalization, in its current form, is closing off important domestic policy options (Article 10.3). He acknowledges the dangers, for example, of so-called "free trade" agreements that include provisions allowing investors to sue governments for policies that reduce their profits. MacEwan, however, argues that such constraints on policy have a much bigger effect on smaller, less powerful countries than on countries like the United States.

John Miller (Article 10.4) looks at the worker-safety accord put in place in Bangladesh in the wake of the 2013 Rana Plaza disaster, a factory collapse that killed over 1,100 workers. Miller argues that the legal liability of major clothing companies (who outsource clothing production to subcontractor companies) is a major positive step for worker safety. He also notes, however, that most major U.S. clothing companies have so far refused to sign onto the accord.

The next article turns to the current debt crisis in Puerto Rico (Article 10.5). Arthur MacEwan argues that Puerto Rico has suffered not only from particular U.S. government policies—reflected, for example, in lower net federal-government transfers to Puerto Rico than to many U.S. states—but also to its underlying "colonial" subordination to the U.S. economy. The Puerto Rico economy, MacEwan notes, has developed more slowly than those of comparable independent countries.

Ellen Frank's "Should Developing Countries Embrace Protectionism?" (Article 10.6), points out that, contrary to the claims of globalization advocates and the theory of comparative advantage, the historical record suggests that protectionism may be a better strategy for economic development. In fact, it is hard to provide an example of successful economic growth and development from countries that "got prices right" as opposed to those that "got prices wrong"—but to their trading advantage.

Finally, Jawied Nawabi (Article 10.7) focuses on land reform and its importance to economic development. Part of the case for land reform, he notes, is "economic"—for example, small farms actually produce more output per acre than large landholdings. However, the crux of the case is not narrowly economic, but "socio-political." Land reform is so essential to economic development because the power of large landlords stands in the way of needed development policies.

Discussion Questions

1. (Article 10.1) Under what conditions might the mainstream argument about the advantages of specialization based on comparative advantage break down?

2. (Article 10.2) Palley argues that the relative benefits and costs of globalization are not evenly distributed. Some folks gain from globalization and others lose. What is Palley's "globalization clock"? Explain in detail the metaphor and mechanism.

3. (Article 10.2) Does Palley's assessment of globalization differ at all from your textbook's? What time is it in the United States according to Palley's "globalization clock"?

4. (Article 10.3) If "investor-state dispute settlement" provisions in international agreements give investors a way to sidestep courts and challenge government

policies that they oppose, why doesn't MacEwan agree that "trade agreements foreclose progressive policy"?

5. (Article 10.4) Opponents of international labor standards argue that workers in very low-income countries just need jobs, and will only be hurt by well-intentioned efforts to raise wages or improve working conditions. How do such arguments hold up to the experience in Bangladesh since the Rana Plaza disaster?

6. (Article 10.5) MacEwan argues that Puerto Rico's is a "colonial" economy. What does he mean by this? Do you agree?

7. (Article 10.6) What is the basic argument made by mainstream economists in favor of free trade? Frank argues that free trade can prevent poorer countries from developing, rather than helping them do so. (The same argument applies to poorer regions within richer countries like the United States.) What is her reasoning? How do you think a pro-free-trade economist would respond?

8. (Article 10.7) Nawabi argues that land reform is important mainly for "sociopolitical" reasons—that it is necessary to break landlords' stranglehold on political power in order to adopt needed economic development policies. What is the rationale of this argument? Are there analogous arguments to be made for societies that are mostly urban and industrial, rather than rural and agricultural?

Article 10.1

COMPARATIVE ADVANTAGE

BY RAMAA VASUDEVAN
July/August 2007

> Dear Dr. Dollar:
> *When economists argue that the outsourcing of jobs might be a plus for the U.S. economy, they often mention the idea of comparative advantage. So free trade would allow the United States to specialize in higher-end service-sector businesses, creating higher-paying jobs than the ones that would be outsourced. But is it really true that free trade leads to universal benefits?*
> —David Goodman, Boston, Mass.

You're right: The purveyors of the free trade gospel do invoke the doctrine of comparative advantage to dismiss widespread concerns about the export of jobs. Attributed to 19th-century British political-economist David Ricardo, the doctrine says that a nation always stands to gain if it exports the goods it produces *relatively* more cheaply in exchange for goods that it can get *comparatively* more cheaply from abroad. Free trade would lead to each country specializing in the products it can produce at *relatively* lower costs. Such specialization allows both trading partners to gain from trade, the theory goes, even if in one of the countries production of *both* goods costs more in absolute terms.

For instance, suppose that in the United States the cost to produce one car equals the cost to produce 10 bags of cotton, while in the Philippines the cost to produce one car equals the cost to produce 100 bags of cotton. The Philippines would then have a comparative advantage in the production of cotton, producing one bag at a cost equal to the production cost of 1/100 of a car, versus 1/10 of a car in the United States; likewise, the United States would hold a comparative advantage in the production of cars. Whatever the prices of cars and cotton in the global market, the theory goes, the Philippines would be better off producing only cotton and importing all its cars from the United States, and the United States would be better off producing only cars and importing all of its cotton from the Philippines. If the international terms of trade—the relative price—is one car for 50 bags, then the United States will take in 50 bags of cotton for each car it exports, 40 more than the 10 bags it forgoes by putting its productive resources into making the car rather than growing cotton. The Philippines is also better off: it can import a car in exchange for the export of 50 bags of cotton, whereas it would have had to forgo the production of 100 bags of cotton in order to produce that car domestically. If the price of cars goes up in the global marketplace, the Philippines will lose out in relative terms—but will still be better off than if it tried to produce its own cars.

The real world, unfortunately, does not always conform to the assumptions underlying comparative-advantage theory. One assumption is that trade is balanced. But many countries are running persistent deficits, notably the United States, whose trade deficit is now at nearly 7% of its GDP. A second premise, that there is full employment within the trading nations, is also patently unrealistic. As global trade intensifies, jobs created in the export sector do not necessarily compensate for the jobs lost in the sectors wiped out by foreign competition.

The comparative advantage story faces more direct empirical challenges as well. Nearly 70% of U.S. trade is trade in similar goods, known as *intra-industry trade*: for example, exporting Fords and importing BMWs. And about one third of U.S. trade as of the late 1990s was trade between branches of a single corporation located in different countries (*intra-firm trade*). Comparative advantage cannot explain these patterns.

Comparative advantage is a static concept that identifies immediate gains from trade but is a poor guide to economic development, a process of structural change over time which is by definition dynamic. Thus the comparative advantage tale is particularly pernicious when preached to developing countries, consigning many to "specialize" in agricultural goods or be forced into a race to the bottom where cheap sweatshop labor is their sole source of competitiveness.

The irony, of course, is that none of the rich countries got that way by following the maxim that they now preach. These countries historically relied on tariff walls and other forms of protectionism to build their industrial base. And even now, they continue to protect sectors like agriculture with subsidies. The countries now touted as new models of the benefits of free trade—South Korea and the other "Asian tigers," for instance—actually flouted this economic wisdom, nurturing their technological capabilities in specific manufacturing sectors and taking advantage of their lower wage costs to *gradually* become effective competitors of the United States and Europe in manufacturing.

The fundamental point is this: contrary to the comparative-advantage claim that trade is universally beneficial, nations as a whole do not prosper from free trade. Free trade creates winners and losers, both within and between countries. In today's context it is the global corporate giants that are propelling and profiting from "free trade": not only outsourcing white-collar jobs, but creating global commodity chains linking sweatshop labor in the developing countries of Latin America and Asia (Africa being largely left out of the game aside from the export of natural resources such as oil) with ever-more insecure consumers in the developed world. Promoting "free trade" as a political cause enables this process to continue.

It is a process with real human costs in terms of both wages and work. People in developing countries across the globe continue to face these costs as trade liberalization measures are enforced; and the working class in the United States is also being forced to bear the brunt of the relentless logic of competition. ❑

Sources: Arthur MacEwan, "The Gospel of Free Trade: The New Evangelists," *Dollars & Sense*, July/August 2002; Ha-Joon Chang, *Kicking away the Ladder: The Real History of Fair Trade*, Foreign Policy in Focus, 2003; Anwar Shaikh, "Globalization and the Myths of Free Trade," in *Globalization and the Myths of Free Trade: History, Theory, and Empirical Evidence*, ed. Anwar Shaikh, Routledge 2007.

Article 10.2

THE GLOBALIZATION CLOCK
Why corporations are winning and workers are losing.

BY THOMAS PALLEY
May/June 2006

Political economy has historically been constructed around the divide between capital and labor, with firms and workers at odds over the division of the economic pie. Within this construct, labor is usually represented as a monolithic interest, yet the reality is that labor has always suffered from internal divisions—by race, by occupational status, and along many other fault lines. Neoliberal globalization has in many ways sharpened these divisions, which helps to explain why corporations have been winning and workers losing.

One of these fault lines divides workers from themselves: since workers are also consumers, they face a divide between the desire for higher wages and the desire for lower prices. Historically, this identity split has been exploited to divide union from nonunion workers, with anti-labor advocates accusing union workers of causing higher prices. Today, globalization is amplifying the divide between people's interests as workers and their interests as consumers through its promise of ever-lower prices.

Consider the debate over Wal-Mart's low-road labor policies. While Wal-Mart's low wages and skimpy benefits have recently faced scrutiny, even some liberal commentators argue that Wal-Mart is actually good for low-wage workers because they gain more as consumers from its "low, low prices" than they lose as workers from its low wages. But this static, snapshot analysis fails to capture the full impact of globalization, past and future.

Globalization affects the economy unevenly, hitting some sectors first and others later. The process can be understood in terms of the hands of a clock. At one o'clock is the apparel sector; at two o'clock the textile sector; at three the steel sector; at six the auto sector. Workers in the apparel sector are the first to have their jobs shifted to lower-wage venues; at the same time, though, all other workers get price reductions. Next, the process picks off textile sector workers at two o'clock. Meanwhile, workers from three o'clock onward get price cuts, as do the apparel workers at one o'clock. Each time the hands of the clock move, the workers taking the hit are isolated. In this fashion globalization moves around the clock, with labor perennially divided.

Manufacturing was first to experience this process, but technological innovations associated with the Internet are putting service and knowledge workers in the firing line as well. Online business models are making even retail workers vulnerable—consider Amazon.com, for example, which has opened a customer support center and two technology development centers in India. Public sector wages are also in play, at least indirectly, since falling wages mean falling tax revenues. The problem is that each time the hands on the globalization clock move forward, workers are divided: the majority is made slightly better off while the few are made much worse off.

Globalization also alters the historical divisions within capital, creating a new split between bigger internationalized firms and smaller firms that remain nationally centered. This division has been brought into sharp focus with the debate over the trade deficit and the overvalued dollar. In previous decades, manufacturing as a whole opposed running trade deficits and maintaining an overvalued dollar because of the adverse impact of increased imports. The one major business sector with a different view was retailing, which benefited from cheap imports.

However, the spread of multinational production and outsourcing has divided manufacturing in wealthy countries into two camps. In one camp are larger multinational corporations that have gone global and benefit from cheap imports; in the other are smaller businesses that remain nationally centered in terms of sales, production and input sourcing. Multinational corporations tend to support an overvalued dollar since this makes imports produced in their foreign factories cheaper. Conversely, domestic manufacturers are hurt by an overvalued dollar, which advantages import competition.

This division opens the possibility of a new alliance between labor and those manufacturers and businesses that remain nationally based—potentially a potent one, since there are approximately seven million enterprises with sales of less than $10 million in the United States, versus only 200,000 with sales greater than $10 million. However, such an alliance will always be unstable as the inherent labor-capital conflict over income distribution can always reassert itself. Indeed, this pattern is already evident in the internal politics of the National Association of Manufacturers, whose members have been significantly divided regarding the overvalued dollar. As one way to address this division, the group is promoting a domestic "competitiveness" agenda aimed at weakening regulation, reducing corporate legal liability, and lowering employee benefit costs—an agenda designed to appeal to both camps, but at the expense of workers.

Solidarity has always been key to political and economic advance by working families, and it is key to mastering the politics of globalization. Developing a coherent story about the economics of neoliberal globalization around which working families can coalesce is a key ingredient for solidarity. So too is understanding how globalization divides labor. These narratives and analyses can help counter deep cultural proclivities to individualism, as well as other historic divides such as racism. However, as if this were not difficult enough, globalization creates additional challenges. National political solutions that worked in the past are not adequate to the task of controlling international competition. That means the solidarity bar is further raised, calling for international solidarity that supports new forms of international economic regulation. ❏

DO TRADE AGREEEMENTS FORECLOSE PROGRESSIVE POLICY?

BY ARTHUR MacEWAN
May/June 2016

> Dear Dr. Dollar:
> *Doesn't the increasing liberalization of U.S. international economic policies foreclose the possibilities for progressive policies in this country? Don't these policies undercut the effectiveness of fiscal policy efforts to stimulate employment and output? And don't they virtually rule out many progressive reforms, such as a single payer health care system or new environmental regulations?* —Anonymous, via voicemail

The simple answer to this set of questions is yes and no. But let's step back for a minute.

From the North American Free Trade Agreement (NAFTA), adopted in the early 1990s, to the Trans-Pacific Partnership (TPP) and the Transatlantic Trade and Investment Partnership (TTIP) being advanced today, criticism has focused on the negative impacts of these agreements on employment in many U.S. industries. These negative impacts are real and are one factor contributing to the decline of manufacturing in the United States, to the stagnation of wages, and to the hollowing out of the "middle class."

Yet, another impact of these agreements generally gets ignored—namely their negative impacts on progressive economic and social policies. Here too the impacts are real, but they are not absolute.

Take the issue of fiscal stimulus—that is, when the government runs a budget deficit, spending more than it is taking in as taxes, in order to increase output and create jobs. In 1970, imports of goods and services were only 6.3% as large as GDP, but in 2014, imports were equal to 18.2% of GDP. This implies that in the earlier era, of a dollar spent on goods and services in general, only 6.3% would go towards imports. Today, as liberalization of trade has brought about the larger role for imports in GDP, a much larger share would go for the stimulation of jobs and output abroad. That is, the impact would in part "leak" out of the U.S. economy.

However, stimulus spending need not be spending "in general." If the government focused its spending on physical infrastructure (roads, bridges, public transport systems) and early childhood education, for example, less of the impact would "leak" out of the country. And certainly there are great needs for spending on infrastructure and early childhood education. (There would still be "leakage" in the later rounds of spending, as those who received the government funds—for example, construction companies and workers, preschools and early-childhood teachers—spent what they had received.)

To an extent, the American Recovery and Reinvestment Act of 2009 (ARRA) did focus spending on infrastructure investment. And, while there is controversy

---

NAFTA, UPS, and Canada: It's All about Money

In 2000, under provisions in NAFTA, the U.S. courier company UPS sued Canada Post (Canada's public postal service), claiming $230 million in lost profits. UPS argued that Canada Post had an unfair advantage because it used the public postal system to support its own courier business. In 2007, UPS finally lost its suit, leading the president of Canada Post to comment: "This dispute was all about money. The United Parcel Service of America is attempting to force postal administrations around the world out of the parcel and courier business in order to increase their market share."

Source: "Canada Post claims victory at NAFTA over UPS," CBC News, Jan. 13, 2007 (cbc.ca).

---

regarding its impact, it did seem to have a positive, though limited impact (it wasn't big enough) in contributing to the recovery from the severe recession of 2007–2008.

The constraints that the liberalization of U.S. economic activity, over the decades, has placed on social programs is related to investmeent, not trade. Various agreements—like NAFTA, TPP, and TTIP—incorporate provisions that derive from the General Agreement on Trade in Services (GATS), a treaty of the World Trade Organization (WTO) that came into force in 1995. These agreements allow firms from outside a country to sue the government of that country if it imposes "over-burdensome" regulations or policies that undermine the firm's profits.

For example, a mining firm based in one country could sue the government of another county in which it is operating if environmental protection regulations are put in place that harm the firm's profits. Or, for a second example, a private health care firm based abroad could sue if the establishment of a single-payer health care system were established in the United States, harming the firm's profits. The threat of such suits could deter the government from implementing these sorts of programs. It might seem, then, that the government's hands would be tied, preventing the enactment of progressive programs.

But let's not forget what government we are talking about here. These profit-protecting provisions of the WTO and particular international economic agreements have been largely the creation of the world's most powerful government—i.e., the U.S. government. If the U.S. government wanted to change those provisions—that is, if it wanted to clear the way for progressive programs—it would not have great problems in doing so. If it is not unrealistic to believe that a U.S. government would want to create a single-payer health care system or a strong set of environmental protection regulations, it is not unrealistic to believe that it could also abrogate or get around those profit-protecting provisions.

The example described in the sidebar above shows the real threat to public services that is created by the provisions in trade agreements. It also shows how in a relatively rich country—Canada in this case—with the resources and expertise to fight such a threat, a government can prevail. The situation of less-powerful, low-income countries is very different.

So, yes, the liberalization of U.S. international commerce does create constraints on progressive economic policies and social programs. But, no, these constraints are by no means absolute. Ultimately, the constraints are political, not technical constraints of economic agreements. ❑

Sources: Elizabeth Warren, "The Trans-Pacific Partnership clause everyone should oppose," *Washington Post*, Feb. 25, 2015 (washingtonpost.com); "The Economic Impact of the American Recovery and Reinvestment Act Five Years Later," Final Report to Congress, Executive Office of the President, Council of Economic Advisers, February 2014 (whitehouse.gov).

Article 10.4

AFTER HORROR, CHANGE?
Taking Stock of Conditions in Bangladesh's Garment Factories

BY JOHN MILLER
September/October 2014

On April 24, 2013, the Rana Plaza factory building, just outside of Bangladesh's capital city of Dhaka, collapsed—killing 1,138 workers and inflicting serious long-term injuries on at least 1,000 others.

While the collapse of Rana Plaza was in one sense an accident, the policies that led to it surely were not. Bangladesh's garment industry grew to be the world's second largest exporter, behind only China's, by endangering and exploiting workers. Bangladesh's 5,000 garment factories paid rock-bottom wages, much lower than those in China, and just half of those in Vietnam. One foreign buyer told The Economist magazine, "There are no rules whatsoever that can not be bent." Cost-saving measures included the widespread use of retail buildings as factories—including at Rana Plaza—adding weight that sometimes exceeded the load-bearing capacity of the structures.

As Scott Nova, executive director of the Worker Rights Consortium, testified before Congress, "the danger to workers in Bangladesh has been apparent for many years." The first documented mass-fatality incident in the country's export garment sector occurred in December 1990. In addition to those killed at Rana Plaza, more than 600 garment workers have died in factory fires in Bangladesh since 2005. After Rana Plaza, however, Bangladesh finally reached a crossroads. The policies that had led to the stunning growth of its garment industry had so tarnished the "Made in Bangladesh" label that they were no longer sustainable.

But just how much change has taken place since Rana Plaza? That was the focus of an International Conference at Harvard this June, bringing together government officials from Bangladesh and the United States, representatives of the Bangladesh garment industry, the international brands, women's groups, trade unions, the International Labor Organization (ILO), and monitoring groups working in Bangladesh.

How Much Change On the Ground?

Srinivas B. Reddy of the ILO spoke favorably of an "unprecedented level of ... practical action" toward workplace safety in Bangladesh.

The "practical action" on the ground, however, has been much more of a mixed bag than Reddy suggests. In the wake of massive protests and mounting international pressure, Bangladesh amended its labor laws to remove some obstacles to workers forming unions. Most importantly, the new law bars the country's labor ministry from giving factory owners lists of workers who want to organize.

But formidable obstacles to unionization still remain. At least 30% of the workers at an entire company are required to join a union before the government will grant recognition. This is a higher hurdle than workers face even in the not-so-union-friendly United States, where recognition is based at the level of the workplace, not the company. Workers in special export-processing zones (the source of about 16% of Bangladesh's exports), moreover, remain ineligible to form unions.

The Bangladesh government did register 160 new garment unions in 2013 and the first half of this year, compared to just two between 2010 and 2012. Nonetheless, collective bargaining happens in only 3% of garment plants. And employers have responded with firings and violence to workers registering for union recognition or making bargaining demands. Union organizers have been kidnapped, brutally beaten, and killed.

After protests that shut down over 400 factories last fall, the Bangladesh government raised the minimum wage for garment workers from the equivalent of $38 a month to $68. The higher minimum wage, however, fell short of the $103 demanded by workers.

The government and the garment brands have also set up the Rana Plaza Donor Trust Fund to compensate victims and their families for their losses and injuries. But according to the fund's website, it stood at just $17.9 million at the beginning of August, well below its $40 million target. Only about half of the 29 international brands that had their clothes sewn at Rana Plaza have made contributions. Ineke Zeldenrust of the Amsterdam-based labor-rights group Clean Clothes Campaign estimates that those 29 brands are being asked to contribute less than 0.2% of their $22 billion in total profits for 2013.

The Accord and the Alliance

Following Rana Plaza, a group of mostly European retail chains turned away from the business-as-usual approach of company codes that had failed to ensure safe working conditions in the factories that made their clothes. Some 151 apparel brands and retailers doing business in Bangladesh, including 16 U.S.-based retailers, signed the Accord on Fire and Building Safety in Bangladesh. Together the signatories of this five-year agreement contracted with 1,639 of the 3,498 Bangladesh factories making garments for export.

The Accord broke important new ground. Unlike earlier efforts:

It was negotiated with two global unions, UndustriALL and UNI (Global).

It sets up a governing board with equal numbers of labor and retail representatives, and a chair chosen by the ILO.

Independent inspectors will conduct audits of factory hazards and make their results public on the Accord website, including the name of the factory, detailed information about the hazard, and recommended repairs.

The retailers will provide direct funding for repairs (up to a maximum of $2.5 million per company) and assume responsibility for ensuring that all needed renovations and repairs are paid for.

Most importantly, the Accord is legally binding. Disputes between retailers and union representatives are subject to arbitration, with decisions enforceable by a court of law in the retailer's home country.

But most U.S. retailers doing business in Bangladesh—including giants like Wal-Mart, JCPenney, The Gap, and Sears—refused to sign. They objected to the Accord's open-ended financial commitment and to its legally binding provisions.

Those companies, along with 21 other North American retailers and brands, developed an alternative five-year agreement, called the Alliance For Bangladesh Worker Safety. Some 770 factories in Bangladesh produce garments for these 26 companies.

Unlike the Accord, the Alliance is not legally binding and lacks labor- organization representatives. Moreover, retailers contribute a maximum of $1 million per retailer (less than half the $2.5 million under the Accord) to implement their safety plan and needed repairs, and face no binding commitment to pay for needed improvements beyond that. The responsibility to comply with safety standards falls to factory owners, although the Alliance does offer up to $100 million in loans for these expenses.

Kalpona Akter, executive director of the Bangladesh Center for Worker Solidarity, told the U.S. Senate Foreign Relations Committee, "There is no meaningful difference between the Alliance and the corporate-controlled 'corporate social responsibility' programs that have failed Bangladeshi garment workers in the past, and have left behind thousands of dead and injured workers."

Historic and Unprecedented?

Dan Mozena, U.S. Ambassador to Bangladesh, believes that, despite facing significant obstacles, "Bangladesh is making history as it creates new standards for the apparel industry globally."

While the Accord may be without contemporary precedent, joint liability agreements that make retailers responsible for the safety conditions of their subcontractor's factories do have historical antecedents. As political scientist Mark Anner has documented, beginning in the 1920s the International Ladies Garment Workers Union (ILGWU) began negotiating "jobber agreements" in the United States that held the buyer (or "jobber") for an apparel brand "jointly liable" for wages and working conditions in the contractor's factories. Jobber agreements played a central role in the near-eradication of sweatshops in the United States by the late 1950s. In today's global economy, however, international buyers are once again able to escape responsibility for conditions in the far-flung factories of their subcontractors.

Like jobber agreements, the Accord holds apparel manufacturers and retailers legally accountable for the safety conditions in the factories that make their clothes through agreements negotiated between workers or unions and buyers or brands. The next steps for the Accord model, as Anner has argued, are to address working conditions other than building safety (as jobber agreements had), to get more brands to sign on to the Accord, and to negotiate similar agreements in other countries.

That will be no easy task. But, according to Arnold Zack, who helped to negotiate the Better Factories program that brought ILO monitoring of Cambodian garment factories, "Bangladesh is the lynch pin that can bring an end to the bottom feeding shopping the brands practice." ❑

Sources: Arnold M. Zack, "In an Era of Accelerating Attention to Workplace Equity: What Place for Bangladesh," Boston Global Forum, July 8, 2014; Testimony of Kalpona Akter, Testimony of Scott Nova, Senate Committee on Foreign Relations, Feb. 11, 2014; Mark Anner, Jennifer Bair, and Jeremy Blasi, "Toward Joint Liability in Global Supply Chains," *Comparative Labor Law & Policy Journal*, Vol. 35:1, Fall 2013; Prepared Remarks for Rep. George Miller (D-Calif.), Keynote Remarks by U.S. Ambassador to Bangladesh Dan Mozena, Remarks by Country Director ILO Bangladesh Srinivas B. Reddy, International Conference on Globalization and Sustainability of the Bangladesh Garment Sector, June 14, 2014; "Rags in the ruins," *The Economist*, May 4, 2013; "Bangladesh: Amended Labor Law Falls Short," Human Rights Watch, July 18, 2013; Rana Plaza Donor Trust Fund (ranaplaza-arrangement.org/fund).

Article 10.5

PUERTO RICO'S COLONIAL ECONOMY

BY ARTHUR MacEWAN
May/June 2016

Dear Dr. Dollar:

It seems like Puerto Rico's economic and financial mess came out of nowhere. Until recently, there wasn't much about Puerto Rico in the press, but what there was seemed to portray things as fine, with a generous amount of funds going to the island from Washington. Sometimes, Puerto Rico was held up as a model for economic development. So where did the current mess come from?
—Janet Sands, Chicago, Ill.

Puerto Rico is a colony of the United States. Colonial status, with some exceptions, is not a good basis for economic progress.

Recently, the details of the Puerto Rican economic mess, and especially the financial crisis, have become almost daily fodder for the U.S. press. Yet, the island's colonial status and the economic impact of that status, which lie at the foundation of the current debacle, have been largely ignored.

Puerto Rico, like other colonies, has been administered in the interests of the "mother country." For example, for many years, a provision of the U.S. tax code, Section 936, let U.S. firms operate on the island without incurring taxes on their Puerto Rican profits (as long as those profits were not moved back to the states). This program was portrayed as a job creator for Puerto Rico. Yet the principal beneficiaries were U.S. firms—especially pharmaceutical firms. When this tax provision was in full-force in the late 1980s and early 1990s, it cost the U.S. government on average more than $3.00 in lost tax revenue for each $1.00 in wages paid in Puerto Rico by the pharmaceuticals. (What's more, the pharmaceuticals, while they did produce in Puerto Rico, also located many of their patents with their Puerto Rican subsidiaries, thus avoiding taxes on the profits from these patents.)

Puerto Ricans are U.S. citizens, but residents of the island have no voting representatives in Congress and do not participate in presidential elections. The Puerto Rican government does have a good deal of autonomy, but is ultimately under U.S. law. And without voting representatives in Congress, Puerto Rico is unable to obtain equal status in federal programs or full inclusion in important legislation. A good example of the latter, which has become especially important in the ongoing financial crisis, is that U.S. law excludes the Puerto Rican government from declaring bankruptcy, an option available to U.S. states and their cities.

It is often asserted that the U.S. government provides "generous" benefits to Puerto Rico. Perhaps the largest federal payment to Puerto Ricans is Social Security. Yet Puerto Ricans on the island pay Social Security taxes just like residents of states and the District of Columbia. Likewise, Puerto Ricans pay Medicare taxes just like residents of the states, but, unlike residents of the states, their Medicare benefits are capped at a lower level. Among the important programs from which residents of Puerto Rico are excluded, a big one is the earned income tax credit (EITC). As a result, a two-parent, two-child family in Puerto Rico earning $25,000 a year ends up, after federal taxes and credits, with about $6,000 less income than a family in the states with the same earnings and family structure.

Opponents of extending the EITC to residents of Puerto Rico argue that they should not get the EITC because they are not liable for federal income taxes. Yet many EITC recipients in the states pay no federal income taxes simply because their incomes are so low (e.g., the family in the above example). Moreover, the EITC was established to offset the burden on low-income families of Social Security and Medicare taxes, which Puerto Rico residents do pay, and to reduce poverty, of which Puerto Ricans have more than their share.

If Puerto Rico gets "generous" benefits from Washington, several states are treated more generously. In particular, if states are ranked in terms of their "net receipts" per capita from the federal government—that is, funds received from the federal government minus federal taxes—in a typical year about one-third of the states rank above Puerto Rico (though the number varies somewhat in different years). In 2010, for example, West Virginia received $8,365 per capita more in federal expenditures than were paid from the state in federal taxes; Kentucky $7,812 more; Vermont $6,713 more; and Alaska and Hawaii topped the list with $11,123 per capita and $10,733 per capita more, respectively, from the federal government than they paid to the federal government. That year Puerto Rico received on net $4,697 per capita.

Beyond these particular disadvantages of colonial status, Puerto Rico suffers from a pervaisive condition of "dependency." In setting economic policy, the Puerto Rican government has continually looked beyond the island, to investments by U.S. firms and favors from Washington. As James Dietz has usefully summed up the situation in his 2003 book *Puerto Rico: Negotiating Development and Change*: "Puerto Rico's strategy of development lacked a focus on the systematic support or fostering of local entrepreneurs and local sources of finance." As a consequence "the central role of domestic entrepreneurs, skilled workers and technological progress that underlies sustained economic progress" has been weaker in Puerto Rico than in sovereign nations where sustained economic progress has proceeded more rapidly. Moreover, government policy and decisions by investors tend to be short-sighted, failing to build the foundation for long-term economic progress. The poor condition of the public schools and the weak physical infrastructure are examples of the consequences.

All of these factors have retarded the Puerto Rican economy for decades. The island did experience a burst of economic activity in the post-World War II period, heavily dependent on low-wage labor, privileged access to the U.S. market, and federal and local tax breaks for U.S. firms. As wages rose and other parts of the world gained access to the U.S. market, the economy faltered. From the mid-1970s into the early 2000s, Puerto Rico lost economic ground compared to the states.

The severe recession that then emerged in 2006 and that Puerto Rico has suffered under for the past decade, only partially attenuated by heavy government borrowing on the bond market, was an outcome to be expected from the economy's long-term weakness and, in fact, was precipitated by that heavy government borrowing.

By 2006, the Puerto Rican public debt was 70% as large as GNP. (Now it is slightly more than 100%.) Under this debt pressure, in an effort to cut its expenditures, the government temporarily laid off without pay 100,000 workers (almost 10% of the total work force). Had the Puerto Rican economy not been so weak and had the U.S. economy not soon entered the Great Recession, perhaps the downturn from this layoff shock would have been brief. But the weak economy and then recession in the states undercut any basis for quick recovery. In 2009 and 2010, Puerto Rico did receive a share of the funds in the American Recovery and Reinvestment Act (ARRA), which attenuated but did not end the island's recession. The boost from the ARRA funds was too small and too short-lived.

Many commentators and Puerto Rican government officials try to explain the emergence of Puerto Rico's recession by the termination of the Section 936 tax breaks and call for a renewal of 936 provisions to aid the economy. However, for the firms, the tax breaks did not end, but were maintained under other tax code provisions, and there was virtually no decline of employment in 936 firms as the tax provision was being phased out between 1996 and 2006. After 2006, however, the employment provisions of Section 936, as weak as they were, did collapse. As a result, while exports of pharmaceuticals have grown apace in subsequent year, for example, employment in the industry has dropped sharply. Perhaps the termination of 936 contributed to the continuation of the downturn, through its impact on employment, but it was not the primary or major causal factor. Most important, a renewal of 936 provisions is not a solution to Puerto Rico's economic difficulties.

Controversy over Puerto Rico's status has been a dominating theme of the island's politics for decades. Various polls have shown a rough split between maintaining the current status and statehood, with the latter gaining an edge in the 2012 poll associated with the election. The polls show support for independence far behind.

The current colonial status, in addition to its negative economic impact, involves a fundamental violation of human rights and democracy. Puerto Ricans should be given a clear choice between independence and statehood; maintenance of the current colonial status (or a somewhat different colonial status that has some support) should be off the table. Beyond the interests of the Puerto Ricans, how can those of us in the states make a claim to democracy while we hold Puerto Rico as our colony? ❑

Article 10.6

SHOULD DEVELOPING COUNTRIES EMBRACE PROTECTIONISM?

BY ELLEN FRANK
July 2004

> Dear Dr. Dollar:
>
> *Supposedly, countries should produce what they are best at. If the United States makes computers and China produces rice, then the theory of free trade says China should trade its rice for computers. But if China puts tariffs on U.S.-made computers and builds up its own computer industry, then it will become best at making them and can buy rice from Vietnam. Isn't it advantageous for poor countries to practice protectionism and become industrial powers themselves, rather than simply producing mono-crop commodities? I'm asking because local alternative currencies like Ithaca Hours benefit local businesses, though they restrict consumers to local goods that may be more expensive than goods from further away.*
>
> —Matt Cary, Hollywood, Fla.

The modern theory of free trade argues that countries are "endowed" with certain quantities of labor, capital, and natural resources. A country with lots of labor but little capital should specialize in the production of labor-intensive goods, like hand-woven rugs, hand-sewn garments, or hand-picked fruit. By ramping up produc-tion of these goods, a developing country can trade on world markets, earning the foreign exchange to purchase capital-intensive products like computers and cars. Free trade thus permits poor countries (or, to be more precise, their most well-off citizens) to *consume* high-tech goods that they lack the ability to *produce* and so obtain higher living standards. "Capital-rich" countries like the United States benefit from relatively cheap fruit and garments, freeing up their workforce to focus on high-tech goods. Free trade, according to this story, is a win-win game for everyone.

The flaw in this tale, which you have hit upon exactly, is that being "capital-rich" or "capital-poor" is not a natural phenomenon like having lots of oil. Capital is created—typically with plenty of government assistance and protection.

Developing countries can create industrial capacity and train their citizens to manufacture high-tech goods. But doing so takes time. Building up the capacity to manufacture computers, for example, at prices that are competitive with firms in developed countries may take several years. To buy this time, a government needs to keep foreign-made computers from flooding its market and undercutting less-established local producers. It also needs to limit inflows of foreign capital. Studies show that when foreign firms set up production facilities in developing countries, they are unlikely to share their latest techniques, so such foreign investment does not typically build local expertise or benefit local entrepreneurs.

The United States and other rich countries employed these protectionist strategies. In the 1800s, American entrepreneurs traveled to England and France to learn the latest manufacturing techniques and freely appropriated designs for cutting-edge industrial equipment. The U.S. government protected its nascent industries with high tariff walls until they could compete with European manufacturers.

After World War II, Japan effectively froze out foreign goods while building up world-class auto, computer, and electronics industries. Korea later followed Japan's strategy; in recent years, so has China. There, "infant industries" are heavily protected by tariffs, quotas, and other trade barriers. Foreign producers are welcome only if they establish high-tech facilities in which Chinese engineers and production workers can garner the most modern skills.

Development economists like Alice Amsden and Dani Rodrik are increasingly reaching the conclusion that carefully designed industrial policies, combined with protections for infant industries, are most effective in promoting internal development in poor countries. "Free-trade" policies, on the other hand, seem to lock poor countries into producing low-tech goods like garments and agricultural commodities, whose prices tend to decline on world markets due to intense competition with other poor countries.

In the contemporary global economy, however, there are three difficulties with implementing a local development strategy. First, some countries have bargained away their right to protect local firms by entering into free-trade agreements. Second, protectionism means that local consumers are denied the benefits of cheap manufactured goods from abroad, at least in the short run.

Finally, in many parts of the world the floodgates of foreign-made goods have already been opened and, with the middle and upper classes enjoying their computers and cell phones, it may be impossible to build the political consensus to close them. This last concern bears on the prospects for local alternative currencies. Since it is impos-sible to "close off" the local economy, the success of local currencies in bolstering hometown businesses depends on the willingness of local residents to deny themselves the benefits of cheaper nonlocal goods. Like national protectionist polices, local currencies restrict consumer choice.

Ultimately, the success or failure of such ventures rests on the degree of public support for local business. With local currencies, participation is voluntary and attitudes toward local producers often favorable. National protectionist polices, however, entail coerced public participation and generally fail when governments are corrupt and unable to command public support. ❑

Article 10.7

LAND REFORM
A Precondition for Sustainable Economic Development

BY JAWIED NAWABI
May/June 2015

> *It is in the agricultural sector that the battle for long-term economic development will be won or lost.*
>> —Gunnar Myrdal, economist and Nobel laureate

The phrase "land reform" often conjures up memories, for those leaning right, of frightening extreme-left ideologies. On the progressive left, meanwhile, land reform is often treated as a passé topic.

With the advent of rising inequality, climate change, weak government institutions, failed states, terrorism, corruption, and a whole slew of other socio-economic problems—sown or exacerbated by three decades of neoliberal policies in the "developing world" (Global South)—it is high time we revisit the issue of land reform. We need to bring it back to the center of the discussion on sustainable economic development. Land reform is not political extremism; rather, it is a critical policy mechanism for the world to address issues of poverty, hunger, urban slums, and good governance.

What is "land reform"? It is usually defined as the redistribution of large landholdings to smaller ones. Land is transferred from large landlords to those who have been working the land as tenants (such as sharecroppers) or paid agricultural workers, as well as dispossessed underemployed or unemployed urban workers who migrated from rural areas looking for employment and wound up living in urban slums. That is one model of land reform. Another model is redistribution in the form of rural communes or cooperative or collective farms. A combination of the two models is also possible.

Land Reform and Colonization

If we broaden the concept of land reform, the whole process of colonial settlement in North America, Central and South America, Australia, and New Zealand was one big land reform, appropriating the lands of indigenous peoples and distributing it to the European settlers. So land reform can be understood as a much more common experience of the "developed" world than it is usually thought of in the economic literature.

Social protest has led even elite institutions such as the World Bank to acknowledge the issue. The Bank's *World Development Report 2008: Agriculture for Development*, at least rhetorically put agriculture and the productivity of small farmers "at the heart of a global agenda to reduce poverty."

Reemergence of Land Reform Movements

Despite the attempts by international institutions (like the IMF and World Bank) and oligarchic political elites in the global South to suppress land reform policies, there have been growing social movements pushing for land reform in the last two decades. Neoliberal "free trade" policies have exposed small farmers to devastating global competition (especially from giant mechanized industrial farms in the global North), leaving hundreds of millions of them dispossessed, and have forced them into the reserve army of impoverished unemployed or underemployed living in urban slums. From Brazil and Mexico to the Philippines and Zimbabwe, social movements for a more just and fair distribution of wealth—particularly land—are confronting these devastating consequences of neoliberalism.

Agriculture as Technical Problem?

The central tendency of mainstream economic development theory since the 1940s and 1950s has been to view agriculture as a mere stepping stone towards industrialization. Economist Arthur W. Lewis' "dualist" model was particularly influential in casting agricultural labor in developing countries as redundant—with a "surplus" of workers adding little or nothing to agricultural production. This surplus labor force, Lewis argued, should be moved out of the agricultural sector—this would supposedly not reduce output—and into the industrial, which he viewed as the key sector of the economy. Besides moving inefficient peasants out of the rural sector, mainstream development economists proposed to boost agricultural yields by consolidating small farms into large ones—supposedly to take advantages of economies of scale. Thus, instead of reducing land concentration, this would increase it, essentially accomplishing a reverse land reform. Such an industrial model of agriculture would use expensive capital equipment (imported from the global North), petroleum-based fertilizers, herbicides, and pesticides. Today's version of the model increasingly pushes the adoption of genetically modified seeds controlled by corporations like Monsanto.

During the 1960s and 1970s, this frame of thought led many international institutions (such as the World Bank, Asian Development Bank, etc.) and governments in the global South to embrace the "Green Revolution." The Green Revolution was essentially a plan to use "science and technology" to increase crop production in developing countries. The use of fertilizers, pesticides, and high-yield crop varieties was supposed to boost agricultural productivity, reduce rural poverty, solve problems of hunger and malnutrition, and thus avoid peasant movements and rural political instability. This was, as economists James M. Cypher and James L. Dietz put it, a "strategy wherein it was hoped that seed technologies could be substituted for missing land reform and for more radical 'red revolutions' of the socialist variety threatening to sweep across the globe at the time." Viewing agricultural productivity as a purely technical problem, advocates of the Green Revolution did not aim to transform the structure of land inequality and landlord power. To take the case of India, the Green Revolution boosted agricultural yields, making the country technically self-sufficient in food production. However, the changes primarily benefited medium and large-sized landowners who used capital-intensive technologies, high-yielding mono-crop seeds, and large inputs of fertilizers and pesticides. "Rural inequity worsened because of the growing prosperity of the large and medium farmers and the unchanged position of the landless and small farmers," concludes Indian scholar Siddharth Dube. "And because large farms use more capital and less labour per unit of produce than small farms, rural employment grew much less than it would have if land reform had taken place and the increase in production come from smaller farms."

The Economic and Socio-Political Cases for Land Reform

There are two broad arguments for the importance of land reform. The first is based on the widely observed inverse relationship between farm size and output per unit of land area: smaller farms produce more per acre of land than larger farms. Smaller land holdings are more productive and ecologically sustainable for a number of reasons:

1. **Higher labor intensity.** Small farmers use more labor per unit of land, which helps generate more output and more employment per unit.

2. **Higher multiple cropping.** They grow more crops per year on a given piece of land.

3. **Higher intensity of cultivation.** Small farmers leave a lower proportion of land fallow or uncultivated. In addition, they cultivate crops that are higher value-added per unit of land.

4. **Lower negative environmental impacts.** Small farms use fertilizers, pesticides, and other agrochemicals more sparingly than large farms. This reduces negative impacts of harmful chemicals on workers and neighbors. Small farmers, overall, have a greater incentive to employ environmentally sustainable techniques than large industrial ones.

While the economic case for land reform can be construed as a narrow technical argument on how best to boost agricultural productivity—which land-reform opponents could argue is unnecessary due to the advent of the Green Revolution—the socio-political argument is aimed against this kind of narrow technical thinking. The importance of a land reform is in changing the hierarchical structure of agrarian class relations while increasing productivity. The idea is to break the power of landlords, who keep peasants as a captive labor force in rural areas and act as a conservative political force at the local and national levels of the state.

The central mechanism by which landlords wield their power is through patron-client networks that give them control over local and regional government institutions. Landlords keep the poor majority dependent on them for jobs and access to land, while also using them as a captive power base for local elections (in countries where there are elections, such as India and Brazil). This way, they

> ### Good Governance
>
> The "good-governance functions" of the state are policies beneficial to the large majority of the population. Good-governance states exercise control over a certain territory, depend on a broad part of their population for revenue, and in turn provide the population with a wide range of public goods: the rule of law, transportation infrastructure (paved roads, extensive and affordable public transportation, etc.), public utilities (electricity, clean water, sewage systems), human services (health, education systems), and job security or at least temporary unemployment insurance.

can block the development of state programs providing public goods—like public roads, clinics, schools, water systems, etc.—for everyone. Instead, they perpetuate a more narrowly targeted development relying on private goods—fertilizer, pesticides, expensive high-yield seeds, privately controlled water wells, loans that put peasants in ever-deeper debt, etc. They provide, also, a form of private insurance system for those clients who exhibit proper loyalty, in contrast to social support systems available to all—which would reduce the peasants' vulnerability and the landlord's power. The consequence is that the state's good-governance capacities are distorted and corrupted, favoring the narrow interests of the landlords and the political elite that is connected to them (often by kinship).

Transformative socio-political land reform for developing countries is aimed at diminishing wealth inequalities in the initial stages of development and breaking the grip on power of the upper-class elite (including not only landlords but also big industrial, financial, and commercial capitalists generally allied with them). This democratization of society would make it possible to orient the state towards long-term national development policies which can create more conducive socioeconomic and sociopolitical conditions serving the population as a whole, and not just the elite.

The socioeconomic conditions would include a more egalitarian class structure in the rural sector, greater incentives for farmers to increase their productivity due to owning the land they work, greater farmer incomes allowing the farmers to send their children to school, better nutrition due to higher caloric intake, and greater small-farmer purchasing power leading to greater demand for the products of labor-intensive manufacturing. The sociopolitical democratization would mean the breaking of landlord power, political stabilization resulting from the inclusion of the peasant masses in the political system, and democratization of decision making now liberated from landlord capture of local and national state bureaucracies.

Land Reform Is Not Enough

There have been many more failed land reforms than successful ones. Reforms have failed mainly because they have not been thorough enough in breaking the power of the landed elite, and in extending the role of the government in an inclusive development process. Across Latin America—in Mexico, Bolivia, Brazil, Chile, and Peru—land reforms have had partial success, but for the most part have not dislodged rural elites and their industrial counterparts from political dominance. This has contributed to an image of land reform, even among the progressive left, as a tried and failed policy. There are also examples of half-successful land reforms in South and East Asia—in India, the Philippines, Indonesia, and Thailand—where peasants did reap some benefits like reliable ownership titles, which allowed them to borrow on better terms, boosted crop yields, and reduced malnutrition, though without fundamentally altering the class structure. On the other hand, successful land reforms were thorough, extensive, and swift. Key examples in the twentieth century include Japan, Taiwan, South Korea, and China. Land in the first three countries was distributed as family-sized farms. (China initially had a collectivized land reform.) Looking at the Japanese and South Korean cases: In Japan in 1945, 45% of the peasants were landless tenants. By 1955, only 9% were tenants and even they benefited from much-strengthened protective laws. In pre-reform South Korea in 1944, the top 3% of landholders owned about 64% of the land, with an average holding of 26 hectares. By 1956, the top 6% owned just 18% of the land, with an average of about 2.6 hectares. Meanwhile, 51% of family farmers owned about 65% of the land, with an average holding of 1.1 hectares.

Nowhere in Latin America or Africa, nor elsewhere in Asia, did land reforms come so close to such equalization and radical reshaping of traditional social structures. The East Asian land reforms succeeded in bringing about the long-term national development policies by creating more conducive socioeconomic and sociopolitical conditions—breaking the existing power structure, allowing for the emergence of developmentally oriented states (as opposed to neoliberal models that saw state promotion of economic development as anachronistic and "inefficient"). Successful land reforms require follow up—supportive policies investing in rural infrastructure development (irrigation, electricity, roads, health clinics, schools), plus providing services such as clear and legitimate land records, micro-credit at reasonable rates of interest, and training for farmers in the newest skills for sustainable farming. Japan, Taiwan, South Korea, and arguably even China's development paths serve as examples of transformative land reforms in the last fifty years. What these countries achieved was remarkable growth with equity.

Sources: Irma Adelman, "Income Distribution, Economic Development and Land Reform," *American Behavioral Scientist*, Vol. 23, No. 3 (pgs. 437-456), Jan/Feb 1980; Miguel A. Altieri, "No: Poor Farmers Won't Reap The Benefits," *Foreign Policy*, Summer 2000; James K. Boyce, Peter Rosset, Elizabeth A. Stanton, "Land Reform and Sustainable Development," Working Paper Series No. 98, Political Economy Research Institute, University of Massachusetts-Amherst, 2005; Sarah Blaskey and Jessee Chapman, "Palm Oil Oppression," *Dollars & Sense*, May/June 2013; Celia A. Dugger, "World Bank Report Puts Agriculture at Core of Antipoverty Effort," *New York Times*, Oct. 20, 2007; H. Ronald Chilcote, *Power and The Ruling Classes in Northeast Brazil: Juazeiro and Petrolina in Transition*, Cambridge University Press, 1990; Michael Courville and Raj Patel, "The Resurgence of Agrarian Reform in the Twenty-First Century," In Peter Rosset, Raj Patel, and Michael Courville, eds., *Promised Land: Competing Visions Agrarian Reform*, Food First Book, 2006; James M. Cypher and James L. Dietz, *The Process of Economic Development* (3rd ed., Routledge, 2009; Siddarth Dube, *In the Land of Poverty: Memoirs of an Indian Family: 1947-1997*, Zed Books, 1998; Mike Davis, *Planet of Slums*, Verso, 2007; Peter Dorner, *Land Reforms and Economic Development*, Penguin Books, 1972; Peter

Evans, *Embedded Autonomy: States and Industrial Transformation*, Princeton University Press, 1995; Penelope Francks, with Johanna Boestel and Choo Hyop Kim, *Agriculture and Economic Development in East Asia: From Growth to Protectionism in Japan, Korea and Taiwan*, Routledge, 1999; Jayati Ghosh, "Equality, Sustainability, Solidarity," *Dollars & Sense*, Jan/Feb 2015; Keith Griffin, Azizur Rahman Khan, and Amy Ickowitz (GKI), "Poverty and Distribution of Land," *Journal of Agrarian Change*, July 2002; Jonathan M. Harris, *Environmental and Natural Resource Economics: A Contemporary Approach*, Houghton Mifflin Company, 2002; Frances Hagopian, "Traditional Politics Against State Transformation in Brazil," In Joel S. Migdal, Atul Kohli and Vivienne Shue, eds., *State Power and Social Forces: Domination and Transformation in the Third World*, Cambridge University Press, 1994; Yoong-Deok Jeon and Young-Yong Kim, "Land Reform, Income Redistribution, and Agricultural Production in Korea," *Economic Development and Cultural Change*, Vol. 48, No. 2, January 2000; Cristobal Kay, "Why East Asia Overtook Latin America: Agrarian Reform, Industrialization and Development," *Third World Quarterly*, Vol. 23, No. 6, December 2002; John Lie, *Han Unbound: The Political Economy of South Korea*, Stanford University Press, 1998; Moyo Sam and Paris Yeros, eds., *Reclaiming the Land: The Resurgence of Rural Movements in Africa, Asia and Latin America*, Zed Books, 2005; Raj Patel, *Stuffed and Starved: The Hidden Battle for World's Food System*, 2nd ed, Melville House, 2012; James Purzel, "Land Reforms in Asia: Lessons From the Past for the 21st Century," Working Paper Series No. 00-04, London School of Economics Development Studies Institute, 2000; Debraj Ray, *Development Economics*, Princeton University Press, 1998; Peter M. Rosset, "Fixing Our Global Food System: Food Sovereignty and Redistributive Land Reform," In *Agriculture and Food in Crisis: Conflict, Resistance, and Renewal*, Monthly Review Press, 2010; Peter M. Rosset, "The Multiple Functions and Benefits of Small Farm Agriculture," Policy Brief No.4, The Institute For Food and Development Policy, Oakland, California, 1999; Vandana Shiva, *Soil Not Oil: Environmental Justice in an Age of Climate Crisis*, South End Press, 2008; Rehman Sobhan, *Agrarian Reform and Social Transformation: Preconditions for Development*, Zed Books, 1993; Lance Taylor, Santosh Mehrotra, and Enrique Delamonica, "The Links between Economic Growth, Poverty Reduction, and Social Development: Theory and Policy," In Santosh Mehrotra and Richard Jolly, *Development with a Human Face: Experiences in Social Achievement and Economic Growth*, Oxford University Press, 2000; Michael P.Todaro, *Economic Development*, 7th ed., Addison- Wesley, 2000; Jong-Sung You, "Inequality and Corruption: The Role of Land Reform in Korea, Taiwan, and the Philippines," Presented at the Annual Conference of the Association for Asian Studies, Atlanta, April 2008; Jong-Sung You, "Embedded Autonomy or Crony Capitalism? Explaining Corruption in South Korea, Relative to Taiwan and the Philippines, Focusing on the Role of Land Reform and Industrial Policy," Annual Meeting of the American Political Science Association, Washington, D.C., Sept. 1-4, 2005; Tim Wegenast, "The Legacy of Landlords: Educational Distribution and Development in a Comparative Perspective," *Zeitschrift für Vergleichende Politikwissenschaft*, Volume 3, Issue 1, April 2009; Maurice Zeitlin and Richard Earl Ratcliff, *Landlords and Capitalists: The Dominant Class of Chile*, Princeton University Press, 1988.

Chapter 11

POLICY SPOTLIGHT: GENERATIONAL WAR?

INTRODUCTION

If you follow economic news and commentary, you will have heard arguments that there is a "generational war" afoot. What does this mean? Mainly, it is an argument that what we are doing economically today, especially what benefits the current working generation or the generation that has already retired, will harm the economic prospects of today's young people and those who are yet to be born. As some of the articles in this chapter argue, this view is very misleading when it comes to government debt (and has been used as a way to attack popular programs, like Social Security and Medicare, that ensure people will not be left destitute late in life).

The term "generational war" is certainly melodramatic. We would be better off referring to issues of "intergenerational distribution" or "intergenerational equity." While the notion that the current generation is doing future generations wrong may be incorrect when it comes to government finance, issues of intergenerational equity (whether the actions of the current generation are fair to future generations) are worth taking seriously. We do have to think about the world we will leave to our children, grandchildren, and so on.

The chapter begins with Dean Baker's refutation of the "generational war" idea, as it is commonly stated in relation to government spending. In "Are Our Parents Stealing From Our Kids? No, They Are Not" (Article 11.1), Baker points out that higher public spending on programs that benefit seniors actually goes hand in hand with higher spending on programs that benefit the young (both in U.S. history and across different countries). So much for a "zero-sum" game pitting one generation against the other.

The next three articles focus on education. To be sure, young people are getting short shrift in some ways, both in terms of the kind of education they are receiving and the ways it is paid for. (But seniors are not to blame.)

As Arthur MacEwan explains in "Education: Not Just 'Human Capital'" (Article 11.2), corporate-inspired education reforms are focused on making schools more effective "human capital" factories. The students should be tested, the "free market" reformers say, as a measure of quality. The teachers who do not perform should be fired, and "failing" schools should be shut down. This agenda, MacEwan argues, reduces education to the production of an adequately skilled and obedient workforce, underestimates the successes of public schools (when they have adequate resources), and ignores the bigger social problems that impede greater educational achievement.

When it comes to higher education, students today do not need to be told that it can bring crushing student debt. Instead of advocating for an education-financing system that would reduce this burden, explains John Miller (Article 11.3), the business press has been fighting for a further reduction in federal higher-education grants (Pell Grants) for low- and middle-income students. Far from being cut, Miller argues, Pell Grants should be made a "near universal" support for students.

Next, two proponents of "free higher education" make their case (Article 11.4). Biola Jeje and Belinda Rodriguez argue that, as higher education becomes more and more essential to young people's future opportunities, its costs are creating unfair barriers to those from lower-income families and saddling millions with crushing debt. The time for free higher education, they argue, is now.

Meanwhile, seniors also find themselves under the gun, especially due to attacks on retirement security—from changes in pensions that shift risk from employers onto workers to attacks on Social Security and other federal "entitlement" programs. The next two articles tackle these issues.

In "What Happened to Defined-Benefit Pensions?" (Article 11.5), Arthur MacEwan takes on the dramatic shift from "defined-benefit" pensions, which guarantee workers' retirement income for life, to "defined-contribution" pensions, which make workers actual retirement incomes dependent on stock market returns. The shift in risk from employers to workers, MacEwan argues, reflects a larger shift in bargaining power in employers' favor.

Next, in "Myths of the Deficit" (Article 11.6), Marty Wolfson refutes the idea that federal budget deficits are creating a "burden" on future generations. Debts run up today will be paid back later. Those doing the paying, through future taxes, will be our grandchildren. But most of the people receiving the payments will also be our grandchildren, since most of the debt is owed to the U.S. public. (Current bond owners will leave these assets to their heirs.) The real distributional issues, in other words, are not really between, but within, generations.

Finally, Frank Ackerman puts intergenerational equity issues in a different light: focusing on the issue of long-term environmental sustainability and climate change. In his article, "Climate Economics in Four Easy Pieces" (Article 11.7), he argues that a key reason for aggressive action to avert climate change now is that "our grandchildren's lives are important."

Discussion Questions

1. (Article 11.1) Baker argues that, far from being in opposition to one another, spending on programs for the young and for the old tend to go hand in hand. Why would this be the case? How does this fact relate to other articles in this chapter (which emphasize attacks on both affordable education and secure retirement)?

2. (Article 11.2) Why does MacEwan argue that education is (and should be) about more than "human capital" formation? Why does he think that even employers are not interested only in the technical skills that future workers learn in school?

3. (Article 11.2) Why does MacEwan think that the narrative about public schools failure is wrong? In what ways are public schools successful and in what ways not? How can we tell, if they are not completely successful, why this is the case?

4. (Articles 11.3 and 11.4) Why have student debt burdens increased so much in recent years? What policy responses would you propose?

5. (Article 11.4) Sen. Bernie Sanders argued, "A college degree today ... is the equivalent of what a high-school degree was 50 years ago. And what we said 50 years ago and a hundred years ago is that every kid in this country should be able to get a high-school education regardless of the income of their family. I think we have to say that is true for everybody going to college." Is the case for free college education now the same as that for free high school a century ago? Why or why not?

6. (Article 11.5) Explain the contrast between "defined-benefit" and "defined-contribution" pensions. What does MacEwan mean when he argues that this is the result of a more general "power shift" in favor of employers and against workers?

7. (Article 11.6) If Wolfson is right, and the main distributional effects of government debt are within (rather than between) generations, why is the "generational war" interpretation so widespread? Is this a simple mistake? Or does it reflect some political agenda?

8. (Article 11.7) Ackerman argues that a key issue in making climate policy today is how we weigh the interests of future generations against those of the current generation. Why is this so important? What kind of formula would you use in weighing these different interests?

Article 11.1

ARE OUR PARENTS STEALING FROM OUR KIDS? NO, THEY'RE NOT

BY DEAN BAKER
October 2013; The Business Desk (PBS NewsHour)

A common refrain in debates over Social Security and Medicare is that these programs are putting seniors ahead of children. The implication is that there is a fixed pool of tax revenue. If more of this revenue goes to seniors to pay for their benefits, there is less to cover the cost of child nutrition and health care, daycare, education and other programs that benefit the young. To put in crudely, in this view, a dollar spent on the elderly is a dollar taken away from spending on children.

There is an alternative perspective. The amount of money that the government collects in tax revenue may not be fixed. Understood this way, people's willingness to pay taxes may depend on their perception of the usefulness of the services provided. This could mean, for example, that if the public believes that the government services being provided to both seniors and children are valuable and should be expanded, they would be willing to pay higher taxes to support those services.

If we look at the situation historically in the United States, we have vastly increased the share of GDP going to government programs for both seniors and the young over the last 60 years. In 1950, Social Security payments were less than 1 percent of GDP and Medicare and Medicaid did not even exist. By comparison, we are now spending almost 5% of GDP on Social Security, and more than 5 percent of GDP on Medicare and Medicaid.

PER PERSON SPENDING ON CHILDREN AND SENIORS, PERCENTAGE OF PER CAPITA INCOME

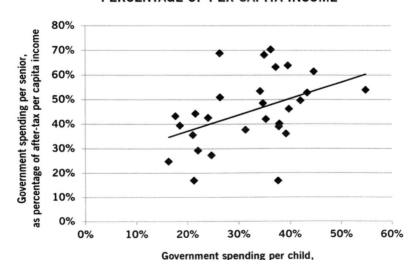

This growth in federal spending for programs that primarily benefit seniors has been accompanied by a huge expansion in programs intended to primarily benefit the young, such as Head Start; the Women, Infants and Children Nutrition Program; and the State Children's Health Insurance Program. In addition, state and local funding for education and other programs that benefit the young has also hugely increased relative to the size of the economy over the last six decades. People have been willing to pay more in taxes to finance programs that benefit both the elderly and the young.

There is a similar story if we look across countries. If the tradeoff view were correct, we should find that countries that are more generous in their support of seniors are stingier when it comes to public support for their children and vice versa. However, the opposite appears to be the case. If we control for the relative income of different countries, it turns out that a dollar of additional spending per kid is associated with 67 cents of additional spending for each senior. (This relationship is statistically significant at the 5% confidence level.)

In short, the data suggest that more spending on seniors is associated with more spending on kids. Presumably this indicates that countries where people rely on the government to ensure that their seniors have a decent standard of living are also inclined to provide the government with resources necessary to ensure that their children's needs are also met.

This evidence suggests that cuts to programs for seniors may be unlikely to end up benefitting our kids. Rather such cuts may be associated with reduced spending on kids as well. If the public does not trust the government to provide good care for seniors, it may also not trust the government to provide good care for children.

In that case, there would be no tradeoff between spending on seniors and spending on kids. If we care about both our seniors and our kids, and trust the government programs designed to provide support at both ends of life, then both sets of programs are likely to be adequately funded. In the opposite case, neither set of programs is likely to be adequately funded. The world where just one set of programs, either those supporting seniors or those supporting kids, receives adequate funding seems largely the invention of politicians. ❑

Article 11.2

EDUCATION: NOT JUST "HUMAN CAPITAL"

BY ARTHUR MacEWAN
January/February 2013

> Dear Dr. Dollar:
> *What's going on with the economics of education? It all seems to be about impos-*
> *ing "standards" to motivate and punish educators. And then there is privatization,*
> *which is supposed to force schools to shape up or die. Help me out here!*
> —Nancy Hernandez, Colorado Springs, Colo.

A great deal of the economics of education reduces schooling to the creation of "human capital." Economists tend to view education as a way of making the individual more productive—like a better-functioning machine that can generate more output. As with any piece of equipment coming off the production line, human capital is subjected to quality control—through standardized testing.

Of course, people are not machines, which presents employers with a problem. A good machine does what it is supposed to do and has no ideas about fair wages and decent working conditions. So in creating human capital, schools have the task of turning out well-behaved workers, people who follow orders and accept their employers' authority. In other words, in economists' human-capital view of education, schools need to prepare pupils for the discipline of the capitalist workplace. Thus, testing is not simply quality-control for technical skills (reading and math) but also for test-taking ability, which teaches discipline, endurance, and not asking too many questions.

Education has—or should have—goals that are much more complex than those involved in building a machine. Education is about the passing on of culture. It is about preparing people both to get the most out of and make the greatest contribution to society. Enabling people to be more economically productive, while important, is only a part of this process. Reducing schooling to its narrowest economic function obscures and undermines the larger roles of education.

But from the perspective of business executives, the narrowest economic function is the important thing, at least in the short run. Complaining that our public schools are failing, elite business groups have pushed an education agenda that would standardize the "products" of the schools, especially through high-stakes standardized testing. These groups (often private foundations, most prominently the Gates Foundation) and many economists argue that testing can create appropriate incentives for the students and their teachers. Students who fail the tests can't graduate and teachers whose students do poorly on the tests don't get raises or get fired.

Likewise, the argument continues, schools with low test scores should be closed down and replaced by other schools—just as private firms that don't produce good products are replaced by other firms. This is the root of the argument for school privatization—sometimes in the form of (formally public) charter schools and sometimes through private schools. Privatized schools eliminate the supposed causes of public schools' failures—public bureaucracy and teachers' unions.

Beyond this ideological drive for privatization, there is also money to be made. For-profit firms such as EdisonLearning, Inc., and Educational Services of America, which run schools and provide services for school systems, are cashing in on the education market. As one consultant recently told a group of potential investors in education: "You start to see entire ecosystems of investment opportunity lining up. It could get really, really big."

There are many problems with the kind of school reform being pushed by many economists and elite business groups. For example:

Our public schools are not failing. We have some marvelous public schools. We also have some terrible schools. No surprise: the good schools tend to be in wealthy areas, the terrible schools in poverty-stricken areas.

To a large extent, the poor academic performance of many kids—in both traditional public schools and charter schools—is rooted in the larger problems of economic inequality and poverty. Poverty undermines children's ability to come to school ready to learn. Poor health, overworked parents, dangerous communities—all this undermines teachers' efforts.

In states where teachers unions exist, both good schools and terrible schools are unionized. Likewise, both good and terrible public schools operate under similar—sometimes the same—bureaucratic structures.

Incentives directed toward the wrong goal (the narrowest economic function) lead people in negative directions. Teaching to the test does not create students who are effective contributors to society.

Charter schools have been operating for decades. Yet there is no evidence that they produce better outcomes than traditional public schools.

Public schools are one of the great social support programs of our society. By themselves, they cannot eliminate poverty and other social ills, but they can move things in a positive direction. However, for the public schools to be an effective social support program, they need effective social support. ❏

Article 11.3

PUTTING THE SCREWS TO GENERATION SCREWED

Wall Street Journal *editors oppose expanded Pell grants.*

BY JOHN MILLER

September/October 2012

- Pell Grants are now so broad that more than half of all undergrads benefit.
- Better-off students often receive the large Pell Grants and apply them to more expensive schools.
- Pell Grants and other student aid are contributing to the ever-higher tuition spiral. Write 100 times on the chalkboard: Student aid raises tuition.
- Overall graduation rates were lower for students who received Pell Grants than for those who didn't.
- The best thing Mr. Obama could do for students, and taxpayers, is to get Pell Grants away from being a broad entitlement and back to their core mission of helping the poorest students.

> —Claims from "Pell Grants Flunk Out: The subsidy program has strayed far from its origins," *Wall Street Journal*, June 18, 2012.

More than $1 trillion of U.S. student debt. Better than nine of ten college graduates with student debt. Over one quarter of the repayments on those loans past due.

"A Generation Hobbled by the Soaring Cost of College" is how the *New York Times* put it in their recent exposé on college debt. And if you mix in the worst economy since the Great Depression, one that has hit those without a college degree especially hard and has left the employment prospects of even college graduates much diminished, this generation is not just hobbled but screwed. Apparently, however, not screwed enough for the editors of the *Wall Street Journal*. The editors rail against the ongoing expansion of Pell Grants, the chief form of federal aid to low- and middle-income students that can reduce the debt burden students incur.

The prospect of Pell Grants becoming an ever-more-universal entitlement must really have the *Wall Street Journal* editors spooked.

Below is a closer look at the predicament of students and former students burdened by debt and exactly why expanding Pell Grants should be supported, not opposed.

Generation Screwed

The cost of college tuition and fees has skyrocketed and student debt along with it. Since 1978, the cost of college tuition and fees has increased eleven-fold, rising faster than even the cost of medical care, and many times faster than family incomes.

Since 1999, student loan debt has increased fivefold. It has eclipsed credit-card debt and is now second only to mortgage debt.

With bankruptcy not an option, borrowers can be stuck repaying their student loans long after leaving college. The federal government is now garnishing the Social Security benefits of an increasing number of retirees with student debt. The Treasury Department reports that in the first seven months of this year, the federal government withheld money from roughly 115,000 retirees' Social Security checks because they had fallen behind on federal student loans. That's nearly double the 60,000 cases in all of 2007. There were just six cases in 2000.

A college degree is now the minimum credential needed for entrance into much of today's economy. "In the mid 1970s, less than 30% of jobs in America required any education beyond high school," reports Jamie P. Merisotis, president and chief executive officer of Lumina Foundation, a private foundation dedicated to expanding higher-education opportunity. "Today, the majority of U.S. jobs require a postsecondary degree or credential." A recent study conducted by the Georgetown Center on Education and the Workforce projects that 63% of job openings in 2018 will require at least some college education.

On top of that, the penalty for not obtaining a college degree has increased dramatically over the last three decades. Beginning with the loss of manufacturing jobs beginning in the late 1970s, the gap between the earnings of college graduates and those with just high school education has steadily widened. The Georgetown study calculated that in 1980 college graduates' lifetime earnings were 44% higher than those of high-school graduates. In 2010 college graduates' lifetime earnings were nearly twice (97% more than) those of high school graduates.

At the same time, the employment prospects of even college graduates are far from bright. First off, having graduated from college is no guarantee of full-time employment. The Economic Policy Institute Briefing Paper on "The Class of 2012" found that the unemployment rate for young college graduates (ages 21 to 24) averaged 9.4% from April 2011 to March 2012. Another 19.1% of of this group was underemployed--unable to find full-time work--during that time period. Second, pay for college grads is down. On average, wages for full-time workers with four-year college degrees fell by 5.4% (adjusted for inflation) between 2000 and 2011. Finally, many graduates do not find the kinds of jobs they wanted. More than a third (37.8%) of college graduates under 25, reports a recent study by economist Andrew Sum of Northeastern University's Center for Labor Market Studies, were working at jobs that did not require a college degree.

For workers without a college degree the numbers are even worse. In May 2012 about one quarter (24%) of new high school graduates from 17 to 20 years old were unemployed, and about half (54% for April 2011 to March 212) were underemployed, unable to get a full time job. Finally, average hourly wages for young high-school graduates plummeted from 2000 to 2011, falling 11.1% after adjusting for inflation.

Pell-Mell

The *WSJ* editors stand four square against providing relief for those hobbled by student debt, especially by expanding Pell Grants to an ever-wider swath of college students. But there is plenty wrong with the editors' long list of complaints about Pell Grants.

To start with, contrary to the editors' complaints, Pell Grants are well targeted. The evidence from a report by the conservative John William Pope Center, which is the source of many of the editors' claims, shows as much. In academic year 2009-2010, a year when the median household income was $51,190, some 94.2% of Pell grant recipients had a family income less than $50,000, and the majority (58.9%) had a family income of less than $20,000.

Nor is it surprising that the graduation rates for Pell Grant recipients are lower than other students. Proportionally, nearly twice as many Pell recipients have parents with only a high school diploma and nearly twice as many come from non-English-speaking homes as other undergraduates. Even the Pope Center recognizes that these are risk factors for dropping out.

The size of Pell Grants is another reason why it is hardly surprising that the graduation rates of Pell recipients are lower than those of other undergraduates. Award amounts for Pell recipients have remained relatively flat in real terms, but covered less and less of college costs. The $5,550 maximum Pell Grant in 2011 covered just one-third of the average cost of attending a public four-year college, just one half the level it covered in 1980-81, according to the Institute for College Access and Success. [Add something like: If Pell Grants covered more of college costs, students from lower-income families would be less likely to drop out due to economic hardship--like being unable to make tuition due to tight family budgets.

In addition, better-off students do not often receive large Pell Grants, as the editors contend. The College Board reports that in academic year 2010-2011 just 1.6% of recipients from families with an income above $60,000 received the maximum Pell Grant of $5,550, well below the 33.8% of the recipients from families with incomes between $15,000 and $20,000 who got the maximum grant. While a bit more than one-fifth of those high-income recipients did apply their Pell Grants to schools that cost $30,000 or more, that amounts to less than one half of one percent of all Pell Grants going to help these high-income recipients attend "more expensive" colleges.

Finally, writing 100 times on the chalkboard "student aid raises tuition," as the editors have suggested, might convince some readers that Pell Grants are driving up tuition. But the evidence is far from conclusive. The Pope Center report states that, "most studies show at least some effect of aid on tuition," which implies that other studies show that student aid has had zero effect on tuition. Indeed they do. For instance, David L. Warren, president of the National Association of Independent Colleges and Universities, reports, "Studies conducted during three successive administrations—Bill Clinton, George W. Bush, and Barack Obama—have found no link between student aid and tuition increases."

One must also ask how Pell Grants with a maximum grant that now covers just one third of the cost of attending a public four-year college, could have fueled the rise in college tuition. What's more, the College Board reports that the average inflation-adjusted net tuition and fees (published tuition and fees minus grants from all sources and federal tax benefits) at private, nonprofit colleges and universities actually dropped from 2006-07 to 2011-12, even as total Pell Grant expenditures more than doubled after correcting for inflation.

A Universal Entitlement

The Obama administration has undertaken some positive steps to expand access to Pell Grants and toward providing debt relief for students. In 2010, the President signed legislation that converted all federally guaranteed student loans (loans issued by private banks to students, with the federal government promising to pay back the loan if the debtor failed to do so) to direct loans administered by the government. This change eliminated fees paid to the private banks that had acted as intermediaries, saving nearly $68 billion over the next 11 years, $36 billion of which is to be used to expand Pell Grants. This year, the Obama Consumer Financial Protection Bureau issued a report recommending that Congress enact legislation letting borrowers discharge their private student loans (those not backed by the federal government) through bankruptcy.

But much more needs to be done. Private student loans account for just 10% of student loans. A good first step toward genuine debt relief would be for Congress to pass the Student Loan Forgiveness Act of 2012, introduced by Representative Hansen Clarke, a Michigan Democrat, which would allow "existing borrowers" to be forgiven up to $45,000 in student debt after the borrower has made ten years of income-based payments (no more than 10% of income).

Pell Grants need to be not only a entitlement, but expanded to a near universal entitlement A recent report from the Pell Institute's newsletter, Postsecondary Education Opportunity, throws into to sharp relief the need to do yet more. Only 10.7% of students from families in the bottom fourth by family income, below $33,050, had attained a bachelor's degree by 24 years of age; among students from families in the second fourth by family income, with incomes between $33,050 and $61,600, only 15%. At the same time, 79.1% of students from the top fourth by family income, above $98,875, had a bachelor's degree by age 24.

As more and more families rely on Pell Grants to reduce the cost of a college education for their children, the more likely it is that Pell Grants will continue to withstand the budget cuts likely to come in the upcoming years. And more fulsome and the more universal Pell Grants will help make merit, not economic means, the determinant of who gets a college degree. ❏

Sources: Anthony Carnevale, Tamara Jayasundera, and Ban Cheah, "The College Advantage: Weathering the Economic Storm," Center on Education and the Workforce, Georgetown University, August 15, 2012; Jenna Ashley Robinson and Duke Cheston, "Pell Grants: Where Does All the Money Go?" John W. Pope Center for Higher Education Policy, June 2012; Rep. Hansen Clarke, The Student Loan Forgiveness Act of 2012; "Public Policy Analysis of Opportunity for Postsecondary Education," Postsecondary Education Opportunity newsletter, January 2012; Heidi Shierholz, Natalie Sabadish, and Hilary Wething, "The Class Of 2012: Labor market for young graduates remains grim," Economic Policy Institute Briefing Paper, May 3, 2012; Meta Brown, Andrew Haughwout, Donghoon Lee, Maricar Mabutas, and Wilbert van der Klaauw, "Federal Student Financial Aid: Grading Student Loans," Federal Reserve Bank of New York, March 05, 2012; Charley Stone, Carl Van Horn, Cliff Zukin, and John J. Heldrich, "Chasing the American Dream: Recent College Graduates and the Great Recession," Center for Workforce Development, May 2012.

Article 11.4

WHY FREE HIGHER ED CAN'T WAIT
Students are rising up to demand free higher education.

BY BIOLA JEJE AND BELINDA RODRIGUEZ
March/April 2016

During the October 2015 Democratic presidential debate, Bernie Sanders offered an accurate assessment of what it will take to make free higher education a reality in the United States. "If we want free tuition at public colleges and universities," Sanders said, "millions of young people are going to have to demand it."

This is exactly what is starting to happen across the country. In recent months, we have witnessed an inspiring upsurge in mobilization around the demand, leading up to the Million Student March. On November 12, 2015, students rose up to demand free higher education, cancelation of all student debt, and a $15 minimum wage for all campus workers. The March marked the beginning of an exciting political moment that included over 100 actions carried out across the country with support from major progressive organizations and labor unions. The mobilizations coincided with a wave of protest in solidarity with students demanding racial justice at the University of Missouri. On many campuses, students combined their protests, producing stunning turnout in the hundreds and even thousands.

Why We Need It

Vermont senator and Democratic presidential hopeful Bernie Sanders has come out in support of free public higher education as part of his campaign platform. Sanders' plan calls for the elimination of tuition at four-year public colleges and universities. This would be paid for through the implementation of a financial transaction tax, which at 0.5% on Wall Street transactions could raise close to $300 billion a year.

Sanders is not alone. For years, students and advocates have been pushing for free higher education, citing many other countries where it has been free for decades. Free education could help us solve some of today's key economic problems. The bar is getting higher for well-paid jobs, with most requiring a college degree, while tuition and fees at universities are rising at staggering rates. Student debt in the United States has reached a record total of over $1.3 trillion. The average individual debt has now grown to $35,000, while wages barely keep up with inflation. The United States is clearly in need of a deep restructuring in terms of how workers are prepared to enter the labor market.

Free—totally free—higher education is key not only to solving the problem of student debt in this country, but also to responding to the demands of our changing economy and the mounting challenges ahead. By "free" we mean four years of tuition-free public higher education, and at the same time expanding financial aid to cover other costs associated with attendance (food, housing, books, etc.).

Senator Sanders summarized the predicament succinctly during the first Democratic debate: "A college degree today ... is the equivalent of what a high-school degree was 50 years ago. And what we said 50 years ago and a hundred years ago is that every kid in this country should be able to get a high-school education regardless of the income of their family. I think we have to say that is true for everybody going to college."

Education, Jobs, and Debt

Until recent years, the main story told by mainstream economists to explain unequal job prospects and growing income inequality was one of "skill-biased technological change." Technological change had reduced the demand for farming labor, manufacturing labor, and routine clerical work, with demand rising for professional and managerial roles that required specialized training. Outsourcing of low-skilled labor, they added, also contributed to this shift.

The trends in manufacturing employment seem to confirm this explanation. In 1990, the manufacturing sector was the leading employer in 37 U.S. states. By 2013, that number dropped to just seven, with health care and social services providing the most jobs in 34 states. Of over 3.85 million job openings in the U.S. in June 2015, only about 300,000 were in manufacturing. Nearly 1 million were in healthcare and education services—with many of those jobs undoubtedly requiring at least a bachelor's degree, and some requiring more advanced degrees.

But that's not the whole story. Demand for "low-skilled" workers has not vanished. "Low-skilled" jobs in retail trade, hospitality, and other sectors have represented a growing share of total employment in recent decades, and accounted for about 1.25 million job openings in June 2015. Despite growth in these sectors, wages are stagnant for middle-income workers and declining for low-wage workers. Economists like former Secretary of Labor Robert Reich, once an advocate of the skill-biased technological change theory (and a campaigner for education and job training as the main cures for economic inequality), have now abandoned the theory—emphasizing instead inequality in market and political power as the key sources of economic inequality.

Economic disparities play a huge role in determining who has access to a college education, and therefore who can compete in our changing economy. Low-income students and students of color are less likely to be able to afford the rising costs of higher education, and are getting shut out of opportunities. Enrollment rates are dropping (down by nearly 2% for the fall 2015 semester, compared to a year earlier), drop-out rates are increasing, and it is taking students longer and longer to complete their degrees due to financial obstacles.

Students who do manage to attend college increasingly rely on loans to finance their education, with students of color taking on a disproportionate debt burden. At public institutions, 63% of white students borrowed to pay for their education compared to 81% of black students. At private institutions, black and Latino students—each of your authors falls into one of these categories—borrow at higher rates than white students, with Latino students taking on the highest average debt. Higher levels of debt are also impacting students in the long term. Those saddled with substantial educational debt are less satisfied with their careers, are saving less for retirement, and are less likely to own homes.

Debt as a Barrier to Change

Debt is even shaping the jobs students pursue after they graduate. Students deeper in debt are more likely to pursue stable, high-salary positions than lower-paid public interest work, compared to their less-indebted counterparts. This finding should be concerning to all of us, considering the enormous collective challenges we face in the years ahead. If we are going to address the deep-rooted causes of racial injustice, climate change, and other social problems, we need to create incentives for students to pursue meaningful work they are passionate about, instead of making it harder and harder for them to do so.

It is particularly concerning that our debt-based system of higher education is depriving people most affected by the flaws in our current political and economic systems of opportunities to participate in reshaping them. People of color, working-class people, survivors of sexual violence, undocumented people, women, and LGBTQIA people deserve to take the lead in crafting solutions to issues that affect their communities. Higher education plays a crucial role in providing access to tools and resources to make this possible, yet people from each of these groups face pervasive barriers to pursuing a degree, graduating, and securing gainful employment. Not all deep-seated social inequalities are perfectly reflected in figures like graduation rates. Women accounted for over 57% of bachelor's degrees awarded in 2009-2010, as well as the majority of master's and doctoral degrees. Still, women face significant barriers to entering some fields, including STEM fields (science, technology, engineering, and math) known for high-paid professional jobs. Universities can and should play a role in advancing opportunities for disenfranchised groups.

Students Speak Out

Art Motta, a student at UC Santa Cruz who studies politics and Latin American & Latino studies, acknowledges that his education has helped him gain the capacity to "analyze institutionalized structures [and] power dynamics," skills critical to help him pursue his passion for advocacy and public service. "[My education] also supplies me with a wealth of background knowledge for real situations that I am bound to encounter as a student of color in a system that was not made for me."

Art represents one of many non-traditional students who had to delay pursuing a college education due to financial barriers. "I had to put my education on hold because the costs became unbearable .... I had to focus on providing for my family." Art was ultimately able to resume his studies but he is very conscious of the fact that these opportunities are not available to most of the people he grew up with. "In my community, graduating from high school was considered a major feat in itself," Art said. Pursuing a four-year degree remains further out of reach "because of the high costs associated with college." The layers upon layers of ways in which our debt-based system of higher education drives inequality are shocking and immoral. But what would things look like if higher education were free? We asked student organizers with the United States Student Association (USSA) to consider what impact free higher education would have on their lives and their communities.

Yareli Castro, a student organizer at UC Irvine who is herself undocumented, noted economic barriers that prevent undocumented students from gaining access to higher education and graduating. "One of the main reasons why my community does not go to college—or, if they do, they drop out—is [because of] financial circumstances. In many states, undocumented students do not get financial aid, loans, or any type of financial support and the burden is very heavy. Undocumented students are very often not allowed to work in this country, so this financial pressure continues mounting. Free higher education would allow my community ... to not have to worry about working many jobs [or] taking out loans, and solely work on their studies."

Filipe de Carvalho, a student organizer at UMass Amherst, reflected on the role free higher education could play in giving students opportunities they can believe in. If higher education were free, "a much larger percentage of my high school ... would see a four-year university as a real option. I believe many of my peers would have cared more about their academics in high school had they believed that they could actually go to college."

Jordan Howzell, a student organizer at UC Santa Cruz, said that free higher education would allow her to "pursue a career rooted in my passions instead of its ability to cover my student loans." If higher education were free, she would study "music and its psychiatric and rehabilitative qualities, and how music is situated in social movements and social justice issues." Several of the students interviewed expressed similar sentiments about how they would choose their majors. Some said they would opt for completely different majors, while others said they would add course work in the humanities to build a balanced worldview and skillset.

John Ashton is a student organizer at Des Moines Area Community College. "When education is expensive, only the rich can obtain it," he says. "When education is free, the disenfranchised can become the best and brightest, and after all is said and done, that is what America is all about. ... Until the cost of higher education is eliminated, [our] higher education system [will never] achieve its full potential, nor will it train enough of the next generation of workers to meet the needs of the country."

The Road Ahead

If we want to end economic inequality and build a better future, we need higher education to be free. Free higher education will not solve all of our problems, but it would be a big step in the right direction. If young people have access to debt-free, high-quality education, it will open up more opportunities for them to use their skills and strengths to build satisfying careers and serve their communities, instead of cramming themselves into thankless and soulless positions just to make ends meet.

This will inevitably take time. Students have been pushing for free higher education for years, and it has only now become a part of the mainstream lexicon. There have been some precedents in U.S. history, including the CUNY system in New York, which offered tuition-free higher education up until the 1970s. In recent years, several elected officials have introduced plans for tuition-free and debt-free college.

New York State Assembly member James Skoufis introduced a 2014 bill offering free undergraduate tuition for all students who fulfill community service and residency requirements after graduation. In Oregon last year, legislators signed off on a bill pushing tuition at community colleges down to just $50. In early 2015, President Obama announced a plan for free community college. Democratic presidential candidates Hillary Clinton and Bernie Sanders have introduced proposals for debt-free and tuition-free higher education, respectively.

It is important that we closely examine these proposals as they come out, and fight to make sure they include all groups affected by the issue. It is even more important that we craft our own narratives about why free higher education matters, and build enough power to secure the win. Young people fighting for progressive change have learned important lessons about what it takes to win over the past few years. There is a widespread understanding that we need to consistently mobilize a large base of young people and win overwhelming public support to make free higher education a reality. ❑

Sources: Dean Baker, Robert Pollin, Travis McArthur, and Matt Sherman, "The Potential Revenue from Financial Transactions Taxes," Center for Economic and Policy Research and the Political Economy Research Institute, December 2009 (cepr.net); Bureau of Labor Statistics, TED: The Economics Daily, "Largest industries by state, 1990-2013," July 28, 2014 (bls.gov); Bureau of Labor Statistics, TED: The Economics Daily, "Job openings, hires, and total separations by industry, June 2015," Aug. 14, 2015 (bls.gov); Lawrence Mishel, Elise Gould, and Josh Bivens, "Wage Stagnation in Nine Charts," Economic Policy Institute, Jan. 6, 2015 (epi.org); Douglas Belkin, "U.S. College Enrollment Has Dropped Nearly 2% Over Last Year," *Wall Street Journal*, May 14, 2015 (wsj.com); Mark Huelsman, "The Debt Divide: The Racial and Class Bias Behind the 'New Normal' of Student Borrowing," Demos, May 19, 2015 (demos.org); Jesse Rothsein and Cecilia Elena Rouse, "Constrained after college: Student loans and early-career occupational choices," *Journal of Public Economics* 95 (2011); National Center for Educational Statistics, Fast Facts, "Degrees conferred by sex and race" (nces.ed.gov); City University of New York, "When Tuition at CUNY Was Free, Sort Of," CUNY Matters, Oct. 12, 2011 (cuny.edu); James Skoufis, "Assemblyman Skoufis Introduces Bill to Provide Free Tuition at SUNY and CUNY," Jan. 27, 2014 (assembly.state.ny.us); Rob Manning. "Thousands to Benefit from Oregon Free Community College Bill," Oregon Public Broadcasting, July 17, 2015 (opb.org); Ashley A. Smith, "Obama Steps Up Push for Free Tuition," *Inside Higher Education*, Sept. 9, 2015 (insidehighered.com); Laura Meckler and Josh Mitchell, "Hillary Clinton Proposes Debt-Free Tuition at Public Colleges," *Wall Street Journal*, Aug. 10, 2015 (wsj.com); Heather Gautney and Adolph Reed Jr., "Bernie Sanders's 'College for All' Plan Is Fair, Smart and Achievable," *The Nation*, Dec. 2, 2015 (thenation.com).

Article 11.5

WHAT HAPPENED TO DEFINED-BENEFIT PENSIONS?

BY ARTHUR MacEWAN
September/October 2013

> Dear Dr. Dollar:
> *What has happened to the defined benefit pensions? Why are they being replaced by defined contribution programs? What are the implications for us (workers!) as we grow older and live longer?* —Susan A. Titus, Detroit, Mich.

In large part, the shift from defined benefit pensions to defined contribution pensions is explained by employers shifting risk from themselves to their employees. Increasingly, in recent decades, for the same reasons that employers have been able to hold down wages, employers have shifted pension plans because they have had the power to do so. (See the box on the next page for definitions of the two types of plans.)

The shift has been dramatic. In 1975, 71% of active workers participating in pension plans had defined benefit plans, and 29% had defined contribution plans. By 2010, the figures had more than reversed: 19% were in defined benefit plans; 81%, in defined contribution plans. Even though the labor force grew by 64% over this 45-year period, the number of workers in defined benefit plans fell by 37%. (See graph.)

In a defined benefit pension system, the employer is obligated to pay the fixed pension regardless of what happens to the economy. The risk for the employer is that bad economic times can make it difficult to make the payments—because the

PERCENTAGE OF NON-RETIRED PENSION-PLAN PARTICIPANTS, DEFINED BENEFIT (DB) VS. DEFINED CONTRIBUTION (DC) PLANS, 1975-2010*

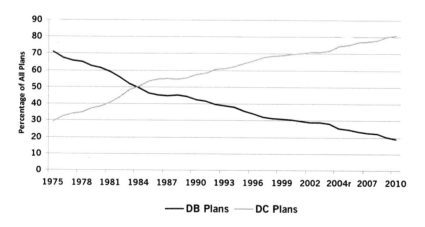

*Many people participate in more than one plan. In 2004 (shown twice) definitions changed.
Sources: U.S. Dept. of Labor, Private Pension Plan Bulletin Historical Tables and Graphs, Nov. 2012.

Defined Benefit: Employer and employees make contributions to a general pension fund managed by the employer. Based on a formula including years of employment and level of salary, each employee receives a fixed annual amount of money after retirement; that fixed amount does not depend on how well the investment of the fund does. The quality of the plan from the perspective of the employee depends on the amount of employee and employer contributions and on the particulars of the formula for determining benefits.

Defined Contribution: Employer and employee make contributions to a fund that is identified with the individual and is managed by an investment firm. The money that the employee receives after retirement depends on the amount of money in the individual's fund. The quality of the plan from the perspective of the employee depends on the amount of employee and employer contributions and on how well the investment does, both up to and after the time of retirement.

investments made with the pension fund have done poorly, because the firm's revenues are less than anticipated, or both. Even if a private firm goes broke, defined benefit pensions are insured by the federal government, so the private-sector employee bears little or no risk. However, for public sector employees, who now account for most defined benefit plans, there is risk in extreme cases such as—you know it well!—Detroit in 2013. When a public employer goes bankrupt, the pensioners and active workers in the pension system are put in line behind the employer's creditors—mainly banks. (The Detroit situation is being disputed in the courts at this writing, but it does not appear likely that things will come out well for people in the public pension system.)

In defined contribution plans, the risk falls on the employee. The contributions (from both the employee and the employer) go into an investment fund for the individual worker, generally with taxes deferred until the money is taken out of the fund (as in a 401k). But if the economy goes sour— for example, if the stock market crashes—the employee has far less for retirement. This is exactly what happened with the crash of 2008.

There could hardly be a clearer case of conflict of interests between employees and employers. As employers have been able to hold down wages over the last several decades, they have shifted the burden of risk onto employees. There are several aspects of this power shift that have favored employers: the large decline in union membership, the way globalization has been structured to favor large firms, the general shift in political power (of which the decline in the minimum wage is a clear marker), and the way technological changes have been used to displace labor. The result has been a worsening of what workers get—stagnant wages and higher risk.

Social Security alone certainly does not provide a good standard of living. In 2012, the average annual Social Security payment from the Old-Age and Survivors Insurance trust fund was a little more than $14,000 per recipient. A person retiring in 2013 at age 65 who had been earning an annual salary of $70,000 (a bit more than the median family income), would receive about $21,000 annually. Even if all the efforts in Washington to cut Social Security benefits fail, it is easy to see why people need some additional form of retirement income to provide them with a reasonable standard of living during retirement.

Beyond Social Security, in 2010, active workers held 90.6 million pension plans, 17.2 million defined benefit plans and 73.4 million defined contribution plans. These figures involve some double counting, as many people have more than one pension plan, but, with a 2010 labor force of 153.9 million, this means that at least 41% of workers had no pension plan at all (other than Social Security). In fact, according to progressive pension expert Teresa Ghilarducci, a majority of workers do not have pension plans at work and over 75% of Americans nearing retirement age in 2010 had less than $30,000 in their retirement accounts.

While the pressure from business groups in Washington is to reduce Social Security, the current dismal state of retirement prospects for the majority of people in fact provides a strong case for a more extensive public pension system. ❑

Sources: Teresa Ghilarducci, "Don't Cut Pensions, Expand Them," *New York Times*, March 15, 2012; Teresa Ghilarducci, "Our Ridiculous Approach to Retirement, *New York Times*, July 21, 2012; Employee Benefit Research Institute, "The Basics of Social Security, Updated With the 2013 Board of Trustees Report," July 2013.

Article 11.6

MYTHS OF THE DEFICIT

BY MARTY WOLFSON
May/June 2010

Nearly 15 million people are officially counted as unemployed in the United States, and more than 6 million of these have been unemployed for more than 26 weeks. Another 11 million are the "hidden" unemployed: jobless workers who have given up looking for work and part-time workers who want full-time jobs. Unemployment has especially affected minority communities; the official black teenage unemployment rate, for example, stands at 42%.

The *moral* case for urgently addressing the unemployment issue is clear. The costs of unemployment, especially prolonged unemployment, are devastating. Self-worth is questioned, homes are lost, families stressed, communities disrupted. Across the land, the number one issue is jobs, jobs, jobs.

The *economic* case for how to address the jobs issue is also clear. As Keynes argued during the Great Depression, federal government spending can directly create jobs. And the $787 billion stimulus package approved by Congress in February 2009 did help pull the economy back from disaster, when it was shedding 20,000 jobs *a day* in late 2008 and early 2009.

But we still have a long way to go. To get back just to where we were when the recession began in December 2007, the economy would need to create 11.1 million jobs: 8.4 million to replace the jobs lost and 2.7 million to absorb new workers who have entered the labor market since then.

Despite a pickup of economic activity recently, long-term projections are that the unemployment rate will fall only gradually over the next several years. The Congressional Budget Office forecast for the unemployment rate for 2012 is a stubbornly high 8%. So why are we not moving more aggressively to reduce unemployment?

The *ideological* opposition to government spending remains a major obstacle. There are those who see an increase in the role of government as something to be avoided at all costs—even if the cost is the jobs of the unemployed.

Even among those who are not subject to such ideological blinders, there is still a *political* argument that resonates strongly. The argument is that government spending to create jobs will create large budget deficits, which will have terrible consequences for the American people. Politicians, pundits, and other commentators—in a frenzied drumbeat of speeches, op-eds, and articles—have asserted that the most urgent priority *now* is to reduce the budget deficit.

It is important to note that this argument is focused on current policy, not just the long-term budgetary situation. There is room for debate about long-term budget deficits, but these are affected more by the explosive growth of health-care costs than by government discretionary spending to create jobs.

Why, then, are people taken in by an argument that says it is more important to reduce the budget deficit now than for the government to spend money to create jobs? Two myths constantly repeated in the public debate have contributed to this situation:

1) Families can't spend more than they have; neither should the government.

It seems to be common sense that a family can't spend more than it has. But of course that is exactly what the family does when it takes out a car loan or a student loan, or does any other kind of borrowing. The government, just like families, should be able to borrow. The real issue is whether or not the debt is affordable. For families, and for the government, that depends on the size of the debt relative to the income available to service the debt; it also depends on the nature of the borrowing.

For the federal government, the relevant debt-income measure is the ratio of outstanding debt of the federal government to gross domestic product. (*Outstanding debt* is the total amount owed at a particular time, roughly the result of debt accumulated over time by annual budget deficits; GDP, the value of goods and services produced, is equal to total income.) In 2009, this ratio was 53%. Although higher than the recent low point of 33% at the end of the 1990s expansion, the ratio in 2009 was still far lower than the record peak of 109% in 1946—after which the U.S. economy in the post-World War II period experienced the strongest economic growth in its history.

The U.S. ratio of 53% actually compares favorably to those of other advanced industrial countries. For example, IMF data indicate the following debt-to-GDP ratios for 2009: France (67%), Germany (70%), Japan (105%), and Italy (113%).

The nature of the borrowing also affects affordability. If a family runs up credit-card debt to finance a lavish lifestyle, after the fancy dinners are eaten the family still needs to figure out how to pay its debt. But if a family member borrows to buy a car to get to work, presumably the job will help provide the income to service the debt.

Likewise for the federal government: If the government borrows to finance tax cuts for the rich, and the rich use their tax cuts to purchase imported luxury goods, then the government still needs to figure out how to pay its debt. On the other hand, if the government borrows to put people to work creating long-term investments that increase the productivity of the U.S. economy, like infrastructure and education, then it is in a much better situation. The income generated by the more productive economy, as well as by the newly employed workers, can help to provide the tax revenue to service the debt.

So it is a myth to say that families can't spend more than they have. They can, and so can the government. And both are justified in borrowing if the size of the debt is manageable and if so doing helps to provide the income necessary to service the debt.

2) Large budget deficits create a burden for our grandchildren.

This is the issue that probably resonates most forcefully with public opinion. If we in the current generation run up a big debt, it may be left to our grandchildren to repay. The only difficulty with this reasoning is that the grandchildren who may be asked to repay the debt are paying it to other grandchildren. When the government incurs a debt, it issues a bond, an obligation to repay the debt to the holder of the bond. If the holders of the bond are U.S. residents, then paying off the debt means paying money to U.S. residents. In other words, debt that is an obligation of future U.S. taxpayers is also a source of income to the U.S. holders of that debt. Thus there is not a generational burden that we today are imposing on "our grandchildren" as a collective entity.

Of course, the obvious exception to this reasoning is the debt held by non-U.S. residents. In that case, it is indeed true that future generations of Americans will need to pay interest to foreign holders of U.S. debt. But the basic reason for this situation is the trade deficit, not the budget deficit. When we pay more for imports than we receive from exports, and when U.S. multinational companies ship production abroad to take advantage of low-cost labor, foreigners are provided with dollars that they can use to invest in U.S. assets. And the real burden that this causes is the same whether foreigners invest in U.S. government debt or whether they invest in U.S. companies, real estate, the U.S. stock market, etc.

Borrowing by the federal government can in some situations create a real burden, but it has less to do with generational transfers and more to do with distributional issues and the nature of economic growth (discussed above). If the grandchildren who are taxed in the future to pay off government debt are poorer than the grandchildren who are paid, the distribution of income becomes more unequal.

Also, cutting taxes for the rich and spending money on wars in Iraq and Afghanistan do not lead to the kind of productive economic growth that generates strong tax revenue. So financing these by debt *does* create a real distributional burden: The rich and military contractors benefit, but the losers are those who might be taxed, or those whose government programs might be squeezed out of the budget, because of the need to pay interest on the debt.

Borrowing money to put people back to work does make sense. It helps people most in need, the unemployed. It provides them with income that they can use to pay taxes and to buy goods and services that create more jobs, more income, and more tax revenue. Indeed, our inability thus far to seriously tackle the unemployment problem is what has worsened the budget problem, as tax receipts have fallen and spending for unemployment benefits and food stamps have risen. An analysis by the Economic Policy Institute reveals that the largest source of the 2009 budget deficit (42%) was actually the recession itself.

We *will* leave a burden for our grandchildren if we don't address the urgent problem of unemployment, if we let parents and grandparents suffer the indignities and financial hardships of lost jobs. We *will* leave a burden for our grandchildren if we don't rebuild our aging infrastructure, break our reliance on fossil fuels, and provide all our children with an excellent education. It makes perfect sense to borrow money now to address these problems, and we shouldn't let myths about budget deficits get in the way of meeting these real needs. ❑

Sources: Congressional Budget Office, "The Budget and Economic Outlook: Fiscal Years 2010 to 2020," January 2010; John Irons, Kathryn Edwards, and Anna Turner, "The 2009 Budget Deficit: How Did We Get Here?" Economic Policy Institute, August 20, 2009; Dean Baker, "The Budget Deficit Scare Story and the Great Recession," Center for Economic and Policy Research, February 2010; Office of Management and Budget, "The President's Budget For Fiscal Year 2011, Historical Tables: Table 7.1, Federal Debt at the End of Year: 1940-2015," February 2010.

Article 11.7

CLIMATE ECONOMICS IN FOUR EASY PIECES
Conventional cost-benefit models cannot inform our decisions about how to address the threat of climate change.

FRANK ACKERMAN
November/December 2008

Once upon a time, debates about climate policy were primarily about the science. An inordinate amount of attention was focused on the handful of "climate skeptics" who challenged the scientific understanding of climate change. The influence of the skeptics, however, is rapidly fading; few people were swayed by their arguments, and doubt about the major results of climate science is no longer important in shaping public policy.

As the climate *science* debate is reaching closure, the climate *economics* debate is heating up. The controversial issue now is the fear that overly ambitious climate initiatives could hurt the economy. Mainstream economists emphasizing that fear have, in effect, replaced the climate skeptics as the intellectual enablers of inaction.

For example, William Nordhaus, the U.S. economist best known for his work on climate change, pays lip service to scientists' calls for decisive action. He finds, however, that the "optimal" policy is a very small carbon tax that would reduce greenhouse gas emissions only 25% below "business-as-usual" levels by 2050—that would, in other words, allow emissions to rise well above current levels by mid-century. Richard Tol, a European economist who has written widely on climate change, favors an even smaller carbon tax of just $2 per ton of carbon dioxide. That would amount to all of $0.02 per gallon of gasoline, a microscopic "incentive" for change that consumers would never notice.

There are other voices in the climate economics debate; in particular, the British government's Stern Review offers a different perspective. Economist Nicholas Stern's analysis is much less wrong than the traditional Nordhaus-Tol approach, but even Stern has not challenged the conventional view enough.

What will it take to build a better economics of climate change, one that is consistent with the urgency expressed by the latest climate science? The issues that matter are big, non-technical principles, capable of being expressed in bumper-sticker format. Here are the four bumper stickers for a better climate economics:

1. Our grandchildren's lives are important.

2. We need to buy insurance for the planet.

3. Climate damages are too valuable to have prices.

4. Some costs are better than others.

1. Our grandchildren's lives are important.

The most widely debated challenge of climate economics is the valuation of the very long run. For ordinary loans and investments, both the costs today and the resulting future benefits typically occur within a single lifetime. In such cases, it makes sense to think in terms of the same person experiencing and comparing the costs and the benefits.

In the case of climate change, the time spans involved are well beyond those encountered in most areas of economics. The most important consequences of today's choices will be felt by generations to come, long after all of us making those choices have passed away. As a result, the costs of reducing emissions today and the benefits in the far future will not be experienced by the same people. The economics of climate change is centrally concerned with our relationship to our descendants whom we will never meet. As a bridge to that unknowable future, consider our grandchildren—the last generation most of us will ever know.

Suppose that you want your grandchildren to receive $100 (in today's dollars, corrected for inflation), 60 years from now. How much would you have to put in a bank account today, to ensure that the $100 will be there 60 years from now? The answer is $55 at 1% interest, or just over $5 at 5%.

In parallel fashion, economists routinely deal with future costs and benefits by "discounting" them, or converting them to "present values"—a process that is simply compound interest in reverse. In the standard jargon, the *present value* of $100, to be received 60 years from now, is $55 at a 1% *discount rate*, or about $5 at a 5% discount rate. As this example shows, a higher discount rate implies a smaller present value.

The central problem of climate economics, in a cost-benefit framework, is deciding how much to spend today on preventing future harms. What should we spend to prevent $100 of climate damages 60 years from now? The standard answer is, no more than the present value of that future loss: $55 at a discount rate of 1%, or $5 at 5%. The higher the discount rate, the less it is "worth" spending today on protecting our grandchildren.

The effect of a change in the discount rate becomes much more pronounced as the time period lengthens. Damages of $1 million occurring 200 years from now have a present value of only about $60 at a 5% discount rate, versus more than $130,000 at a 1% discount rate. The choice of the discount rate is all-important to our stance toward the far future: should we spend as much as $130,000, or as little as $60, to avoid one million dollars of climate damages in the early twenty-third century?

For financial transactions within a single lifetime, it makes sense to use market interest rates as the discount rate. Climate change, however, involves public policy decisions with impacts spanning centuries; there is no market in which public resources are traded from one century to the next. The choice of an intergenerational discount rate is a matter of ethics and policy, not a market-determined result.

Economists commonly identify two separate aspects of long-term discounting, each contributing to the discount rate.

One component of the discount rate is based on the assumption of an upward trend in income and wealth. If future generations will be richer than we are, they will need less help from us, and they will get less benefit from an additional dollar of income than we do. So we can discount benefits that will flow to our wealthier descendants, at a rate based on the expected growth of per capita incomes. Among economists, the income-related motive for discounting may be the least controversial part of the picture.

Setting aside changes in per capita income from one generation to the next, there may still be a reason to discount a sum many years in the future. This component of the discount rate, known as "pure time preference," is the subject of longstanding ethical, philosophical, and economic debate. On the one hand, there are reasons to think that pure time preference is greater than zero: both psychological experiments and common sense suggest that people are impatient, and prefer money now to money later. On the other hand, a pure time preference of zero expresses the equal worth of people of all generations, and the equal importance of reducing climate impacts and other burdens on them (assuming that all generations have equal incomes).

The Stern Review provides an excellent discussion of the debate, explaining Stern's assumption of pure time preference close to zero and an overall discount rate of 1.4%. This discount rate alone is sufficient to explain Stern's support for a substantial program of climate protection: at the higher discount rates used in more traditional analyses, the Stern program would look "inefficient," since the costs would outweigh the present value of the benefits.

2. We need to buy insurance for the planet.

Does climate science predict that things are certain to get worse? Or does it tell us that we are uncertain about what will happen next? Unfortunately, the answer seems to be yes to both questions. For example, the most likely level of sea level rise in this century, according to the latest Intergovernmental Panel on Climate Change reports, is no more than one meter or so—a real threat to low-lying coastal areas and islands that will face increasing storm damages, but survivable, with some adaptation efforts, for most of the world. On the other hand, there is a worst-case risk of an abrupt loss of the Greenland ice sheet, or perhaps of a large portion of the West Antarctic ice sheet. Either one could cause an eventual seven-meter rise in sea level—a catastrophic impact on coastal communities, economic activity, and infrastructure everywhere, and well beyond the range of plausible adaptation efforts in most places.

The evaluation of climate damages thus depends on whether we focus on the most likely outcomes or the credible worst-case risks; the latter, of course, are much larger.

Cost-benefit analysis conventionally rests on average or expected outcomes. But this is not the only way that people make decisions. When faced with uncertain, potentially large risks, people do not normally act on the basis of average outcomes; instead, they typically focus on protection against worst-case scenarios. When you go to the airport, do you leave just enough time for the average traffic delay (so that you would catch your plane, on average, half of the time)? Or do you allow time for some estimate of worst-case traffic jams? Once you get there, of course, you will experience additional delays due to security, which is all about worst cases: your *average* fellow passenger is not a threat to anyone's safety.

The very existence of the insurance industry is evidence of the desire to avoid or control worst-case scenarios. It is impossible for an insurance company to pay out in claims as much as its customers pay in premiums; if it did, there would be no money left to pay the costs of running the company, or the profits received by its owners. People who buy insurance are therefore guaranteed to get back less than they, on average, have paid; they (we) are paying for the security that insurance provides in case the worst should happen. This way of thinking does not apply to every decision: in casino games, people make bets based on averages and probabilities, and no one has any insurance against losing the next round. But life is not a casino, and public policy should not be a gamble.

Should climate policy be based on the most likely outcomes, or on the worst-case risks? Should we be investing in climate protection as if we expect sea level rise of one meter, or as if we are buying insurance to be sure of preventing a seven-meters rise?

In fact, the worst-case climate risks are even more unknown than the individual risks of fire and death that motivate insurance purchases. You do not know whether or not you will have a fire next year or die before the year is over, but you have very good information about the likelihood of these tragic events. So does the insurance industry, which is why they are willing to insure you. In contrast, there is no body of statistical information about the probability of Greenland-sized ice sheets collapsing at various temperatures; it's not an experiment that anyone can perform over and over again.

A recent analysis by Martin Weitzman argues that the probabilities of the worst outcomes are inescapably unknowable—and this deep uncertainty is more important than anything we do know in motivating concern about climate change. There is a technical sense in which the expected value of future climate damages can be infinite because we know so little about the probability of the worst, most damaging possibilities. The practical implication of infinite expected damages is that the most likely outcome is irrelevant; what matters is buying insurance for the planet, i.e., doing our best to understand and prevent the worst-case risks.

3. Climate damages are too valuable to have prices.

To decide whether climate protection is worthwhile, in cost-benefit terms, we would need to know the monetary value of everything important that is being protected. Even if we could price everything affected by climate change, the prices would conceal a critical form of international inequity. The emissions that cause climate change have come predominantly from rich countries, while the damages will be felt first and worst in some of the world's poorest, tropical countries (although no one will be immune from harm for long). There are, however, no meaningful prices for many of the benefits of health and environmental protection. What is the dollar value of a human life saved? How much is it worth to save an endangered species from extinction, or to preserve a unique location or ecosystem? Economists have made up price tags for such priceless values, but the results do not always pass the laugh test.

Is a human life worth $6.1 million, as estimated by the Clinton administration, based on small differences in the wages paid for more and less risky jobs? Or is it worth $3.7 million, as the (second) Bush administration concluded on the basis of question- naires about people's willingness to pay for reducing small, hypothetical risks? Are lives of people in rich countries worth much more than those in poor countries, as some economists infamously argued in the IPCC's 1995 report? Can the value of an endangered species be determined by survey research on how much people would pay to protect it? If, as one study found, the U.S. population as a whole would pay $18 bil- lion to protect the existence of humpback whales, would it be acceptable for someone to pay $36 billion for the right to hunt and kill the entire species?

The only sensible response to such nonsensical questions is that there are many crucially important values that do not have meaningful prices. This is not a new idea: as the eighteenth-century philosopher Immanuel Kant put it, some things have a price, or relative worth, while other things have a dignity, or inner worth. No price tag does justice to the dignity of human life or the natural world.

Since some of the most important benefits of climate protection are priceless, any monetary value for total benefits will necessarily be incomplete. The corollary is that preventive action may be justified even in the absence of a complete monetary measure of the benefits of doing so.

4. Some costs are better than others.

The language of cost-benefit analysis embodies a clear normative slant: benefits are good, costs are bad. The goal is always to have larger benefits and smaller costs. In some respects, measurement and monetary valuation are easier for costs than for benefits: implementing pollution control measures typically involves changes in such areas as manufacturing, construction, and fuel use, all of which have well- defined prices. Yet conventional economic theory distorts the interpretation of costs in ways that exaggerate the burdens of environmental protection and hide the posi- tive features of some of the "costs."

Average Risks or Worst-Case Scenarios?

You don't have to look far to find situations in which the sensible policy is to address worst- case outcomes rather than average outcomes. The annual number of residential fires in the United States is about 0.4% of the number of housing units. This means that a fire occurs, on average, about once every 250 years in each home—not even close to once per lifetime. By far the most likely number of fires a homeowner will experience next year, or even in a lifetime, is zero. Why don't these statistics inspire you to cancel your fire insurance? Unless you are extremely wealthy, the loss of your home in a fire would be a devastating financial blow; despite the low probability, you cannot afford to take any chances on it.

What are the chances of the ultimate loss? The probability that you will die next year is under 0.1% if you are in your twenties, under 0.2% in your thirties, under 0.4% in your for- ties. It is not until age 61 that you have as much as a 1% chance of death within the coming year. Yet most U.S. families with dependent children buy life insurance. Without it, the risk to children of losing their parents' income would be too great—even though the parents are, on average, extraordinarily likely to survive.

For instance, empirical studies of energy use and carbon emissions repeatedly find significant opportunities for emissions reduction at zero or negative net cost—the so-called "no regrets" options.

According to a longstanding tradition in economic theory, however, cost-free energy savings are impossible. The textbook theory of competitive markets assumes that every resource is productively employed in its most valuable use—in other words, that every no-regrets option must already have been taken. As the saying goes, there are no free lunches; there cannot be any $20 bills on the sidewalk because someone would have picked them up already. Any new emissions reduction measures, then, must have positive costs. This leads to greater estimates of climate policy costs than the bottom-up studies that reveal extensive opportunities for costless savings.

In the medium term, we will need to move beyond the no-regrets options; how much will it cost to finish the job of climate protection? Again, there are rival interpretations of the costs based on rival assumptions about the economy. The same economic theory that proclaimed the absence of $20 bills on the sidewalk is responsible for the idea that all costs are bad. Since the free market lets everyone spend their money in whatever way they choose, any new cost must represent a loss: it leaves people with less to spend on whatever purchases they had previously selected to maximize their satisfaction in life. Climate damages are one source of loss, and spending on climate protection is another; both reduce the resources available for the desirable things in life.

But are the two kinds of costs really comparable? Is it really a matter of indifference whether we spend $1 billion on bigger and better levees or lose $1 billion to storm damages? In the real-world economy, money spent on building levees creates jobs and incomes. The construction workers buy groceries, clothing, and so on, indirectly creating other jobs. With more people working, tax revenues increase while unemployment compensation payments decrease.

None of this happens if the levees are not built and the storm damages are allowed to occur. The costs of prevention are good costs, with numerous indirect benefits; the costs of climate damages are bad costs, representing pure physical destruction. One worthwhile goal is to keep total costs as low as possible; another is to have as much as possible of good costs rather than bad costs. Think of it as the cholesterol theory of climate costs.

In the long run, the deep reductions in carbon emissions needed for climate stabilization will require new technologies that have not yet been invented, or at best exist only in small, expensive prototypes. How much will it cost to invent, develop, and implement the low-carbon technologies of the future?

Lacking a rigorous theory of innovation, economists modeling climate change have often assumed that new technologies simply appear, making the economy inexorably more efficient over time. A more realistic view observes that the costs of producing a new product typically decline as industry gains more experience with it, in a pattern called "learning by doing" or the "learning curve" effect. Public investment is often necessary to support the innovation process in its early, expensive stages. Wind power is now relatively cheap and competitive, in suitable locations; this is a direct result of decades of public investment in the United States and Europe, starting when wind turbines were still quite expensive. The costs of climate policy, in the long run, will include doing the same for other promising new technologies, investing public resources in jump-starting a set of slightly different industries than we might have chosen in the absence of climate change. If this is a cost, many communities would be better off with more of it.

Saving the Planet

A widely publicized, conventional economic analysis recommends inaction on climate change, claiming that the costs currently outweigh the benefits for anything more than the smallest steps toward reducing carbon emissions. Put our "four easy pieces" together, and we have the outline of an economics that complements the science of climate change and endorses active, large-scale climate protection.

How realistic is it to expect that the world will shake off its inertia and act boldly and rapidly enough to make a difference? This may be the last generation that will have a real chance at protecting the earth's climate. Projections from the latest IPCC reports, the Stern Review, and other sources suggest that it is still possible to save the planet—if we start at once. ❑

Sources: Frank Ackerman, *Can We Afford the Future? Economics for a Warming World*, Zed Books, 2008; Frank Ackerman, *Poisoned for Pennies: The Economics of Toxics and Precaution*, Island Press, 2008; Frank Ackerman and Lisa Heinzerling, *Priceless: On Knowing the Price of Everything and the Value of Nothing*, The New Press, 2004; J. Creyts, A. Derkach, S. Nyquist, K. Ostrowski and J. Stephenson, *Reducing U.S. Greenhouse Gas Emissions: How Much at What Cost?*, McKinsey & Co., 2007; P.-A. Enkvist, T. Naucler and J. Rosander, "A Cost Curve for Greenhouse Gas Reduction," *The McKinsey Quarterly*, 2007; Immanuel Kant, *Groundwork for the Metaphysics of Morals*, translated by Thomas K. Abbot, with revisions by Lara Denis, Broadview Press, 2005 [1785]; B. Lomborg, *Cool It: The Skeptical Environmentalist's Guide to Global Warming*, Alfred A. Knopf, 2007; W.D. Nordhaus, *A Question of Balance: Economic Modeling of Global Warming*, Yale University Press, 2008; F.P. Ramsey, "A mathematical theory of saving," *The Economic Journal* 138(152): 543-59, 1928; Nicholas Stern et al., *The Stern Review: The Economics of Climate Change*, HM Treasury, 2006; U.S. Census Bureau, "Statistical Abstract of the United States." 127th edition. 2008; M.L. Weitzman, "On Modeling and Interpreting the Economics of Catastrophic Climate Change," December 5, 2007 version, www.economics.harvard.edu/faculty/weitzman/files/modeling.pdf.

CONTRIBUTORS

Frank Ackerman is an economist with Synapse Energy Economics and a founder of *Dollars & Sense*.

Gar Alperovitz is a professor of political economy at the University of Maryland and co-author, with Lew Daly, of *Unjust Deserts: How the Rich Are Taking Our Common Inheritance and Why We Should Take It Back* (New Press, 2009).

Eileen Appelbaum is a senior economist at the Center for Economic and Policy Research and a visiting professor at the University of Leicester, UK

Dean Baker is co-director of the Center for Economic and Policy Research.

Peter Barnes, co-founder of Working Assets, is a senior fellow at the Tomales Bay Institute.

Rosemary Batt is the Alice Hanson Cook Professor of Women and Work at the Industrial and Labor Relations School, Cornell University, and a *Dollars & Sense* Associate.

Sarah Blaskey is a student at the University of Wisconsin-Madison and a member of the Student Labor Action Coalition.

James K. Boyce is a professor of economics at the University of Massachusetts-Amherst and co-director of the Political Economy Research Institute (PERI) Program on Development, Peacebuilding, and the Environment.

Sasha Breger Bush is a lecturer at the Josef Korbel School of International Studies at the University of Denver and author of *Derivatives and Development: A Political Economy of Global Finance, Farming, and Poverty* (Palgrave Macmillan, 2012).

Marc Breslow is co-chair of the Massachusetts Climate Action Network and a former *Dollars & Sense* collective member.

Marie Brill is the executive director of ActionAid USA.

Jim Campen is professor emeritus of economics at the University of Massachusetts-Boston, and former executive director of Americans for Fairness in Lending.

Lew Daly is a senior fellow at Demos and co-author, with Gar Alperovitz, of *Unjust Deserts: How the Rich Are Taking Our Common Inheritance and Why We Should Take It Back* (New Press, 2009).

Deborah M. Figart is a professor or education and economics at the Richard Stockton College of New Jersey.

Nancy Folbre is a professor emerita of economics at the University of Massachusetts-Amherst. She contributes regularly to the *New York Times* Economix blog.

Ellen Frank teaches economics at the University of Massachusetts-Boston and is a *Dollars & Sense* collective member.

Gerald Friedman is a professor of economics at the University of Massachusetts-Amherst.

Heidi Garrett-Peltier is a research fellow at the Political Economy Research Institute at the University of Massachusetts-Amherst.

Phil Gasper teaches at Madison College and writes the "Critical Thinking" column for *International Socialist Review*.

Mark Haggerty is an associate professor in the Honors College at the University of Maine and a member of its Sustainable Foods Systems Research Collaborative.

Lisa Heinzerling is a professor of law at Georgetown University Law School, specializing in environmental law.

Edward Herman is an economist and co-author of *The Global Media: The New Missionaries of Corporate Capitalism*.

Biola Jeje is a cofounder of New York Students Rising, a statewide student network at state and city colleges, and now works as a full time digital media organizer in the labor movement.

Rob Larson teaches economics at Tacoma Community College in Tacoma, Wash., and is the author of *Bleakonomics* (Pluto Press).

Arthur MacEwan, a *Dollars & Sense* Associate, is professor emeritus of economics at the University of Massachusetts-Boston.

John Miller, a *Dollars & Sense* collective member, teaches economics at Wheaton College.

Jawied Nawabi is a professor of economics and sociology at CUNY Bronx Community College and a member of the *Dollars & Sense* collective.

Thomas Palley is an economist who has held positions at the AFL-CIO, Open Society Institute, and the U.S./China Economic and Security Review Commission.

Stephen Pressman is a professor of economics at Colorado State University and the author of *Fifty Major Economists*.

Alejandro Reuss (co-editor of this volume) is co-editor of *Dollars & Sense* and an instructor at the Labor Relations and Research Center at UMass-Amherst.

Belinda Rodriguez is a climate justice activist and organizer. She sits on the board of the Energy Action Coalition and most recently served as Training Director at United States Student Association.

Helen Scharber is an assistant professor of economics at Hampshire College in Amherst, Mass.

Juliet Schor is a professor of sociology at Boston College and the author of *The Overworked American*, *The Overspent American*, and *True Wealth*.

Zoe Sherman is an assistant professor at Merrimack College and a member of the *Dollars & Sense* collective.

Bryan Snyder (co-editor of this volume) is a senior lecturer in economics at Bentley University.

Chris Sturr (co-editor of this volume) is co-editor of *Dollars & Sense*.

Chris Tilly is a *Dollars & Sense* Associate and director of UCLA's Institute for Research on Labor and Employment and professor in the Urban Planning Department.

Ramaa Vasudevan teaches economics at Colorado State University and is a *Dollars & Sense* Associate.

Craig Watts is a chicken producer for Perdue in Fairmont, N.C.

Jeannette Wicks-Lim is an economist and research fellow at the Political Economy Research Institute at the University of Massachusetts-Amherst.

Timothy A. Wise is director of the Research and Policy Program at the Global Development and Environment Institute, Tufts University.

Marty Wolfson is a professor of economics at the University of Notre Dame.

Earn your **Master's Degree** in **Applied Economics**

at the University of Massachusetts Boston

Would you like to do applied economic research? Our program will provide you with both critical analytical thinking and quantitative problem-solving skills.

You will:

- Gain insights from alternative and traditional economic approaches.
- Learn and practice applied research techniques.
- Study with a progressive and diverse economics faculty whose interests include urban economics, political economy, feminist economics, and ecological economics.
- Pay affordable tuition at a great public university in a beautiful city.
- Study part-time or full-time in a 32 credit program designed for working adults.

Learn more at **www.economics.umb.edu**

UMASS
BOSTON

CPSIA information can be obtained at www.ICGtesting.com
Printed in the USA
BVOW01s1209140816

458515BV00004B/10/P